Better Homes and Gardens®

the *ultimate*
slow
cooker
book

WILEY

John Wiley & Sons, ____

D1059074

Copyright © 2010 by Meredith Corporation, Des Moines, IA. All rights reserved

Published by John Wiley & Sons, Inc., Hoboken, New Jersey

Published simultaneously in Canada

For general information on our other products and services or for technical support, please contact our Customer Care Department within the United States at (800) 762–2974, outside the United States at (317) 572–3993 or fax (317) 572–4002.

Wiley also publishes its books in a variety of electronic formats. Some content that appears in print may not be available in electronic books. For more information about Wiley products, visit our web site at www.wiley.com.

Library of Congress Cataloging-in-Publication Data

The ultimate slow cooker book : more than 400 recipes from appetizers to desserts.
    p. cm.
  At head of title: Better homes and gardens
  Includes bibliographical references and index.
  ISBN 978-0-470-54032-9 (pbk.)
  ISBN 978-0-470-58765-2 (special edition)
  1. Electric cookery, Slow. I. Meredith Corporation. II. Better homes and gardens. III. Title: Better homes and gardens. IV. Title: Slow cooker book.
  TX827.U45 2010
  641.5'884—dc22

                              2009035862

Printed in the United States of America

10 9 8 7 6 5 4 3 2 1

Meredith Corporation

Editor: Jan Miller

Contributing Editors: Lisa Kingsley, Waterbury Publishing and Kristi Thomas

Recipe Development and Testing: Better Homes and Gardens® Test Kitchen

John Wiley & Sons, Inc.

Publisher: Natalie Chapman

Associate Publisher: Jessica Goodman

Executive Editor: Anne Ficklen

Editor: Adam Kowit

Production Director: Diana Cisek

Senior Production Editor: Jacqueline Beach

Cover and Interior Design: Jill Budden

Layout: Jill Budden and Holly Wittenberg

Manufacturing Manager: Tom Hyland

Our seal assures you that every recipe in *The Ultimate Slow Cooker Book* has been tested in the Better Homes and Gardens® Test Kitchen. This means that each recipe is practical and reliable and meets our high standards of taste appeal. We guarantee your satisfaction with this book for as long as you own it.

Cover photography: Kritsada Panichgul
Food stylist: Nicole Peterson
Prop stylist: Sue Mitchell
Pictured (top row, from left): Farmer's Market Vegetable Soup, page 90, Sherried Fruit, page 74, Aztec Hot Chocolate, page 56; (middle row, from left): Buffalo Wings with Blue Cheese Dip, page 31, Raspberry Fudgy Brownies, page 467, Meatball Sliders, page 43; (bottom row, from left): Bean-and-Rice-Stuffed Peppers, page 392, Pesto Chicken Sandwich, page 189, Country-Style Pork Ribs, page 349.

table of
contents

Chicken
and White
Bean Stew,
page 112

These days convenience and economy are top of mind for everyone, especially working moms. So what could be more necessary than your slow cooker? It's a busy family's most invaluable kitchen tool. It makes menu planning easier because many recipes are complete meals. Furthermore, there is such a variety of recipes you can make in a slow cooker that you'll never run out of ideas. And, if you choose to make a big batch, leftovers are inevitable and economical. Slow cookers can also take an inexpensive tough cut of meat and turn it into a melt-in- your-mouth masterpiece. And as a timesaver, you can simply put all of the ingredients in the cooker in the morning or afternoon, and your dinner is just hours away— without your constant attention!

But the best part of all is the slow cooker's versatility. If your slow cooker has been limited to the occasional pot roast, you'll love this collection of recipes. From appetizers, beverages, breakfast dishes, main dishes, sides, and desserts, you will have a plethora of recipes to serve for any occasion or weeknight meal. We have to admit, what you hold in your hands is the ultimate slow cooker cookbook—complete with answers to any questions you might have regarding slow cooking. We've even included full-color photos of hundreds of the recipes!

In-a-Hurry
Chicken Curry,
page 198

HOT SURFACE

Proctor Silex®

slow cooking

sm

It doesn't take a lot of cooking know-how to make a tasty slow cooker meal—that's the beauty of a slow cooker! However, a few easy tips and some slow cooker basics will help you make a sensational meal every time.

arts

type
matters

There are two basic types of slow cookers.

The first type has a crockery insert and two temperature settings: low (about 200°F) and high (about 300°F). The heating coils wrap around the sides of the cooker. This allows for the continuous slow cooking needed for the recipes in this book. It cooks foods at a very low wattage. The liner may or not be removable. The second type has an adjustable thermostat indicating temperature in degrees. The heating coil is located in the bottom of the cooker—the only place heat is applied—and the element cycles on and off during cooking.

When buying a slow cooker, look for these features:

* **A snug-fitting, see-through lid.**

* **A removable ceramic or stainless-steel insert or liner.** They are easier to clean if you can take them out of the cooker. The insert should also have large, sturdy handles to make it easier (and safer) to remove it from the base. A "stove-top-safe" insert is an excellent feature for one-pan browning. Consider a stainless-steel insert if a ceramic insert feels too heavy.

* **A programmable timer** to set the cooker to start if you will be gone all day. (Note: The cooker should be set to start within 2 hours of filling it.) Some timers can be programmed to cook on high for a set time and then switch to low.

* **Cookers with wraparound heating** elements heat more evenly than those with the element on the bottom.

* **Oval-shaped cookers** are better suited to oblong cuts of meat and are easier to pour from than round cookers.

Cooker Size and Use

Check out this chart for guidelines on how to select the right size cooker for your recipe. All recipes in this book indicate the size of the cooker needed for the amount of ingredients called for.

If you are . . .	Use this size cooker	For . . .
Single	1½ -quart	▪ Cooking two meals at once. (You can freeze most leftovers.) ▪ Keeping casual party foods warm.
A couple	1½-quart or 2-quart	▪ Dinners for two—no leftovers. ▪ Keeping casual party foods warm.
	3½-quart	▪ Cooking a small (2- to 2½-pound) roast. (Freeze leftovers to use in salads or sandwiches.)
Small family (3 or 4)	3½- to 4½-quart	▪ Cooking all-time favorites for 3 or 4, including soups, stews, chili, meat and vegetables.
Large family (5 to 7)	4½- to 5-quart	▪ Family-size meals plus leftovers for 5 to 7 to freeze and serve later.
Cooking for 8 or more	6- to 8-quart	▪ Dinners with friends. ▪ Keeping casual party foods or beverages warm. ▪ Potlucks.

Don't peek!

(Keep a lid on it.) Lifting the lid releases valuable moisture and heat.

slow-cooker savvy

It's safe to toss ingredients in a slow cooker and walk away because the long cooking time and the steam that forms in the tightly covered container destroy any bacteria. Follow the easy tips below to ensure your slow cooker meal is not only safe but delicious as well.

* Clean the cooker and all utensils before you start. Do not use the slow cooker for large pieces of meat. Cut in half any roasts larger than 2½ pounds.

* Save time in the morning by preparing ingredients for tomorrow's dinner the night before. Place chopped ingredients in tightly sealed containers (except for partially cooked meats) in your refrigerator overnight. Be sure to cover cut-up potatoes with water so they don't discolor before cooking. It's okay to brown ground meat and refrigerate overnight because browning fully cooks the meat. However, if your recipe calls for a roast or cubed meat for stew, brown the meat just before plugging in your slow cooker as browning doesn't completely cook those cuts.

* Schedule your cooking by using a plug-in timer. Be sure ingredients in the cooker are well chilled, and set the timer to start within two hours. Do not use this delayed cooking method for recipes that include frozen fish or poultry.

* Add herbs at the right time to the slow cooker. Because dried herbs have more staying power, crush and add them at the beginning of cooking. Add fresh herbs just minutes before serving—except for rosemary, which can survive long hours in a cooker.

* Ensure that your slow cooker is safe if it is older or you are unsure of its heating ability. Fill it half to two-thirds with water. Heat it on the low-heat setting, covered, for 8 hours, and then check the water temperature with an accurate food thermometer. It should be about 185°F. It it's not, it's time to retire the cooker.

* Fill the cooker at least half full and no more than two-thirds full.

* Browning meat before adding it to the slow cooker adds extra flavor and color. If you're in a hurry, skip the browning.

* Never toss frozen raw meat directly into your slow cooker. Bacteria grow most rapidly between 40°F and 140°F. Because the slow cooking process brings fresh or thawed meat up to temperature at a slow rate, frozen meat placed in the cooker hovers within the danger zone for far too long, putting you and others who eat it at risk.

* Allow your meals to cook as long as specified in the recipe.

* Never place a hot insert on a cool surface. Likewise, an insert that has been refrigerated should not be placed in a hot base unit. A sudden change in temperature could cause the insert to crack.

* To avoid burns from hot steam that is created on the inside of the lid during cooking, lift the lid gently and straight up without tilting.

* Leave disposable nylon liners and the cooking liquids in the slow cooker insert until they have cooled to a safe handling temperature. However, when making a bread pudding or stuffing in the slow cooker, the edges of the nylon liner can be carefully grasped to lift the pudding out of the insert (wear oven mitts) and transfer it to a

cutting board. Then, just peel back or cut the liner and slice the pudding into wedges for serving.

*When you live at high altitudes. add about 30 extra minutes for each hour of cooking time called for in a slow cooking recipe. If the recipe suggests a cooking time of 5 hours, for example, cook it for 7½ hours.

Add dried crushed herbs at the beginning of cooking. Fresh herbs are more delicate so add them minutes before serving.

Freezer Sense

One of the great things about cooking many of the recipes in this book is that you can freeze leftovers to reheat and enjoy on another day. To successfully freeze foods and maintain good flavor, here are a few pointers.

Choose freezer-safe containers or bags. Look for moisture-proof and vapor-proof materials that can withstand temperatures of 0°F or below and can be tightly sealed. For liquid or semiliquid foods, use rigid plastic containers, bags, or wide-top jars designed for freezing. Regular jars seldom are tempered to withstand freezer temperatures.

Cool hot foods quickly. Divide soups and stews into portions that are 2 to 3 inches deep and stir while cooling. Divide roasts and whole poultry into portions that are 2 to 3 inches thick. Place the food in the refrigerator. When thoroughly chilled, transfer food to freezer containers. Arrange containers in a single layer in the freezer to allow cold air to circulate around them. Once the food is frozen, stack the containers for storage.

Remove excess air. This will help prevent freezer burn. There is an exception: When freezing cooked food, you'll want to leave about ½ inch of space between the top of the food and the rim of its container. This will provide room for the food to expand while it freezes without breaking the container or causing the lid to pop off.

Be label conscious. Include the name of the recipe, the quantity, the date it was frozen, and the number of servings.

Maximum Freeze Times

Roasts and Meat Dishes (Cooked): 3 months

Poultry Dishes (Cooked): 4 months

Soups and Stews: 6 months

toting foods safely

Don't risk ruining a wonderful potluck or family gathering by ignoring some basic food safety. Here are some tips to keep in mind.

* Plan to have your food finish cooking just as you're ready to leave home.

* Wrap the covered slow cooker in several layers of newspaper or a heavy towel. Place in an insulated cooler for transport. The food should stay hot for up to 2 hours. If you are using an electric slow cooker, plug it in when you arrive at your destination and the food will keep warm on the low-heat setting for hours.

* Use your cooker to transport. Depending on the type of food you are toting, the slow cooker is a perfect transporter for soups, stews, and some casseroles. Again, plug the cooker in as soon as you arrive at your destination.

Cleaning Your Slow Cooker

To keep your slow cooker working properly, follow a few guidelines when cleaning it.

* Unplug the slow cooker and fill the liner with hot soapy water (do not add cold water when the crockery liner is hot) as soon as your remove the food from the cooker. Let the liner soak while you're eating. Never immerse the cooker or cord in water.

* Be careful during cleaning not to hit the crockery liner on the faucets or hard surfaces of your sink. Crockery chips easily.

* If soaking does not remove all the food residue, use a sponge, cloth, plastic cleaning pad, or nonabrasive cleaner to clean the crockery liner.

* If your cooker has a removable crockery liner, wash it, after soaking, in a dishwasher or by hand.

* For a cooker with a nonremovable crockery liner, wipe the liner clean with a dishcloth and soapy water after soaking. Rinse carefully and wipe dry.

* Both glass and plastic cooker lids are dishwasher safe, but be sure to put plastic lids only on the top rack of your dishwasher.

* Wipe the outside of the cooker's metal shell with a damp soft cloth and dry it with a towel.

With a little tweaking, you can cook many of your favorite conventional soups, stews, and roasts in your slow cooker.

»Choosing a recipe: Use recipes that call for less tender cuts of meat, such as beef chuck roast, beef brisket, pork shoulder, and stew meat. Use a sample recipe as a guide to estimate ingredient quantities and timings.

»Quantities: The slow cooker must be at least half full and no more than two-thirds full. If necessary, add an extra potato, carrot, or onion to fill the cooker to the halfway point.

»Vegetables: Cut potatoes, carrots, parsnips, and other dense vegetables into bite-size pieces; place them in the bottom of the cooker. Add tender vegetables, such as fresh or frozen broccoli, green beans, or peas, at the end of the cooking time and cook on the high-heat setting for 30 minutes or until tender.

»Meat: Trim any fat from the cut roasts larger than 2½ pour desired, brown the meat. Place on top of the vegetables.

»Poultry: Remove skin from poultry pieces before cooking.

»Ground meats, poultry, and sausage: Brown all ground meats, poultry, and sausage in a skillet over medium heat. These products must be completely cooked before you place them in the slow cooker.

»Liquids: Reduce by about half the total amount of the liquid in your recipe.

crockery conversions

Thickeners: Use quick-cooking tapioca for thickening stews and sauces, or thicken the juices with cornstarch and flour in a saucepan at the end of cooking. For each cup of liquid, use 1 tablespoon cornstarch or 2 tablespoons all-purpose flour. Quick-cooking tapioca (crushed) is most often added to a recipe in the beginning because it doesn't break down during the long cooking time.

Dairy products: Milk, cream, and natural cheeses break down when cooked for long periods of time; stir them in near the end of cooking time. Canned condensed cream soups and packaged white sauce mixeswork well to add creaminess to your recipe. Evaporated milk also can be used if you add it during the last 30 to 60 minutes of cooking time.

Dried beans: Rinse beans and place in saucepan. Add enough water to cover beans by 2 inches. Bring to boiling; reduce heat. Simmer, uncovered, for 10 minutes. Remove from heat. Cover and let stand for about 1 hour. Drain and rinse beans before adding them to slow cooker.

And you thought your slow cooker was just for main dishes. Not so. Here we've included a variety of dishes that are just right for your next party. From Asiago Cheese Dip, Spicy Sausage Pizza Dip, or Fruit-Glazed Ham Balls to Polynesian-Glazed Wings or Mulled Ginger-Apple Tea, your guests will be impressed.

appetizers & beve

2

rages

Cayenne pepper adds heat to this sugar-and-spice nut mix. Four types of nuts are suggested, but use whatever kind you like best.

sweet-and-hot nuts

prep: 15 minutes   **cook:** 2 hours (low)   **cool:** 1 hour   **makes:** 22 (¼-cup) servings

1   cup whole cashews
1   cup whole almonds, toasted*
1   cup pecan halves, toasted*
1   cup hazelnuts, toasted and skins removed*
½   cup sugar
⅓   cup butter, melted
1   teaspoon ground ginger
½   teaspoon salt
½   teaspoon ground cinnamon
¼   teaspoon ground cloves
¼   teaspoon cayenne pepper

1 Place nuts in a 2- to 3½-quart slow cooker. In a small bowl combine sugar, butter, ginger, salt, cinnamon, cloves, and cayenne pepper. Add to slow cooker, tossing to coat.

2 Cover and cook on low-heat setting for 2 hours, stirring after 1 hour. Stir nuts again. Spread in a single layer on buttered foil; let cool for at least 1 hour. (Nuts may appear soft after cooking but will crisp upon cooling.) Store in a tightly covered container at room temperature for up to 3 weeks.

nutrition facts per serving: 147 cal., 13 g total fat (3 g sat. fat), 7 mg chol., 73 mg sodium, 8 g carbo., 2 g dietary fiber, 3 g protein.

*test kitchen tip: To toast nuts, spread nuts in a single layer in a shallow baking pan. Bake in a 350°F oven for 10 to 15 minutes or until light golden brown, watching carefully and stirring once or twice. To remove the papery skin from hazelnuts, rub the nuts with a clean dish towel.

Cooked in hoisin sauce with garlic and crushed red pepper, bite-size button mushrooms pack a surprisingly big jolt of flavor.

hoisin-garlic mushrooms

prep: 15 minutes   cook: 5 to 6 hours (low) or 2½ to 3 hours (high)
makes: 10 servings

½   cup bottled hoisin
     sauce
¼   cup water
2   tablespoons bottled
     minced garlic
¼   to ½ teaspoon
     crushed red pepper
24 ounces whole fresh
     button mushrooms,
     trimmed

1 In a 3½- or 4-quart slow cooker combine hoisin sauce, the water, garlic, and crushed red pepper. Add mushrooms, stirring to coat.

2 Cover and cook on low-heat setting for 5 to 6 hours or on high-heat setting for 2½ to 3 hours. Using a slotted spoon, remove mushrooms from cooking liquid to serve. Discard cooking liquid. Serve warm mushrooms with decorative toothpicks.

nutrition facts per serving: 43 cal., 1 g total fat (0 g sat. fat), 0 mg chol., 211 mg sodium, 9 g carbo., 1 g dietary fiber, 3 g protein.

Generally herbs are added at the end of cooking time; however, rosemary can hold up to long cooking. Marjoram is a bit more delicate, so sprinkle more fresh atop the dip before serving.

white bean spread

prep: 15 minutes **cook:** 3 to 4 hours (low) **makes:** 20 (2-tablespoon) servings

2 15-ounce cans
Great Northern or
cannellini beans
(white kidney beans),
rinsed and drained
½ cup canned chicken
or vegetable broth
1 tablespoon olive oil
3 cloves garlic, minced
1 teaspoon snipped
fresh marjoram or
¼ teaspoon dried
marjoram, crushed
½ teaspoon snipped
fresh rosemary or
⅛ teaspoon dried
rosemary, crushed
⅛ teaspoon ground
black pepper
Olive oil (optional)
Fresh marjoram leaves
Fresh rosemary
(optional)
Pita Chips

1 In a 1½-quart slow cooker combine beans, broth, 1 tablespoon oil, garlic, 1 teaspoon snipped marjoram, ½ teaspoon snipped rosemary, and pepper.

2 Cover and cook on low-heat setting for 3 to 4 hours.

3 Slightly mash bean mixture using a potato masher. Spoon bean mixture into a serving bowl. If desired, drizzle with additional oil and sprinkle with fresh marjoram and rosemary. Serve warm or at room temperature with Pita Chips.

nutrition facts per serving (spread only): 70 cal., 1 g total fat (0 g sat. fat), 0 mg chol., 33 mg sodium, 11 g carbo., 3 g dietary fiber, 4 g protein.

pita chips: Split 2 pita bread rounds horizontally in half; cut each circle into 6 wedges. Place pita wedges in a single layer on a large baking sheet. Combine 2 tablespoons olive oil, 2 teaspoons snipped fresh oregano, and ¼ teaspoon kosher salt; brush pita wedges with oil mixture. Bake in a 350°F oven for 12 to 15 minutes or until crisp and light brown. Remove from baking sheet; cool on a wire rack. Makes 24 chips.

Small rye bread slices topped with this corned beef dip create a hearty appetizer. Cream cheese adds a wonderful richness to the dip.

reuben spread

prep: 15 minutes   cook: 2½ to 3 hours (low)   makes: 20 (¼-cup) servings

1 pound cooked corned beef, finely chopped

1 16-ounce can sauerkraut, rinsed, drained, and snipped

1 cup bottled Thousand Island salad dressing

1½ cups shredded Swiss cheese (6 ounces)

1 3-ounce package cream cheese, cut into cubes

1 tablespoon prepared horseradish

1 teaspoon caraway seeds

Party rye bread slices, toasted, or rye crackers

1 In a 3½- or 4-quart slow cooker combine corned beef, sauerkraut, salad dressing, Swiss cheese, cream cheese, horseradish, and caraway seeds.

2 Cover and cook on low-heat setting for 2½ to 3 hours.

3 Serve immediately or keep covered on warm or low-heat setting for up to 2 hours. Stir occasionally. Serve with assorted dippers.

nutrition facts per serving (spread only): 157 cal., 13 g total fat (5 g sat. fat), 38 mg chol., 531 mg sodium, 3 g carbo., 1 g dietary fiber, 7 g protein.

What's not to like? Smoky bacon and blue cheese are new invitees to this classic dip. One such as this should be part of any top-notch appetizer tray.

spinach-artichoke dip
with blue cheese and bacon

prep: 25 minutes cook: 3 to 4 hours (low) makes: 24 (¼-cup) servings

4   slices bacon
1   cup sweet onion, coarsely chopped (1 large)
2   14-ounce cans artichoke hearts, drained and coarsely chopped
1   10-ounce box frozen chopped spinach, thawed and well drained
1   cup chopped red sweet pepper
1   cup light mayonnaise dressing (do not use regular mayonnaise)
8   ounces cream cheese, cut into cubes
4   ounces blue cheese, crumbled
3   cloves garlic, minced
½   teaspoon dry mustard
    Assorted crackers

1 In a skillet cook bacon until crisp. Drain on paper towels. Crumble bacon; cover and chill until ready to use. Cook onion in 1 tablespoon bacon drippings for about 5 minutes or until tender.

2 In a 3½- or 4-quart slow cooker combine onion, artichoke hearts, spinach, red sweet pepper, mayonnaise, cream cheese, blue cheese, garlic, and dry mustard.

3 Cover and cook on low-heat setting for 3 to 4 hours or until cheese melts and mixture is heated through. Stir in bacon. Serve with assorted crackers.

nutrition facts per serving (dip only): 128 cal., 11 g total fat (4 g sat. fat), 22 mg chol., 341 mg sodium, 4 g carbo., 2 g dietary fiber, 4 g protein.

Yum. Creamy and delicious, this sublime dip is wonderful served on a simple toasted slice of baguette.

asiago cheese dip

prep: 15 minutes cook: 3 to 4 hours (low) or 1½ to 2 hours (high)
makes: 28 (¼-cup) servings

1   cup chicken broth
    or water
4   ounces dried
    tomatoes (not
    oil-packed)
4   8-ounce cartons dairy
    sour cream
1¼ cups mayonnaise
½   of an 8-ounce
    package cream
    cheese, cut into
    cubes
1   cup sliced fresh
    mushrooms
1   cup thinly sliced
    green onions (8)
1½ cups shredded
    Asiago cheese
    (6 ounces)
    Thinly sliced green
    onion
    Toasted baguette
    slices

1 In a medium saucepan bring broth to boiling. Remove from heat and add dried tomatoes. Cover and let stand for 5 minutes. Drain and discard the liquid; chop tomatoes (about 1¼ cups).

2 Meanwhile, in a 3½- or 4-quart slow cooker combine sour cream, mayonnaise, cream cheese, mushrooms, 1 cup green onions, and Asiago cheese. Stir in chopped tomatoes. Cover and cook on low-heat setting for 3 to 4 hours or on high-heat setting for 1½ to 2 hours. Stir before serving and sprinkle with additional sliced green onion. Serve immediately or keep warm on low-heat setting for 1 to 2 hours. Serve with toasted baguette slices.

nutrition facts per serving (dip only): 194 cal., 18 g total fat (8 g sat. fat), 29 mg chol., 237 mg sodium, 5 g carbo., 1 g dietary fiber, 4 g protein.

A trio of beans, cheese, and vegetables combine for a tomato-studded queso dip that will satisfy the Mexican food lovers at your next party.

vegetable chili con queso

prep: 20 minutes cook: 6 to 7 hours (low) or 3 to 3½ hours (high)
makes: 32 servings

1 15-ounce can pinto beans, rinsed and drained
1 15-ounce can black beans, rinsed and drained
1 15-ounce can chili beans with chili gravy
1 10-ounce can chopped tomatoes and green chile peppers, undrained
1 medium zucchini, chopped
1 medium yellow summer squash, chopped
1 cup chopped onion (1 large)
¼ cup tomato paste
2 to 3 teaspoons chili powder
4 cloves garlic, minced
3 cups shredded Colby and Monterey Jack cheese (12 ounces)
   Tortilla or corn chips

1 In a 3½- or 4-quart slow cooker combine pinto beans, black beans, chili beans, tomatoes, and green chile peppers, zucchini, summer squash, onion, tomato paste, chili powder, and garlic.

2 Cover and cook on low-heat setting for 6 to 7 hours or on high-heat setting for 3 to 3½ hours. Stir in cheese until melted. Serve immediately or keep warm on low-heat setting for up to 1 hour. Serve with tortilla chips.

nutrition facts per serving (dip only): 81 cal., 4 g total fat (2 g sat. fat), 9 mg chol., 231 mg sodium, 8 g carbo., 2 g dietary fiber, 5 g protein.

Here is a dip for those who adore big flavors. Cream cheese, cheddar cheese, bacon, green onion, and, of course, horseradish aren't for the faint of tongue.

bacon-horseradish dip

prep: 25 minutes   cook: 4 to 5 hours (low) or 2 to 2½ hours (high)
makes: 20 (¼-cup) servings

3 8-ounce packages
   cream cheese,
   cut into cubes and
   softened
3 cups shredded
   cheddar cheese
   (12 ounces)
1 cup half-and-half
   or light cream
⅓ cup chopped green
   onions (3)
1 tablespoon
   Worcestershire
   sauce
3 cloves garlic, minced
½ teaspoon coarsely
   ground black
   pepper
12 slices bacon, crisp-
   cooked, cooled,
   and finely crumbled
   (1 cup)
3 tablespoons prepared
   horseradish
   Corn chips, toasted
   baguette slices,
   toasted pita wedges,
   or assorted crackers

1 In a 3½- or 4-quart slow cooker combine cream cheese, cheddar cheese, half-and-half, green onions, Worcestershire sauce, garlic, and pepper.

2 Cover and cook on low-heat setting for 4 to 5 hours or on high-heat setting for 2 to 2½ hours, stirring once halfway through cooking. Stir in the bacon and horseradish. Serve with corn chips.

nutrition facts per serving (dip only): 227 cal., 21 g total fat (13 g sat. fat), 63 mg chol., 282 mg sodium, 2 g carbo., 0 g dietary fiber, 8 g protein.

How can you go wrong with something that tastes like pizza in a dip? For a cheesy side of the expected, serve with mozzarella cheese sticks. De-lish.

spicy sausage pizza dip

prep: 15 minutes   cook: 5 to 6 hours (low) or 2½ to 3 hours (high)
makes: 14 (¼-cup servings)

1	pound bulk Italian sausage
⅔	cup chopped onion
4	cloves garlic, minced
2	15-ounce cans tomato sauce
1	14.5-ounce can diced tomatoes, undrained
1	6-ounce can tomato paste
1	tablespoon dried oregano, crushed
1	tablespoon dried basil, crushed
2	teaspoons sugar
¼	teaspoon crushed red pepper
½	cup chopped black olives
	Breadsticks, breaded mozzarella cheese sticks, and/or green sweet pepper strips

1 In a large skillet cook Italian sausage, onion, and garlic over medium heat until sausage is brown and onion is tender. Drain off fat.

2 In a 3½- or 4-quart slow cooker, combine sausage mixture, tomato sauce, tomatoes, tomato paste, oregano, basil, sugar, and crushed red pepper; mix well. Cover and cook on low-heat setting for 5 to 6 hours or on high-heat setting for 2½ to 3 hours. Stir in olives. Serve with assorted dippers.

nutrition facts per serving: 143 cal., 8 g total fat (3 g sat. fat), 22 mg chol., 548 mg sodium, 8 g carbo., 1 g dietary fiber, 6 g protein.

to store reserves: After serving, transfer any leftovers to freezer containers and freeze for up to 3 months. Thaw and reheat in a saucepan.

Not hot enough for you? If you like your dips to have a bit of extra heat, use hot salsa or Monterey Jack cheese with jalapeño peppers.

rio grande dip

prep: 15 minutes   cook: 3 to 4 hours (low) or 1½ to 2 hours (high)
makes: 24 (¼-cup) servings

8   ounces bulk Italian
    sausage
⅓   cup finely chopped
    onion (1 small)
2   15-ounce cans refried
    black beans
1½ cups bottled salsa
1   4-ounce can diced
    green chile peppers,
    undrained
1½ cups shredded
    Monterey Jack
    cheese (6 ounces)
    Tortilla chips or large
    corn chips

1 In a large skillet cook the sausage and onion over medium heat until meat is brown and onion is tender. Drain off fat. In a 3½- or 4-quart slow cooker stir together the meat mixture, refried beans, salsa, and chile peppers. Stir in cheese.

2 Cover and cook on low-heat setting for 3 to 4 hours or on high-heat setting for 1½ to 2 hours.

3 Serve immediately or keep covered on warm or low-heat setting for up to 2 hours. Stir occasionally. Serve with tortilla chips.

nutrition facts per serving (dip only): 90 cal., 5 g total fat (2 g sat. fat), 13 mg chol., 238 mg sodium, 6 g carbo., 2 g dietary fiber, 5 g protein.

Chicken, three kinds of cheese, white kidney beans, chile-studded tomatoes, fajita seasoning, and cilantro join to make this a dip you'll remember.

spicy **chicken-bean** dip

prep: 15 minutes   cook: 2½ to 3 hours (low)   makes: 26 (¼-cup) servings

2   8-ounce tubs cream cheese spread with chive and onion
1   10-ounce can chopped tomatoes and green chile peppers, undrained
¼   cup milk
1   teaspoon ground cumin
½   teaspoon fajita seasoning
2   cups finely chopped cooked chicken
2   cups shredded American cheese (8 ounces)
2   cups shredded Monterey Jack cheese (8 ounces)
1   15-ounce can cannellini beans (white kidney beans) or small white beans, rinsed and drained
2   tablespoons snipped fresh cilantro
     Pita wedges, toasted, and/or tortilla chips

1 In a 3½- or 4-quart slow cooker combine cream cheese, tomatoes and green chile peppers, milk, cumin, and fajita seasoning. Stir in chicken, American cheese, Monterey Jack cheese, and beans.

2 Cover and cook on low-heat setting for 2½ to 3 hours. Serve immediately or keep covered on warm or low-heat setting for up to 2 hours. Just before serving, stir in cilantro. Serve with toasted pita wedges.

nutrition facts per serving (dip only): 153 cal., 11 g total fat (7 g sat. fat), 39 mg chol., 324 mg sodium, 5 g carbo., 1 g dietary fiber, 8 g protein.

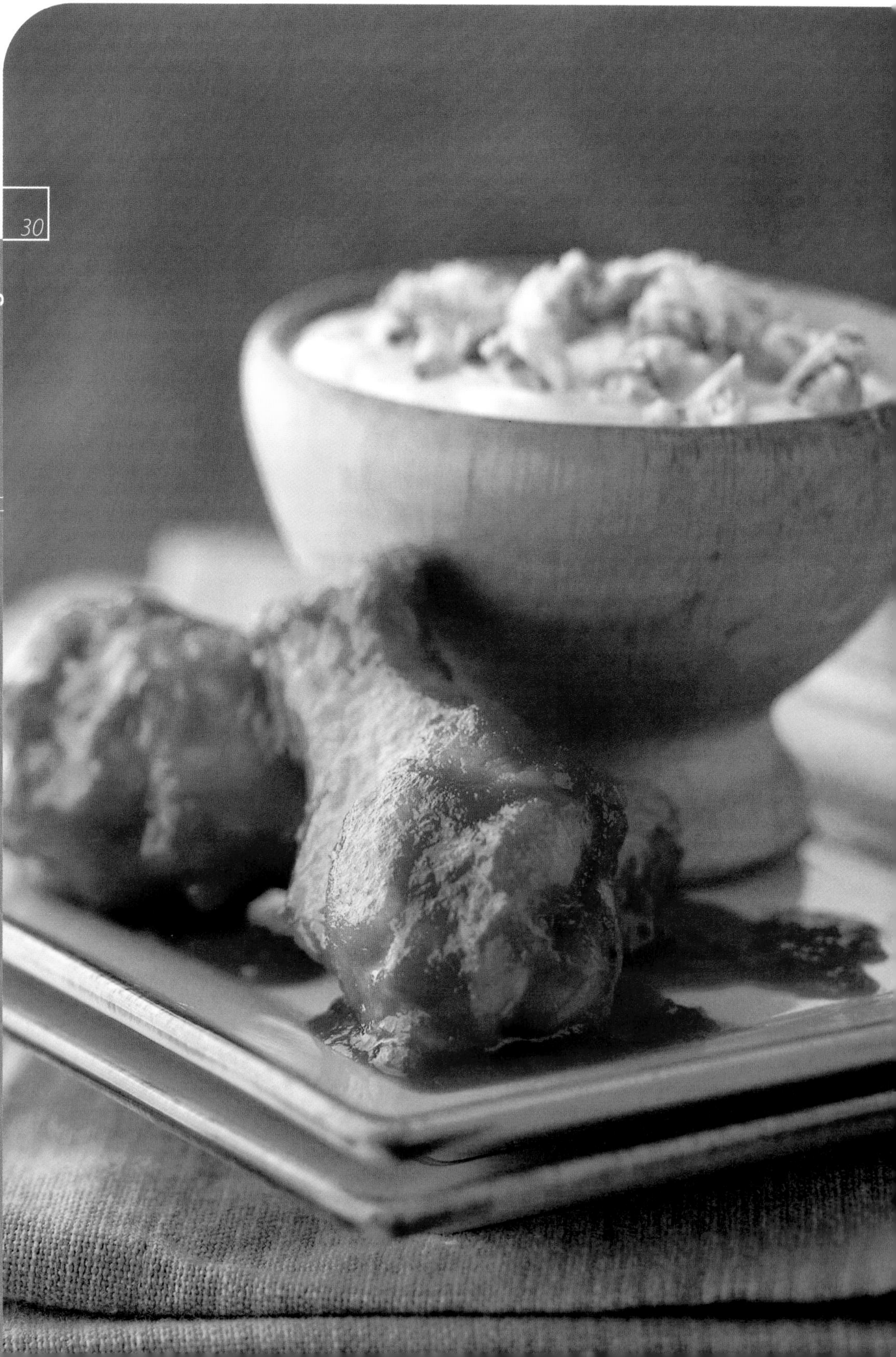

Just two ingredients take chicken wings from ho-hum to yum.
If time permits, make the homemade dip. It will make the wings
even more appetizing.

buffalo wings
with blue cheese dip

prep: 35 minutes broil: 12 minutes cook: 4 to 5 hours (low) or 2 to 2½ hours (high)
makes: 32 servings

16   chicken wings
       (about 3 pounds)
1¼ cups bottled chili
       sauce
2   tablespoons bottled
       hot pepper sauce
       Blue Cheese Dip or
       bottled ranch salad
       dressing

1 Cut off and discard tips of chicken wings. Cut wings at joints to form 32 pieces. Place chicken pieces on the unheated rack of a broiler pan. Broil 3 to 4 inches from the heat for about 12 minutes or until light brown, turning once. Place chicken pieces in a 3½- or 4-quart slow cooker.

2 In a small bowl combine chili sauce and hot pepper sauce. Pour over chicken.

3 Cover and cook on low-heat setting for 4 to 5 hours or on high-heat setting for 2 to 2½ hours. Serve chicken wings with Blue Cheese Dip.

nutrition facts per serving: 108 cal., 8 g total fat (3 g sat. fat), 21 mg chol., 217 mg sodium, 3 g carbo., 0 g dietary fiber, 6 g protein.

blue cheese dip: In a blender combine one 8-ounce carton dairy sour cream; ½ cup mayonnaise or salad dressing; ½ cup (2 ounces) crumbled blue cheese; 1 clove garlic, minced; and 1 tablespoon white wine vinegar or white vinegar. Cover and blend until smooth. Cover and chill for up to 1 week. If desired, top with additional crumbled blue cheese before serving.

You can't go wrong when you combine crab, shrimp, cheese, cream, and mayo. Add a spicy kick and the flavor just can't get any better.

spicy slow-cooked
seafood dip

prep: 25 minutes cook: 1½ hours (high) makes: 16 to 20 (¼-cup) servings

4   cups shredded
    Monterey Jack
    cheese with
    jalapeño peppers
    (16 ounces)
2   6-ounce packages
    refrigerated crab
    claw meat, drained
7   to 8 ounces peeled
    and deveined
    cooked baby shrimp
¾   cup finely chopped
    red sweet pepper
    (1 medium)
⅔   cup mayonnaise
½   cup finely chopped
    onion (1 medium)
½   cup whipping cream
2   tablespoons finely
    chopped jalapeño
    pepper* (1 medium;
    optional)
2   tablespoons
    all-purpose flour
1   teaspoon paprika
    Sliced chile peppers
    Toasted Crostini,
    sliced vegetables,
    and/or breadsticks

1 In a 3½- or 4-quart slow cooker combine cheese, crab, shrimp, red sweet pepper, mayonnaise, onion, cream, jalapeño pepper, flour, and paprika; mix well.

2 Cover and cook on high-heat setting for 1½ hours, until melted and bubbly. Serve immediately or keep covered on warm or low-heat setting for up to 2 hours. Garnish with sliced chile peppers. Serve with Toasted Crostini.

nutrition facts per serving (dip only): 241 cal., 20 g total fat (9 g sat. fat), 95 mg chol., 358 mg sodium, 2 g carbo., 0 g dietary fiber, 14 g protein.

✱test kitchen tip: Because chile peppers, such as jalapeños, contain volatile oils that can burn your skin and eyes, avoid direct contact with chiles as much as possible. When working with chile peppers, wear plastic or rubber gloves. If your bare hands do touch the chile peppers, wash your hands well with soap and water.

toasted crostini: Cut a baguette crosswise into thirds. Slice lengthwise into thin slices. Brush lightly with 3 tablespoons olive oil. Place in a single layer on an extra-large baking sheet. Bake in a 425°F oven for 12 to 15 minutes or until light brown, turning once.

Poblanos, a milder chile pepper, are fairly large and dark green. If you can't find them, use an Anaheim or a couple of jalapeños.

queso verde dip

prep: 15 minutes **cook:** 3 to 3½ hours (low) or 1½ to 1¾ hours (high)
makes: 22 (¼-cup) servings

1	pound ground turkey
¾	cup chopped onion (1 large)
1	tablespoon cooking oil
1	16-ounce jar green salsa (salsa verde)
1	8-ounce package cream cheese, cut into cubes
2	cups shredded Monterey Jack cheese (8 ounces)
1	medium poblano chile pepper, seeded and chopped (see tip, page 32)
1	tablespoon Worcestershire-style marinade for chicken
1	teaspoon ground cumin
2	cloves garlic, minced
1	tablespoon snipped fresh cilantro
	Tortilla chips

1 In a large skillet cook ground turkey and onion in hot oil over medium heat until turkey is no longer pink and onion is tender. Drain off fat.

2 In a 3½- or 4-quart slow cooker combine turkey mixture, salsa, cream cheese, Monterey Jack cheese, poblano pepper, Worcestershire marinade, cumin, and garlic.

3 Cover and cook on low-heat setting for 3 to 3½ hours or on high-heat setting for 1½ to 1¾ hours. Stir until cream cheese is blended. Serve immediately or keep covered on warm or low-heat setting for up to 2 hours. Stir before serving. Sprinkle with cilantro. Serve with tortilla chips.

nutrition facts per serving (dip only): 122 cal., 9 g total fat (5 g sat. fat), 37 mg chol., 146 mg sodium, 3 g carbo., 0 g dietary fiber, 7 g protein.

appetizers & beverages

Crabmeat in a can makes this a convenient dip. Parmesan cheese, cream cheese, and mayonnaise make this an extra-creamy delight.

hot crab dip

prep: 15 minutes   cook: 1½ to 2 hours (low) or 1 to 1½ hours (high)
makes: 20 (2-tablespoon) servings

Nonstick cooking spray
12 ounces cream cheese, cut into cubes
½ cup mayonnaise or salad dressing
½ cup finely shredded Parmesan cheese (2 ounces)
¼ cup thinly sliced green onions (2)
1 tablespoon Worcestershire sauce for chicken
2 6-ounce cans crabmeat, drained, flaked, and cartilage removed
Snipped fresh chives or green onions
Toasted pita bread wedges or assorted crackers

1 Coat the inside of a 1½-quart slow cooker with nonstick cooking spray; set aside.

2 In a medium bowl combine cream cheese, mayonnaise, Parmesan cheese, ¼ cup green onions, and Worcestershire sauce. Stir in crabmeat. Transfer mixture to prepared slow cooker.

3 Cover and cook on low-heat setting for 1½ to 2 hours or on high-heat setting for 1 to 1½ hours. Stir well before serving. Serve immediately or keep covered on warm or low-heat setting for up to 2 hours. Sprinkle with chives before serving. Serve with pita bread wedges.

nutrition facts per serving (dip only): 125 cal., 11 g total fat (5 g sat. fat), 37 mg chol., 183 mg sodium, 1 g carbo., 0 g dietary fiber, 6 g protein.

Cocktail wieners are the quintessential party food. Here, Caribbean jerk seasoning and pineapple preserves give them a tropical twist.

caribbean cocktail sausages

prep: 15 minutes cook: 4 hours (low) makes: 12 servings

1   16-ounce package
    cocktail wieners
    or small, cooked
    smoked sausage
    links
1   12-ounce jar
    pineapple preserves
½   teaspoon finely
    shredded lime peel
1   tablespoon lime juice
1   teaspoon Jamaican
    jerk seasoning
1   teaspoon ground
    ginger
2   cloves garlic, minced
    Few dashes bottled
    hot pepper sauce

In a 1½-quart slow cooker combine wieners, pineapple preserves, lime peel, lime juice, jerk seasoning, ginger, garlic, and hot pepper sauce. Cover and cook on low-heat setting for 4 hours. Serve immediately or keep covered on warm or low-heat setting for up to 2 hours. Serve wieners with wooden toothpicks.

nutrition facts per serving: 194 cal., 10 g total fat (4 g sat. fat), 24 mg chol., 421 mg sodium, 21 g carbo., 0 g dietary fiber, 5 g protein.

to serve 24: Use two 16-ounce packages of cocktail sausages and place in a 3½- or 4-quart slow cooker. Cover and cook on low-heat setting for 4 hours or on high-heat setting for 2 hours.

A mere three ingredients create a dynamic sauce for cocktail wieners. A whisper of bourbon is called for, but if little ones are on board, use the orange juice.

bourbon-glazed
cocktail sausages

prep: 5 minutes   cook: 4 hours (low)   makes: 12 servings

1   16-ounce package cocktail wieners or small, cooked smoked sausage links
½   cup apricot preserves
¼   cup maple syrup
1   tablespoon bourbon or orange juice

In a 1½-quart slow cooker combine cocktail wieners, apricot preserves, maple syrup, and bourbon. Cover and cook on low-heat setting for 4 hours. Serve immediately or keep warm on low-heat setting for up to 1 hour. Serve wieners with wooden toothpicks.

nutrition facts per serving: 170 cal., 10 g total fat (4 g sat. fat), 23 mg chol., 383 mg sodium, 14 g carbo., 0 g dietary fiber, 5 g protein.

increasing the recipe: Double all ingredient amounts, using 1 package cocktail wieners and 1 package small cooked smoked sausage links; place in a 3½- or 4-quart slow cooker. Cover and cook on low-heat setting for 4 hours.

Grind your own ham in your food processor to make these marvelous meatballs. If you can't find ground pork, go ahead and grind your own, too.

fruit-glazed ham balls

prep: 20 minutes **bake:** 20 minutes **cook:** 4 to 5 hours (low) or 1½ to 2 hours (high) **oven:** 350°F **makes:** 30 meatballs

½ cup graham cracker crumbs
1 egg, lightly beaten
2 tablespoons unsweetened pineapple juice
1 teaspoon dry mustard
¼ teaspoon salt
½ pound ground cooked ham
½ pound ground pork
½ cup snipped dried apricots
1 18-ounce jar pineapple preserves
⅓ cup unsweetened pineapple juice
1 tablespoon cider vinegar
½ teaspoon ground ginger

1 For meatballs, in a large bowl combine graham cracker crumbs, egg, 2 tablespoons pineapple juice, dry mustard, and salt. Add ground ham, ground pork, and apricots; mix well. Shape into 30 meatballs. In a 15x10x1-inch baking pan arrange meatballs in a single layer. Bake, uncovered, in a 350°F oven for 20 minutes. Drain off fat. In a 3½- or 4-quart slow cooker place cooked meatballs.

2 In a small bowl combine pineapple preserves, ⅓ cup pineapple juice, vinegar, and ginger. Pour over meatballs.

3 Cover and cook on low-heat setting for 4 to 5 hours or on high-heat setting for 1½ to 2 hours. Serve immediately or keep covered on warm or low-heat setting for up to 2 hours. Stir gently just before serving. Serve ham balls with wooden toothpicks.

nutrition facts per serving: 97 cal., 3 g total fat (1 g sat. fat), 17 mg chol., 153 mg sodium, 15 g carbo., 0 g dietary fiber, 3 g protein.

These are definitely for the adult-only party! Whiskey, maple syrup, and a bit o' butter is all you need for these sweet wings.

chicken wings
in maple-whiskey sauce

prep: 15 minutes bake: 20 minutes cook: 4 to 5 hours (low) or 2 to 2½ hours (high) oven: 375°F makes: 16 servings

3 pounds chicken wings (about 16)
½ cup maple syrup
½ cup whiskey
2 tablespoons butter or margarine, melted

1 Preheat oven to 375°F. Cut off and discard tips of chicken wings. Cut wings at joints to form 32 pieces. Line a 15x10x1-inch baking pan with foil. Arrange chicken wings in a single layer in prepared pan. Bake for 20 minutes. Drain off fat.

2 In a 3½- or 4-quart slow cooker combine maple syrup, whiskey, and melted butter. Add chicken wings, stirring to coat.

3 Cover and cook on low-heat setting for 4 to 5 hours or on high-heat setting for 2 to 2½ hours. Serve immediately or keep covered on warm or low-heat setting for up to 2 hours.

nutrition facts per serving: 180 cal., 11 g total fat (3 g sat. fat), 62 mg chol., 67 mg sodium, 7 g carbo., 0 g dietary fiber, 10 g protein.

Asked to bring an appetizer to a party? A combo of chicken wings and meatballs glazed with a tangy-sweet sauce is a welcomed contribution.

cherry-ginger
sticks and stones

prep: 20 minutes broil: 12 to 15 minutes cook: 3 to 4 hours (low) or 1½ to 2 hours (high) makes: about 20 servings

2   pounds chicken
     wings
1½   cups frozen pitted
     tart red cherries,
     thawed
½   cup ketchup
¼   cup packed brown
     sugar
2   teaspoons ground
     ginger
½   teaspoon ground
     allspice
½   teaspoon salt
¼   teaspoon ground
     black pepper
1   12-ounce package
     frozen cooked
     Swedish-style
     meatballs

1 Cut off and discard tips of chicken wings. Cut wings at joints to form 24 pieces. Place wing pieces on the unheated rack of a broiler pan. Broil 4 to 5 inches from the heat for 12 to 15 minutes or until light brown, turning once.

2 In a blender or food processor combine cherries, ketchup, brown sugar, ginger, allspice, salt, and pepper. Cover and blend or process until smooth.

3 Place wings and meatballs in a 3½- or 4-quart slow cooker. Add cherry mixture, stirring to coat.

4 Cover and cook on low-heat setting for 3 to 4 hours or on high-heat setting for 1½ to 2 hours.

nutrition facts per serving: 100 cal., 5 g total fat (2 g sat. fat), 24 mg chol., 205 mg sodium, 8 g carbo., 1 g dietary fiber, 6 g protein.

Chorizo is a pork sausage flavored with chile pepper and garlic. Look for it with other sausages in the supermarket or Mexican markets.

mexican-style meatballs and smokies

prep: 30 minutes bake: 15 minutes cook: 3 to 4 hours (low) or 1½ to 2 hours (high) oven: 350°F makes: 25 servings (about 100 pieces)

1   egg, lightly beaten
¼   cup fine dry bread crumbs
¼   cup finely chopped onion
3   cloves garlic, minced
½   teaspoon salt
8   ounces lean ground beef
8   ounces chorizo (casing removed, if necessary)
1   16-ounce jar salsa
1   12-ounce jar chili sauce
1   16-ounce package small fully cooked smoked sausage links
2   tablespoons snipped fresh cilantro

1 In a medium mixing bowl combine egg, bread crumbs, onion, garlic, and salt. Add ground beef and chorizo; mix well. Shape meat mixture into thirty-eight 1-inch balls. Arrange meatballs in a single layer in an ungreased 15x10x1-inch baking pan. Bake, uncovered, in a 350°F oven for 20 minutes. Drain off fat.

2 In a 3½- or 4-quart slow cooker combine salsa and chili sauce. Add cooked meatballs and sausage links, stirring gently to coat.

3 Cover and cook on low-heat setting for 3 to 4 hours or on high-heat setting for 1½ to 2 hours. Sprinkle with cilantro before serving. Serve with decorative toothpicks.

nutrition facts per serving: 148 cal., 11 g total fat (4 g sat. fat), 34 mg chol., 648 mg sodium, 6 g carbo., 1 g dietary fiber, 7 g protein.

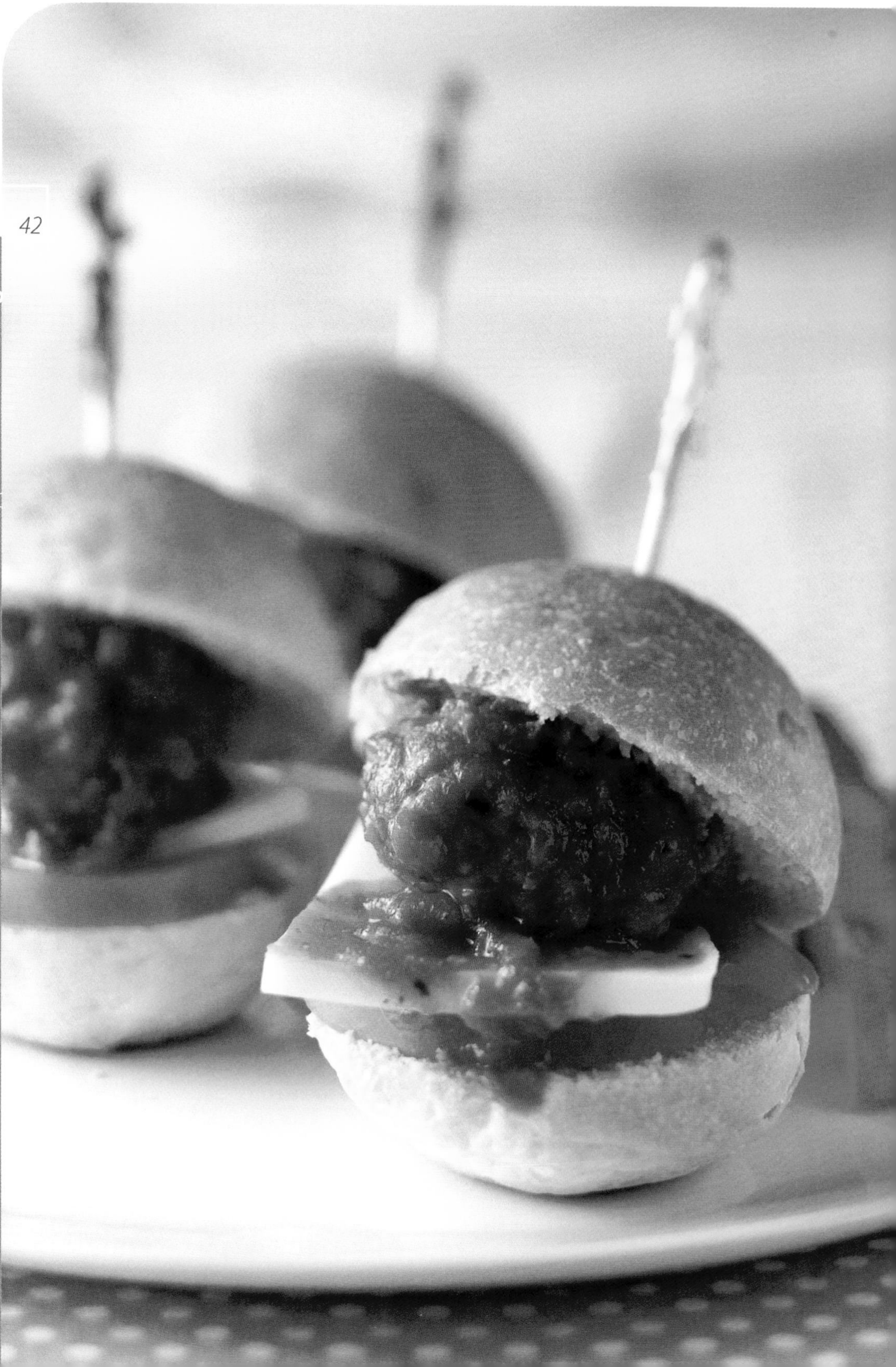

Sliders are small bites of flavor in a bun. Here meatballs are smothered in a classic Italian marinara sauce. Don't forget the provolone cheese.

meatball sliders

prep: 10 minutes cook: 4 to 5 hours (low) or 2 to 2½ hours (high)
makes: 24 appetizers

1 large red onion, cut into thin wedges (1½ cups)
2 12-ounce packages frozen cooked Italian meatballs (24)
1 24- to 26-ounce jar marinara or pasta sauce (about 2¼ cups)
1 tablespoon balsamic vinegar
½ teaspoon crushed red pepper
6 slices provolone cheese, quartered (6 ounces)
4 roma tomatoes, sliced
24 cocktail buns, split and toasted, if desired

1 Place onion wedges in a 3½- or 4-quart slow cooker. Top with meatballs. In a medium bowl combine marinara sauce, balsamic vinegar, and crushed red pepper. Pour over meatballs.

2 Cover and cook on low-heat setting for 4 to 5 hours or on high-heat setting for 2 to 2½ hours.

3 Gently stir through mixture in cooker. Place a slice of provolone cheese and a slice of tomato on each cocktail bun bottom. Top each with a meatball and bun tops.

nutrition facts per serving: 217 cal., 11 g total fat (5 g sat. fat), 24 mg chol., 516 mg sodium, 20 g carbo., 2 g dietary fiber, 10 g protein.

Although this recipe calls for a package of 16 meatballs, various brands contain a different count. Just look for the total weight, even if it isn't a 16 count.

plum-good
sausage and meatballs

prep: 10 minutes cook: 5 to 6 hours (low) or 2½ to 3 hours (high)
makes: 16 servings

1   10- or 12-ounce
    jar plum jam or
    preserves
1   18-ounce bottle
    barbecue sauce
1   16-ounce link cooked
    jalapeño pepper
    smoked sausage
    or smoked sausage,
    sliced into bite-size
    pieces
1   16- to 18-ounce
    package Italian-
    style or regular
    frozen cooked
    meatballs, thawed

1 In a 3½- or 4-quart slow cooker combine jam, barbecue sauce, sausage, and meatballs.

2 Cover and cook on low-heat setting for 5 to 6 hours or on high-heat setting for 2½ to 3 hours.

3 Serve immediately or keep covered on warm or low-heat setting for up to 2 hours. Stir occasionally.

nutrition facts per serving: 267 cal., 16 g total fat (6 g sat. fat), 38 mg chol., 898 mg sodium, 19 g carbo., 2 g dietary fiber, 12 g protein.

To make uniform-size meatballs, pat the meat mixture into a 6-inch square and cut into 36 pieces. Shape each piece into a ball.

sweet, hot, and sour
meatballs

prep: 35 minutes   bake: 25 minutes   cook: 3 to 4 hours (low) or 1½ to 2 hours (high)
oven: 375°F   makes: 36 meatballs

2	eggs
½	cup fine dry bread crumbs
½	cup finely chopped onion (1 medium)
¼	cup milk
½	teaspoon salt
½	teaspoon ground black pepper
1	pound bulk pork sausage
1	pound ground beef
¾	cup apple jelly
⅓	cup spicy brown mustard
⅓	cup whiskey or apple juice
1½	teaspoons Worcestershire sauce
	Dash bottled hot pepper sauce

1 Preheat oven to 375°F. In a large bowl beat eggs with a fork. Stir in bread crumbs, onion, milk, salt, and pepper. Add sausage and beef; mix well. Shape into 36 meatballs. Place in a shallow baking pan. Bake for 25 to 30 minutes or until meatballs are cooked through (160°F). Drain off fat.

2 Place meatballs in a 3½- or 4-quart slow cooker. In a small bowl stir together jelly, mustard, whiskey, Worcestershire sauce, and hot pepper sauce. Pour over meatballs.

3 Cover and cook on low-heat setting for 3 to 4 hours or on high-heat setting for 1½ to 2 hours. Serve immediately or keep covered on warm or low-heat setting for up to 2 hours.

nutrition facts per meatball: 112 cal., 7 g total fat (3 g sat. fat), 28 mg chol., 195 mg sodium, 6 g carbo., 0 g dietary fiber, 5 g protein.

Flavors from the islands of the Pacific dominate in these scrumptious chicken wings. Add crushed red pepper to your taste for a subtle bit of heat.

polynesian glazed
wings

prep: 20 minutes broil: 15 minutes cook: 3 to 4 hours (low) or 1½ to 2 hours (high) makes: 32 servings

3 pounds chicken wings (about 16)
1 10-ounce bottle sweet-and-sour sauce (about 1¼ cups)
2 tablespoons soy sauce
2 teaspoons grated fresh ginger
¼ to ½ teaspoon crushed red pepper
Thinly sliced green onions (optional)

1 Cut off and discard tips of chicken wings. Cut wings at joints to make 32 pieces. Place wing pieces on the unheated rack of a broiler pan. Broil 4 to 5 inches from heat for 15 minutes or until wings are brown, turning once.

2 In a 3½- or 4-quart slow cooker combine sweet-and-sour sauce, soy sauce, ginger, and crushed red pepper. Add wings, stirring to coat.

3 Cover and cook on low-heat setting for 3 to 4 hours or on high-heat setting for 1½ to 2 hours. Transfer to serving plate and sprinkle with green onions, if desired.

nutrition facts per serving: 61 cal., 5 g total fat (1 g sat. fat), 29 mg chol., 112 mg sodium, 2 g carbo., 0 g dietary fiber, 5 g protein.

Spicy brown mustard flavors these mini tortilla-wrapped bites. Modify the taste next time with one of the multitudes of flavored mustards available.

spicy mustard stir-fry bites

prep: 25 minutes cook: 6 to 7 hours (low) makes: about 25 appetizers

Nonstick cooking spray
1 pound packaged chicken, pork, or beef stir-fry strips
½ cup water
½ cup spicy brown mustard
4 teaspoons fajita seasoning
5 7- to 8-inch flour tortillas, warmed*
1 medium red, green, or yellow sweet pepper, seeded and cut into thin strips
Snipped fresh cilantro and/or sliced green onion (optional)

1 Lightly coat a large skillet with cooking spray. Heat skillet over medium-high heat; add stir-fry strips. Cook and stir until brown. Drain off fat.

2 In a 1½-quart slow cooker stir together the water, mustard, and fajita seasoning. Add stir-fry strips, stirring to coat.

3 Cover and cook on low-heat setting for 6 to 7 hours. Using a slotted spoon, transfer meat to a cutting board. Discard cooking liquid.

4 Divide meat mixture evenly among the warmed tortillas. Top with sweet pepper strips and, if desired, cilantro and/or green onion. Roll up tortillas. Using a serrated knife, cut filled tortillas crosswise into bite-size pieces. If desired, skewer with decorative toothpicks.

nutrition facts per appetizer: 60 cal., 2 g total fat (0 g sat. fat), 12 mg chol., 311 mg sodium, 6 g carbo., 0 g dietary fiber, 5 g protein.

*test kitchen tip: To warm tortillas, stack tortillas and wrap tightly in foil. Heat in a 350°F oven for about 10 minutes or until heated through.

to serve 50: Double all ingredients. Place in a 3½- or 4-quart slow cooker. Cover and cook for 6 to 7 hours on low or for 3 to 3½ hours on high. Continue as directed.

To make the ribs easier to eat, ask your butcher to cut the ribs in half crosswise (across the bones) to make smaller portions.

flamin' cajun riblets

prep: 20 minutes   cook: 5 to 6 hours (low) or 2½ to 3 hours (high)
makes: 12 servings

3   pounds pork loin
    back ribs
1   tablespoon Cajun
    seasoning
1   cup bottled chili
    sauce
1   medium onion, finely
    chopped
1   serrano chile pepper,
    seeded and finely
    chopped (see tip,
    page 32)
2   tablespoons quick-
    cooking tapioca,
    crushed
1   teaspoon finely
    shredded lemon
    peel
1   tablespoon lemon
    juice
1   to 2 teaspoons
    bottled hot pepper
    sauce
    Snipped fresh parsley
    (optional)

1 Sprinkle ribs with Cajun seasoning and rub in with your fingers. Cut ribs into single rib portions. Place ribs in a 3½- or 4-quart slow cooker.

2 In a medium bowl combine chili sauce, onion, serrano pepper, tapioca, lemon peel, lemon juice, and hot pepper sauce. Pour over ribs.

3 Cover and cook on low-heat setting for 5 to 6 hours or on high-heat setting for 2½ to 3 hours. Serve immediately or keep covered on warm or low-heat setting for up to 2 hours. (Remove any bones without meat.) If desired, sprinkle with parsley.

nutrition facts per serving: 231 cal., 17 g total fat (6 g sat. fat), 57 mg chol., 369 mg sodium, 7 g carbo., 1 g dietary fiber, 12 g protein.

Five spices, chili sauce, dried apricots, and a serrano pepper make up this finger-licking sauce. If you like it, cilantro adds a crowning freshness.

maharajah **riblets**

prep: 25 minutes   cook: 5 to 6 hours (low) or 2½ to 3 hours (high)
makes: 12 servings

1 teaspoon curry
   powder
1 teaspoon ground
   ginger
½ teaspoon ground
   cumin
½ teaspoon ground
   cinnamon
¼ teaspoon ground
   cardamom
3 pounds pork loin
   back ribs*
1 12-ounce bottle
   chili sauce
1 medium onion,
   finely chopped
1 serrano chile pepper,
   seeded and finely
   chopped (see tip,
   page 32)
¼ cup snipped dried
   apricots
2 tablespoons quick-
   cooking tapioca,
   crushed
1 teaspoon finely
   shredded lemon
   peel
1 tablespoon lemon
   juice
   Chopped fresh
   cilantro (optional)

1 In a small bowl combine curry powder, ginger, cumin, cinnamon, and cardamom. Sprinkle the ribs with the spice mixture and rub in with your fingers. Cut ribs into single rib portions. Place ribs in a 3½- or 4-quart slow cooker. In a medium bowl combine chili sauce, onion, serrano pepper, apricots, tapioca, lemon peel, and lemon juice. Pour over ribs, stirring to coat.

2 Cover and cook on low-heat setting for 5 to 6 hours or on high-heat setting for 2½ to 3 hours. Serve immediately or keep covered on warm or low-heat setting for up to 2 hours. Using tongs, remove ribs from cooking liquid to serve. If desired, sprinkle with fresh cilantro.

nutrition facts per serving: 126 cal., 1 g total fat (0 g sat. fat), 31 mg chol., 878 mg sodium, 12 g carbo., 1 g dietary fiber, 15 g protein.

*test kitchen tip: To make eating the ribs easier, have your butcher saw the ribs in half crosswise (across the bone) for smaller rib portions.

Peach preserves from a jar make this an easy sauce. A touch of bourbon rounds out the wonderful flavor.

georgia peach ribs

prep: 15 minutes cook: 5 to 6 hours (low) or 2½ to 3 hours (high)
makes: 12 servings

2½ pounds pork loin back ribs*
1 12-ounce jar peach preserves
½ cup finely chopped onion (1 medium)
1 tablespoon bourbon
1 tablespoon yellow mustard
1 tablespoon cider vinegar
¼ teaspoon salt
¼ teaspoon cayenne pepper

1 Cut ribs into single-rib portions. Place ribs in a 3½- or 4-quart slow cooker. In a medium bowl combine peach preserves, onion, bourbon, mustard, vinegar, salt, and cayenne pepper. Pour over ribs, tossing to coat.

2 Cover and cook on low-heat setting for 5 to 6 hours or on high-heat setting for 2½ to 3 hours. Serve immediately or keep covered on warm or low-heat setting for up to 2 hours. Use tongs to remove ribs from cooking liquid to serve.

nutrition facts per serving: 205 cal., 13 g total fat (5 g sat. fat), 47 mg chol., 80 mg sodium, 10 g carbo., 0 g dietary fiber, 10 g protein.

*test kitchen tip: To make eating the ribs easier, have your butcher saw the ribs in half crosswise (across the bone) for smaller rib portions.

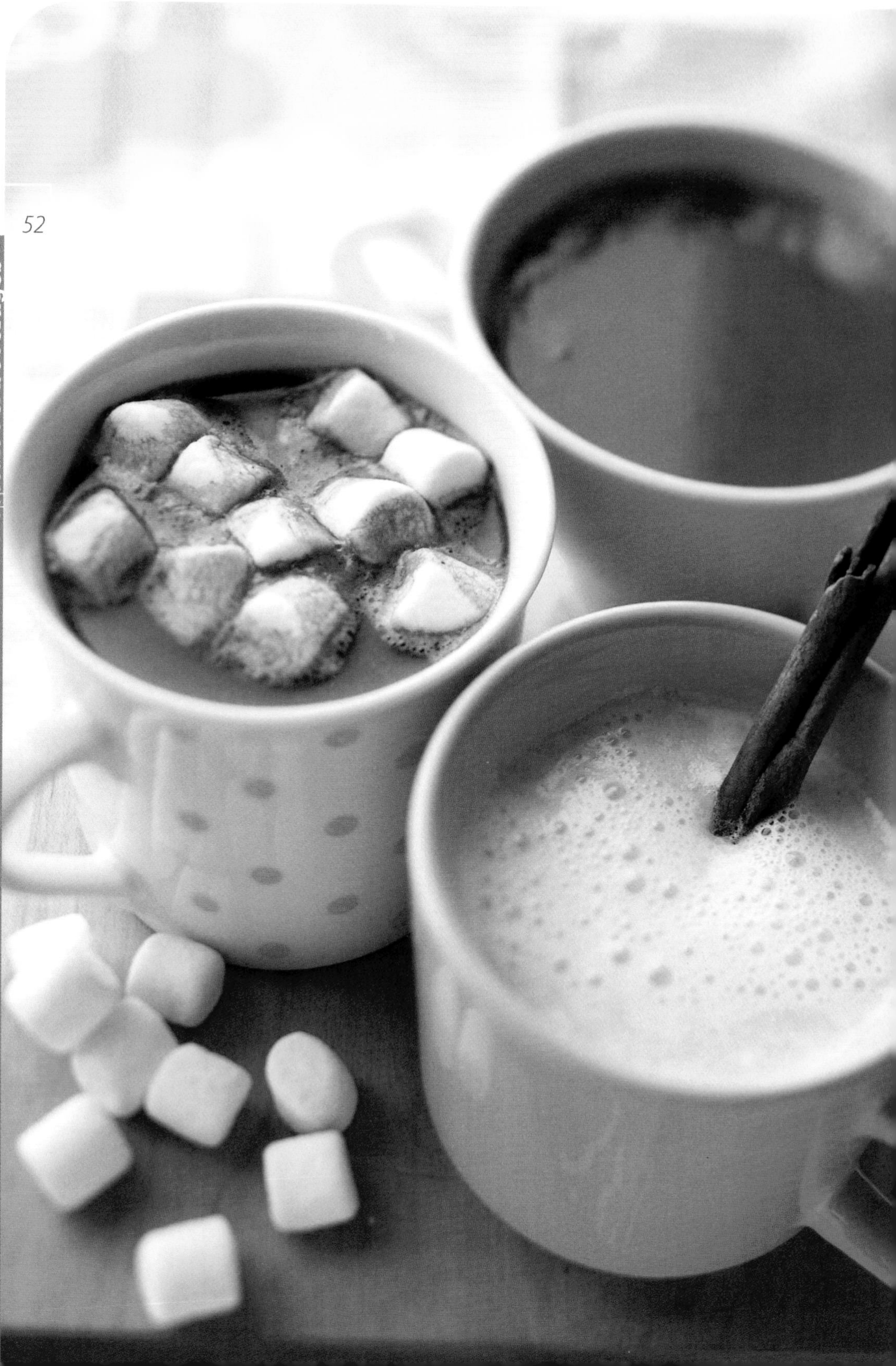

Here's a hot beverage that is a nice change from typical hot chocolate. White baking pieces flavor this brew.

white hot chocolate

prep: 10 minutes cook: 4 hours (low) or 2 hours (high)
makes: 8 (¾-cup) servings

3 cups milk
3 cups half-and-half
   or light cream
1½ cups white baking
   pieces
6 inches stick
   cinnamon
8 cardamom pods,
   cracked
1 vanilla bean, split, or
   2 teaspoons vanilla
Additional cinnamon
   sticks (optional)

1 In a 3- to 4-quart slow cooker, stir together the milk, half-and-half, and baking pieces. For a spice bag, cut an 8-inch square from a double thickness of 100-percent-cotton cheesecloth. Place the 6 inches cinnamon, cardamom, and vanilla bean, if using, in the center of the cheesecloth square. Bring up corners of the cheesecloth; tie closed with clean 100-percent-cotton kitchen string. Add spice bag to mixture in cooker.

2 Cover and cook on low-heat setting for 4 hours or on high-heat setting for 2 hours, stirring halfway through cooking time. Remove spice bag and discard. Stir in vanilla, if using. If necessary, whisk until smooth. If desired, serve with additional cinnamon sticks.

nutrition facts per serving: 403 cal., 24 g total fat (18 g sat. fat), 41 mg chol., 134 mg sodium, 35 g carbo., 0 g dietary fiber, 6 g protein.

Bittersweet chocolate makes this hot drink a favorite of chocolate lovers. Use either chocolate chips or chopped chocolate.

bittersweet hot chocolate

prep: 5 minutes cook: 5 to 6 hours (low) or 2½ to 3 hours (high)
makes: 12 (¾-cup) servings

4   cups half-and-half
    or light cream
4   cups milk
6   inch stick cinnamon,
    broken
1   12-ounce package
    bittersweet
    chocolate pieces
    or two 6-ounce
    packages bittersweet
    chocolate, chopped
1   tablespoon vanilla
    Marshmallows
    (optional)

1 In a 3- to 4-quart slow cooker combine half-and-half, milk, and cinnamon sticks. Cover and cook on low-heat setting for 5 to 6 hours or on high-heat setting for 2½ to 3 hours.

2 Remove and discard cinnamon sticks. Stir in chocolate pieces; whisk until chocolate is melted and smooth. Stir in vanilla. Serve immediately in mugs or keep covered on warm or low-heat setting for up to 2 hours. If desired, top with marshmallows.

nutrition facts per serving: 284 cal., 21 g total fat (13 g sat. fat), 36 mg chol., 68 mg sodium, 23 g carbo., 2 g dietary fiber, 7 g protein.

Kids will love this peanut buttery cocoa that can be made in a snap. Peanut allergies? Use sunflower butter spread, which tastes a lot like peanut butter.

peanut butter cocoa

prep: 10 minutes   cook: 3 to 4 hours (low) or 1½ to 2 hours (high)
makes: 9 (1-cup) servings

1 cup instant milk chocolate or chocolate fudge cocoa mix

8 cups hot water

¾ cup chocolate-flavor syrup

¼ cup smooth peanut butter

1½ teaspoons vanilla

1 Place cocoa mix in a 3½- or 4-quart slow cooker. Carefully stir in the hot water. Stir in chocolate syrup.

2 Cover and cook on low-heat setting for 3 to 4 hours or on high-heat setting for 1½ to 2 hours. Whisk in peanut butter and vanilla until smooth.

nutrition facts per serving: 248 cal., 5 g total fat (2 g sat. fat), 0 mg chol., 172 mg sodium, 48 g carbo., 1 g dietary fiber, 3 g protein.

Coffee, cinnamon, and ground chipotle chile pepper explains this hot chocolate's Mexican moniker.

aztec hot chocolate

prep: 15 minutes   cook: 4 hours (low) or 2 hours (high)
makes: 12 (½-cup) servings

4   cups milk
2   cups half-and-half
1½ cups semisweet
      chocolate pieces
1   teaspoon instant
      espresso powder
1   teaspoon ground
      cinnamon
½   teaspoon ground
      chipotle chile
      pepper
    Sweetened whipped
      cream (optional)
    Ground cinnamon
      (optional)

1 In a 3½- or 4-quart slow cooker combine milk, half-and-half, chocolate pieces, espresso powder, 1 teaspoon cinnamon, and ground chipotle chile pepper.

2 Cover and cook on low-heat setting for 4 hours or on high-heat setting for 2 hours, whisking vigorously once halfway through cooking time. Whisk well before serving in mugs. If desired, top with whipped cream and sprinkle with cinnamon.

nutrition facts per serving: 197 cal., 13 g total fat (8 g sat. fat), 21 mg chol., 53 mg sodium, 19 g carbo., 1 g dietary fiber, 5 g protein.

When you want to serve mulled wine without the wine, this drink will satisfy. Fruity and spicy, it's a perfect drink for those designated drivers at the party.

teetotaler's mulled wine

prep: 20 minutes cook: 5 to 6 hours (low) or 2½ to 3 hours (high)
makes: 10 (¾-cup) servings

1	orange
4	inches stick cinnamon, broken
12	whole cloves
12	whole allspice
4	cups cranberry juice
2	cups pomegranate juice
2	cups cherry juice blend or raspberry juice blend
¼	cup packed brown sugar
	Cinnamon sticks (optional)

1 Use a vegetable peeler to remove peel in wide strips from the orange, avoiding the bitter white pith underneath. Reserve the orange flesh for another use.

2 For spice bag, cut a 6-inch square from a double thickness of 100-percent-cotton cheesecloth. Place orange peel, broken cinnamon sticks, cloves, and allspice in the center of the cheesecloth square. Bring up corners of the cheesecloth; tie closed with clean 100-percent-cotton kitchen string.

3 In a 3½- or 4-quart slow cooker combine cranberry juice, pomegranate juice, cherry juice, and brown sugar. Add spice bag to mixture in cooker.

4 Cover and cook on low-heat setting for 5 to 6 hours or on high-heat setting for 2½ to 3 hours. Remove spice bag and discard. To serve, ladle beverage into cups. If desired, garnish servings with additional cinnamon sticks.

nutrition facts per serving: 131 cal., 0 g total fat (0 g sat. fat), 0 mg chol., 20 mg sodium, 33 g carbo., 0 g dietary fiber, 0 g protein.

The beautiful crimson color of this hot punch lends itself to the holiday season or a winter wedding. The spice bag will make it easy to remove the whole spices.

mulled cranberry punch

prep: 15 minutes   cook: 4 to 6 hours (low) or 2 to 2½ hours (high)
makes: 12 (¾-cup) servings

1   orange
8   inches stick
     cinnamon, broken
8   whole cloves
4   whole allspice
1   32-ounce bottle
     cranberry juice
1   11.5-ounce can frozen
     white grape–
     raspberry juice
     concentrate
4   cups water

1 Use a vegetable peeler to remove several 2- to 3-inch-long sections of orange peel from the orange, avoiding the bitter white pith underneath. Juice the orange.

2 For a spice bag, cut a 6-inch square from a double thickness of 100-percent-cotton cheesecloth. Place orange peel, cinnamon sticks, cloves, and allspice in the center of the square. Bring up corners of the cheesecloth; tie closed with clean 100-percent-cotton kitchen string.

3 In a 3½- or 4-quart slow cooker combine cranberry juice, grape-raspberry juice concentrate, the water, and orange juice. Add spice bag to mixture in cooker.

4 Cover and cook on low-heat setting for 4 to 6 hours or on high-heat setting for 2 to 2½ hours. Remove spice bag and discard. Serve immediately or keep warm on low-heat setting for up to 2 hours.

nutrition facts per serving: 114 cal., 0 g total fat (0 g sat. fat), 0 mg chol., 7 mg sodium, 29 g carbo., 1 g dietary fiber, 0 g protein.

This hot tea calls for tea bags, with no flavor suggestion. Use plain tea bags or another flavor of your choice. Today, there's a plethora of flavors.

ginger-apple tea

prep: 15 minutes   cook: 5 to 6 hours (low) or 2½ to 3 hours (high)
stand: 5 minutes   makes: 8 to 10 (1-cup) servings

1   lemon
⅓   cup coarsely chopped
      fresh ginger
4   inches stick cinnamon,
      broken
½   teaspoon whole
      cloves
1   quart apple juice
      or apple cider
1   quart water
6   tea bags
      Lemon slices
      (optional)
      Sugar or honey
      (optional)

1 Use a vegetable peeler to remove peel in wide strips from the lemon, avoiding the bitter white pith underneath. Juice the lemon; cover and chill juice until needed.

2 For spice bag, cut an 8-inch square from a double thickness of 100-percent-cotton cheesecloth. Place lemon peel, ginger, cinnamon sticks, and cloves in the center of the cheesecloth square. Bring up corners of the cheesecloth; tie closed with clean 100-percent-cotton kitchen string. In a 3½- or 4-quart slow cooker combine apple juice and the water. Add spice bag to the mixture in cooker.

3 Cover and cook on low-heat setting for 5 to 6 hours or on high-heat setting for 2½ to 3 hours. Turn off cooker. Remove and discard spice bag. Add tea bags* and chilled lemon juice to the cooker. Let stand for 5 minutes. Remove tea bags, squeezing gently to remove liquid; discard tea bags.

4 If desired, garnish tea with lemon slices and sweeten to taste with sugar.

nutrition facts per serving: 67 cal., 0 g total fat (0 g sat. fat), 0 mg chol., 9 mg sodium, 17 g carbo., 1 g dietary fiber, 0 g protein.

*test kitchen tip: For easy removal, allow the strings of the tea bags to hang over the side of the slow cooker and use the lid to hold the strings in place.

If you can't find star anise at your supermarket, use anise seeds instead. They both have a black licorice–like flavor.

mulled cranberry cider

prep: 15 minutes cook: 5 to 6 hours (low) or 2½ to 3 hours (high)
makes: 10 (¾-cup) servings

8   cups cranberry-
     raspberry juice
     blend
¼   cup packed brown
     sugar
6   inch stick cinnamon,
     broken
3   star anise
1   teaspoon whole
     cloves
     Orange peel strips
     (optional)

1 In a 3½- to 5-quart slow cooker combine cranberry-raspberry juice blend and brown sugar.

2 For a spice bag, cut an 8-inch square from a double thickness of 100-percent-cotton cheesecloth. Place cinnamon sticks, star anise, and cloves in the center of the cheesecloth square. Bring up corners of the cheesecloth; tie closed with clean 100-percent-cotton kitchen string. Add spice bag to mixture in cooker.

3 Cover and cook on low-heat setting for 5 to 6 hours or on high-heat setting for 2½ to 3 hours. Remove spice bag and discard. Ladle cider into cups. If desired, garnish with orange peel strips.

nutrition facts per serving: 152 cal., 0 g total fat (0 g sat. fat), 0 mg chol., 30 mg sodium, 37 g carbo., 0 g dietary fiber, 0 g protein.

This is the ultimate adult wintertime beverage. Real butter lends the flavor you are looking for, so don't be tempted to substitute.

hot buttered apple rum

prep: 10 minutes cook: 7 to 8 hours (low) or 3 to 4 hours (high)
makes: 10 (¾-cup) servings

4   inches stick
    cinnamon, broken
1   teaspoon whole
    allspice
1   teaspoon whole
    cloves
7   cups apple cider
    or apple juice
1½ to 2 cups rum
⅓   to ½ cup packed
    brown sugar
    Butter

1 For a spice bag cut a 6-inch square from a double thickness of 100-percent-cotton cheesecloth. Place cinnamon sticks, allspice, and cloves in the center of the cheesecloth square. Bring up corners of the cheesecloth; tie closed with clean 100-percent-cotton kitchen string.

2 In a 3½- to 6-quart slow cooker combine apple cider, rum, and brown sugar. Add spice bag to mixture in cooker.

3 Cover and cook on low-heat setting for 7 to 8 hours or on high-heat setting for 3 to 4 hours.

4 Remove spice bag and discard. Float about ½ teaspoon butter on each serving.

nutrition facts per serving: 214 cal., 2 g total fat (1 g sat. fat), 5 mg chol., 29 mg sodium, 27 g carbo., 0 g dietary fiber, 0 g protein.

A beautiful golden color emerges when you blend the ingredients for this delightful drink. When purchasing fresh ginger, look for firm, unshriveled roots.

citrus cider

prep: 10 minutes   cook: 5 to 6 hours (low) or 2½ to 3 hours (high)
makes: about 13 (¾-cup) servings

2	quarts apple cider or apple juice
1	cup orange juice*
½	cup lemon juice*
¼	cup honey
8	inches stick cinnamon, broken
8	whole cloves
3	slices fresh ginger

1 In a 3½- or 4-quart slow cooker combine cider, orange juice, lemon juice, and honey. Stir to dissolve honey.

2 For a spice bag, cut a 6-inch square from a double thickness of 100-percent-cotton cheesecloth. Place cinnamon sticks, cloves, and ginger in the center of the cheesecloth square. Bring up corners of the cheesecloth; tie closed with clean 100-percent-cotton kitchen string. Add spice bag to mixture in cooker.

3 Cover and cook on low-heat setting for 5 to 6 hours or on high-heat setting for 2½ to 3 hours. Remove spice bag and discard.

nutrition facts per serving: 89 cal., 0 g total fat (0 g sat. fat), 0 mg chol., 1 mg sodium, 10 g carbo., 0 g dietary fiber, 0 g protein.

*test kitchen tip: If you squeeze fresh oranges and lemons for the juice, use a vegetable peeler to cut several wide strips of peel from the fruit, avoiding the white pith underneath. Add the peel to the spice bag.

Brandy or rum livens up this holiday classic. Cranberry, raspberry, lemon, and apple juices all contribute to the snappy flavor.

holiday wassail

prep: 10 minutes   cook: 4 to 6 hours (low) or 2 to 3 hours (high)
makes: 16 (¾-cup) servings

6   inches stick
     cinnamon, broken
12   whole cloves
6   cups water
1   12-ounce can frozen
     cranberry juice
     cocktail concentrate
1   12-ounce can frozen
     raspberry juice
     blend concentrate
1   12-ounce can
     frozen apple juice
     concentrate
1   cup brandy or rum
⅓   cup lemon juice
¼   cup sugar
     Orange slices (optional)

1 For spice bag cut a 6-inch square from a double thickness of 100-percent-cotton cheesecloth. Place cinnamon sticks and cloves in center of the cheesecloth square. Bring up corners of the cheesecloth; tie closed with clean 100-percent-cotton kitchen string.

2 In a 4- to 6-quart slow cooker combine the water, juice concentrates, brandy, lemon juice, and sugar. Add spice bag to mixture in cooker.

3 Cover and cook on low-heat setting for 4 to 6 hours or on high-heat setting for 2 to 3 hours. Remove spice bag and discard. To serve, ladle wassail into cups. If desired, garnish with orange slices.

nutrition facts per serving: 178 cal., 0 g total fat (0 g sat. fat), 0 mg chol., 12 mg sodium, 37 g carbo., 0 g dietary fiber, 0 g protein.

Brandy, triple sec (an orange-flavored liqueur), pineapple-orange juice, and spices take a bottle of red wine from good to great.

wine to warm you

prep: 15 minutes   cook: 4 to 5 hours (low) or 2 to 2½ hours (high)
makes: about 22 (½-cup) servings

1	orange
1	lemon
4	slices fresh ginger
3	inches stick cinnamon, broken
8	whole allspice
8	whole cloves
1	750-milliliter bottle Bordeaux or Beaujolais wine
4	cups water
1	12-ounce can frozen pineapple-orange juice concentrate
½	cup brandy
½	cup sugar
¼	cup triple sec
	Star anise
	Cinnamon sticks

1 Using a vegetable peeler, cut wide strips of peel from the orange and lemon, avoiding the bitter white pith underneath. Juice the orange and lemon.

2 For a spice bag, cut a 6-inch square from a double thickness of 100-percent-cotton cheesecloth. Place lemon peel, orange peel, ginger, cinnamon sticks, allspice, and cloves in the center of the cheesecloth square. Bring up corners of the cheesecloth; tie closed with clean 100-percent-cotton kitchen string.

3 In a 4- to 5-quart slow cooker combine wine, the water, juice concentrate, brandy, sugar, triple sec, and citrus juices. Add spice bag to mixture in cooker.

4 Cover and cook on low-heat setting for 4 to 5 hours or on high-heat setting for 2 to 2½ hours. Remove spice bag and discard. Garnish each serving with star anise and cinnamon sticks.

nutrition facts per serving: 103 cal., 0 g total fat (0 g sat. fat), 0 mg chol., 8 mg sodium, 15 g carbo., 0 g dietary fiber, 0 g protein.

3

brilliant

break

French toast in your slow cooker? Yes! Of course hot cereals make perfect partners to slow cookers, but Spanish Strata, Italian Breakfast Burritos, or Tropical Fruit Casserole are all breakfast options, too. So for your next brunch or special breakfast, break out the slow cooker.

fasts

With 8 grams of fiber, this cereal contributes almost one-third of your fiber for the day. With wheat berries, barley, and oats, it's a fiber powerhouse.

four-grain hot cereal

prep: 15 minutes   **cook:** 6 to 7 hours (low)   **makes:** 6 to 8 servings

Disposable slow-
   cooker liner
3 cups water
2½ cups apple juice
½ cup regular barley
   (not quick-cooking)
½ cup steel-cut oats
½ cup dried cranberries
½ cup dried apricots,
   chopped
¼ cup wheat berries
¼ cup quinoa
¼ teaspoon salt
¼ cup honey
   Toasted sliced
   almonds
   Honey (optional)

1 Line a 3½- or 4-quart slow cooker with a disposable slow-cooker liner. In prepared slow cooker combine the water, apple juice, barley, oats, cranberries, apricots, wheat berries, quinoa, and salt.

2 Cover and cook on low-heat setting for 6 to 7 hours. Stir in ¼ cup honey. Sprinkle each serving with almonds, and, if desired, drizzle with additional honey.

nutrition facts per serving: 331 cal., 5 g total fat (1 g sat. fat), 0 mg chol., 108 mg sodium, 70 g carbo., 8 g dietary fiber, 7 g protein.

Granny Smith, Jonathan, Newtown Pippin, and McIntosh apples are all suitable for this delicious applesauce.

chunky applesauce

prep: 20 minutes   cook: 6 to 8 hours (low) or 3 to 4 hours (high)
makes: 10 servings

3   pounds tart cooking apples, peeled, cored, and sliced
1   cup snipped dried apples
½   cup packed brown sugar
½   cup water
¼   cup frozen apple juice concentrate, thawed
1   teaspoon finely shredded lemon peel
3   tablespoons lemon juice
6   inches stick cinnamon, broken into 1-inch pieces

1 In a 3½- or 4-quart slow cooker combine sliced apples, dried apples, brown sugar, the water, apple juice concentrate, lemon peel, lemon juice, and cinnamon. Cover and cook on low-heat setting for 6 to 8 hours or on high-heat setting for 3 to 4 hours. Remove and discard cinnamon. Using a potato masher, coarsely mash apples.

2 If storing applesauce for later use, slightly cool. Ladle into airtight containers; seal. Chill for up to 1 week or freeze for up to 8 months.

nutrition facts per serving: 159 cal., 0 g total fat (0 g sat. fat), 0 mg chol., 29 mg sodium, 41 g carbo., 2 g dietary fiber, 1 g protein.

Slow-cooker liners help keep your ceramic insert clean, eliminating the need for use of harsh chemicals, scrubbing, or soaking.

crème brûlée french toast

prep: 15 minutes   **chill:** 4 hours   **cook:** 7 to 8 hours (low)   **stand:** 30 minutes
makes: 12 servings

Disposable slow-
    cooker liner
12 ounces challah or
    sweet bread (such
    as Portuguese or
    Hawaiian sweet
    bread), cut into
    1-inch cubes (about
    9 cups)
4 cups milk
½ cup sugar
3 eggs, or ¾ cup
    refrigerated or
    frozen egg product,
    thawed
1 teaspoon vanilla
¼ teaspoon salt
    Caramel ice cream
    topping, warmed

1 Line a 3½- or 4-quart slow cooker with a disposable slow-cooker liner. Place bread cubes in prepared slow cooker.

2 In a large mixing bowl whisk together milk, sugar, eggs, vanilla, and salt. Pour over bread cubes in cooker. Press bread lightly with back of a large spoon to moisten bread completely. Cover and chill in the refrigerator for 4 to 24 hours.

3 Remove from refrigerator. Cover and cook on low-heat setting for 7 to 8 hours or until a knife inserted in the center comes out clean. Turn off cooker. Let stand for 30 minutes. Carefully lift liner from cooker, using a plate to transfer French toast to a cutting board. If desired, slice French toast to serve or spoon it into serving dishes. Top with ice cream topping.

nutrition facts per serving: 231 cal., 5 g total fat (2 g sat. fat), 33 mg chol., 287 mg sodium, 39 g carbo., 1 g dietary fiber, 7 g protein.

Serve this warm fruit mixture for brunch or serve it spooned over Belgian waffles. It's better than syrup, guaranteed.

tropical fruit casserole

prep: 15 minutes cook: 3½ to 4 hours (low) or 1½ to 2 hours (high)
makes: 12 to 14 servings

1 24-ounce jar
    refrigerated mango
    slices, drained
    and cut into 1-inch
    pieces
1 20-ounce can
    pineapple chunks
    in juice, drained
1 16-ounce package
    frozen unsweetened
    peach slices
1 12-ounce package
    soft coconut
    macaroon cookies,
    crumbled
½ cup dried cherries
¼ cup packed brown
    sugar
¼ cup butter, melted
1 teaspoon finely
    shredded lemon
    peel
2 tablespoons lemon
    juice

1 In a 3½- or 4-quart slow cooker combine mango, pineapple, peaches, crumbled macaroons, and cherries. In a small bowl stir together brown sugar, butter, lemon peel, and lemon juice. Pour over fruit mixture.

2 Cover and cook on low-heat setting for 3½ to 4 hours or on high-heat setting for 1½ to 2 hours.

nutrition facts per serving: 271 cal., 10 g total fat (8 g sat. fat), 10 mg chol., 102 mg sodium, 46 g carbo., 3 g dietary fiber, 2 g protein.

brilliant **breakfasts**

When you have 15 minutes some Saturday evening, prepare this cereal. Wake up in the morning to a hot cereal that will make you wish every day was oatmeal day.

cranberry-maple
oatmeal with pears

prep: 15 minutes   cook: 6 to 7 hours (low)   makes: 8 servings

Nonstick cooking
  spray
4¾ cups water
1½ cups steel-cut oats
 ¾ cup maple syrup
 ⅓ cup golden raisins
 ⅓ cup dried cranberries
 ⅓ cup chopped dried
       pears
  1 teaspoon ground
       cinnamon or
       Chinese five-spice
       powder
  1 teaspoon vanilla
 ½ teaspoon salt
     Milk (optional)

1 Lightly coat the inside of a 3½- or 4-quart slow cooker with cooking spray. In prepared slow cooker combine the water, oats, syrup, raisins, cranberries, pears, cinnamon, vanilla, and salt.

2 Cover and cook on low-heat setting for 6 to 7 hours. If desired, serve with milk.

nutrition facts per serving: 242 cal., 2 g total fat (0 g sat. fat), 0 mg chol., 154 mg sodium, 56 g carbo., 4 g dietary fiber, 5 g protein.

A dollop of vanilla yogurt and granola are musts for this fruited oatmeal-and-spice hot cereal.

good morning oatmeal

prep: 15 minutes cook: 6 to 7 hours (low) makes: 10 servings

1 In a 3½- or 4-quart slow cooker combine the water, apple juice, oats, pear, dried fruit bits, brown sugar, salt, and cinnamon.

2 Cover and cook on low-heat setting for 6 to 7 hours. To serve, top with yogurt and granola.

3 cups water
1¾ cups apple juice
1½ cups steel-cut oats
1 medium pear, cored and chopped
1 7-ounce package mixed dried fruit bits
⅓ cup packed brown sugar
½ teaspoon salt
½ teaspoon ground cinnamon
2 6-ounce cartons vanilla yogurt
1 cup low-fat granola

nutrition facts per serving: 281 cal., 3 g total fat (0 g sat. fat), 2 mg chol., 185 mg sodium, 59 g carbo., 6 g dietary fiber, 7 g protein.

Keep this hot multifruit combo reserved for the adults. Sweet sherry adds an interesting flavor dimension to a simple mix of fruits.

sherried fruit

prep: 25 minutes   cook: 3½ to 4 hours (low) or 1½ to 2 hours (high)
makes: 12 to 14 servings

1   20-ounce can
     pineapple chunks in
     juice, undrained
3   medium firm ripe
     plums, pitted
     and cut into thick
     wedges
2   medium cooking
     apples, cored and
     cut into 1-inch
     pieces
2   medium pears, cored
     and cut into 1-inch
     pieces
½   cup dried apricots,
     halved
⅓   cup packed brown
     sugar
¼   cup butter, melted
¼   cup sherry
2   tablespoons quick-
     cooking tapioca,
     crushed
¼   teaspoon salt

1 In a 3½- or 4-quart slow cooker combine pineapple, plums, apples, pears, and apricots. In a small bowl combine brown sugar, melted butter, sherry, tapioca, and salt. Pour brown sugar mixture over fruit; stir to combine.

2 Cover and cook on low-heat setting for 3½ to 4 hours or on high-heat setting for 1½ to 2 hours.

nutrition facts per serving: 148 cal., 4 g total fat (2 g sat. fat), 10 mg chol., 79 mg sodium, 28 g carbo., 2 g dietary fiber, 1 g protein.

Just when you thought you couldn't eat another bowl of hot oatmeal you get a bite of this. You're hooked. Now every day is a good day for a hearty bowl of hot cereal.

six-grain hot cereal

prep: 15 minutes   cook: 6 to 7 hours (low)   makes: 8 servings

1 In a 3 ½- or 4-quart slow cooker combine the water, dried fruit, ginger, steel-cut oats, cracked wheat, brown rice, barley, millet, cornmeal, cinnamon, vanilla, and salt.

2 Cover and cook on low-heat setting for 6 to 7 hours. Stir before serving. If too thick, stir in a bit of boiling water. If desired, serve hot porridge topped with milk, yogurt, maple syrup, and/or coconut.

nutrition facts per serving: 142 cal., 1 g total fat (0 g sat. fat), 0 mg chol., 93 mg sodium, 32 g carbo., 3 g dietary fiber, 3 g protein.

5   cups water
1   cup mixed dried fruit, coarsely snipped, and/or dried cranberries, dried tart cherries, and/or raisins (about 7 ounces)
¼   cup chopped crystallized ginger
3   tablespoons steel-cut oats
3   tablespoons cracked wheat
3   tablespoons regular brown rice
2   tablespoons regular pearled barley (not quick-cooking)
2   tablespoons millet or regular brown rice
2   tablespoons yellow cornmeal
1   teaspoon ground cinnamon
1   teaspoon vanilla
¼   teaspoon salt
    Milk and/or desired flavor yogurt (optional)
    Maple syrup and/or shredded coconut (optional)

This refined burrito contains spinach, basil, artichoke hearts, shallots, and prosciutto in an egg base. Don't forget the marinara sauce.

italian **breakfast** burritos

prep: 30 minutes   cook: 4½ to 5 hours (low)   makes: 10 servings

1 In a 3½- or 4-quart slow cooker combine eggs, mozzarella cheese, spinach, artichoke hearts, milk, shallots, basil, prosciutto, garlic, and pepper. Cover and cook on low-heat setting for 4½ to 5 hours.

2 Wrap tortillas in white microwave-safe paper towels; heat in microwave oven on 100 percent power (high) for 1 to 1½ minutes or just until warmed. Spread pesto over each tortilla to within 1 inch of edge. Evenly divide egg mixture among tortillas, breaking it up as necessary; roll up, tucking in ends. Serve burritos with warm marinara sauce.

nutrition facts per serving: 455 cal., 22 g total fat (7 g sat. fat), 25 mg chol., 1190 mg sodium, 38 g carbo., 4 g dietary fiber, 24 g protein.

- 16 eggs, lightly beaten, or 4 cups refrigerated or frozen egg product, thawed
- 1½ cups shredded mozzarella cheese (6 ounces)
- 1 10-ounce package frozen chopped spinach, thawed and squeezed dry
- 1 6-ounce jar marinated artichoke hearts, drained and coarsely chopped
- ½ cup milk
- 3 shallots, finely chopped
- ½ cup fresh basil, snipped
- 3 ounces prosciutto, chopped
- 2 cloves garlic, minced
- ¼ teaspoon ground black pepper
- 10 10-inch flour tortillas
- 1 cup purchased basil pesto
- 1 15-ounce container refrigerated marinara sauce, heated

Sweet and savory ingredients come together for this bread pudding–like breakfast. Make it the night before, and then cook it in the morning.

morning casserole

prep: 25 minutes chill: 8 hours cook: 5½ to 6 hours (low)
stand: 30 minutes makes: 10 servings

1 pound bulk pork
  sausage
  Disposable slow-
  cooker liner
1 16-ounce loaf raisin
  bread, cubed
6 eggs, or 1½ cups
  refrigerated or
  frozen egg product,
  thawed
1½ cups milk
1½ cups half-and-half
  or light cream
1 teaspoon vanilla
¼ teaspoon ground
  nutmeg
¼ teaspoon ground
  cinnamon
1 cup coarsely chopped
  pecans, toasted
  (optional)

1 In a medium skillet cook sausage over medium heat until brown. Drain off fat. Line a 4- to 5-quart slow cooker with a disposable slow-cooker liner. Place sausage and bread cubes in prepared slow cooker; mix well.

2 In a large bowl whisk together the eggs, milk, half-and-half, vanilla, nutmeg, and cinnamon. Pour over sausage and bread cubes. Press bread lightly with back of a large spoon to moisten bread completely. Cover and refrigerate for 8 hours or overnight.

3 Cover and cook on low-heat setting for 5½ to 6 hours. Turn off cooker; let stand for 30 minutes. Carefully lift liner from cooker, using a plate to transfer casserole to a cutting board. Slice casserole to serve. If desired, sprinkle each serving with pecans.

nutrition facts per serving: 381 cal., 23 g total fat (9 g sat. fat), 174 mg chol., 565 mg sodium, 29 g carbo., 2 g dietary fiber, 15 g protein.

Serve this dish for brunch amigos and amigas who love foods with a Mexican flair. Cornbread muffins and a fruit salad make perfect sides.

breakfast migas

prep: 25 minutes cook: 5 to 6 hours (low) makes: 6 servings

Disposable slow-
  cooker liner
1 pound bulk breakfast
  sausage, browned
  and drained
1 4.5-ounce package
  tostada shells,
  coarsely broken
¾ cup chopped red
  sweet pepper
  (1 medium)
½ cup chopped onion
  (1 medium)
1 4-ounce can diced
  green chiles,
  undrained
12 eggs, or 3½ cups
  refrigerated or
  frozen egg product
1 10.75-ounce can
  condensed nacho
  cheese soup
¼ teaspoon ground
  black pepper
2 avocados, chopped
2 cups refrigerated
  fresh salsa
1 8-ounce carton sour
  cream

1 Line a 3½ or 4-quart slow cooker with a disposable slow-cooker liner. In an extra-large bowl combine sausage, tostada shells, red sweet pepper, onion, and diced green chiles. In a large bowl whisk together eggs, soup, and pepper. Pour over sausage mixture; transfer to prepared slow cooker.

2 Cover and cook on low-heat setting for 5 to 6 hours. Serve with avocados, salsa, and sour cream.

nutrition facts per serving: 591 cal., 37 g total fat (13 g sat. fat), 482 mg chol., 1578 mg sodium, 33 g carbo., 7 g dietary fiber, 31 g protein.

Wake up to an all-in-one breakfast. Put this casserole on the night before (on low) and treat your family to a wonderful meal when they rise.

ham, gouda, and potato bake

prep: 20 minutes cook: 6 to 7 hours (low) makes: 8 servings

1 In a 3½- or 4-quart slow cooker combine hash browns, ham, red sweet pepper, onion, and Gouda cheese. Toss together to combine. In a medium mixing bowl whisk together eggs, soup, milk, and pepper. Pour over potato mixture.

2 Cover and cook on low-heat setting for 6 to 7 hours. To serve, spoon potato mixture over English muffin halves.

nutrition facts per serving: 417 cal., 13 g total fat (6 g sat. fat), 199 mg chol., 1292 mg sodium, 52 g carbo., 4 g dietary fiber, 24 g protein.

4   cups frozen diced hash brown potatoes
½   pound cooked ham, chopped
¾   cup chopped red sweet pepper (1 medium)
½   cup chopped onion (1 medium)
1½   cups shredded Gouda cheese (6 ounces)
6   eggs, lightly beaten, or 1½ cups refrigerated or frozen egg product, thawed
1   10.75-ounce can condensed cream of potato soup
½   cup milk
⅛   teaspoon ground black pepper
8   English muffins, split and toasted

Strata in the slow cooker? What a great idea! This version boasts ingredients of Spain—Manchego cheese and smoked chorizo.

spanish strata

prep: 25 minutes cook: 5½ to 6 hours (low) stand: 15 minutes
makes: 8 servings

Disposable slow-
    cooker liner
4   cups country-style
    bread, cut into
    1-inch pieces
1½ cups frozen diced
    hash brown
    potatoes with
    onions and peppers
1   cup shredded
    Manchego cheese
    (4 ounces)
½   cup coarsely chopped
    sweet onion
    (1 small)
½   cup coarsely chopped
    roasted red sweet
    pepper
2   ounces serrano ham
    or cooked smoked
    chorizo, chopped
2   cloves garlic, minced
2   cups milk
4   eggs, or 1 cup
    refrigerated or
    frozen egg product,
    thawed
½   teaspoon salt
¼   teaspoon crushed
    red pepper

1 Line a 3½- or 4-quart slow cooker with a disposable slow-cooker liner. In a large mixing bowl combine bread, hash browns, Manchego cheese, onion, red sweet pepper, ham, and garlic. Spoon bread mixture into prepared cooker. In the same bowl whisk together milk, eggs, salt, and crushed red pepper. Pour over bread mixture in cooker.

2 Cover and cook on low-heat setting for 5½ to 6 hours. Turn off cooker. Let stand for 15 to 30 minutes. Carefully lift liner from cooker, using a plate to transfer strata to a cutting board. To serve, slice strata.

nutrition facts per serving: 230 cal., 11 g total fat (5 g sat. fat), 126+ mg chol., 569 mg sodium, 20 g carbo., 1 g dietary fiber, 13 g protein.

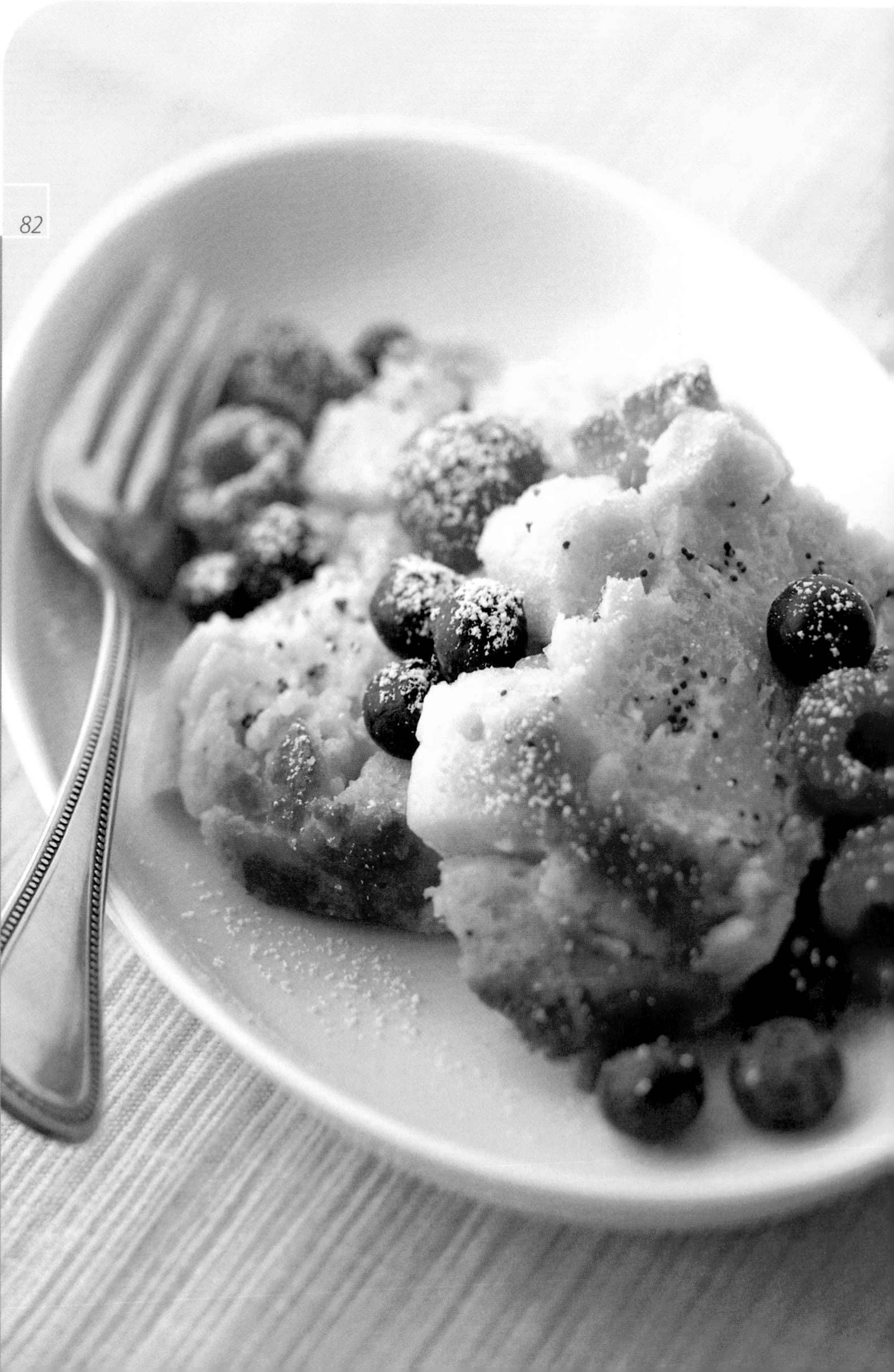

Making French toast for a crowd just got easier. Lemon curd, cream cheese, and cubed bread transform into a morning favorite in your slow cooker.

lemon–poppy seed
french toast

prep: 25 minutes chill: 4 hours cook: 7 to 8 hours (low) stand: 30 minutes
makes: 8 to 10 servings

Disposable slow-
cooker liner
12 ounces country-style
bread, cut in 1-inch
pieces (about 9 cups)
1 8-ounce package
cream cheese,
softened
½ cup lemon curd
4 cups milk
¼ cup granulated sugar
3 eggs, or ¾ cup
refrigerated or
frozen egg product,
thawed
1 tablespoon poppy
seeds
¼ teaspoon almond
extract
¼ teaspoon salt
Confectioner's sugar
(optional)
Fresh raspberries,
blueberries, and/
or blackberries
(optional)

1 Line a 3½- or 4-quart slow cooker with a disposable slow-cooker liner. Place bread cubes in prepared slow cooker. In a large bowl beat together cream cheese and lemon curd with a wooden spoon until smooth. Whisk in milk, sugar, eggs, poppy seeds, almond extract, and salt. Pour mixture over bread cubes in cooker. Cover and chill for 4 to 24 hours.

2 Cover and cook on low-heat setting for 7 to 8 hours or until a knife inserted near the center comes out clean. Turn off cooker. Let stand for 30 minutes. Carefully lift liner from cooker, using a plate to transfer French toast to a cutting board. To serve, slice French toast. If desired, sprinkle with confectioner's sugar and serve with fresh berries.

nutrition facts per serving: 392 cal., 17 g total fat (9 g sat. fat), 135 mg chol., 496 mg sodium, 49 g carbo., 3 g dietary fiber, 12 g protein.

Bold flavors dominate this appetizing strata. Chèvre cheese and marinated tomato bits craft a dish that is bold and delicious.

artichoke strata
with sun-dried tomatoes and chèvre

prep: 20 minutes bake: 10 minutes cook: 6 to 7 hours (low)
stand: 15 minutes oven: 350°F makes: 6 to 8 servings

8 cups 1-inch sourdough bread cubes
   Disposable slow-cooker liner
1 14-ounce can artichoke hearts, drained and chopped
½ cup chopped green onions (4)
1⅓ to 1½ cups crumbled goat cheese (chèvre) (5 to 6 ounces)
¼ cup chopped oil-pack dried tomatoes
2 cups half-and-half or whole milk
6 eggs, or 1½ cups refrigerated or frozen egg product, thawed
3 cloves garlic, minced
½ teaspoon dried basil, crushed
¼ teaspoon salt
¼ teaspoon crushed red pepper

1 Preheat oven to 350°F. Spread bread cubes evenly in a 15x10x1-inch baking pan. Bake for 10 to 15 minutes or until bread cubes are dry, stirring twice; cool. (The bread cubes will continue to dry and crisp as they cool.) Or let bread cubes stand loosely covered at room temperature for 8 to 10 hours.

2 Line a 3½- or 4-quart slow cooker with a disposable slow-cooker liner. Place bread cubes, artichoke hearts, green onions, 1 cup goat cheese, and dried tomatoes in prepared slow cooker; toss gently to combine. In a medium bowl whisk together half-and-half, eggs, garlic, basil, salt, and crushed red pepper. Pour evenly over bread mixture.

3 Cover and cook on low-heat setting for 6 to 7 hours. Turn off cooker. Sprinkle with remaining goat cheese. Let stand for 15 to 30 minutes. Carefully lift liner from cooker, using a plate to transfer strata to a cutting board. To serve, slice strata or spoon onto serving plates.

nutrition facts per serving: 436 cal., 21 g total fat (11 g sat. fat), 252 mg chol., 889 mg sodium, 41 g carbo., 4 g dietary fiber, 21 g protein.

Fresh beets are a tasty surprise in this classic favorite.

red flannel hash

prep: 20 minutes   cook: 6 to 7 hours (low) or 3 to 3½ hours (high)
makes: 6 servings

1½ pounds beets, peeled
    and chopped
1½ pounds round red
    potatoes, peeled
    and chopped
    (4½ cups)
12 ounces cooked
    corned beef from
    deli (about ¾-inch-
    thick chunk),
    chopped
1 cup chopped onion
    (1 large)
¼ cup beef or chicken
    broth
2 tablespoons spicy
    brown mustard
2 tablespoons butter,
    melted
1 tablespoon honey
1 tablespoon cider
    vinegar
½ teaspoon salt
½ teaspoon bottled
    hot pepper sauce
¼ teaspoon ground
    black pepper

1 In a 3½- or 4-quart slow cooker combine beets, potatoes, corned beef, onion, broth, mustard, melted butter, honey, vinegar, salt, hot pepper sauce, and pepper.

2 Cover and cook on low-heat setting for 6 to 7 hours or on high-heat setting for 3 to 3½ hours. Stir before serving.

nutrition facts per serving: 258 cal., 5 g total fat (3 g sat. fat), 35 mg chol., 1021 mg sodium, 39 g carbo., 6 g dietary fiber, 15 g protein.

Completely loaded with all your breakfast usuals, these hash browns will quickly become a family favorite.

loaded hash browns

prep: 15 minutes   cook: 8 to 9 hours (low) or 4 to 4½ hours (high)
makes: 8 servings

1   pound bulk pork
     sausage
½   cup chopped onion
     (1 medium)
     Disposable slow-
     cooker liner
5   cups frozen diced
     hash brown
     potatoes
1   cup shredded
     Monterey Jack
     cheese with
     jalapeño peppers
     (4 ounces)
1   small red sweet
     pepper, chopped
1   4-ounce can sliced
     mushrooms,
     drained
1   10.75-ounce can
     condensed nacho
     cheese soup
¼   cup water
     Shredded Monterey
     Jack cheese with
     jalapeño peppers
     (optional)
     Thinly sliced fresh
     jalapeño pepper
     (see tip, page 32)
     (optional)
     Salsa and/or sour
     cream (optional)

1 In a large skillet cook sausage and onion over medium heat until sausage is brown and onion is tender. Drain off fat.

2 Line a 3½- or 4-quart slow cooker with a disposable slow-cooker liner. Place sausage mixture, hash browns, 1 cup Monterey Jack cheese, red sweet pepper, and mushrooms in prepared slow cooker; mix well. In a medium bowl, combine soup and the water. Pour over hash brown mixture; stir to combine.

3 Cover and cook on low-heat setting for 8 to 9 hours or on high-heat setting for 4 to 4½ hours. Stir before serving. If desired, top with additional cheese and sliced jalapeño. If desired, serve with salsa and/or sour cream.

nutrition facts per serving: 381 cal., 25 g total fat (11 g sat. fat), 64 mg chol., 1015 mg sodium, 24 g carbo., 3 g dietary fiber, 16 g protein.

simmering **soups**

The variety of soups and stews that simmer to perfection in a slow cooker is amazing! This collection will keep your menu planned throughout the cool months. Your family will love Pesto-Meatball Stew, Cheesy Ham and Vegetable Chowder, Teriyaki Beef-Noodle Soup, White and Green Chili, or Split Pea Soup, to name only a few.

4

&stews

When fall gives way to the cold winter months, come home to a colorful slow-simmered meatless vegetable soup.

farmer's market
vegetable soup

prep: 30 minutes **cook:** 8 to 9 hours (low) or 4 to 4½ hours (high) + 20 to 30 minutes **makes:** 4 servings

2 cups ½-inch pieces peeled rutabaga (½ of a small)
1½ cups coarsely chopped red-skinned potatoes (2 medium)
1 cup chopped roma tomatoes (2 large)
1 cup ½-inch pieces carrots or peeled parsnips (2 medium)
⅔ cup chopped leeks (2 medium)
1 teaspoon fennel seeds, crushed
½ teaspoon dried sage, crushed
½ to ¼ teaspoon ground black pepper
1 14-ounce can vegetable broth or chicken broth
½ cup dried tiny bow-tie pasta
3 cups fresh baby spinach leaves or torn spinach
   Garlic Toast (optional)

1 In a 3½- or 4-quart slow cooker combine rutabaga, potatoes, tomatoes, carrots, and leeks. Sprinkle with fennel seeds, sage, and pepper. Pour broth over mixture in cooker.

2 Cover and cook on low-heat setting for 8 to 9 hours or on high-heat setting for 4 to 4½ hours.

3 If using low-heat setting, turn to high-heat setting. Stir in uncooked pasta. Cover and cook for 20 to 30 minutes more or until pasta is tender. Just before serving, stir in spinach. If desired, float a Garlic Toast on each serving.

nutrition facts per serving: 198 cal., 2 g total fat (0 g sat. fat), 0 mg chol., 1313 mg sodium, 41 g carbo., 8 g dietary fiber, 8 g protein.

garlic toast: Brush both sides of eight ½-inch baguette slices with 1 tablespoon garlic-flavor olive oil. Arrange on a baking sheet. Broil 3 to 4 inches from the heat for 1 minute. Turn; sprinkle with 2 teaspoons grated Parmesan cheese. Broil for 1 to 2 minutes more or until lightly toasted.

The cornmeal and Parmesan cheese dumplings hike this vegetable stew up a notch or two on the yummy scale.

vegetable stew
with cornmeal dumplings

prep: 25 minutes **cook:** 8 to 10 hours (low) or 4 to 5 hours (high) + 50 minutes
makes: 6 servings

3 cups ½-inch cubes peeled and seeded butternut or acorn squash (1½ pounds)

2 cups sliced fresh mushrooms

2 14.5-ounce cans diced tomatoes, undrained

1 15-ounce can Great Northern beans, rinsed and drained

1 cup water

4 cloves garlic, minced

1 teaspoon dried Italian seasoning, crushed

¼ teaspoon ground black pepper

½ cup all-purpose flour

⅓ cup yellow cornmeal

2 tablespoons grated Parmesan cheese

1 tablespoon snipped fresh parsley

1 teaspoon baking powder

¼ teaspoon salt

1 egg

2 tablespoons milk

2 tablespoons cooking oil

1 9-ounce package frozen Italian green beans or frozen cut green beans
Paprika

1 In a 3½- or 4-quart slow cooker combine squash, mushrooms, tomatoes, Great Northern beans, the water, garlic, Italian seasoning, and pepper.

2 Cover and cook on low-heat setting for 8 to 10 hours or on high-heat setting for 4 to 5 hours.

3 For dumplings, in a medium bowl combine flour, cornmeal, Parmesan cheese, parsley, baking powder, and salt. In a small bowl whisk together egg, milk, and oil. Add egg mixture to flour mixture; stir with a fork just until combined.

4 If using low-heat setting, turn to high-heat setting. Stir in green beans. Spoon dough formed into six mounds on top of stew. Sprinkle dough with paprika. Cover and cook for 50 minutes more. (Do not lift lid while dumplings are cooking.)

nutrition facts per serving: 288 cal., 7 g total fat (2 g sat. fat), 37 mg chol., 442 mg sodium, 45 g carbo., 7 g dietary fiber, 12 g protein.

Spices borrowed from India give this soup an Indian flair. Use grated fresh ginger if you can. It lends the soup a wonderful flavor.

indian vegetable soup

prep: 30 minutes **cook:** 9 to 10 hours (low) or 4½ to 5 hours (high)
makes: 6 servings

1 medium eggplant, cut
   into ½-inch cubes
   (5 to 6 cups)
2 14-ounce cans
   vegetable broth
1 pound tiny new
   potatoes, cut into
   1-inch pieces
2 cups chopped
   tomatoes or one
   14½-ounce can
   no-salt-added
   diced tomatoes,
   undrained
1 15-ounce can
   garbanzo beans
   (chickpeas), rinsed
   and drained
2 teaspoons grated
   fresh ginger or
   ½ teaspoon ground
   ginger
1½ teaspoons curry
   powder
1 teaspoon ground
   coriander
¼ teaspoon salt
¼ teaspoon ground
   black pepper
2 tablespoons snipped
   fresh cilantro
   (optional)

1 In a 5- to 6-quart slow cooker combine eggplant, broth, potatoes, tomatoes, garbanzo beans, ginger, curry powder, coriander, salt, and pepper.

2 Cover and cook on low-heat setting for 9 to 10 hours or on high-heat setting for 4½ to 5 hours. If desired, sprinkle individual servings with cilantro.

nutrition facts per serving: 186 cal., 1 g total fat (0 g sat. fat), 0 mg chol., 837 mg sodium, 39 g carbo., 9 g dietary fiber, 7 g protein.

The hearty barley grain and red beans add bulk to this meatless vegetable soup. You'll feel full and satisfied long after eating it.

barley-vegetable soup

prep: 25 minutes **cook:** 8 to 10 hours (low) or 4 to 5 hours (high)
makes: 6 servings

1	cup chopped onion (1 large)
½	cup bias-sliced carrot (1 medium)
½	cup sliced celery (1 stalk)
2	cups sliced fresh mushrooms
1	15-ounce can red beans, rinsed and drained
1	14.5-ounce can stewed tomatoes, undrained
1	10-ounce package frozen whole kernel corn
½	cup regular barley (not quick-cooking)
2	teaspoons dried Italian seasoning, crushed
¼	teaspoon ground black pepper
3	cloves garlic, minced
5	cups vegetable or chicken broth

1 In a 3½- to 5-quart slow cooker combine onion, carrot, celery, mushrooms, red beans, tomatoes, corn, barley, Italian seasoning, pepper, and garlic. Pour broth over mixture in cooker.

2 Cover and cook on low-heat setting for 8 to 10 hours or on high-heat setting for 4 to 5 hours.

nutrition facts per serving: 228 cal., 2 g total fat (0 g sat. fat), 0 mg chol., 1212 mg sodium, 47 g carbo., 8 g dietary fiber, 9 g protein.

A spoonful of pesto and a sprinkling of Parmesan cheese are optional additions to the final bowl of soup, but they definitely add a crowning touch.

italian vegetable soup

prep: 20 minutes   cook: 6 to 8 hours (low) or 3 to 4 hours (high)
makes: 6 to 8 side-dish servings

1   9-ounce package
    frozen cut green
    beans
½   of a 16-ounce
    package frozen
    cauliflower
1   14.5-ounce can diced
    tomatoes with basil,
    garlic, and oregano,
    undrained
½   cup chopped onion
    (1 medium)
½   cup sliced celery
    (1 stalk)
¼   cup regular barley
    (not quick-cooking)
1   clove garlic, minced
¼   teaspoon ground
    black pepper
3   cups reduced-sodium
    chicken broth
1½ cups reduced-sodium
    vegetable juice
¼   cup purchased basil
    pesto (optional)
    Finely shredded
    Parmesan cheese
    (optional)

1 In a 3½- or 4-quart slow cooker combine green beans, cauliflower, tomatoes, onion, celery, barley, garlic, and pepper. Pour broth and vegetable juice over mixture in cooker.

2 Cover and cook on low-heat setting for 6 to 8 hours or on high-heat setting for 3 to 4 hours. If desired, top each serving with pesto and Parmesan cheese.

nutrition facts per serving: 81 cal., 0 g total fat (0 g sat. fat), 0 mg chol., 520 mg sodium, 17 g carbo., 3 g dietary fiber, 4 g protein.

Lots of veggies, beans, and spices makes a chili that will surely satisfy. One serving contains a hefty dose of fiber, too.

spicy vegetable chili

prep: 25 minutes **cook:** 9 to 10 hours (low) or 4½ to 5 hours (high)
makes: 10 to 12 servings

2   28-ounce cans
     diced tomatoes,
     undrained
2   15-ounce cans dark
     red kidney beans,
     rinsed and drained
2   15-ounce cans pinto
     beans, rinsed and
     drained
2   cups chopped onions
     (2 large)
2   cups chopped green
     sweet peppers
1   15.25-ounce can
     whole kernel corn,
     drained
1   cup chopped celery
     (2 stalks)
1   cup water
1   6-ounce can tomato
     paste
2   tablespoons chili
     powder
8   cloves garlic, minced
1   tablespoon
     Worcestershire
     sauce
1   teaspoon ground
     cumin
1   teaspoon dried
     oregano, crushed
1   teaspoon bottled hot
     pepper sauce
¼   teaspoon cayenne
     pepper (optional)
     Snipped fresh chives
     (optional)

1 In a 6- to 7-quart slow cooker combine tomatoes, kidney beans, pinto beans, onions, green sweet peppers, corn, celery, the water, tomato paste, chili powder, garlic, Worcestershire sauce, cumin, oregano, hot pepper sauce, and, if desired, cayenne pepper.

2 Cover and cook on low-heat setting for 9 to 10 hours or on high-heat setting for 4½ to 5 hours. If desired, sprinkle each serving with chives.

nutrition facts per serving: 229 cal., 1 g total fat (0 g sat. fat), 0 mg chol., 733 mg sodium, 48 g carbo., 11 g dietary fiber, 12 g protein.

Meaty portobellos give the illusion of actually eating meat. Serve this chili with warm-from-the-oven cornbread for a satisfying meal.

portobello chili

prep: 15 minutes **cook:** 6 to 8 hours (low) or 3 to 4 hours (high)
makes: 4 servings

2   15-ounce cans red
kidney beans,
rinsed and drained
2   14.5-ounce cans diced
tomatoes with
basil and oregano,
undrained
6   cups coarsely
chopped portobello
mushrooms
(1 pound)
1   cup chopped onion
(1 large)
1   tablespoon chili
powder
2   teaspoons ground
cumin
2   cloves garlic, minced
Sour cream (optional)

1 In a 3½- or 4-quart slow cooker combine red kidney beans, tomatoes, mushrooms, onion, chili powder, cumin, and garlic.

2 Cover and cook on low-heat setting for 6 to 8 hours or on high-heat setting for 3 to 4 hours. If desired, top each serving with sour cream.

nutrition facts per serving: 322 cal., 2 g total fat (0 g sat. fat), 0 mg chol., 1816 mg sodium, 63 g carbo., 18 g dietary fiber, 18 g protein.

Toasting the cumin seeds brings out a deep, nutty flavor. You'll know the cumin is ready when your kitchen is filled with its fragrant aroma.

white bean and cumin
chili

prep: 20 minutes   cook: 9 to 10 hours (low) or 4½ to 5 hours (high)
makes: 4 servings

1   cup chopped onion
    (1 large)
3   cloves garlic, minced
2   tablespoons cooking
    oil
2   14.5-ounce cans
    diced tomatoes,
    undrained
1   12-ounce can beer or
    nonalcoholic beer
1   chipotle chile pepper
    in adobo sauce,
    chopped
1   tablespoon cumin
    seed, toasted*
1   teaspoon sugar
½   teaspoon salt
2   19-ounce cans
    cannellini beans
    (white kidney
    beans), rinsed and
    drained
1½ cups coarsely
    chopped, peeled,
    and seeded Golden
    Nugget or acorn
    squash (about
    12 ounces)
½   cup dairy sour cream
2   tablespoons lime
    juice
1   tablespoon snipped
    fresh chives
    Lime wedges
    (optional)

1 In a 3½ or 4-quart slow cooker combine onion, garlic, oil, tomatoes, beer, chipotle pepper, cumin, sugar, and salt. Stir in beans and squash.

2 Cover and cook on low-heat setting for 9 to 10 hours or on high-heat setting for 4½ to 5 hours. Meanwhile, combine sour cream, lime juice, and chives; cover and chill until ready to serve.

3 To serve, ladle chili into bowls. Top with sour cream mixture. If desired, garnish with lime wedges.

nutrition facts per serving: 365 cal., 15 g total fat (5 g sat. fat), 13 mg chol., 995 mg sodium, 52 g carbo., 13 g dietary fiber, 17 g protein.

*test kitchen tip: To toast cumin seeds, place seeds in a dry skillet over low heat. Cook for about 8 minutes or until fragrant, stirring frequently. Remove from heat; allow to cool before grinding in a spice grinder or with a mortar and pestle.

Strong brewed coffee adds a bold richness to this black bean chili. Serve it over rice and don't forget the avocado and sour cream.

black bean chili
with joe

prep: 20 minutes cook: 7 to 9 hours (low) or 3½ to 4½ hours (high)
makes: 6 servings

2 15-ounce cans black beans, rinsed and drained
1 28-ounce can crushed tomatoes
1 cup hot strong coffee
1 cup chicken broth
½ cup finely chopped onion (1 medium)
4 cloves garlic, minced
2 tablespoons packed brown sugar
1 tablespoon chili powder
1½ teaspoons ground cumin
¼ teaspoon ground cloves
¼ teaspoon salt
⅓ cup snipped fresh cilantro
   Hot cooked rice
   Chopped avocado
   Sour cream

1 In a 3½- or 4-quart slow cooker combine black beans, tomatoes, coffee, broth, onion, garlic, brown sugar, chili powder, cumin, cloves, and salt.

2 Cover and cook on low-heat setting for 7 to 9 hours or on high-heat setting for 3½ to 4½ hours. Stir in cilantro. Serve over rice; top with avocado and sour cream.

nutrition facts per serving: 324 cal., 8 g total fat (2 g sat. fat), 5 mg chol., 1160 mg sodium, 55 g carbo., 13 g dietary fiber, 14 g protein.

Be sure to use regular barley in this chili rather than quick-cooking. The chili is probably unlike any chili you're accustomed to eating, but it is delicious.

sweet potato
and barley chili

prep: 20 minutes **cook:** 6 to 7 hours (low) or 3 to 3½ hours (high)
makes: 6 servings

1 28-ounce can crushed tomatoes
1 medium sweet potato, peeled and cut into 1-inch cubes (1½ cups)
1 15- to 16-ounce can red beans, rinsed and drained
1 14-ounce can chicken broth
¾ cup chopped red sweet pepper (1 medium)
½ cup chopped onion (1 medium)
½ cup regular pearled barley (not quick-cooking)
½ cup water
3 cloves garlic, minced
1 tablespoon chili powder
1 tablespoon lime juice
1 teaspoon ground cumin
½ teaspoon dried oregano, crushed
½ teaspoon salt
¼ teaspoon ground black pepper
   Lime wedges and/ or snipped fresh cilantro (optional)

1 In a 3½- or 4-quart slow cooker combine tomatoes, sweet potato, red beans, broth, red sweet pepper, onion, barley, the water, garlic, chili powder, lime juice, cumin, oregano, salt, and pepper.

2 Cover and cook on low-heat setting for 6 to 7 hours or on high-heat setting for 3 to 3½ hours.

3 If desired, serve with lime wedges and/or top each serving with cilantro.

nutrition facts per serving: 198 cal., 1 g total fat (0 g sat. fat), 1 mg chol., 930 mg sodium, 41 g carbo., 11 g dietary fiber, 9 g protein.

Maple syrup lends a subtle sweetness to this creamy soup. If you have some fresh sage, snip some and scatter it over the top of each bowl before serving.

new england
sweet potato soup

prep: 25 minutes   **cook:** 6 to 8 hours (low) or 3 to 4 hours (high)
makes: 6 servings

2½	to 3 pounds sweet potatoes, peeled and cut into 1-inch pieces
½	cup chopped onion (1 medium)
¼	cup maple syrup
1	clove garlic, minced
½	teaspoon dried sage, crushed
¼	teaspoon salt
⅛	teaspoon ground black pepper
2	14-ounce cans chicken broth
1	cup water
½	cup half-and-half, light cream, or whole milk
	Crisp-cooked crumbled bacon (optional)
	Sliced green onions (optional)

1 In a 3½- or 4-quart slow cooker combine sweet potatoes, onion, syrup, garlic, sage, salt, and pepper. Pour broth and the water over mixture in cooker.

2 Cover and cook on low-heat setting for 6 to 8 hours or on high-heat setting for 3 to 4 hours.

3 Using a potato masher, mash the soup to desired consistency.* Stir in half-and-half. If desired, sprinkle each serving with bacon and green onions.

nutrition facts per serving: 192 cal., 3 g total fat (1 g sat. fat), 9 mg chol., 712 mg sodium, 39 g carbo., 4 g dietary fiber, 3 g protein.

*test kitchen tip: For a smoother texture, use an immersion blender to puree the soup.

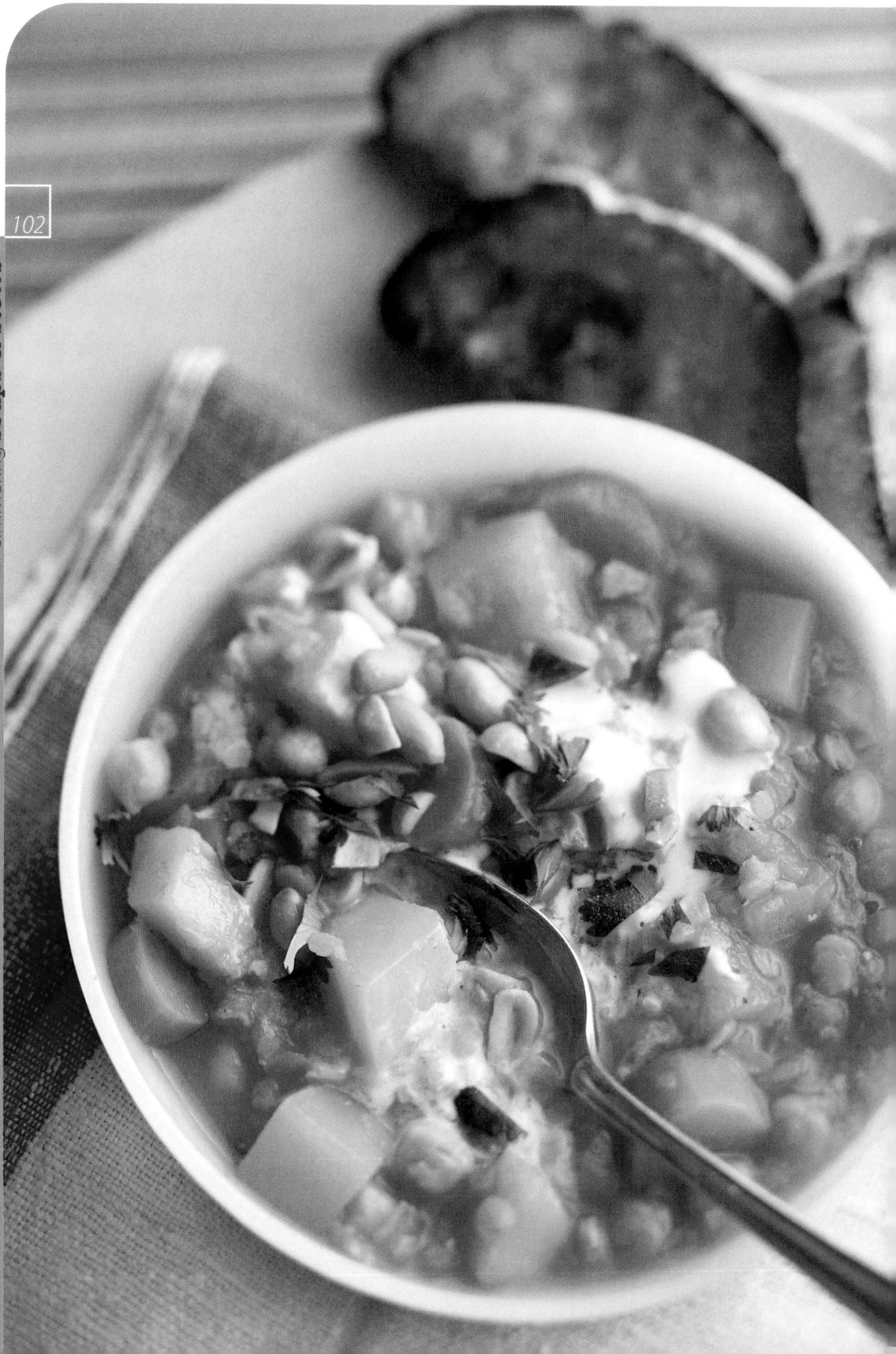

Red lentils are actually more salmon in color than red and have a mild earthy flavor. Like other legumes, lentils are high in fiber and protein.

pumpkin, chickpea, and red lentil stew

prep: 25 minutes **cook:** 8 to 10 hours (low) or 4 to 5 hours (high)
makes: 6 servings

1 pound pie pumpkin or winter squash, peeled, seeded, and cut into 1-inch cubes

1 15-ounce can garbanzo beans (chickpeas), rinsed and drained

3 medium carrots, sliced ½ inch thick

1 cup chopped onion (1 large)

1 cup dried red lentils, rinsed and drained

2 tablespoons tomato paste

1 tablespoon grated fresh ginger

1 tablespoon lime juice

1 teaspoon ground cumin

¼ teaspoon salt

¼ teaspoon ground turmeric

¼ teaspoon ground black pepper

4 cups chicken or vegetable broth

¼ cup chopped peanuts

2 tablespoons snipped fresh cilantro

Plain nonfat yogurt (optional)

1 In a 3½- or 4-quart slow cooker combine pumpkin, garbanzo beans, carrots, onion, lentils, tomato paste, ginger, lime juice, cumin, salt, turmeric, and pepper. Pour broth over mixture in cooker.

2 Cover and cook on low-heat setting for 8 to 10 hours or on high-heat setting for 4 to 5 hours. Top each serving with peanuts, cilantro, and, if desired, yogurt.

nutrition facts per serving: 275 cal., 4 g total fat (1 g sat. fat), 2 mg chol., 1027 mg sodium, 46 g carbo., 10 g dietary fiber, 14 g protein.

simmering **soups & stews**

Lentils are a great source of protein, making this dish perfect for a vegetarian meal. A fresh jalapeño adds a spicy kick to the soup.

curried lentil soup

prep: 20 minutes **cook:** 8 to 10 hours (low) or 4 to 5 hours (high)
makes: 4 to 6 servings

3 cups ¾-inch pieces peeled sweet potatoes (2 medium)
1 cup dried brown or yellow lentils, rinsed and drained
½ cup chopped onion (1 medium)
3 cloves garlic, minced
1 tablespoon finely chopped fresh jalapeño pepper (see tip, page 32)
3 14-ounce cans vegetable broth
1 14.5-ounce can diced tomatoes, undrained
1 tablespoon curry powder
1 teaspoon grated fresh ginger
   Plain yogurt or sour cream (optional)
   Small fresh jalapeño peppers and/or crushed red pepper (optional)

1 In a 4- or 5-quart slow cooker combine sweet potatoes, lentils, onion, garlic, and 1 tablespoon jalapeño pepper. Stir in broth, tomatoes, curry powder, and ginger.

2 Cover and cook on low-heat setting for 8 to 10 hours or on high-heat setting for 4 to 5 hours. If desired, top each serving with yogurt and garnish with a small jalapeño pepper.

nutrition facts per serving: 316 cal., 2 g total fat (0 g sat. fat), 0 mg chol., 1425 mg sodium, 60 g carbo., 18 g dietary fiber, 18 g protein.

You probably already have the ingredients for this flavorful soup in your pantry, so it can be made on the fly.

cha-cha corn chowder

prep: 15 minutes **cook:** 6 to 8 hours (low) or 3 to 4 hours (high)
makes: 6 servings

3 cups ½-inch pieces red-skinned potatoes (3 medium)
2 14.75-ounce cans cream-style corn
1 14-ounce can chicken broth with roasted garlic
1 11-ounce can whole kernel corn with sweet peppers, drained
1 4-ounce can diced green chiles, undrained
¼ teaspoon ground black pepper
Cracked black pepper (optional)
Saltine crackers (optional)

1 In a 3½- or 4-quart slow cooker combine potatoes, cream-style corn, broth, corn, green chiles, and ground black pepper.

2 Cover and cook on low-heat setting for 6 to 8 hours or on high-heat setting for 3 to 4 hours. If desired, top each serving with cracked black pepper and serve with crackers.

nutrition facts per serving: 202 cal., 1 g total fat (0 g sat. fat), 1 mg chol., 898 mg sodium, 49 g carbo., 5 g dietary fiber, 5 g protein.

A white sauce mix adds flavor and creaminess to this delightful soup. Baby spinach added at the end of cooking adds an eye-catching freshness.

creamy tortellini soup

prep: 20 minutes **cook:** 5 to 6 hours (low) + 1 hour or 2½ to 3 hours (high) + 45 minutes **makes:** 4 servings

4 cups water
1 1.8-ounce envelope white sauce mix
1 14-ounce can vegetable broth
1½ cups sliced fresh mushrooms
½ cup chopped onion (1 medium)
3 cloves garlic, minced
½ teaspoon dried basil, crushed
¼ teaspoon salt
¼ teaspoon dried oregano, crushed
⅛ teaspoon cayenne pepper
1 7- to 8-ounce package dried cheese tortellini (about 2 cups)
6 cups fresh baby spinach leaves or torn spinach
1 12-ounce can evaporated milk
   Ground black pepper (optional)
   Finely shredded Parmesan cheese (optional)

1 In a 3½- or 4-quart slow cooker combine the water and sauce mix. Stir in broth, mushrooms, onion, garlic, basil, salt, oregano, and cayenne pepper.

2 Cover and cook on low-heat setting for 5 to 6 hours or on high-heat setting for 2½ to 3 hours.

3 Stir in tortellini. Cover and cook on low-heat setting for 1 hour more or on high-heat setting for 45 minutes more.

4 Stir in spinach and evaporated milk. If desired, sprinkle each serving with black pepper and Parmesan cheese.

nutrition facts per serving: 450 cal., 18 g total fat (7 g sat. fat), 34 mg chol., 1710 mg sodium, 53 g carbo., 2 g dietary fiber, 22 g protein.

Frozen stir-fry vegetables help make this an easy throw-together dinner. Convenient tortilla strips (sold as salad toppers) can be purchased for more ease.

chicken tortilla soup

prep: 15 minutes **cook:** 6 to 7 hours (low) or 3 to 3½ hours (high) **bake:** 10 minutes **oven:** 350°F **makes:** 4 servings

2   14-ounce cans reduced-sodium chicken broth

1   14.5-ounce can no-salt-added stewed tomatoes, undrained

2   cups chopped cooked chicken breast

2   cups frozen sweet pepper and onion stir-fry vegetables

3   cloves garlic, minced

¼   teaspoon crushed red pepper

4   6-inch corn tortillas

½   of an avocado, pitted, peeled, and sliced (optional)

¼   cup chopped fresh cilantro (optional)

¼   cup light sour cream (optional)

Sliced fresh jalapeño peppers (see tip, page 32) (optional)

Crushed red pepper (optional)

1 In a 3½- or 4-quart slow cooker combine broth, tomatoes, chicken, frozen vegetables, garlic, and ¼ teaspoon crushed red pepper.

2 Cover and cook on low-heat setting for 6 to 7 hours or on high-heat setting for 3 to 3½ hours.

3 Before serving, preheat oven to 350°F. Cut tortillas into ½-inch strips. Place in a single layer on a baking sheet. Bake for 10 to 12 minutes or until golden brown and crisp. Cool on baking sheet.

4 If desired, top each serving with avocado, cilantro, sour cream, jalapeño peppers, and/or additional crushed red pepper. Sprinkle with tortilla strips.

nutrition facts per serving: 229 cal., 3 g total fat (1 g sat. fat), 60 mg chol., 579 mg sodium, 23 g carbo., 4 g dietary fiber, 27 g protein.

Dried Japanese somen noodles are an angel hair pasta look-alike that can be found wrapped in bundles in the ethnic section of your supermarket.

soy-ginger soup
with chicken

prep: 20 minutes **cook:** 2 to 3 hours (high) + 3 minutes **makes:** 6 servings

1 pound skinless, boneless chicken thighs, cut into 1-inch pieces
1 cup coarsely shredded carrots (2 medium)
2 tablespoons dry sherry (optional)
1 tablespoon soy sauce
1 tablespoon rice vinegar
1 teaspoon grated fresh ginger or ½ teaspoon ground ginger
¼ teaspoon ground black pepper
3 14-ounce cans reduced-sodium chicken broth
1 cup water
2 ounces dried somen (thin white noodles)
1 6-ounce package frozen snow pea pods, thawed
Soy sauce

1 In a 3½- to 6-quart slow cooker combine chicken, carrots, sherry (if desired), 1 tablespoon soy sauce, vinegar, ginger, and pepper. Stir in broth and the water.

2 Cover and cook on high-heat setting for 2 to 3 hours. Stir in somen and snow pea pods. Cover and cook for 3 minutes more.

3 To serve, ladle soup into bowls and serve with soy sauce.

nutrition facts per serving: 175 cal., 5 g total fat (1 g sat. fat), 72 mg chol., 1246 mg sodium, 12 g carbo., 2 g dietary fiber, 19 g protein.

Imagine making dinner using just five ingredients. That's what this soup offers, along with family appeal, of course.

nacho cheese
chicken chowder

prep: 10 minutes **cook:** 4 to 5 hours (low) or 2 to 2½ hours (high)
makes: 6 servings

1   pound skinless, boneless chicken breast halves, cut into ½-inch pieces
2   14.5-ounce cans Mexican-style stewed tomatoes, undrained
1   10.75-ounce can condensed nacho cheese soup
1   10-ounce package frozen whole kernel corn, thawed
    Shredded Mexican-style or cheddar cheese

1 In a 3½- or 4-quart slow cooker combine chicken, tomatoes, nacho cheese soup, and corn.

2 Cover and cook on low-heat setting for 4 to 5 hours or on high-heat setting for 2 to 2½ hours. Sprinkle each serving with shredded cheese.

nutrition facts per serving: 244 cal., 6 g total fat (3 g sat. fat), 55 mg chol., 347 mg sodium, 24 g carbo., 2 g dietary fiber, 23 g protein.

This company-special soup will make you think you're in New Orleans. Look for spicy andouille sausage next to the bratwurst at your supermarket.

smokin' jambalaya

prep: 30 minutes   cook: 6 to 8 hours (low) or 3 to 4 hours (high) + 30 minutes
makes: 6 servings

1½   pounds skinless, boneless chicken thighs, cut into 1-inch pieces
4   ounces andouille or cooked smoked chorizo sausage, cut into 1-inch pieces
1   cup chopped onion (1 large)
1   cup sliced celery
1   14.5-ounce can fire-roasted diced tomatoes,* undrained
1   cup chicken broth
2   tablespoons tomato paste
2   tablespoons quick-cooking tapioca, crushed
1   tablespoon Worcestershire sauce
1   tablespoon lemon juice
1   tablespoon finely chopped fresh serrano chile pepper (see tip, page 32)
3   cloves garlic, minced
½   teaspoon dried thyme, crushed
½   teaspoon dried oregano, crushed
¼   teaspoon salt
¼   teaspoon cayenne pepper

1   8-ounce package frozen peeled and deveined medium shrimp
2   cups frozen cut okra (optional)
½   cup chopped yellow sweet pepper (1 small)
1   14-ounce pouch boil-in-bag long-grain rice

1 In a 3½- or 4-quart slow cooker combine chicken, sausage, onion, and celery. Stir in undrained tomatoes, broth, tomato paste, tapioca, Worcestershire sauce, lemon juice, serrano pepper, garlic, thyme, oregano, salt, and cayenne pepper.

2 Cover and cook on low-heat setting for 6 to 8 hours or on high-heat setting for 3 to 4 hours.

3 If using low-heat setting, turn to high-heat setting. Stir in frozen shrimp and, if desired, okra. Add sweet pepper. Cover and cook for about 30 minutes more or until shrimp are opaque.

4 Prepare rice according to package directions. Serve rice with each serving.

nutrition facts per serving: 398 cal., 12 g total fat (3 g sat. fat), 149 mg chol., 789 mg sodium, 32 g carbo., 2 g dietary fiber, 34 g protein.

*test kitchen tip: If you can't find fire-roasted diced tomatoes, use plain diced tomatoes and add ¼ teaspoon liquid smoke.

Creamy Alfredo sauce supplies richness to this stew. It will remind you of white chicken chili with its green chile peppers and cumin.

chicken and white bean stew

prep: 35 minutes   **cook:** 4 to 5 hours (low) or 2 to 2½ hours (high)
makes: 8 servings

2   pounds skinless,
     boneless chicken
     thighs, cut into
     1-inch pieces
2   teaspoons ground
     cumin
⅛   teaspoon ground
     black pepper
1   tablespoon olive oil
2   10-ounce packages
     refrigerated light
     Alfredo sauce
1   15-ounce can Great
     Northern or
     cannellini beans
     (white kidney
     beans), rinsed and
     drained
1   cup reduced-sodium
     chicken broth
½   cup chopped red
     onion (1 medium)
1   4-ounce can diced
     green chile peppers,
     undrained
4   cloves garlic, minced
¼   cup shredded sharp
     cheddar cheese
     or Monterey Jack
     cheese (1 ounce)
     (optional)
    Fresh parsley leaves
     (optional)

1 Sprinkle chicken with cumin and black pepper. In a large skillet heat oil over medium heat. Cook chicken, half at a time, in hot oil until brown. Place chicken in a 3½- or 4-quart slow cooker. Stir in Alfredo sauce, Great Northern beans, broth, onion, chile peppers, and garlic.

2 Cover and cook on low-heat setting for 4 to 5 hours or on high-heat setting for 2 to 2½ hours. If desired, sprinkle each serving with cheddar cheese and parsley.

nutrition facts per serving: 360 cal., 16 g total fat (8 g sat. fat), 122 mg chol., 918 mg sodium, 20 g carbo., 3 g dietary fiber, 31 g protein.

Chop up a couple of cups of leftover chicken for this soup or buy a rotisserie chicken from the deli and tear the meat into pieces.

creamy chicken noodle soup

prep: 15 minutes **cook:** 6 to 8 hours (low) or 3 to 4 hours (high) + 20 minutes
makes: 6 to 8 servings

1 In a 3½- or 4-quart slow cooker combine the water and chicken-mushroom soup. Stir in chicken, vegetables, and pepper.

2 Cover and cook on low-heat setting for 6 to 8 hours or on high-heat setting for 3 to 4 hours.

3 If using low-heat setting, turn slow cooker to high-heat setting. Stir in uncooked noodles. Cover and cook for 20 to 30 minutes more or just until noodles are tender.

- 5 cups water
- 2 10.75-ounce cans condensed creamy chicken-mushroom soup
- 2 cups chopped cooked chicken (about 10 ounces)
- 1 9- to 10-ounce package frozen mixed vegetables (cut green beans, corn, diced carrots, and peas)
- 1 teaspoon seasoned pepper or garlic-pepper seasoning
- 1½ cups dried egg noodles

nutrition facts per serving: 262 cal., 12 g total fat (3 g sat. fat), 63 mg chol., 908 mg sodium, 21 g carbo., 3 g dietary fiber, 19 g protein.

This has "kid-worthy" written all over it. Chunks of chicken, tender corn kernels, and added cream will make this soup a family pleaser.

chicken-corn chowder

prep: 15 minutes   **cook:** 4 to 6 hours (low) or 2 to 3 hours (high)
makes: 6 servings

1 pound skinless, boneless chicken thighs, cut into ½- to ¾-inch pieces
2 10.75-ounce cans condensed cream of potato or cream of chicken soup
1 11-ounce can whole kernel corn with sweet peppers, undrained
1½ cups sliced celery
1 cup water
1 cup half-and-half, light cream, or whole milk

1 In a 3½- or 4-quart slow cooker combine chicken, cream of potato soup, corn, celery, and the water.

2 Cover and cook on low-heat setting for 4 to 6 hours or on high-heat setting for 2 to 3 hours. Stir in half-and-half.

nutrition facts per serving: 261 cal., 10 g total fat (5 g sat. fat), 86 mg chol., 1029 mg sodium, 24 g carbo., 3 g dietary fiber, 19 g protein.

If you like, try cream of chicken with herbs, cream of onion, or cream of potato soup to change up the flavor of this easy everyday soup.

creamed
chicken and corn soup

prep: 20 minutes   **cook:** 5 to 6 hours (low) or 2½ to 3 hours (high)
makes: 4 to 6 servings

12   ounces skinless,
      boneless chicken
      thighs
 1   26-ounce can
      condensed cream
      of chicken soup
 1   14.75-ounce can
      cream-style corn
 1   14-ounce can
      reduced-sodium
      chicken broth
 1   cup chopped carrots
      (2 medium)
 1   cup finely chopped
      onion (1 large)
 1   cup frozen whole
      kernel corn
 ½   cup chopped celery
      (1 stalk)
 ½   cup water
 2   slices bacon, crisp-
      cooked, drained,
      and crumbled

1 In a 3½- or 4-quart slow cooker combine chicken, cream of chicken soup, cream-style corn, broth, carrots, onion, corn, celery, and the water.

2 Cover and cook on low-heat setting for 5 to 6 hours or on high-heat setting for 2½ to 3 hours.

3 Remove chicken from cooker; cool slightly. Chop chicken; stir back into soup mixture. Sprinkle each serving with bacon.

nutrition facts per serving: 447 cal., 17 g total fat (5 g sat. fat), 90 mg chol., 2056 mg sodium, 50 g carbo., 5 g dietary fiber, 28 g protein.

Turkey sausage and chicken thighs pair up for this bean-studded soup. A jar of pasta sauce supplies the robust flavor.

chicken cassoulet-style soup

prep: 25 minutes **cook:** 5 to 7 hours (low) or 2½ to 3½ hours (high)
makes: 6 servings

1 pound boneless, skinless chicken thighs, cut into ½-inch pieces

8 ounces smoked turkey sausage, cut into ½-inch slices

1 26-ounce jar pasta sauce with red wine and herbs

1 15- to 19-ounce can cannellini beans (white kidney beans), rinsed and drained

1⅓ cups water

1 teaspoon dried oregano, crushed

1 In a 3½- or 4-quart slow cooker combine chicken, sausage, pasta sauce, cannellini beans, the water, and oregano.

2 Cover and cook on low-heat setting for 5 to 7 hours or on high-heat setting for 2½ to 3½ hours.

nutrition facts per serving: 286 cal., 7 g total fat (2 g sat. fat), 88 mg chol., 1178 mg sodium, 33 g carbo., 9 g dietary fiber, 30 g protein.

Be sure to remember to prepare the dried beans ahead of time for this soup. The beans can be prepped, covered, and chilled for up to 24 hours.

turkey sausage
and bean soup

prep: 25 minutes **stand:** 1 hour **cook:** 10 hours (low) or 5 hours (high) + 1 hour
makes: 10 to 12 servings

1   pound dried beans (such as cranberry, kidney, Great Northern, and/or pinto beans)
8   cups water
4   cups water
1   32-ounce carton chicken broth
3   cups cubed red-skinned potatoes (3 medium)
4   cloves garlic, minced
1   tablespoon chili powder
1   pound smoked turkey sausage, halved lengthwise and cut into ½-inch pieces
2   cups frozen cut green beans
1   teaspoon salt

1 Rinse dried beans; drain. In a large Dutch oven combine beans and the 8 cups water. Bring to boiling; reduce heat. Simmer, uncovered, for 10 minutes. Remove from heat. Cover and let stand for 1 hour (or cool, then transfer to an extra-large bowl, cover, and chill for up to 24 hours). Drain and rinse beans.

2 In a 6- to 7-quart slow cooker combine beans, the 4 cups water, broth, potatoes, garlic, and chili powder. Cover and cook on low-heat setting for 10 hours or on high-heat setting for 5 hours. Using a potato masher or the back of a wooden spoon, mash beans slightly.

3 If using low-heat setting, turn to high-heat setting. Stir in sausage, green beans, and salt. Cover and cook for 1 hour more.

nutrition facts per serving: 270 cal., 5 g total fat (2 g sat. fat), 25 mg chol., 1038 mg sodium, 39 g carbo., 13 g dietary fiber, 19 g protein.

Frozen meatballs are a busy mom's best find. Toss together the meatballs and a few other ingredients and you have a dinner ready to cook in just minutes.

mexican meatball stew

prep: 10 minutes   **cook:** 6 to 7 hours (low) or 3 to 3½ hours (high)
makes: 8 to 10 servings

2   14.5-ounce cans
    Mexican-style
    stewed tomatoes,
    undrained
2   12-ounce packages
    frozen cooked
    turkey meatballs,
    thawed
1   15-ounce can black
    beans, rinsed and
    drained
1   14-ounce can chicken
    broth with roasted
    garlic
1   10-ounce package
    frozen whole kernel
    corn, thawed

1 In a 4- to 5-quart slow cooker combine tomatoes, meatballs, black beans, broth, and corn.

2 Cover and cook on low-heat setting for 6 to 7 hours or on high-heat setting for 3 to 3½ hours.

nutrition facts per serving: 287 cal., 13 g total fat (6 g sat. fat), 37 mg chol., 1134 mg sodium, 30 g carbo., 6 g dietary fiber, 16 g protein.

Shredded coleslaw mix is a clever time-saver for many recipes. Here it adds crisp-tender texture and fresh flavor to this sausage soup.

sausage
and tortellini soup

prep: 10 minutes   **cook:** 8 to 10 hours (low) or 4 to 5 hours (high) + 15 minutes
makes: 10 to 12 servings

2   14.5-ounce cans Italian-style stewed tomatoes, undrained
3   cups water
2   cups frozen cut green beans or Italian green beans
1   10.5-ounce can condensed French onion soup
8   ounces cooked smoked turkey sausage, halved lengthwise and cut into ½-inch pieces
2   cups packaged shredded cabbage with carrot (coleslaw mix)
1   9-ounce package refrigerated cheese-filled tortellini
    Shaved Parmesan cheese (optional)

1 In a 4- to 5-quart slow cooker combine tomatoes, the water, green beans, French onion soup, and sausage.

2 Cover and cook on low-heat setting for 8 to 10 hours or on high-heat setting for 4 to 5 hours.

3 If using low-heat setting, turn to high-heat setting. Stir in cabbage and tortellini. Cover and cook for 15 minutes more. If desired, top each serving with Parmesan cheese.

nutrition facts per serving: 176 cal., 5 g total fat (1 g sat. fat), 28 mg chol., 717 mg sodium, 23 g carbo., 2 g dietary fiber, 9 g protein.

This soup is like a stir-fry in a bowl! Rice, chicken, vegetables, and classic Asian flavors are slow cooked into a satisfying soup.

asian turkey and rice soup

prep: 25 minutes   **cook:** 7 to 8 hours (low) or 3½ to 4 hours (high) + 10 minutes
makes: 6 servings

1   pound turkey breast tenderloin or skinless, boneless chicken breast halves, cut into 1-inch pieces
2   cups sliced fresh mushrooms (such as shiitake or button)
1   cup carrots cut into thin bite-size strips (2 medium)
½   cup chopped onion (1 medium)
2   14-ounce cans reduced-sodium chicken broth
1½ cups water
2   tablespoons reduced-sodium soy sauce
2   teaspoons minced fresh ginger
2   teaspoons minced garlic
1½ cups sliced bok choy
1   cup uncooked instant brown rice
    Chow mein noodles (optional)

1 In a 3½- or 4-quart slow cooker combine turkey, mushrooms, carrots, and onion. Pour broth and the water over mixture in cooker. Stir in soy sauce, ginger, and garlic.

2 Cover and cook on low-heat setting for 7 to 8 hours or on high-heat setting for 3½ to 4 hours.

3 If using low-heat setting, turn to high-heat setting. Stir in bok choy and rice. Cover and cook for 10 to 15 minutes more or until rice is tender. If desired, top each serving with chow mein noodles.

nutrition facts per serving: 166 cal., 2 g total fat (0 g sat. fat), 45 mg chol., 572 mg sodium, 15 g carbo., 2 g dietary fiber, 22 g protein.

Winter nights call for hearty soups. This soup—with chunks of beef, potatoes, cabbage, and beets—will surely fill the bill.

bowl of borscht

prep: 45 minutes   **cook:** 8 to 9 hours (low) or 4 to 4½ hours (high) + 30 minutes
makes: 8 servings

1	pound boneless beef chuck steak
¼	cup all-purpose flour
¼	teaspoon salt
¼	teaspoon ground black pepper
2	tablespoons olive oil
1	pound beets with leafy tops (4 medium)
1	cup ½-inch pieces red-skinned potato
1	cup ½-inch pieces peeled turnip
½	cup chopped onion
¼	cup dried porcini mushrooms, rinsed, drained, and broken
1	14.5-ounce can diced tomatoes, undrained
2	14-ounce cans beef broth
1	tablespoon red wine vinegar
1	tablespoon tomato paste
1	tablespoon snipped fresh dill
½	teaspoon salt
¼	teaspoon caraway seeds
2	cups finely shredded cabbage
½	cup coarsely shredded carrot
1	tablespoon lemon juice
½	cup sour cream

1 Trim fat from meat. Cut meat into 1-inch pieces. In a plastic bag combine flour, ¼ teaspoon salt, and the pepper. Add meat pieces, a few at a time, shaking to coat. In a large skillet heat 1 tablespoon of the oil over medium-high heat. Cook meat, half at a time, in hot oil until brown. Drain off fat.

2 Cut tops from beets; wash and drain tops. Cut beet tops into fine shreds; set aside. Scrub beets; trim off root ends. Peel beets and cut into 1-inch pieces.

3 In a 5- to 6-quart slow cooker combine beet pieces, potato, turnip, onion, and mushrooms. Add meat. Stir in tomatoes, broth, vinegar, tomato paste, 1 tablespoon dill, ½ teaspoon salt, and caraway seeds.

4 Cover and cook on low-heat setting for 8 to 9 hours or on high-heat setting for 4 to 4½ hours. If using low-heat setting, turn to high-heat setting. Stir in cabbage and carrot. Cover and cook for about 30 minutes more or until tender.

5 Toss beet greens with remaining 1 tablespoon oil and lemon juice. Season to taste with salt and pepper. To serve, top each serving with beet greens and sour cream.

nutrition facts per serving: 249 cal., 11 g total fat (4 g sat. fat), 42 mg chol., 829 mg sodium, 24 g carbo., 5 g dietary fiber, 16 g protein.

True Burgundy wine comes from the Burgundy region of France.
However, some American red wines are just called "burgundy."
Pinot noir can also be used.

burgundy beef stew

prep: 20 minutes   **cook:** 10 to 12 hours (low) or 5 to 6 hours (high)
makes: 6 servings

2   pounds boneless beef
     chuck pot roast
½   teaspoon salt
¼   teaspoon ground
     black pepper
2   tablespoons
     vegetable oil
     (optional)
6   medium carrots, cut
     into 1½-inch pieces
1   9-ounce package
     frozen cut green
     beans
2   cups frozen small
     whole onions
     (½ of a 16-ounce
     package)
2   cloves garlic, minced
2   tablespoons quick-
     cooking tapioca
1   14-ounce can
     reduced-sodium
     beef broth
1   cup dry red wine
     (such as Burgundy)
     Hot cooked egg
     noodles (optional)
4   slices bacon, crisp-
     cooked, drained,
     and crumbled
     Snipped fresh parsley
     (optional)

1 Trim fat from meat. Cut meat into 1-inch pieces. Sprinkle meat with salt and pepper. If desired, in a large skillet heat oil over medium-high heat. Cook meat, one-third at a time, in hot oil until brown. Drain off fat.

2 In a 3½- or 4-quart slow cooker combine carrots, green beans, onions, and garlic. Add meat. Sprinkle with tapioca. Pour broth and wine over mixture in cooker.

3 Cover and cook on low-heat setting for 10 to 12 hours or on high-heat setting for 5 to 6 hours. If desired, serve over noodles. Sprinkle each serving with bacon and, if desired, parsley.

nutrition facts per serving: 317 cal., 8 g total fat (3 g sat. fat), 95 mg chol., mg sodium, 16 g carbo., 3 g dietary fiber, 37 g protein.

To add a unique flavor to this stew, try smoked paprika instead of regular for a change. Tender cubed beef stars in this caraway- and paprika-flavored stew.

paprika beef stew

prep: 20 minutes cook: 8 to 9 hours (low) or 4 to 4½ hours (high)
makes: 6 servings

2 pounds boneless beef chuck pot roast
1½ cups chopped onions (3 medium)
3 cloves garlic, minced
1 14-ounce can reduced-sodium beef broth
1½ cups water
1 6-ounce can tomato paste
1 tablespoon paprika
1 tablespoon caraway seeds
2 teaspoons dried marjoram, crushed
¼ teaspoon ground black pepper
2 cups coarsely chopped green and/or red sweet peppers (about 2 large)
½ cup light sour cream

1 Trim fat from meat. Cut meat into ¾-inch pieces. In a 3½- or 4-quart slow cooker combine meat, onions, garlic, broth, the water, tomato paste, paprika, caraway seeds, marjoram, and black pepper.

2 Cover and cook on low-heat setting for 8 to 9 hours or on high-heat setting for 4 to 4½ hours. Stir in sweet peppers for the last 45 minutes of cooking. Top each serving with sour cream.

nutrition facts per serving: 280 cal., 8 g total fat (3 g sat. fat), 96 mg chol., 259 mg sodium, 15 g carbo., 3 g dietary fiber, 37 g protein.

A hint of allspice and plenty of vegetables make this a test kitchen all-time favorite. Add the green beans at the end to keep them from overcooking.

fireside beef stew

prep: 25 minutes **cook:** 8 to 10 hours (low) or 4 to 5 hours (high) + 15 minutes
makes: 6 servings

1½ pounds boneless beef chuck pot roast
2½ cups 1-inch pieces peeled and seeded butternut squash (1 pound)
2 small onions, cut into wedges
2 cloves garlic, minced
1 14-ounce can reduced-sodium beef broth
1 8-ounce can tomato sauce
2 tablespoons Worcestershire sauce
1 teaspoon dry mustard
¼ teaspoon ground black pepper
⅛ teaspoon ground allspice
2 tablespoons cold water
4 teaspoons cornstarch
1 9-ounce package frozen Italian green beans
   Freshly ground black pepper (optional)

1 Trim fat from meat. Cut meat into 1-inch pieces. In a 3½- to 4½-quart slow cooker combine meat, squash, onions, and garlic. Stir in broth, tomato sauce, Worcestershire sauce, dry mustard, ¼ teaspoon black pepper, and allspice.

2 Cover and cook on low-heat setting for 8 to 10 hours or on high-heat setting for 4 to 5 hours.

3 If using low-heat setting, turn to high-heat setting. In a small bowl combine the cold water and cornstarch. Stir cornstarch mixture and green beans into the cooker. Cover and cook for about 15 minutes more or until thickened. If desired, sprinkle each serving with freshly ground black pepper.

nutrition facts per serving: 206 cal., 4 g total fat (1 g sat. fat), 67 mg chol., 440 mg sodium, 15 g carbo., 3 g dietary fiber, 27 g protein.

Although red wine is part of the title of this delicious soup, you can substitute beef broth if you want to make this kid-friendly.

beef stew
with red wine gravy

prep: 30 minutes **cook:** 12 to 14 hours (low) or 6 to 7 hours (high)
makes: 6 servings

2 pounds boneless beef chuck pot roast
¼ cup all-purpose flour
2 teaspoons dried Italian seasoning
1 teaspoon salt
½ teaspoon ground black pepper
2 tablespoons olive oil
2 large onions, cut into thin wedges
1 large parsnip, peeled, quartered lengthwise, and halved
1 large carrot, quartered lengthwise and halved
1½ cups ¾-inch pieces peeled Jerusalem artichokes (sunchokes)
1 cup red wine (such as Cabernet Sauvignon) or beef broth
½ cup beef broth
¼ cup tomato paste
Chopped roma tomatoes, golden raisins, and/or red wine vinegar or balsamic vinegar
Crusty bread (optional)

1 Trim fat from meat. Cut meat into 1-inch pieces. In a plastic bag combine flour, Italian seasoning, salt, and pepper. Add meat pieces, a few at a time, shaking to coat. In a large skillet heat oil over medium-high heat. Cook meat, one-third at a time, in hot oil until brown. Drain off fat.

2 In a 4½- to 6-quart slow cooker combine onions, parsnip, carrot, and Jerusalem artichokes. Add meat. Pour wine and broth over mixture in cooker.

3 Cover and cook on low-heat setting for 12 to 14 hours or on high-heat setting for 6 to 7 hours. Stir in tomato paste. Top each serving with tomatoes, raisins, and/or vinegar. If desired, serve with bread.

nutrition facts per serving: 356 cal., 9 g total fat (2 g sat. fat), 90 mg chol., 601 mg sodium, 26 g carbo., 4 g dietary fiber, 35 g protein.

Sometimes you can take a can of soup and "doctor it up" to personalize it and make it "yours." That's especially true with this hearty, quick-to-prepare soup.

minestrone plus

prep: 20 minutes   **cook:** 7 to 8 hours (low) or 3½ to 4 hours (high)
makes: 6 servings

1   pound lean ground beef, ground pork, or sweet Italian sausage
½   cup chopped onion (1 medium)
2   19-ounce cans chunky minestrone soup
1   15-ounce can navy beans, rinsed and drained
2   cups water
¼   cup finely shredded Parmesan cheese (1 ounce)

1 In a large skillet cook meat and onion over medium heat until meat is brown and onion is tender. Drain off fat. In a 3½- or 4-quart slow cooker combine meat mixture, minestrone, navy beans, and the water.

2 Cover and cook on low-heat setting for 7 to 8 hours or on high-heat setting for 3 ½ to 4 hours. Sprinkle each serving with Parmesan cheese.

nutrition facts per serving: 378 cal., 18 g total fat (9 g sat. fat), 67 mg chol., 1175 mg sodium, 27 g carbo., 8 g dietary fiber, 31 g protein.

Ancho chile pepper, a dominant flavor in this stew, can be found with the spices at most supermarkets. If not, check any Mexican market or specialty spice store.

ancho-beef stew

prep: 15 minutes   **cook:** 8 to 9 hours (low) or 4 to 4½ hours (high)
makes: 4 servings

1	pound boneless beef chuck pot roast
1	tablespoon ground ancho chile pepper
1	tablespoon vegetable oil
1	16-ounce package frozen stew vegetables
1	cup frozen whole kernel corn
1	16-ounce jar salsa
½	cup water
	Cornbread (optional)

1 Trim fat from meat. Cut meat into 1-inch pieces. Sprinkle meat with ancho chile pepper, tossing to coat all sides. In a large skillet heat oil over medium-high heat. Cook meat, half at a time, in hot oil until brown. Drain off fat.

2 In a 3½- or 4-quart slow cooker combine frozen stew vegetables and corn. Add meat. Pour salsa and the water over mixture in cooker.

3 Cover and cook on low-heat setting for 8 to 9 hours or on high-heat setting for 4 to 4½ hours. If desired, serve with cornbread.

nutrition facts per serving: 302 cal., 9 g total fat (2 g sat. fat), 50 mg chol., 1311 mg sodium, 28 g carbo., 5 g dietary fiber, 30 g protein.

Classic ingredients make up this beef soup. If you prefer, use frozen cut green beans or soybeans (edamame) instead of the peas.

busy-day
beef-vegetable soup

prep: 20 minutes   cook: 8 to 10 hours (low) or 4 to 5 hours (high)
makes: 4 servings

1   pound boneless beef
      chuck pot roast
1½ cups ½-inch pieces
      carrots (3 medium)
1   cup ½-inch pieces
      peeled potatoes
      (2 small)
½   cup chopped onion
      (1 medium)
½   teaspoon salt
½   teaspoon dried
      thyme, crushed
1   bay leaf
2   14.5-ounce cans
      diced tomatoes,
      undrained
1   cup water
½   cup frozen peas
      Fresh parsley sprigs
      (optional)

1 Trim fat from meat. Cut meat into ¾-inch pieces. In 3½- or 4-quart slow cooker combine meat, carrots, potatoes, and onion. Sprinkle with salt and thyme; add bay leaf. Pour tomatoes and the water over mixture in cooker.

2 Cover and cook on low-heat setting for 8 to 10 hours or on high-heat setting for 4 to 5 hours. Remove and discard bay leaf. Stir in peas. If desired, garnish each serving with parsley.

nutrition facts per serving: 269 cal., 4 g total fat (1 g sat. fat), 67 mg chol., 746 mg sodium, 29 g carbo., 4 g dietary fiber, 28 g protein.

Barley adds a toothsome texture to this juicy beef soup. Try using lamb instead of beef—it's a great match for the barley.

barley-beef soup

prep: 25 minutes **cook:** 8 to 10 hours (low) or 4 to 5 hours (high)
makes: 8 (1⅓-cup) servings

1	tablespoon vegetable oil
12	ounces beef or lean lamb stew meat, cut into ¾- to 1-inch pieces
4	14-ounce cans beef broth
1	14.5-ounce can diced tomatoes, undrained
1	cup chopped onion (1 large)
1	cup ½-inch slices peeled parsnip or ½-inch pieces peeled potato
1	cup frozen mixed vegetables
⅔	cup quick-cooking barley
½	cup chopped celery (1 stalk)
1	teaspoon dried oregano or basil, crushed
¼	teaspoon ground black pepper
2	cloves garlic, minced
1	bay leaf

1 In a large skillet heat oil over medium-high heat. Cook meat in hot oil until brown. Drain off fat.

2 In a 5- or 6-quart slow cooker combine meat, broth, tomatoes, onion, parsnip, frozen mixed vegetables, barley, celery, oregano, pepper, garlic, and bay leaf.

3 Cover and cook on low-heat setting for 8 to 10 hours or on high-heat setting for 4 to 5 hours. Remove and discard bay leaf.

nutrition facts per serving: 171 cal., 4 g total fat (1 g sat. fat), 25 mg chol., 865 mg sodium, 20 g carbo., 4 g dietary fiber, 13 g protein.

Here is a five-ingredient beef stew that can easily be made in a few minutes. If you buy precut stew meat, cut up the bigger pieces if necessary.

beef and bean ragout

prep: 10 minutes **cook:** 8 to 10 hours (low) or 4 to 5 hours (high)
makes: 6 servings

1 pound beef stew
    meat, cut into ¾- to
    1-inch pieces
1 16-ounce can kidney
    beans, rinsed and
    drained
1 15-ounce can tomato
    sauce with onion
    and garlic
1 14.5-ounce can
    Italian-style
    stewed tomatoes,
    undrained
½ of a 28-ounce
    package frozen
    diced hash brown
    potatoes with
    onions and peppers
    (about 4 cups)
    Fresh oregano leaves
    (optional)

1 In a 3½- or 4-quart slow cooker combine meat, kidney beans, tomato sauce, tomatoes, and potatoes.

2 Cover and cook on low-heat setting for 8 to 10 hours or on high-heat setting for 4 to 5 hours. If desired, garnish each serving with oregano.

nutrition facts per serving: 260 cal., 3 g total fat (1 g sat. fat), 45 mg chol., 835 mg sodium, 35 g carbo., 7 g dietary fiber, 23 g protein.

Here's a classic, home-style winter warmer. Store extra barley in tightly covered containers for up to a year in a cool, dry place.

beef and vegetable soup

prep: 20 minutes **cook:** 9 to 11 hours (low) or 4½ to 5½ hours (high)
makes: 6 servings

1½ pounds boneless beef
      sirloin steak
2 14-ounce cans beef
      broth
1 14.5-ounce can
      stewed tomatoes,
      undrained
1½ cups ½-inch slices
      carrots (3 medium)
2 small onions, cut into
      thin wedges
½ cup regular barley
½ cup water
1 teaspoon dried
      thyme, crushed
2 cloves garlic, minced
1 bay leaf

1 Trim fat from meat. Cut meat into ¾-inch pieces. In a 3½- or 4-quart slow cooker combine meat, broth, tomatoes, carrots, onions, barley, the water, thyme, garlic, and bay leaf.

2 Cover and cook on low-heat setting for 9 to 11 hours or on high-heat setting for 4½ to 5½ hours. Remove and discard bay leaf.

nutrition facts per serving: 254 cal., 5 g total fat (1 g sat. fat), 53 mg chol., 710 mg sodium, 22 g carbo., 5 g dietary fiber, 28 g protein.

White wine, garlic, rosemary, white beans, and beef create a French soup that is high in flavor and comfort.

french country soup

prep: 20 minutes **stand:** 1 hour **cook:** 8 to 10 hours (low) or 4 to 5 hours (high)
makes: 6 servings

8 ounces dried navy,
   Great Northern,
   or cannellini beans
   (white kidney
   beans)
6 cups water
1 pound beef or lean
   lamb stew meat,
   cut into ¾- to 1-inch
   pieces
4 cups reduced-sodium
   chicken broth
2 medium carrots, cut
   into 1-inch pieces
2 stalks celery, cut into
   1-inch pieces
1 large onion, cut into
   thin wedges
1 cup dry white wine
6 cloves garlic, minced
3 bay leaves
1½ teaspoons dried
   rosemary, crushed
½ teaspoon salt
¼ teaspoon ground
   black pepper
   French bread slices,
   toasted (optional)

1 Rinse and drain navy beans. In a 4-quart Dutch oven combine beans and the water. Bring to boiling; reduce heat. Simmer, uncovered, for 10 minutes. Remove from heat. Cover and let stand for 1 hour. Drain and rinse beans.

2 In a 3½- to 6-quart slow cooker combine beans, meat, broth, carrots, celery, onion, wine, garlic, bay leaves, rosemary, salt, and pepper.

3 Cover and cook on low-heat setting for 8 to 10 hours or on high-heat setting for 4 to 5 hours. Remove and discard bay leaves. If desired, serve with bread.

nutrition facts per serving: 288 cal., 3 g total fat (1 g sat. fat), 45 mg chol., 652 mg sodium, 31 g carbo., 11 g dietary fiber, 27 g protein.

Paprikash is a Hungarian dish made with meat, onions, and—as its name implies—paprika. This long-braising stew is perfect for the slow cooker.

hungarian paprikash

prep: 20 minutes **cook:** 8 to 10 hours (low) or 4 to 5 hours (high)
makes: 8 servings

2   pounds beef stew meat, cut into ¾- to 1-inch pieces
2   medium onions, sliced
1   cup chopped red or green sweet pepper (1 large)
1   4.5-ounce jar (drained weight) sliced mushrooms, drained
1   14.5-ounce can diced tomatoes, drained
1   10.75-ounce can condensed cream of mushroom soup
1   tablespoon Hungarian paprika or paprika
1   teaspoon dried thyme, crushed
¼   teaspoon coarsely ground black pepper
    Hot cooked noodles or spaetzle
    Sour cream

1 In a 3½- or 4-quart slow cooker combine meat, onions, red sweet pepper, and drained mushrooms.

2 In a medium bowl combine drained tomatoes, cream of mushroom soup, paprika, thyme, and pepper. Pour tomato mixture over mixture in cooker.

3 Cover and cook on low-heat setting for 8 to 10 hours or on high-heat setting for 4 to 5 hours. Serve over noodles and top each serving with sour cream.

nutrition facts per serving: 452 cal., 12 g total fat (4 g sat. fat), 126 mg chol., 503 mg sodium, 50 g carbo., 4 g dietary fiber, 34 g protein.

Pot-au-feu translates as "pot on the fire." Any combo of meats and veggies can be used. Here, smoked pork chops add a smoky flavor.

french pot-au-feu

prep: 50 minutes   cook: 7 to 8 hours (low) or 3½ to 4 hours (high)
makes: 6 servings

1 tablespoon vegetable oil
3 boneless beef short ribs (1¼ pounds)
1 medium onion, halved
2 stalks celery with leaves
2 medium leeks
4 cloves garlic, unpeeled
2 sprigs fresh thyme
½ teaspoon whole peppercorns
2 bay leaves
6 large or 12 small whole fingerling potatoes (10 ounces)
4 small carrots,* cut into 2-inch pieces
1 medium turnip, peeled and cut into 2-inch pieces
3 whole chicken legs (drumstick and thigh), skinned (2 pounds)
3 boneless smoked pork chops (8 ounces)
2 14-ounce cans chicken broth
   Coarse salt (such as kosher or sea salt)
   Freshly cracked black pepper
1 recipe Sauce Verte
   Dijon-style mustard
   Cornichons

1 In a large skillet heat oil over medium-high heat. Cook ribs on all sides in hot oil until brown. Remove ribs from skillet; set aside. Add onion to skillet, cut sides down, and cook until deeply brown. Remove onion from skillet; set aside.

2 Cut celery into 2-inch pieces, reserving leaves. Cut white parts of leeks into 2-inch pieces, reserving green tops.

3 For a bouquet garni, cut a 12x10-inch piece from a double thickness of 100-percent-cotton cheesecloth. Place onion, celery leaves, leek tops, garlic, thyme, peppercorns, and bay leaves in the center of the cheesecloth piece. Bring up corners of the cheesecloth; tie closed with clean 100-percent-cotton kitchen string.

4 In a 6-quart slow cooker combine celery pieces, leek pieces, potatoes, carrots, and turnip. Top with ribs, chicken legs, and smoked pork chops. Add bouquet garni to mixture in cooker. Pour broth over mixture in cooker.

5 Cover and cook on low-heat setting for 7 to 8 hours or on high-heat setting for 3½ to 4 hours. Remove bouquet garni and discard.

6 To serve, ladle broth into shallow bowls and serve with portions of meat and vegetables. Sprinkle each serving with coarse salt and cracked black pepper. Serve with Sauce Verte, mustard, and cornichons.

sauce verte: In a saucepan cook ½ cup fresh spinach and ¼ cup Italian (flat-leaf) parsley leaves in boiling water for 1 minute. Drain and immediately place in ice water. Drain again and pat dry with paper towels. In a blender or food processor combine 1 cup mayonnaise, blanched spinach and parsley, 1 teaspoon snipped fresh tarragon, 1 teaspoon lemon juice, 1 anchovy fillet, and 1 clove garlic, halved. Cover and blend or process until smooth. Stir in 2 teaspoons capers, drained.

nutrition facts per serving: 656 cal., 44 g total fat (10 g sat. fat), 135 mg chol., 1709 mg sodium, 22 g carbo., 3 g dietary fiber, 39 g protein.

Your kids will love this cheese-based soup with ground beef, potatoes, and carrots. Serve with some crackers and plump red grapes.

cheeseburger soup

prep: 25 minutes **cook:** 10 to 11 hours (low) or 5 to 5½ hours (high)
makes: 6 servings

1   pound ground beef
½   cup chopped onion
      (1 medium)
2   cloves garlic, minced
2   cups ½-inch pieces
      peeled russet
      potatoes (2 medium)
½   cup coarsely
      shredded carrot
      (1 medium)
¼   cup ketchup
2   tablespoons yellow
      mustard
1   tablespoon finely
      chopped fresh
      serrano chile
      pepper (see tip,
      page 32)
¼   teaspoon salt
¼   teaspoon ground
      black pepper
2   14-ounce cans beef
      broth
1   10.75-ounce can
      condensed cheddar
      cheese soup
½   cup shredded
      cheddar cheese
      (4 ounces)
      Dill pickle spears
      (optional)

1 In a large skillet cook meat, onion, and garlic over medium heat until meat is brown and onion is tender. Drain off fat.

2 In a 4- to 5-quart slow cooker combine meat mixture, potatoes, carrot, ketchup, mustard, serrano pepper, salt, and pepper. Stir in broth and cheddar cheese soup.

3 Cover and cook on low-heat setting for 10 to 11 hours or on high-heat setting for 5 to 5½ hours.

4 Top each serving with cheddar cheese, and, if desired, serve with pickles.

nutrition facts per serving: 417 cal., 31 g total fat (13 g sat. fat), 81 mg chol., 1311 mg sodium, 17 g carbo., 2 g dietary fiber, 18 g protein.

Authentic Cincinnati chili is served over spaghetti. Onions and beans can be served as toppers, but this version contains these ingredients in the chili.

cincinnati chili

prep: 30 minutes **cook:** 8 to 10 hours (low) or 4 to 5 hours (high)
makes: 6 servings

- 1 bay leaf
- ½ teaspoon whole allspice
- ½ teaspoon whole cloves
- 2 pounds lean ground beef
- 2 cups chopped onions (2 large)
- 1 15-ounce can dark red kidney beans, rinsed and drained
- 1 15-ounce can tomato sauce
- 1½ cups water
- 4 cloves garlic, minced
- 3 tablespoons chili powder
- 1 teaspoon Worcestershire sauce
- ¾ teaspoon ground cumin
- ¾ teaspoon ground cinnamon
- ½ teaspoon salt
- ¼ teaspoon cayenne pepper
- ½ ounce unsweetened chocolate, chopped
- 12 ounces dried spaghetti, cooked and well drained
- 1 cup shredded cheddar cheese (4 ounces)

1 For a spice bag, cut a 4-inch square from a double thickness of 100-percent-cotton cheesecloth. Place bay leaf, allspice, and cloves in the center of the cheesecloth square. Bring up corners of the cheesecloth; tie closed with clean 100-percent-cotton kitchen string; set aside.

2 In a large skillet cook meat over medium heat until brown. Drain off fat. In a 3½- or 4-quart slow cooker combine meat, onions, red kidney beans, tomato sauce, the water, garlic, chili powder, Worcestershire sauce, cumin, cinnamon, salt, and cayenne pepper. Add spice bag to mixture in cooker.

3 Cover and cook on low-heat setting for 8 to 10 hours or on high-heat setting for 4 to 5 hours. Stir in chocolate for the last 30 minutes of cooking. Remove spice bag and discard.

4 To serve, ladle chili over spaghetti. Sprinkle each serving with cheddar cheese.

nutrition facts per serving: 743 cal., 32 g total fat (14 g sat. fat), 123 mg chol., 953 mg sodium, 69 g carbo., 10 g dietary fiber, 48 g protein.

If you purchase beef stir-fry strips, your work will be half done for this tasty soup. Look for plain Chinese noodles in the Asian food section of the supermarket.

teriyaki beef-noodle soup

prep: 20 minutes **cook:** 6 to 8 hours (low) or 3 to 4 hours (high)
stand: 5 minutes **makes:** 6 servings

1 pound beef stir-fry
  strips
2 14-ounce cans beef
  broth
2 cups water
2 medium red or green
  sweet peppers, cut
  into ½-inch pieces
1 8-ounce can sliced
  water chestnuts,
  drained and
  chopped
6 green onions, cut into
  1-inch pieces
3 tablespoons soy
  sauce
1 teaspoon ground
  ginger
¼ teaspoon ground
  black pepper
5 to 6 ounces dried
  Chinese egg
  noodles or fine
  egg noodles
  Green onion strips
  (optional)

1 In a 3½- or 4-quart slow cooker combine meat, broth, the water, red sweet peppers, water chestnuts, green onion pieces, soy sauce, ginger, and black pepper.

2 Cover and cook on low-heat setting for 6 to 8 hours or on high-heat setting for 3 to 4 hours.

3 Turn off cooker. Stir in uncooked noodles. Cover and let stand for 5 minutes. If desired, sprinkle each serving with green onion strips.

nutrition facts per serving: 230 cal., 4 g total fat (1 g sat. fat), 46 mg chol., 1628 mg sodium, 26 g carbo., 3 g dietary fiber, 22 g protein.

It may be exaggerating slightly to say this great-tasting chili is so easy you could do it in your sleep, but it truly is incredibly simple.

in-your-sleep chili

prep: 15 minutes **cook:** 4 to 6 hours (low) or 2 to 3 hours (high)
makes: 6 servings

1 pound ground beef
1 cup chopped onion
   (1 large)
2 15-ounce cans chili
   beans in chili gravy
1 14.5-ounce can diced
   tomatoes and green
   chiles, undrained
11 1½-ounce can
   hot-style vegetable
   juice
   Sliced green onions,
   sour cream, and/or
   shredded cheddar
   cheese (optional)

1 In a large skillet cook meat and onion until meat is brown and onion is tender. Drain off fat.

2 In a 3½- or 4-quart slow cooker combine meat mixture, chili beans, tomatoes, and vegetable juice.

3 Cover and cook on low-heat setting for 4 to 6 hours on high-heat setting for 2 to 3 hours. If desired, top each serving with green onions, sour cream, and/or cheddar cheese.

nutrition facts per serving: 332 cal., 12 g total fat (4 g sat. fat), 51 mg chol., 873 mg sodium, 31 g carbo., 9 g dietary fiber, 23 g protein.

Pasta is a tasty addition to this chili soup. It's definitely tried-and-true when it comes to being delicious.

tried-and-true chili mac

prep: 25 minutes **cook:** 4 to 6 hours (low) or 2 to 3 hours (high)
makes: 6 servings

1½ pounds ground beef
1 cup chopped onion
   (1 large)
3 cloves garlic, minced
1 15-ounce can chili
   beans in chili gravy,
   undrained
1 14.5-ounce can diced
   tomatoes and green
   chiles, undrained
1 cup beef broth
¾ cup chopped green
   sweet pepper
   (1 medium)
2 teaspoons chili
   powder
1 teaspoon ground
   cumin
¼ teaspoon salt
8 ounces dried
   cavatappi pasta
   or macaroni
   Shredded cheddar
   cheese (optional)
   Chopped green
   onions (optional)

1 In a large skillet cook meat, onion, and garlic over medium heat until meat is brown and onion is tender. Drain off fat.

2 In a 3½- or 4-quart slow cooker combine meat mixture, chili beans, tomatoes, broth, green sweet pepper, chili powder, cumin, and salt.

3 Cover and cook on low-heat setting for 4 to 6 hours or on high-heat setting for 2 to 3 hours.

4 Meanwhile, cook pasta according to package directions; drain. Stir cooked pasta into meat mixture. If desired, top each serving with cheddar cheese and green onion.

nutrition facts per serving: 576 cal., 27 g total fat (10 g sat. fat), 85 mg chol., 829 mg sodium, 51 g carbo., 8 g dietary fiber, 31 g protein.

Most green salsas contain tomatillos, a fruit that looks like a green tomato. The salsa will add a hint of tanginess to your chili.

white and green chili

prep: 20 minutes **cook:** 7 to 8 hours (low) or 3½ to 4 hours (high)
makes: 6 servings

1½ pounds lean ground pork
1 cup chopped onion (1 large)
2 15-ounce cans Great Northern beans, rinsed and drained
1 16-ounce jar green salsa
1 14-ounce can chicken broth
1½ teaspoons ground cumin
2 tablespoons snipped fresh cilantro
⅓ cup sour cream (optional)
Snipped fresh cilantro (optional)

1 In a large skillet cook meat and onion over medium heat until meat is brown and onion is tender. Drain off fat.

2 In a 3½- or 4-quart slow cooker combine meat mixture, Great Northern beans, salsa, broth, and cumin.

3 Cover and cook on low-heat setting for 7 to 8 hours or on high-heat setting for 3½ to 4 hours. Stir in 2 tablespoons cilantro.

4 If desired, top each serving with sour cream and cilantro.

nutrition facts per serving: 258 cal., 9 g total fat (4 g sat. fat), 54 mg chol., 816 mg sodium, 27 g carbo., 8 g dietary fiber, 23 g protein.

simmering **soups & stews**

This is true campsite fare. Sloppy joe flavor, two kinds of beans, and ground beef come together for a slow-cooker classic that's hearty and tangy.

pioneer bean stew

prep: 15 minutes cook: 4 to 6 hours (low) or 2 to 3 hours (high)
makes: 8 servings

1½ pounds lean ground
     beef
4 or 5 slices bacon,
     chopped (4 ounces)
2 15.5-ounce cans
     sloppy joe sauce
2 15-ounce cans red
     kidney beans,
     rinsed and drained
1 15-ounce can butter
     beans, rinsed and
     drained
2 cups water

1 In a large skillet cook meat and bacon until meat is brown. Drain off fat.

2 In a 4- to 6-quart slow cooker combine meat mixture, sloppy joe sauce, red kidney beans, and butter beans. Pour the water over mixture in cooker.

3 Cover and cook on low-heat setting for 4 to 6 hours or on high-heat setting for 2 to 3 hours.

nutrition facts per serving: 446 cal., 19 g total fat (7 g sat. fat), 66 mg chol., 1692 mg sodium, 41 g carbo., 8 g dietary fiber, 26 g protein.

Black-eyed peas and a trio of beans give this soup a high fiber dossier. A dollop of sour cream on each serving provides a cooldown from the spices.

taco soup

prep: 15 minutes   cook: 6 to 8 hours (low) or 3 to 4 hours (high)
makes: 8 servings

1   pound ground beef
1   15-ounce can
    black-eyed peas,
    undrained
1   15-ounce can black
    beans, undrained
1   15-ounce can
    garbanzo beans
    (chickpeas),
    undrained
1   15-ounce can chili
    beans in chili gravy,
    undrained
1   14.5-ounce can
    Mexican-style
    stewed tomatoes,
    undrained
1   11-ounce can whole
    kernel corn with
    sweet peppers,
    undrained
1   1.25-ounce envelope
    taco seasoning mix
    Sour cream (optional)
    Tortilla chips
    (optional)

1 In a large skillet cook meat over medium heat until brown. Drain off fat.

2 In a 3½- to 6-quart slow cooker combine meat, black-eyed peas, black beans, garbanzo beans, chili beans, tomatoes, corn, and taco seasoning mix.

3 Cover and cook on low-heat setting for 6 to 8 hours or on high-heat setting for 3 to 4 hours. If desired, top each serving with sour cream and tortilla chips.

nutrition facts per serving: 349 cal., 10 g total fat (3 g sat. fat), 36 mg chol., 1372 mg sodium, 45 g carbo., 11 g dietary fiber, 25 g protein.

Pork, beans, hominy, and a tequila-lime salsa go together for a stew you won't soon forget.

hominy-pork stew

prep: 15 minutes   **cook:** 8 to 9 hours (low) or 4 to 4½ hours (high)
makes: 4 servings

2   pounds boneless pork shoulder roast
1½   teaspoons ground cumin
1   tablespoon vegetable oil
   Disposable slow-cooker liner
1   15- to 16-ounce can navy beans, rinsed and drained
1   15- to 15.5-ounce can hominy, rinsed and drained
1   16-ounce jar tequila-lime salsa
1¼   cups water
   Lime wedges (optional)

1 Trim fat from meat. Cut meat into 1-inch pieces. In a medium bowl toss meat with cumin. In a large skillet heat oil over medium-high heat. Cook meat, half at a time, in hot oil until brown. Drain off fat.

2 Line a 3½- or 4-quart slow cooker with a disposable slow cooker liner. In the prepared cooker combine meat, navy beans, and hominy. In a large bowl combine salsa and the water. Pour salsa mixture over mixture in cooker.

3 Cover and cook on low-heat setting for 8 to 9 hours or on high-heat setting for 4 to 4½ hours. If desired, serve with lime wedges.

nutrition facts per serving: 557 cal., 20 g total fat (6 g sat. fat), 151 mg chol., 1186 mg sodium, 41 g carbo., 8 g dietary fiber, 52 g protein.

Pork and Polish sausage couldn't be happier together than in this bean-studded, thyme-flavored stew.

hearty pork stew

prep: 30 minutes **cook:** 8 to 10 hours (low) or 4 to 5 hours (high)
makes: 8 servings

1½ pounds boneless pork
    shoulder roast
1 pound cooked
    kielbasa (Polska
    Kielbasa) or cooked,
    smoked Polish
    sausage, cut into
    ½-inch slices
2 15- to 19-ounce cans
    cannellini beans
    (white kidney
    beans), rinsed and
    drained
6 carrots, peeled and
    sliced into 1-inch
    pieces
2 cups chopped onions
    (2 large)
1 14-ounce can
    reduced-sodium
    chicken broth*
    or 1¾ cups water
3 tablespoons tomato
    paste
2 tablespoons snipped
    fresh thyme or
    1 teaspoon dried
    thyme, crushed
2 cloves garlic, minced
½ teaspoon freshly
    ground black
    pepper

1 Trim fat from meat. Cut meat into 1-inch pieces. In a 6- to 7-quart slow cooker combine meat, kielbasa, cannellini beans, carrots, onions, broth, tomato paste, thyme, garlic, and pepper.

2 Cover and cook on low-heat setting for 8 to 10 hours or on high-heat setting for 4 to 5 hours.

nutrition facts per serving: 430 cal., 20 g total fat (6 g sat. fat), 95 mg chol., 1063 mg sodium, 32 g carbo., 8 g dietary fiber, 36 g protein.

*test kitchen tip: If desired, replace ½ cup of the chicken broth with ½ cup dry white wine.

Apple juice and caraway seeds, classic flavor complements to pork, season the meat and the rich brown gravy of this stew.

german-style pork stew

prep: 25 minutes   **cook:** 7 to 8 hours (low) or 3½ to 4 hours (high)
makes: 4 servings

2   to 2¼ pounds
    boneless pork
    shoulder roast
    or boneless beef
    chuck pot roast
    Nonstick cooking
    spray
1   16- to 20-ounce
    package
    refrigerated diced
    potatoes
2   12-ounce jars
    mushroom gravy
1½ cups apple juice
2   teaspoons caraway
    seeds

1 Trim fat from meat. Cut meat into ¾-inch pieces. Lightly coat a large skillet with cooking spray. Heat over medium heat. Cook pork pieces, one-third at a time, until light brown, stirring often. Drain off fat.

2 In a 3½- or 4-quart slow cooker combine pork, potatoes, mushroom gravy, apple juice, and caraway seeds.

3 Cover and cook on low-heat setting for 7 to 8 hours or on high-heat setting for 3½ to 4 hours.

nutrition facts per serving: 462 cal., 16 g total fat (5 g sat. fat), 101 mg chol., 1150 mg sodium, 44 g carbo., 3 g dietary fiber, 34 g protein.

When winter has worn out its welcome, let this meatball stew warm you from the inside out. Basil pesto punches up the flavor.

pesto meatball stew

prep: 10 minutes **cook:** 5 to 7 hours (low) or 2½ to 3½ hours (high)
makes: 6 servings

1   16-ounce package
    frozen cooked
    Italian-style
    meatballs (32),
    thawed
2   14.5-ounce cans
    Italian-style
    stewed tomatoes,
    undrained
1   15- to 19-ounce can
    cannellini beans
    (white kidney
    beans), rinsed and
    drained
½   cup water
¼   cup purchased basil
    pesto
½   cup finely shredded
    Parmesan cheese
    (2 ounces)

1 In a 3½- or 4-quart slow cooker combine thawed meatballs, tomatoes, cannellini beans, the water, and pesto.

2 Cover and cook on low-heat setting for 5 to 7 hours or on high-heat setting for 2½ to 3½ hours. Sprinkle each serving with Parmesan cheese.

nutrition facts per serving: 408 cal., 27 g total fat (10 g sat. fat), 34 mg chol., 1201 mg sodium, 24 g carbo., 6 g dietary fiber, 17 g protein.

Edamame are green soybeans. Fresh edamame may be difficult to find, but the frozen version is readily available in the frozen foods section of your supermarket.

pork and edamame soup

prep: 25 minutes   **cook:** 7 to 8 hours (low) or 3½ to 4 hours (high) + 5 minutes
makes: 6 servings

2 pounds boneless pork shoulder
1 tablespoon vegetable oil
2 14-ounce cans chicken broth
1 12-ounce package frozen green soybeans (edamame)
1 8-ounce can sliced water chestnuts, drained
1 cup chopped red sweet pepper (1 large)
2 tablespoons reduced-sodium soy sauce
1 tablespoon bottled hoisin sauce
6 cloves garlic, minced
2 teaspoons grated fresh ginger
¼ to ½ teaspoon crushed red pepper
1 3-ounce package ramen noodles, broken
   Sliced green onions (optional)

1 Trim fat from meat. Cut meat into 1-inch pieces. In a large skillet heat oil over medium-high heat. Cook meat, half at a time, in hot oil until brown. Drain off fat.

2 In a 3½- to 4½-quart slow cooker combine meat, broth, soybeans, water chestnuts, red sweet pepper, soy sauce, hoisin sauce, garlic, ginger, and crushed red pepper.

3 Cover and cook on low-heat setting for 7 to 8 hours or on high-heat setting for 3½ to 4 hours. Skim off fat. Stir in noodles (reserve seasoning packet for another use). Cover and cook for 5 minutes more. If desired, top each serving with green onions.

nutrition facts per serving: 400 cal., 15 g total fat (4 g sat. fat), 111 mg chol., 906 mg sodium, 22 g carbo., 7 g dietary fiber, 41 g protein.

Balsamic vinegar and roasted red peppers add an Italian take to this up-to-date soup. Zucchini added at the end of cooking freshens up the soup.

pork and red pepper
soup

prep: 25 minutes cook: 6 to 8 hours (low) or 3 to 4 hours (high) + 15 minutes
makes: 6 servings

1½ pounds boneless pork
     shoulder roast
2   14-ounce cans beef
     broth
1   14.5-ounce can diced
     tomatoes with basil,
     oregano, and garlic,
     undrained
1   cup bottled roasted
     red sweet peppers,
     drained and cut into
     bite-size strips
½   cup chopped onion
     (1 medium)
2   tablespoons balsamic
     vinegar
¼   teaspoon ground
     black pepper
2   medium zucchini,
     halved lengthwise
     and sliced

1 Trim fat from meat. Cut meat into 1-inch pieces. In a 3½- or 4-quart slow cooker combine meat, broth, tomatoes, roasted sweet peppers, onion, vinegar, and black pepper.

2 Cover and cook on low-heat setting for 6 to 8 hours or on high-heat setting for 3 to 4 hours.

3 If using low-heat setting, turn to high-heat setting. Stir in zucchini. Cover and cook for about 15 minutes more or until zucchini is crisp-tender.

nutrition facts per serving: 177 cal., 6 g total fat (2 g sat. fat), 51 mg chol., 887 mg sodium, 12 g carbo., 2 g dietary fiber, 18 g protein.

This cheesy, smoky chowder will surely appeal to everyone around your table. It's a classic that's always a favorite.

cheesy ham and vegetable chowder

prep: 20 minutes **cook:** 6 to 7 hours (low) or 3 to 3½ hours (high) + 20 minutes
makes: 6 servings

2   cups chopped red-skinned potatoes (2 large)
8   ounces cooked ham, diced
1   cup chopped onion (1 large)
1   cup sliced carrots (2 medium)
1   14.75-ounce can cream-style corn
¼   teaspoon cayenne pepper
2   14-ounce cans reduced-sodium chicken broth
½   cup half-and-half or whole milk
2   tablespoons all-purpose flour
1½ cups shredded American cheese (6 ounces)
1   cup frozen peas

1 In a 4- to 5-quart slow cooker combine potatoes, ham, onion, carrots, corn, and cayenne pepper. Pour broth over mixture in cooker.

2 Cover and cook on low-heat setting for 6 to 7 hours or on high-heat setting for 3 to 3½ hours.

3 In a screw-top jar combine half-and-half and flour; shake well to mix. Stir into chowder along with American cheese and peas. If using low-heat setting, turn to high-heat setting. Cover and cook for 20 minutes more. Stir again before serving.

nutrition facts per serving: 306 cal., 13 g total fat (8 g sat. fat), 51 mg chol., 1609 mg sodium, 31 g carbo., 4 g dietary fiber, 20 g protein.

Look for diced ham and already cut-up
vegetables at your supermarket.

lentil-ham soup

prep: 20 minutes **cook:** 7 to 8 hours (low) or 3½ to 4 hours (high)
makes: 6 servings

3 cups reduced-sodium
   chicken broth
3 cups water
1 medium onion, cut
   into thin wedges
1½ cups chopped celery
   (3 stalks)
1½ cups thinly sliced
   carrots (3 medium)
1 cup brown lentils,
   rinsed and drained
6 ounces cooked ham,
   diced
1½ teaspoons dried
   thyme, crushed
3 cups shredded fresh
   spinach
1 ounce Parmesan
   cheese, shaved

1 In a 4- to 5-quart slow cooker combine
broth, the water, onion, celery, carrots,
lentils, ham, and thyme.

2 Cover and cook on low-heat setting
for 7 to 8 hours or on high-heat setting
for 3½ to 4 hours.

3 Stir in spinach. Top each serving with
Parmesan cheese.

nutrition facts per serving: 186 cal., 2 g total fat
(1 g sat. fat), 14 mg chol., 849 mg sodium, 26 g carbo.,
12 g dietary fiber, 17 g protein.

Cream of potato soup is the base flavor for this classic soup. Leave the skin on the potatoes for added nutrition and fiber.

ham and potato stew

prep: 15 minutes   **cook:** 8 to 10 hours (low) or 4 to 5 hours (high)
stand: 5 minutes   **makes:** 8 servings

3   cups cubed cooked
     ham
3   cups 1-inch pieces
     red-skinned
     potatoes
1   16-ounce package
     frozen small whole
     onions
1   16-ounce package
     peeled baby carrots
1   cup sliced celery
     (2 stalks)
2   10.75-ounce cans
     condensed cream
     of potato soup
1   14-ounce can chicken
     broth
1   teaspoon dried
     thyme, crushed
¼   teaspoon ground
     black pepper
1   cup frozen peas

1 In a 4- or 5-quart slow cooker combine ham, potatoes, onions, carrots, and celery. Stir in cream of potato soup, broth, thyme, and pepper.

2 Cover and cook on low-heat setting for 8 to 10 hours on high-heat setting for 4 to 5 hours. Stir in peas. Let stand for 5 minutes before serving.

nutrition facts per serving: 257 cal., 7 g total fat (3 g sat. fat), 29 mg chol., 1570 mg sodium, 33 g carbo., 6 g dietary fiber, 14 g protein.

If you need a simple meal to feed your hungry crew, turn to this one. Not only is it tasty, it's inexpensive too.

spicy ham and garbanzo bean soup

prep: 15 minutes **cook:** 7 to 9 hours (low) or 3½ to 4½ hours (high)
makes: 6 servings

simmering **soups & stews**

2 cups sliced carrots
(4 medium)
1 15-ounce can
garbanzo beans
(chickpeas), rinsed
and drained
1½ cups cubed cooked
ham (8 ounces)
1 cup sliced celery
(2 stalks)
4 cups hot-style
vegetable juice
1 cup water

1 In a 3½- to 4½-quart slow cooker combine carrots, garbanzo beans, ham, and celery. Pour vegetable juice and the water over mixture in cooker.

2 Cover and cook on low-heat setting for 7 to 9 hours or on high-heat setting for 3½ to 4½ hours.

nutrition facts per serving: 187 cal., 5 g total fat (1 g sat. fat), 22 mg chol., 1272 mg sodium, 23 g carbo., 5 g dietary fiber, 12 g protein.

The easiest way to crush tapioca is to use a mortar and pestle. If you don't have one, place tapioca in a small plastic bag and crush it with a rolling pin.

irish stew

prep: 25 minutes **cook:** 10 to 11 hours (low) or 5 to 5½ hours (high)
makes: 6 servings

1 pound lean boneless lamb
2 tablespoons vegetable oil
2½ cups ½-inch pieces peeled turnips (2 medium)
1½ cups ½-inch pieces carrots (3 medium)
1½ cups ½-inch pieces peeled potatoes (2 medium)
2 medium onions, cut into thin wedges
¼ cup quick-cooking tapioca, crushed
½ teaspoon salt
¼ teaspoon ground black pepper
¼ teaspoon dried thyme, crushed
2 14-ounce cans beef broth

1 Cut meat into 1-inch pieces. In a large skillet heat oil over medium heat. Cook meat in hot oil until brown. Drain off fat.

2 In a 3½- or 4-quart slow cooker combine meat, turnips, carrots, potatoes, onions, tapioca, salt, pepper, and thyme. Pour broth over mixture in cooker.

3 Cover and cook on low-heat setting for 10 to 11 hours or on high-heat setting for 5 to 5½ hours.

nutrition facts per serving: 234 cal., 8 g total fat (2 g sat. fat), 49 mg chol., 784 mg sodium, 21 g carbo., 3 g dietary fiber, 19 g protein.

Now you can stay at home and have your favorite Asian soup. This hot-and-sour soup rivals any restaurant version.

hot-and-sour soup

prep: 20 minutes   **cook:** 9 to 11 hours (low) or 3 to 4 hours (high) + 50 minutes
makes: 8 servings

4   cups chicken broth
1   8-ounce can bamboo
     shoots, drained
1   8-ounce can sliced
     water chestnuts,
     drained
1   4-ounce can (drained
     weight) sliced
     mushrooms, drained
3   tablespoons quick-
     cooking tapioca
3   tablespoons rice wine
     vinegar or vinegar
1   tablespoon soy sauce
1   teaspoon sugar
½   teaspoon ground
     black pepper
1   8-ounce package
     frozen peeled and
     deveined medium
     shrimp
4   ounces firm tofu
     (fresh bean curd),
     drained and cubed
1   egg, lightly beaten
2   tablespoons snipped
     fresh parsley or
     fresh coriander

1 In a 3½- or 4-quart slow cooker combine broth, bamboo shoots, water chestnuts, mushrooms, tapioca, vinegar, soy sauce, sugar, and pepper.

2 Cover and cook on low-heat setting for 9 to 11 hours or on high-heat setting for 3 to 4 hours. Add frozen shrimp and drained tofu. Cover and cook on low- or high-heat setting for about 50 minutes more or until shrimp are opaque.

3 Pour beaten egg slowly into soup in a thin stream. Stir soup gently so that egg forms fine strands instead of clumps. Sprinkle each serving with parsley.

nutrition facts per serving: 114 cal., 2 g total fat (1 g sat. fat), 83 mg chol., 664 mg sodium, 9 g carbo., 1 g dietary fiber, 13 g protein.

Canned white tuna is an inexpensive and versatile protein source.
As an added plus, it's a good source of omega-3 fatty acids.

manhattan tuna chowder

prep: 20 minutes **cook:** 6 to 7 hours (low) or 3 to 3½ hours (high)
stand: 5 minutes **makes:** 6 servings

1 In a 3½- or 4-quart slow cooker combine broth, potatoes, tomatoes, celery, onion, carrot, thyme, cayenne pepper, and black pepper.

2 Cover and cook on low-heat setting for 6 to 7 hours or on high-heat setting for 3 to 3½ hours. Gently stir in drained tuna. Let stand for 5 minutes before serving.

2   14-ounce cans chicken broth
2   cups chopped red-skinned potatoes (2 large)
1   14.5-ounce can diced tomatoes, undrained
1   cup chopped celery (2 stalks)
½   cup chopped onion (1 medium)
½   cup coarsely shredded carrot (1 medium)
1   teaspoon dried thyme, crushed
⅛   teaspoon cayenne pepper
⅛   teaspoon ground black pepper
1   12-ounce can chunk white tuna (water pack), drained and broken into chunks

nutrition facts per serving: 40 cal., 2 g total fat (0 g sat. fat), 25 mg chol., 900 mg sodium, 14 g carbo., 3 g dietary fiber, 16 g protein.

Seafood is best when cooked quickly, so it's rarely added at the beginning of the cooking time.

clam chowder

prep: 25 minutes   **cook:** 4½ to 5 hours (low) or 2 to 2½ hours (high) + 30 minutes
makes: 8 servings

3   cups chopped celery
    (6 stalks)
1½ cups chopped onions
    (3 medium)
1   cup chopped carrots
    (2 medium)
2   8-ounce bottles clam
    juice
1   14-ounce can
    reduced-sodium
    chicken broth
1½ teaspoons dried
    thyme, crushed
½   teaspoon salt
½   teaspoon coarsely
    ground black
    pepper
1   cup fat-free half-and-
    half
2   tablespoons
    cornstarch
2   6.5-ounce cans
    chopped clams,
    drained
2   tablespoons dry
    sherry (optional)
4   slices turkey bacon,
    crisp-cooked,
    drained, and
    crumbled
    Sliced green onions
    (optional)

1 In a 3- to 4-quart slow cooker combine celery, onions, carrots, clam juice, broth, thyme, salt, and pepper.

2 Cover and cook on low-heat setting for 4½ to 5 hours or on high-heat setting for 2 to 2½ hours.

3 If using low-heat setting, turn to high-heat setting. In a small bowl combine half-and-half and cornstarch. Stir half-and-half mixture, clams, and, if desired, sherry into cooker. Cover and cook for 30 minutes more.

4 Sprinkle each serving with crumbled bacon and, if desired, green onions.

nutrition facts per serving: 144 cal., 2 g total fat (0 g sat. fat), 38 mg chol., 309 mg sodium, 14 g carbo., 2 g dietary fiber, 15 g protein.

A sprinkling of shredded red cabbage adds freshness to this sauerkraut-filled soup. Toss leftover cabbage into salads for great color and fiber.

german potato soup

prep: 10 minutes **cook:** 7 to 9 hours (low) or 3½ to 4½ hours (high)
makes: 6 to 8 servings

1   pound cooked smoked sausage, halved lengthwise and cut into ½-inch slices
4   cups frozen diced hash brown potatoes with onions and peppers (½ of a 28-ounce package)
1   16-ounce jar sauerkraut, rinsed and drained
2   tablespoons stone-ground mustard
3   14-ounce cans chicken broth
    Shredded red cabbage or very thinly sliced red onion

1 In a 4- to 5-quart slow cooker combine sausage, potatoes, sauerkraut, and mustard. Pour broth over mixture in cooker.

2 Cover and cook on low-heat setting for 7 to 9 hours or on high-heat setting for 3½ to 4½ hours. Top each serving with red cabbage.

nutrition facts per serving: 322 cal., 22 g total fat (7 g sat. fat), 48 mg chol., 2063 mg sodium, 18 g carbo., 4 g dietary fiber, 12 g protein.

Serve this superbly flavorful stew with warm flour tortillas and lime wedges. If desired, top with sour cream to temper the heat.

texas two-step stew

prep: 20 minutes   cook: 4 to 6 hours (low) or 2 to 3 hours (high) + 45 minutes
makes: 6 servings

8   ounces uncooked
     chorizo sausage
½   cup chopped onion
     (1 medium)
1   15-ounce can
     spicy chili beans,
     undrained
1   15-ounce can hominy
     or one 11-ounce
     can whole kernel
     corn with sweet
     peppers, drained
1   6.75-ounce package
     Spanish rice mix
6   cups water

1 In a medium skillet cook sausage and onion over medium heat until sausage is brown and onion is tender. Drain off fat.

2 In a 3½- or 4-quart slow cooker combine sausage mixture, chili beans, hominy, and the seasoning packet from rice mix, if present (set aside the remaining rice mix). Pour the water over mixture in cooker.

3 Cover and cook on low-heat setting for 4 to 6 hours or on high-heat setting for 2 to 3 hours.

4 If using low-heat setting, turn to high-heat setting. Stir in the remaining rice mix. Cover and cook for 45 minutes more.

nutrition facts per serving: 325 cal., 17 g total fat (6 g sat. fat), 33 mg chol., 1069 mg sodium, 29 g carbo., 5 g dietary fiber, 15 g protein.

Lots of herbs and crushed fennel seeds bump up the flavor of this simple soup. Sprinkle each serving with shredded basil to freshen it up, if you like.

italian sausage soup

prep: 25 minutes **cook:** 8 to 10 hours (low) or 4 to 5 hours (high) + 20 minutes
makes: 8 servings

1   pound Italian
    sausage, casings
    removed if present
1   cup chopped onion
    (1 large)
1   clove garlic, minced
1   cup chopped carrots
    (2 medium)
½   cup chopped celery
    (1 stalk)
1   14.5-ounce can
    diced tomatoes,
    undrained
1   8-ounce can tomato
    sauce
1   teaspoon dried
    oregano, crushed
½   teaspoon dried
    rosemary, crushed
½   teaspoon dried basil,
    crushed
¼   teaspoon dried
    thyme, crushed
¼   teaspoon fennel
    seeds, crushed
1   bay leaf
3   14-ounce cans
    reduced-sodium
    chicken broth
½   cup dried orzo pasta
    or finely broken
    capellini pasta
    Finely shredded
    Parmesan cheese
    (optional)

1 In a large skillet cook Italian sausage, onion, and garlic over medium heat until sausage is brown, stirring often. Drain off fat.

2 In a 4½- to 6-quart slow cooker combine carrots and celery. Place sausage mixture on top. In a medium bowl combine tomatoes, tomato sauce, oregano, rosemary, basil, thyme, fennel seeds, and bay leaf. Pour over mixture in cooker. Pour broth over.

3 Cover and cook on low-heat setting for 8 to 10 hours or on high-heat setting for 4 to 5 hours.

4 If using low-heat setting, turn to high-heat setting. Add uncooked pasta. Cover and cook for about 20 minutes more or until pasta is tender. Remove bay leaf and discard. If desired, top each serving with Parmesan cheese.

nutrition facts per serving: 250 cal., 13 g total fat (5 g sat. fat), 38 mg chol., 923 mg sodium, 17 g carbo., 2 g dietary fiber, 12 g protein.

This recipe takes a can of soup and dresses it up with carrots, sausage, and diced canned tomatoes. Garlic and onion in the tomatoes saves you chopping time.

split pea soup

prep: 15 minutes   **cook:** 7 to 9 hours (low) or 3½ to 4½ hours (high)
makes: 6 servings

3   cups water
2   11.5-ounce cans
      condensed split pea
      with ham soup
1   14.5-ounce can diced
      tomatoes with
      onion and garlic,
      undrained
8   ounces cooked
      smoked sausage,
      sliced
1   cup coarsely
      shredded carrots
      (2 medium)

1 In a 3½- or 4-quart slow cooker combine the water, split pea soup, tomatoes, sausage, and carrot.

2 Cover and cook on low-heat setting for 7 to 9 hours or on high-heat setting for 3½ to 4½ hours.

nutrition facts per serving: 330 cal., 16 g total fat (6 g sat. fat), 32 mg chol., 1724 mg sodium, 30 g carbo., 3 g dietary fiber, 18 g protein.

This stew is loaded with flavor! It's also loaded with potatoes, cabbage, and sweet pepper. Use any type of sausage, such as weisswurst, bockwurst, or kielbasa.

loaded **bratwurst** stew

prep: 20 minutes **cook:** 6 to 7 hours (low) or 3 to 3½ hours (high)
makes: 6 servings

4 cups coarsely chopped green cabbage (about ½ of a head)

1 pound cooked (smoked) bratwurst, cut into ½-inch slices

1½ cups coarsely chopped red-skinned potatoes (2 medium)

¾ cup chopped red sweet pepper (1 medium)

1 medium onion, cut into thin wedges

2 14-ounce cans chicken broth

1 tablespoon spicy brown mustard

1 tablespoon cider vinegar

¼ teaspoon salt

¼ teaspoon ground black pepper

⅛ teaspoon celery seeds

Shredded Swiss cheese (optional)

1 In a 5- to 6-quart slow cooker combine cabbage, bratwurst, potatoes, red sweet pepper, and onion. In a large bowl combine broth, mustard, vinegar, salt, black pepper, and celery seeds. Pour over mixture in cooker.

2 Cover and cook on low-heat setting for 6 to 7 hours or on high-heat setting for 3 to 3½ hours. If desired, top each serving with Swiss cheese.

nutrition facts per serving: 315 cal., 23 g total fat (8 g sat. fat), 49 mg chol., 1348 mg sodium, 15 g carbo., 3 g dietary fiber, 12 g protein.

America's favorite meat just got better. The slow cooker turns chicken into a multitude of delicious family dishes or even dinner with friends. Chicken Merlot with Mushrooms or Herbed Balsamic Chicken will certainly win raves at your next dinner party, while Kickin' Chicken Taco Salad or Easy Chicken Tetrazzini will thrill the kids. Does your family like turkey, duck, or pheasant? We've got you covered.

pleasing pou

5

ltry

A citrus combo plus a good dose of chili powder brightens the flavor of this chicken-zucchini entrée.

lemon-lime chili chicken

prep: 15 minutes   cook: 5 to 6 hours (low) or 2½ to 3 hours (high)
makes: 6 to 8 servings

2   tablespoons chili
     powder
1   teaspoon salt
½   teaspoon ground
     black pepper
3   to 3½ pounds
     meaty chicken
     pieces (breast
     halves, thighs,
     and drumsticks),
     skinned
1   medium zucchini
     or yellow summer
     squash, halved
     lengthwise and cut
     into 1-inch pieces
1   medium onion, cut
     into wedges
¼   cup reduced-sodium
     chicken broth
¼   cup lime juice
¼   cup lemon juice
2   cloves garlic, minced

1 In a small bowl combine chili powder, salt, and pepper. Sprinkle over chicken and rub in with your fingers. Place chicken in a 4- to 5-quart slow cooker. Add zucchini and onion. In a small bowl combine broth, lime juice, lemon juice, and garlic. Pour over mixture in cooker.

2 Cover and cook on low-heat setting for 5 to 6 hours or on high-heat setting for 2½ to 3 hours.

3 Using a slotted spoon, transfer chicken and vegetables to a serving platter. Discard cooking liquid.

nutrition facts per serving: 156 cal., 4 g total fat (1 g sat. fat), 76 mg chol., 525 mg sodium, 6 g carbo., 1 g dietary fiber, 24 g protein.

Serve this no-fuss meal with a side of polenta to soak up all the delicious juices. Either make polenta from the boxed variety or buy the slice-and-heat type.

easy italian chicken

prep: 20 minutes cook: 6 to 7 hours (low) or 3 to 3½ hours (high)
makes: 4 to 6 servings

½ of a medium head cabbage, cut into wedges

1 medium onion, sliced and separated into rings

1 4.5-ounce jar (drained weight) sliced mushrooms, drained

2 tablespoons quick-cooking tapioca

2 to 2½ pounds meaty chicken pieces (breast halves, thighs, and drumsticks), skinned

2 cups purchased meatless spaghetti sauce
   Grated Parmesan cheese
   Hot cooked polenta or pasta (optional)

1 In a 3½- to 6-quart slow cooker combine cabbage, onion, and mushrooms. Sprinkle with tapioca. Top with chicken. Pour spaghetti sauce over mixture in cooker.

2 Cover and cook on low-heat setting for 6 to 7 hours or on high-heat setting for 3 to 3½ hours.

3 Transfer to a serving platter. Sprinkle with Parmesan cheese. If desired, serve with hot cooked polenta or pasta.

nutrition facts per serving: 300 cal., 9 g total fat (3 g sat. fat), 94 mg chol., 662 mg sodium, 24 g carbo., 4 g dietary fiber, 35 g protein.

Want to save money and enjoy your Asian meal even more? Then make this tangy sweet-and-sour classic at home.

saucy sweet-and-sour chicken

prep: 20 minutes   cook: 6 to 7 hours (low) or 3 to 3½ hours (high)
makes: 4 to 6 servings

2½ to 3 pounds meaty chicken pieces (breast halves, thighs, and drumsticks), skinned

¼ teaspoon salt

½ of a 12-ounce can (about ¾ cup) frozen lemonade concentrate, thawed

3 tablespoons packed brown sugar

3 tablespoons ketchup

1 tablespoon vinegar

2 tablespoons cornstarch

2 tablespoons cold water

2 to 3 cups hot cooked rice or fried rice

1 Place chicken in a 3½- or 4-quart slow cooker; sprinkle with salt. In a medium bowl combine lemonade concentrate, brown sugar, ketchup, and vinegar. Pour over chicken.

2 Cover and cook on low-heat setting for 6 to 7 hours or on high-heat setting for 3 to 3½ hours. Transfer chicken to a serving platter; cover and keep warm.

3 For sauce, pour cooking liquid into a medium saucepan. Skim off fat. In a small bowl combine cornstarch and the cold water; stir into liquid in saucepan. Cook and stir over medium heat until thickened and bubbly. Cook and stir for 2 minutes more. Spoon sauce over chicken. Serve with hot cooked rice.

nutrition facts per serving: 480 cal., 9 g total fat (3 g sat. fat), 115 mg chol., 381 mg sodium, 57 g carbo., 1 g dietary fiber, 40 g protein.

Chicken pieces cook to tender perfection in a broth of Merlot, basil, mushroom, onions, and garlic. Before serving, thicken the sauce with cornstarch.

chicken merlot
with mushrooms

prep: 25 minutes cook: 5 to 6 hours (low) or 2½ to 3 hours (high) + 15 minutes
makes: 6 servings

3 cups sliced fresh mushrooms (8 ounces)

1 cup chopped onion (1 large)

2 cloves garlic, minced

2½ to 3 pounds meaty chicken pieces (breast halves, thighs, and drumsticks), skinned

¾ cup reduced-sodium chicken broth

1 6-ounce can tomato paste

¼ cup Merlot or other dry red wine or chicken broth

1½ teaspoons dried basil, crushed

½ teaspoon salt

¼ teaspoon ground black pepper

2 tablespoons cornstarch

2 tablespoons cold water

1 In a 3½- to 5-quart slow cooker combine mushrooms, onion, and garlic. Top with chicken. In a medium bowl combine broth, tomato paste, wine, basil, salt, and pepper. Pour over mixture in cooker.

2 Cover and cook on low-heat setting for 5 to 6 hours or on high-heat setting for 2½ to 3 hours.

3 Transfer chicken and vegetables to a serving platter. Cover chicken and vegetables and keep warm.

4 If using low-heat setting, turn to high-heat setting. For sauce, in a small bowl combine cornstarch and the cold water. Stir into cooking liquid. Cover and cook for about 15 minutes more or until thickened. Spoon sauce over chicken.

nutrition facts per serving: 249 cal., 8 g total fat (4 g sat. fat), 75 mg chol., 639 mg sodium, 13 g carbo., 2 g dietary fiber, 30 g protein.

Moroccan cooking often includes dried fruit, such as raisins and apricots, in savory dishes. The result? A dish with more complex flavor.

moroccan chicken

prep: 30 minutes   cook: 6½ to 7 hours (low) or 3½ to 4 hours (high)
makes: 4 servings

2   large onions, halved
      and thinly sliced
2   cups sliced carrots
      (4 medium)
3   pounds meaty
      chicken pieces
      (breast halves,
      thighs, and
      drumsticks),
      skinned
½   teaspoon salt
½   cup raisins
½   cup dried apricots,
      coarsely snipped
1   14-ounce can chicken
      broth
¼   cup tomato paste
2   tablespoons all-
      purpose flour
2   tablespoons lemon
      juice
1½ teaspoons ground
      cumin
1½ teaspoons ground
      ginger
1   teaspoon ground
      cinnamon
2   cloves garlic, minced
¾   teaspoon ground
      black pepper
2   cups hot cooked
      couscous
      Toasted pine nuts

1 In a 5- to 6-quart slow cooker combine onions and carrots. Add chicken; sprinkle with salt. Add raisins and dried apricots. In a medium bowl whisk together broth, tomato paste, flour, lemon juice, cumin, ginger, cinnamon, garlic, and pepper. Pour over mixture in cooker.

2 Cover and cook on low-heat setting for 6½ to 7 hours or on high-heat setting for 3½ to 4 hours.

3 Serve in shallow bowls with hot cooked couscous. Sprinkle with pine nuts.

nutrition facts per serving: 600 cal., 15 g total fat (3 g sat. fat), 139 mg chol., 997 mg sodium, 65 g carbo., 8 g dietary fiber, 52 g protein.

Capers and olives are what give this sauce its spirited, southern Italian flair. If you like, substitute your favorite pasta for the tiny almond-shaped orzo.

puttanesca chicken

prep: 20 minutes   cook: 6 to 7 hours (low) or 3 to 3½ hours (high)
makes: 6 servings

2½   to 3 pounds meaty
      chicken pieces
      (breast halves,
      thighs, and
      drumsticks),
      skinned
¼   teaspoon salt
⅛   teaspoon ground
      black pepper
1   26-ounce jar pasta
      sauce with olives
2   tablespoons drained
      capers
1   teaspoon finely
      shredded lemon
      peel
3   cups hot cooked orzo
      pasta

1 Place chicken in a 3½- or 4-quart slow cooker. Sprinkle with salt and pepper. In a medium bowl stir together pasta sauce, capers, and lemon peel. Pour over chicken.

2 Cover and cook on low-heat setting for 6 to 7 hours or on high-heat setting for 3 to 3½ hours. Serve over hot cooked orzo.

nutrition facts per serving: 315 cal., 8 g total fat (2 g sat. fat), 77 mg chol., 638 mg sodium, 31 g carbo., 3 g dietary fiber, 30 g protein.

The chives are optional, but they add a bright green color and fresh flavor that make them a worthwhile topper.

saucy chicken
with mushrooms

prep: 20 minutes   cook: 4 to 5 hours (low)   makes: 4 servings

8   ounces fresh button
     mushrooms,
     quartered
6   ounces fresh shiitake
     mushrooms, stems
     removed and caps
     sliced
4   skinless, boneless
     chicken breast
     halves (about
     1½ pounds total)
¼   cup butter or
     margarine
1   0.7-ounce packet
     Italian dry salad
     dressing mix
1   10.75-ounce can
     condensed golden
     mushroom soup
½   cup dry white wine
½   of an 8-ounce tub
     cream cheese spread
     with chives and onion
     Hot cooked rice or
     angel hair pasta
     Snipped fresh chives
     (optional)

1 In a 3½- or 4-quart slow cooker combine button and shiitake mushrooms. Top with chicken. In medium saucepan melt butter over medium heat; stir in dry dressing mix. Stir in soup, wine, and cream cheese. Stir until cream cheese melts; pour over chicken.

2 Cover and cook on low-heat setting for 4 to 5 hours.

3 Serve chicken and sauce over hot cooked rice. If desired, sprinkle each serving with chives.

nutrition facts per serving: 405 cal., 17 g total fat (9 g sat. fat), 110 mg chol., 1043 mg sodium, 26 g carbo., 1 g dietary fiber, 32 g protein.

Couscous is a busy person's go-to side dish because it cooks in just 5 minutes. With all the flavor varieties available, it is as much a household staple as rice.

greek chicken
with couscous

prep: 15 minutes cook: 5 to 6 hours (low) or 2½ to 3 hours (high)
stand: 5 minutes makes: 8 servings

2   pounds skinless, boneless chicken breast halves, cut into ½-inch pieces
2   14.5-ounce cans diced tomatoes with basil, garlic, and oregano, undrained
1½ cups water
2   6-ounce packages toasted pine nut–flavor couscous mix
1   cup crumbled feta cheese (4 ounces)
½   cup pitted Kalamata olives, coarsely chopped

1 Place chicken in a 3½- or 4-quart slow cooker. Add tomatoes and the water.

2 Cover and cook on low-heat setting for 5 to 6 hours or on high-heat setting for 2½ to 3 hours.

3 Stir in couscous and flavor packet if present. Cover and let stand for 5 minutes. Fluff couscous with a fork. Sprinkle each serving with feta cheese and olives.

nutrition facts per serving: 377 cal., 8 g total fat (4 g sat. fat), 82 mg chol., 1226 mg sodium, 41 g carbo., 3 g dietary fiber, 36 g protein.

A combination of five spices dominates in this Moroccan-inspired dish. Serve the savory juices over either brown rice or couscous.

moroccan-spiced
chicken

prep: 10 minutes   cook: 6 to 8 hours (low) or 3 to 4 hours (high)
makes: 6 servings

½   cup reduced-sodium
     chicken broth
1½ teaspoons ground
     cumin
 1   teaspoon salt
½   teaspoon ground
     cinnamon
½   teaspoon ground
     coriander
¼   teaspoon ground
     turmeric
¼   teaspoon ground
     black pepper
3½ to 4 pounds meaty
     chicken pieces
     (breast halves,
     thighs, and
     drumsticks),
     skinned

1 Pour broth into a 3½- or 4-quart slow cooker. In a small bowl combine cumin, salt, cinnamon, coriander, turmeric, and pepper. Sprinkle over chicken and rub in with your fingers. Place chicken in cooker.

2 Cover and cook on low-heat setting for 6 to 8 hours or on high-heat setting for 3 to 4 hours.

nutrition facts per serving: 155 cal., 4 g total fat (1 g sat. fat), 89 mg chol., 534 mg sodium, 1 g carbo., .4 g dietary fiber, 27 g protein.

The sweet flavor of balsamic vinegar has fairly recently captured the interest of many, although Italians have been using it for centuries. Its complex flavor is developed through a long aging process in oak barrels.

herbed
balsamic chicken

prep: 20 minutes   cook: 4½ hours (low) or 2 hours (high) + 30 minutes
makes: 6 servings

1	medium onion, cut into thin wedges
1	tablespoon quick-cooking tapioca, crushed
6	chicken breast halves (3½ to 4 pounds), skinned
1	teaspoon dried rosemary, crushed
1	teaspoon dried thyme, crushed
½	teaspoon salt
¼	teaspoon ground black pepper
¼	cup balsamic vinegar
2	tablespoons chicken broth
1	9-ounce package frozen Italian green beans
1	cup red sweet pepper strips (1 medium)

1 Place onion in a 3½- or 4-quart slow cooker. Sprinkle with tapioca. Top with chicken. Sprinkle with rosemary, thyme, salt, and pepper. Pour vinegar and broth over chicken.

2 Cover and cook on low-heat setting for 4½ hours or on high-heat setting for 2 hours.

3 If using low-heat setting, turn to high-heat setting. Add green beans and red sweet pepper. Cover and cook for 30 minutes more.

4 Using a slotted spoon, transfer chicken and vegetables to a serving platter. Spoon some of the cooking liquid over chicken and vegetables. Pass the remaining cooking liquid.

nutrition facts per serving: 234 cal., 2 g total fat (1 g sat. fat), 100 mg chol., 308 mg sodium, 10 g carbo., 2 g dietary fiber, 41 g protein.

With chicken instead of beef, white beans instead of red, and a
windfall of colorful vegetables, this is a whole new bowl of chili!

kickin' chicken chili

prep: 25 minutes   cook: 4 to 5 hours (low) or 2 to 2½ hours (high)
makes: 4 servings + reserves

2   pounds skinless,
     boneless chicken
     breast halves or
     thighs, cut into
     1-inch pieces
2   teaspoons ground
     cumin
¼   teaspoon salt
1   tablespoon olive oil
     or vegetable oil
1   16-ounce package
     frozen sweet
     pepper and onion
     stir-fry vegetables
1   16-ounce jar green
     salsa
1   15-ounce can
     cannellini beans
     (white kidney
     beans), rinsed and
     drained
1   14.5-ounce can diced
     tomatoes with
     onion and garlic,
     undrained
     Sour cream (optional)
     Shredded cheese
     (optional)

1 In a large bowl combine chicken, cumin,
and salt; toss gently to coat. In a large
skillet heat oil over medium-high heat. Cook
chicken, half at a time, in hot oil until light
brown. Drain off fat. In a 4- to 5-quart slow
cooker combine chicken, frozen vegetables,
salsa, drained beans, and tomatoes.

2 Cover and cook on low-heat setting for
4 to 5 hours or on high-heat setting for
2 to 2½ hours. Reserve 3 cups of the chili;
store as directed below.

3 Serve the remaining chili while still warm.
If desired, top each serving with sour
cream and cheese.

nutrition facts per serving: 305 cal., 5 g total fat
(1 g sat. fat), 88 mg chol., 914 mg sodium, 24 g carbo.,
6 g dietary fiber, 41 g protein.

to store reserves: Place chili in an airtight
container. Seal and chill for up to 3 days.
Use in Kickin' Chicken Taco Salad, page 177.

Give the usual taco salad extra kick by starting with Kickin' Chicken Chili. In a hurry? Use a container of baby romaine and don't bother halving the tomatoes.

kickin' chicken taco salad

start to finish: 30 minutes makes: 4 servings

Reserved Kickin'
  Chicken Chili*
  (page 176)
6 cups torn romaine
  lettuce
1 large avocado, pitted,
  peeled, and chopped
1 cup grape tomatoes
  or cherry tomatoes,
  halved
½ cup chopped red
  onion (1 medium)
1½ cups coarsely
  crushed lime-flavor
  or plain tortilla
  chips
½ cup sour cream
  (optional)
¼ cup chopped fresh
  cilantro or parsley
  (optional)

1 In a medium saucepan heat the reserved chili over medium-low heat until hot, stirring occasionally. In an extra-large bowl combine lettuce, avocado, tomatoes, and red onion. Add heated chili; toss gently to combine.

2 Divide lettuce mixture among large salad bowls. Sprinkle with chips. If desired, in a small bowl stir together sour cream and cilantro; spoon onto salads.

nutrition facts per serving: 283 cal., 10 g total fat (2 g sat. fat), 44 mg chol., 537 mg sodium, 27 g carbo., 7 g dietary fiber, 23 g protein.

*test kitchen tip: There should be about 3 cups reserved chili.

A vinaigrette-dressed mixture of greens, tomatoes, Kalamata olives, and feta cheese creates a vibrant bed for the flavorful tender chicken.

thyme-garlic chicken breasts

prep: 20 minutes   cook: 6 to 7 hours (low) or 3 to 3½ hours (high)
makes: 6 to 8 servings

3	to 4 pounds chicken breast halves, skinned
6	cloves garlic, minced
1½	teaspoons dried thyme, crushed
½	teaspoon salt
¼	cup orange juice
1	tablespoon balsamic vinegar
1	8- to 10-ounce package mixed salad greens
½	cup cherry tomatoes, halved or quartered
¼	cup pitted Kalamata olives, halved
¼	cup crumbled feta cheese (1 ounce)
½	cup bottled vinaigrette salad dressing

1 Place chicken in a 3½- or 4-quart slow cooker. Sprinkle with garlic, thyme, and salt. Pour orange juice and vinegar over chicken.

2 Cover and cook on low-heat setting for 6 to 7 hours or on high-heat setting for 3 to 3½ hours. Remove chicken from cooker; cover and keep warm. Discard cooking liquid.

3 In a large bowl toss together salad greens, tomato, olives, and feta cheese. Divide salad among dinner plates. Slice chicken from bones; discard bones. Arrange sliced chicken on top of salads. Drizzle with dressing.

nutrition facts per serving: 252 cal., 8 g total fat (2 g sat. fat), 90 mg chol., 660 mg sodium, 8 g carbo., 1 g dietary fiber, 36 g protein.

Legend has it that Chicken Tetrazzini was created for a famous Italian opera singer. Purchased Alfredo sauce heightens the convenience factor of this version.

easy chicken tetrazzini

prep: 20 minutes cook: 5 to 6 hours (low) or 2½ to 3 hours (high)
makes: 8 servings

2½ pounds skinless, boneless chicken breast halves and/or thighs, cut into 1-inch pieces
2 4.5-ounce jars (drained weight) sliced mushrooms, drained
1 16-ounce jar Alfredo pasta sauce
¼ cup chicken broth or water
2 tablespoons dry sherry (optional)
¼ teaspoon ground nutmeg
¼ teaspoon ground black pepper
10 ounces dried spaghetti or linguine
⅔ cup grated Parmesan cheese
¾ cup thinly sliced green onions (6)
    Toasted French bread slices (optional)

1 In a 3½- or 4-quart slow cooker combine chicken and mushrooms. In a medium bowl stir together pasta sauce, broth, sherry (if desired), nutmeg, and pepper. Pour over mixture in cooker.

2 Cover and cook on low-heat setting for 5 to 6 hours or on high-heat setting for 2½ to 3 hours. Meanwhile, cook spaghetti according to package directions; drain.

3 Stir Parmesan cheese into chicken mixture. Serve over hot cooked spaghetti. Sprinkle each serving with green onions. If desired, serve with French bread.

nutrition facts per serving: 430 cal., 14 g total fat (6 g sat. fat), 121 mg chol., 753 mg sodium, 32 g carbo., 2 g dietary fiber, 42 g protein.

This is company fare at its best. It is a colorful meal that showcases the flavors of spring. Serve it with garlic mashed potatoes instead of orzo, if you like.

creamy basil chicken

prep: 25 minutes   cook: 6 to 7 hours (low) or 3 to 3½ hours (high) + 30 minutes
makes: 4 servings + reserves

2   cups sliced fresh
     mushrooms
2   cups red and/or
     yellow sweet pepper
     strips (2 medium)
1   large onion, sliced
4   ounces cooked
     pancetta or bacon,
     chopped
8   cloves garlic, minced
3   tablespoons quick-
     cooking tapioca,
     crushed
8   skinless, boneless
     chicken breast
     halves (about
     2½ pounds)
1   cup chicken broth
¼   cup dry white wine
     or dry vermouth
1   pound fresh
     asparagus or
     one 10-ounce
     package frozen cut
     asparagus, thawed
½   cup chopped fresh
     basil or 1 tablespoon
     dried basil, crushed
⅓   cup whipping cream
2   cups hot cooked orzo
     pasta
2   tablespoons snipped
     fresh basil
2   tablespoons grated
     Parmesan cheese
     Toasted pine nuts
     (optional)

1 In a 5- to 6-quart slow cooker combine mushrooms, sweet peppers, onion, pancetta, and garlic. Sprinkle with tapioca. Top with chicken. Pour broth and wine over mixture in cooker.

2 Cover and cook on low-heat setting for 6 to 7 hours or on high-heat setting for 3 to 3½ hours.

3 Meanwhile, snap off and discard woody bases from fresh asparagus. If desired, scrape off scales. Cut into 2-inch lengths. If using low-heat setting, turn to high-heat setting. Stir in asparagus, ½ cup fresh basil or the dried basil, and cream. Cover and cook for 30 minutes more.

4 Reserve four chicken breast halves; store as directed below. Serve the remaining chicken, vegetables, and sauce with hot cooked orzo. Sprinkle with 2 tablespoons fresh basil, Parmesan cheese, and, if desired, pine nuts.

nutrition facts per serving: 556 cal., 21 g total fat (9 g sat. fat), 132 mg chol., 892 mg sodium, 43 g carbo., 5 g dietary fiber, 47 g protein.

to store reserves: Place chicken in an airtight container. Seal and chill for up to 3 days. (Or freeze for up to 3 months. Thaw in the refrigerator overnight before using.) *Use in Chicken and Wild Rice Chowder, page 181.*

If you couldn't resist and ate all of the chicken from Creamy Basil Chicken, buy some roasted deli chicken breasts and cut it off the bone for this chowder.

chicken
and wild rice chowder

prep: 20 minutes cook: 20 minutes makes: 4 servings

Reserved chicken
from Creamy Basil
Chicken* (page 180)
3 tablespoons butter
or margarine
1 cup sliced carrots
(2 medium)
1 cup sliced celery
(2 stalks)
1 cup quartered fresh
mushrooms
3 tablespoons all-
purpose flour
2 14-ounce cans
chicken broth
¾ cup cooked wild rice
¼ teaspoon ground
black pepper
1½ cups half-and-half
or light cream
2 tablespoons dry
sherry (optional)

1 Chop reserved chicken; set aside. In a large saucepan melt butter over medium heat. Cook carrots, celery, and mushrooms in hot butter until tender. Stir in flour. Add chopped chicken, broth, wild rice, and pepper.

2 Cook and stir until mixture is slightly thickened and bubbly. Stir in half-and-half and, if desired, sherry; heat through.

nutrition facts per serving: 445 cal., 22 g total fat (13 g sat. fat), 140 mg chol., 1019 mg sodium, 21 g carbo., 2 g dietary fiber, 40 g protein.

*test kitchen tip: There should be four chicken breast halves.

Leeks, related to onions and garlic, have a mellower flavor. Be sure to clean them well. Cut the leek stalk lengthwise and wash out any sand that is present.

garlic-lemon chicken with leeks

prep: 30 minutes cook: 4 to 4½ hours (low) or 2 to 2½ hours (high)
makes: 6 servings

pleasing **poultry**

- ⅓ cup all-purpose flour
- ½ teaspoon salt
- ½ teaspoon ground black pepper
- 6 skinless, boneless chicken breast halves (2¼ to 2½ pounds)
- 3 tablespoons butter or margarine
- 2 cups thinly sliced leeks (6 medium)
- 10 cloves garlic, thinly sliced
- 2 tablespoons quick-cooking tapioca, crushed
- ¼ teaspoon salt
- 1 lemon
- 1½ cups chicken broth
- 2 cups hot cooked mashed potatoes
  Snipped fresh parsley

1 In a shallow dish combine flour, ½ teaspoon salt, and pepper. Dip chicken in flour mixture, turning to coat. In a large skillet heat butter over medium-high heat. Cook chicken, half at a time, in hot butter until brown.

2 Meanwhile, place leeks and garlic in a 4- to 5-quart slow cooker. Sprinkle with tapioca and ¼ teaspoon salt. Top with chicken. Peel lemon, removing all of the white pith; discard peel. Thinly slice lemon and remove any seeds. Place lemon slices on top of chicken. Pour broth over mixture in cooker.

3 Cover and cook on low-heat setting for 4 to 4½ hours or on high-heat setting for 2 to 2½ hours.

4 Transfer chicken to dinner plates. Using a slotted spoon, remove leeks from cooker and spoon over chicken. Serve with mashed potatoes. If desired, spoon some of the cooking liquid over each serving. Sprinkle with parsley.

nutrition facts per serving: 454 cal., 13 g total fat (6 g sat. fat), 126 mg chol., 1172 mg sodium, 38 g carbo., 3 g dietary fiber, 44 g protein.

Two doses of cheese—rich cream cheese and mild mozzarella—bring extra flavor to this dish. Four cloves of garlic make the flavors really soar.

cheesy garlic chicken

prep: 20 minutes cook: 3½ to 4½ hours (low) or 1½ to 2 hours (high) + 30 minutes
stand: 10 minutes makes: 6 servings

2   pounds skinless, boneless chicken breast halves, cut into 1½-inch pieces
1½ cups cauliflower florets
¾   cup reduced-sodium chicken broth
2   tablespoons quick-cooking tapioca
¼   teaspoon salt
4   cloves garlic, minced
1½ cups frozen cut green beans
½   of an 8-ounce package reduced-fat cream cheese (Neufchâtel), cut into cubes
½   cup shredded part-skim mozzarella cheese (2 ounces)
⅔   cup chopped roma tomatoes (2 medium)

1 In a 3½- or 4-quart slow cooker combine chicken, cauliflower, broth, tapioca, salt, and garlic.

2 Cover and cook on low-heat setting for 3½ to 4½ hours or on high-heat setting for 1½ to 2 hours.

3 If using low-heat setting, turn to high-heat setting. Add green beans to mixture in cooker. Cook for 30 minutes more. Turn off cooker.

4 Stir cream cheese into cooker. Cover and let stand for 10 minutes. Remove cover and gently stir until cream cheese is melted and sauce is smooth. Sprinkle each serving with mozzarella cheese and tomatoes.

nutrition facts per serving: 283 cal., 8 g total fat (4 g sat. fat), 108 mg chol., 393 mg sodium, 10 g carbo., 2 g dietary fiber, 41 g protein.

Buy chicken thighs when they go on sale and make this 6-cup master recipe for the next four recipes. Keep it on hand for effortless menu planning.

shredded chicken
master recipe

prep: 20 minutes cook: 7 to 8 hours (low) or 3½ to 4 hours (high)
makes: 3 (2-cup) portions chicken and 3 (2-cup) portions broth

4½ to 5 pounds chicken
    thighs, skinned
4 fresh thyme sprigs
4 fresh parsley sprigs
2 bay leaves
2 cloves garlic, halved
½ teaspoon whole black
    peppercorns
1 32-ounce carton
    chicken broth

1 Place chicken in a 4- to 5-quart slow cooker. For bouquet garni, cut an 8-inch square from a double thickness of 100-percent-cotton cheesecloth. Place thyme, parsley, bay leaves, garlic, and peppercorns in the center of the cheesecloth square. Bring up corners of the cheesecloth and tie closed with clean 100-percent-cotton kitchen string. Add bouquet garni to mixture in cooker. Pour broth over chicken.

2 Cover and cook on low-heat setting for 7 to 8 hours or on high-heat setting for 3½ to 4 hours. Remove bouquet garni and discard.

3 Using a slotted spoon, transfer chicken to a large bowl. Remove meat from bones; discard bones. Using two forks, pull chicken apart into shreds. Strain cooking liquid and skim off fat. Add enough of the cooking liquid to chicken to moisten. Reserve the remaining cooking liquid to use for chicken broth.

4 Place 2-cup portions of chicken and broth in separate airtight containers. Seal and chill for up to 3 days. (Or freeze for up to 3 months. Thaw overnight in the refrigerator before using.)

nutrition facts per cup: 229 cal., 7 g total fat (2 g sat. fat), 161 mg chol., 213 mg sodium, 0 g carbo., 0 g dietary fiber, 38 g protein.

Change the flavor of this chicken salad sandwich by replacing cilantro with fresh basil or tarragon and using orange juice rather than lime.

caramelized onion
chicken salad sandwich

prep: 30 minutes   cook: 16 minutes   makes: 5 sandwiches

1   tablespoon butter or margarine
1   cup chopped sweet onion (1 large)
2   cups Shredded Chicken Master Recipe (page 184)
½   cup coarsely chopped walnuts, toasted
¼   cup sliced green onions (2)
½   cup mayonnaise or salad dressing
1   tablespoon snipped fresh cilantro
1   tablespoon lime juice
     Salt (optional)
     Ground black pepper (optional)
10 slices sourdough bread, toasted
10 slices tomato
¾   cup baby spinach leaves
     Pimiento-stuffed green olives (optional)

1 In a large skillet melt butter over medium-low heat. Add chopped onion. Cover and cook for 13 to 15 minutes or until tender, stirring occasionally. Uncover; cook and stir over medium-high heat for 3 to 5 minutes more or until golden.

2 In a large bowl combine cooked onion, shredded chicken, walnuts, and green onions. Add mayonnaise, cilantro, and lime juice, tossing to coat. If desired, season to taste with salt and pepper.

3 Place about ½ cup of the chicken mixture on each of five bread slices. Top each with two slices tomato and some of the spinach. Top with the remaining bread slices. If desired, halve each sandwich, secure with a skewer, and garnish with an olive.

nutrition facts per sandwich: 518 cal., 32 g total fat (6 g sat. fat), 78 mg chol., 555 mg sodium, 36 g carbo., 3 g dietary fiber, 24 g protein.

Of course, bourbon is an optional ingredient in these sandwiches. Apricot and mustard complement each other very well in the chicken mixture.

apricot-mustard
chicken sandwiches

start to finish: 20 minutes   makes: 6 sandwiches

1 tablespoon vegetable oil
1 cup finely chopped onion (1 large)
2 cloves garlic, minced
2 cups Shredded Chicken Master Recipe (page 184)
¼ cup spicy brown mustard
¼ cup apricot preserves
1 tablespoon cider vinegar
1 tablespoon bourbon (optional)
¼ teaspoon cayenne pepper
6 hamburger buns, split and toasted
Dill pickle slices
Thinly sliced red onion

1 In a large skillet heat oil over medium heat. Cook chopped onion and garlic in hot oil for about 4 minutes or until tender. Stir in shredded chicken, mustard, apricot preserves, vinegar, bourbon (if desired), and cayenne pepper. Heat through. If necessary, simmer, uncovered, for about 5 minutes or to desired consistency.

2 Place chicken mixture on bun bottoms. Top with pickle slices and red onion slices. Cover with bun tops.

nutrition facts per sandwich: 423 cal., 10 g total fat (2 g sat. fat), 80 mg chol., 770 mg sodium, 52 g carbo., 3 g dietary fiber, 26 g protein.

Barbecue meets Mexico in a quesadilla with surprising barbecue flavors. Salsa and chile peppers contribute the flavors of Mexican cuisine.

bbq chicken
and cheddar quesadillas

prep: 20 minutes   cook: 4 minutes per batch   makes: 4 servings
oven: 300°F

2 cups Shredded Chicken Master Recipe (page 184)
½ cup bottled barbecue sauce
1 4-ounce can diced green chile peppers, drained
4 8-inch flour tortillas
   Nonstick cooking spray
1 cup shredded extra-sharp cheddar cheese or Mexican cheese blend (4 ounces)
1 cup bottled salsa
¼ cup sour cream
¼ cup sliced green onions (2)

1 In a medium saucepan combine shredded chicken, barbecue sauce, and drained chile peppers. Cook over medium heat until heated through.

2 Coat one side of each tortilla with cooking spray. Place tortillas, sprayed sides down, on cutting board or waxed paper. Sprinkle ¼ cup of the cheddar cheese over half of each tortilla. Top evenly with shredded chicken mixture. Fold tortillas in half, pressing gently.

3 Preheat a large nonstick skillet over medium heat. Cook quesadillas, two at a time, in hot skillet for 4 to 6 minutes or until light brown, turning once. Remove quesadillas from skillet; place on a baking sheet. Keep warm in a 300°F oven. Repeat with remaining quesadillas. To serve, cut each quesadilla into three wedges. Serve with salsa, sour cream, and green onions.

nutrition facts per serving: 415 cal., 18 g total fat (9 g sat. fat), 115 mg chol., 1224 mg sodium, 33 g carbo., 2 g dietary fiber, 30 g protein.

Your master chicken recipe comes into play once again in this Thai-inspired noodle dish. Use spaghetti or be adventurous and try rice noodles.

peanut noodles
with chicken and vegetables

start to finish: 25 minutes makes: 6 servings

8 ounces dried spaghetti

1 16-ounce package frozen sugar snap pea stir-fry vegetables

¼ cup sugar

¼ cup creamy peanut butter

3 tablespoons soy sauce

3 tablespoons water

2 tablespoons vegetable oil

2 cloves garlic, minced

¼ teaspoon crushed red pepper

2 cups Shredded Chicken Master Recipe (page 184)
  Chopped peanuts and/or sliced green onions (optional)

1 In a 4-quart Dutch oven cook spaghetti according to package directions, adding frozen vegetables during the last 2 minutes of cooking; drain.

2 For peanut sauce, in a small saucepan combine sugar, peanut butter, soy sauce, the water, oil, garlic, and crushed red pepper. Cook and stir until sugar is dissolved.

3 In a large bowl combine spaghetti mixture, peanut sauce, and shredded chicken, tossing gently to coat. If desired, top with peanuts and/or green onions.

nutrition facts per serving: 390 cal., 13 g total fat (2 g sat. fat), 54 mg chol., 654 mg sodium, 45 g carbo., 4 g dietary fiber, 22 g protein.

Dine out at home on chicken sandwich wedges just like those served in fancy bistros. Focaccia is available at most supermarkets.

pesto chicken sandwich

prep: 30 minutes   cook: 4 to 5 hours (low) or 2 to 2½ hours (high) + 30 minutes
makes: 6 to 8 servings

1	teaspoon dried Italian seasoning, crushed
¼	teaspoon salt
¼	teaspoon ground black pepper
1	pound skinless, boneless chicken breast halves
3	cups sliced fresh mushrooms (8 ounces)
1	large onion, thinly sliced
2	cloves garlic, minced
1	14.5-ounce can diced tomatoes, undrained
2	tablespoons red wine vinegar
1	medium zucchini or yellow summer squash, halved lengthwise and cut into ¼-inch pieces
1¼	cups yellow, green, and/or red sweet pepper strips (1 large or 2 small)
⅓	cup mayonnaise or salad dressing
2	tablespoons purchased basil pesto
1	9- to 10-inch Italian flatbread (focaccia), cut in half horizontally
	Tomato slices (optional)
2	ounces provolone cheese, shredded (½ cup)

1 In a small bowl combine Italian seasoning, salt, and pepper. Sprinkle over chicken and rub in with your fingers. Place chicken in a 3½- or 4-quart slow cooker. Add mushrooms, onion, and garlic. Pour canned tomatoes and vinegar over mixture in cooker.

2 Cover and cook on low-heat setting for 4 to 5 hours or on high-heat setting for 2 to 2½ hours.

3 If using low-heat setting, turn to high-heat setting. Add zucchini and sweet pepper. Cover and cook for 30 minutes more.

4 Meanwhile, in a small bowl combine mayonnaise and pesto. Spread evenly over cut sides of focaccia.

5 Using a slotted spoon, remove chicken from cooker. Thinly slice chicken. Arrange chicken slices on focaccia bottom. Using a slotted spoon, spoon vegetable mixture onto chicken. Add tomato slices if desired, provolone cheese, and focaccia top. Cut into wedges.

nutrition facts per serving: 439 cal., 18 g total fat (4 g sat. fat), 63 mg chol., 770 mg sodium, 43 g carbo., 3 g dietary fiber, 29 g protein.

Chicken tenders come in handy in this stir-together meal. Carryout never tasted so good.

cashew chicken

prep: 15 minutes   cook: 6 to 8 hours (low) or 3 to 4 hours (high)
makes: 6 servings

1   10.75-ounce can
    condensed golden
    mushroom soup
3   tablespoons soy
    sauce
1   teaspoon ground
    ginger
1½ pounds chicken
    tenders
1   16-ounce package
    frozen broccoli stir-
    fry vegetables
1   4-ounce can (drained
    weight) sliced
    mushrooms,
    drained
½   cup cashews
    Hot cooked brown
    rice* (optional)

1 In a 3½- or 4-quart slow cooker combine mushroom soup, soy sauce, and ginger. Stir in chicken, stir-fry vegetables, and mushrooms.

2 Cover and cook on low-heat setting for 6 to 8 hours or on high-heat setting for 3 to 4 hours.

3 Stir cashews into chicken mixture. If desired, serve over hot cooked rice.

nutrition facts per serving: 256 cal., 8 g total fat (2 g sat. fat), 68 mg chol., 1026 mg sodium, 13 g carbo., 3 g dietary fiber, 31 g protein.

✳test kitchen tip: For really fast rice, use two 8.8-ounce pouches cooked whole grain brown rice and heat them in the microwave according to package directions.

This is comfort food at its best. Cheese-flecked biscuits partner with a cream cheese–rich chicken and vegetable mixture.

chicken and biscuits

prep: 30 minutes bake: 10 minutes cook: 6 to 7 hours (low) or 3 to 3½ hours (high) + 10 minutes oven: 450°F makes: 6 servings

2	cups chopped red-skinned potatoes (2 large)
1	cup coarsely chopped carrots (2 medium)
½	cup coarsely chopped onion (1 medium)
½	cup coarsely chopped celery (1 stalk)
1	4-ounce can (drained weight) sliced mushrooms, drained
2	cloves garlic, minced
½	teaspoon dried thyme, crushed
½	teaspoon dried sage, crushed
¼	teaspoon salt
¼	teaspoon ground black pepper
2	tablespoons quick-cooking tapioca, crushed
1	pound chicken thighs, skinned
1	cup chicken broth
1	cup frozen peas
1	3-ounce package cream cheese, cut into cubes
	Cheesy Biscuits

1 In a 3½- or 4-quart slow cooker combine potatoes, carrots, onion, celery, mushrooms, garlic, thyme, sage, salt, and pepper. Sprinkle tapioca over vegetables. Top with chicken. Pour broth over mixture in cooker.

2 Cover and cook on low-heat setting for 6 to 7 hours or on high-heat setting for 3 to 3½ hours.

3 Using a slotted spoon, remove chicken from cooker. Remove meat from bones and coarsely chop; discard bones. If using low-heat setting, turn to high-heat setting. Return meat to slow cooker. Stir in peas and cream cheese. Cover and cook for 10 minutes. Stir well. Serve over split Cheesy Biscuits.

nutrition facts per serving: 369 cal., 15 g total fat (7 g sat. fat), 63 mg chol., 927 mg sodium, 41 g carbo., 3 g dietary fiber, 18 g protein.

cheesy biscuits: Preheat oven to 450°F. In a medium bowl combine 1⅔ cups packaged biscuit mix and ½ cup shredded cheddar cheese (2 ounces). Stir in ½ cup milk. Turn out onto a floured surface and knead 10 times. Pat into a ½-inch-thick circle. Cut with a floured 3-inch biscuit cutter. Reroll scraps as needed. Place biscuits on an ungreased baking sheet. Bake for 10 to 12 minutes or until golden.

Don't forget to reserve part of this recipe for Bayou Shrimp and Rice, on page 193. You'll love having two meals planned during the busy workweek.

stewed chicken
and andouille

prep: 25 minutes   cook: 6 to 7 hours (low) or 3 to 3½ hours (high)
makes: 4 servings + reserves

1   pound andouille
     sausage, cut into
     ¾-inch slices
1   medium onion, cut
     into thin wedges
8   chicken thighs (2½ to
     3 pounds), skinned
1   16-ounce jar picante
     sauce
⅓   cup water
2   tablespoons quick-
     cooking tapioca
2   teaspoons
     Worcestershire
     sauce
1   teaspoon dried
     thyme, crushed
2   cups frozen cut okra
6   ounces dried egg
     noodles

1 In a large skillet cook sausage over medium heat until brown. Drain off fat.

2 Place onion in a 4- to 5-quart slow cooker. Add sausage, chicken, picante sauce, the water, tapioca, Worcestershire sauce, and thyme. Top with okra.

3 Cover and cook on low-heat setting for 6 to 7 hours or on high-heat setting for 3 to 3½ hours. Meanwhile, cook noodles according to package directions; drain.

4 Reserve 4 chicken thighs and 1 cup of the sausage mixture; store as directed below. Serve the remaining chicken and sausage mixture over hot cooked noodles.

nutrition facts per serving: 419 cal., 8 g total fat (2 g sat. fat), 154 mg chol., 1481 mg sodium, 50 g carbo., 3 g dietary fiber, 36 g protein.

to store reserves: Place chicken and sausage mixture in an airtight container. Seal and chill for up to 3 days. (Or freeze for up to 3 months. Thaw in the refrigerator overnight before using.) *Use in Bayou Shrimp and Rice, page 193.*

Cook some rice revved up with picante sauce, then stir in shrimp plus leftover Stewed Chicken and Andouille and a Cajun dish becomes a Creole dish.

bayou shrimp and rice

prep: 20 minutes cook: 20 minutes makes: 4 servings

12 ounces fresh or frozen medium shrimp
    Reserved chicken and sausage mixture from Stewed Chicken and Andouille* (page 192)
2¼ cups water
1¼ cups bottled picante sauce
2 teaspoons Worcestershire sauce
1 cup long grain rice
    Salt
    Ground black pepper
    Bottled hot pepper sauce (optional)

1 Thaw shrimp, if frozen. Peel and devein shrimp. Remove reserved chicken from bones and chop; discard bones. Set aside.

2 In a large skillet stir together the water, picante sauce, and Worcestershire sauce. Bring to boiling; add uncooked rice. Return to boiling; reduce heat. Cover and simmer for 15 minutes.

3 Add shrimp, chopped chicken, and reserved sausage mixture to rice mixture. Return to boiling; reduce heat. Cover and simmer for about 5 minutes more or until shrimp are opaque and rice is tender. Remove from heat; season to taste with salt and pepper. If desired, serve with hot pepper sauce.

nutrition facts per serving: 437 cal., 7 g total fat (2 g sat. fat), 211 mg chol., 1261 mg sodium, 45 g carbo., 1 g dietary fiber, 44 g protein.

*test kitchen tip: There should be 4 chicken thighs and 1 cup sausage mixture.

Inexpensive chicken thighs and drumsticks generally are a smart buy. Removing the skin before cooking eliminates some of the fat.

cranberry chicken

prep: 15 minutes cook: 5 to 6 hours (low) or 2½ to 3 hours (high)
makes: 6 servings

2½   to 3 pounds chicken
       thighs and/or
       drumsticks, skinned
1   16-ounce can whole
       cranberry sauce
2   tablespoons dry
       onion soup mix
2   tablespoons quick-
       cooking tapioca
3   cups hot cooked rice
       or couscous

1 Place chicken in a 3½- or 4-quart slow cooker. In a small bowl stir together cranberry sauce, dry soup mix, and tapioca. Pour over chicken.

2 Cover and cook on low-heat setting for 5 to 6 hours or on high-heat setting for 2½ to 3 hours. Serve over hot cooked rice.

nutrition facts per serving: 357 cal., 4 g total fat (1 g sat. fat), 89 mg chol., 268 mg sodium, 55 g carbo., 1 g dietary fiber, 23 g protein.

Beefy onion soup mix and red wine combine with chicken for a stew that's luscious and comforting on a cold night.

coq au vin

prep: 25 minutes **cook:** 5 to 6 hours (low) or 2½ to 3 hours (high)
makes: 4 servings

Nonstick cooking spray
3 pounds chicken thighs, skinned
1 envelope (½ of a 2.2-ounce package) dry beefy onion soup mix
2 cups quartered fresh mushrooms
1½ cups frozen small whole onions
3 medium carrots, cut into 3½-inch sticks
½ cup dry red wine
Hot cooked mashed potatoes (optional)
Snipped fresh parsley (optional)

1 Lightly coat an unheated large skillet with cooking spray. Heat skillet over medium heat. Cook chicken thighs, several at a time, in the hot skillet until brown. Drain off fat.

2 Place chicken thighs in a 3½- or 4-quart slow cooker. Sprinkle with dry soup mix. Add mushrooms, onions, and carrots. Pour wine over mixture in cooker.

3 Cover and cook on low-heat setting for 5 to 6 hours or on high-heat setting for 2½ to 3 hours. If desired, serve with mashed potatoes and sprinkle with parsley.

nutrition facts per serving: 320 cal., 8 g total fat (2 g sat. fat), 161 mg chol., 782 mg sodium, 15 g carbo., 2 g dietary fiber, 42 g protein.

No need to cook the rice separately for this one-dish winner. Simply stir the rice into the chicken mixture at the end of cooking time and cook it in the sauce.

easy chicken and rice

prep: 15 minutes   cook: 5 to 6 hours (low) or 2½ to 3 hours (high) + 10 minutes
makes: 4 servings

2 cups sliced fresh mushrooms
1 cup sliced celery (2 stalks)
½ cup chopped onion (1 medium)
1½ teaspoons dried dill
¼ teaspoon ground black pepper
2 pounds chicken thighs, skinned
1 10.75-ounce can condensed cream of mushroom or cream of chicken soup
¾ cup chicken broth
1½ cups uncooked instant rice

1 In a 3½- or 4-quart slow cooker combine mushrooms, celery, onion, dill, and pepper. Top with chicken. In a small bowl whisk together cream of mushroom soup and broth. Pour over mixture in cooker.

2 Cover and cook on low-heat setting for 5 to 6 hours or on high-heat setting for 2½ to 3 hours.

3 If using low-heat setting, turn to high-heat setting. Stir in uncooked rice. Cover and cook for about 10 minutes more or until rice is tender.

nutrition facts per serving: 387 cal., 11 g total fat (2 g sat. fat), 107 mg chol., 795 mg sodium, 42 g carbo., 2 g dietary fiber, 31 g protein.

Chutney, a spicy condiment that originated in the East Indies, is usually served with curry dishes. It provides the major flavor for these saucy chicken thighs.

gingered chutney
chicken

prep: 15 minutes cook: 5 to 6 hours (low) or 2½ to 3 hours (high)
makes: 6 servings

½ cup mango chutney
¼ cup bottled chili sauce
2 tablespoons quick-cooking tapioca
1½ teaspoons grated fresh ginger or ½ teaspoon ground ginger
12 chicken thighs (about 4 pounds), skinned

1 Cut up any large pieces of fruit in the chutney. In a 4- to 5-quart slow cooker combine chutney, chili sauce, tapioca, and ginger. Add chicken, turning to coat.

2 Cover and cook on low-heat setting for 5 to 6 hours or on high-heat setting for 2½ to 3 hours.

nutrition facts per serving: 264 cal., 7 g total fat (2 g sat. fat), 143 mg chol., 494 mg sodium, 16 g carbo., 1 g dietary fiber, 34 g protein.

Frozen stew vegetables eliminate peeling and cutting, keeping prep time to a quick 15 minutes. What a deal!

in-a-hurry chicken curry

prep: 15 minutes   cook: 6 to 7 hours (low) or 3 to 3½ hours (high)
makes: 6 servings

1   16-ounce package
     frozen stew
     vegetables
1½ to 1¾ pounds chicken
     thighs, skinned
     Salt
     Ground black pepper
1   10.75-ounce can
     condensed cream
     of potato soup
2   teaspoons curry
     powder
     Snipped fresh cilantro
     (optional)

1 Place frozen vegetables in a 3½ - or 4-quart slow cooker. Top with chicken. Sprinkle with salt and pepper. In a small bowl stir together cream of potato soup and curry powder. Pour over mixture in cooker.

2 Cover and cook on low-heat setting for 6 to 7 hours or on high-heat setting for 3 to 3½ hours.

3 Using a slotted spoon, remove chicken from cooker. Remove meat from bones and, if desired, break into large pieces; discard bones. Stir chicken back into vegetable mixture. If desired, sprinkle each serving with cilantro.

nutrition facts per serving: 200 cal., 5 g total fat (2 g sat. fat), 97 mg chol., 734 mg sodium, 13 g carbo., 1 g dietary fiber, 24 g protein.

In India, curry powder is ground fresh each day, combining as many as 16 to 20 spices. You can shortcut that step with your favorite ready-to-go blend.

chicken curry

prep: 30 minutes cook: 6 to 8 hours (low) or 3 to 4 hours (high) + 30 minutes
makes: 8 servings

1½ pounds skinless,
    boneless chicken
    breast halves or
    thighs
3 tablespoons
    all-purpose flour
3 tablespoons curry
    powder
1½ teaspoons ground
    cumin
1 teaspoon salt
2 cups chopped
    potatoes (2 large)
1½ cups bias-sliced
    carrots (3 medium)
1 cup coarsely chopped
    cooking apple
    (1 large)
¾ cup chopped onion
    (1 large)
1 fresh jalapeño
    pepper, seeded
    and finely chopped
    (see tip, page 32)
1 teaspoon instant
    chicken bouillon
    granules
2 cloves garlic, minced
½ cup water
1 13.5-ounce can
    unsweetened
    coconut milk
4 cups hot cooked rice
¼ cup raisins
¼ cup chopped peanuts

1 Cut chicken into 1-inch pieces. In a resealable plastic bag combine flour, curry powder, cumin, and salt. Add chicken pieces, a few at a time, shaking to coat.

2 In a 3½- or 4-quart slow cooker combine chicken, potatoes, carrots, apple, onion, jalapeño pepper, bouillon granules, and garlic. Pour the water over mixture in cooker.

3 Cover and cook on low-heat setting for 6 to 8 hours or on high-heat setting for 3 to 4 hours.

4 If using low-heat setting, turn to high-heat setting. Stir in coconut milk. Cover and cook for 30 minutes more.

5 Serve chicken mixture over hot cooked rice. Sprinkle each serving with raisins and peanuts.

nutrition facts per serving: 415 cal., 16 g total fat (11 g sat. fat), 49 mg chol., 490 mg sodium, 44 g carbo., 5 g dietary fiber, 26 g protein.

At first glance, some Indian-inspired recipes look really long. But take another look—many of the ingredients are spices, which take minutes to measure.

indian-spiced
chicken thighs

prep: 20 minutes   cook: 7 to 8 hours (low) or 3½ to 4 hours (high)
makes: 6 servings + reserves

4	medium onions, thinly sliced
¼	cup quick-cooking tapioca
8	cloves garlic, minced
24	to 30 skinless, boneless chicken thighs (4 to 4½ pounds)
1	tablespoon ground cumin
2	teaspoons salt
2	teaspoons curry powder
1½	teaspoons ground coriander
½	teaspoon ground cinnamon
¼	teaspoon ground cloves
¼	teaspoon cayenne pepper
¼	teaspoon ground black pepper
1	14-ounce can chicken broth
1	6-ounce carton plain yogurt
3	cups hot cooked basmati rice
	Snipped fresh mint (optional)
	Finely shredded lemon peel (optional)
	Toasted slivered almonds (optional)

1 Place onions in a 5- to 7-quart slow cooker; sprinkle with tapioca and garlic. Top with chicken. Sprinkle with cumin, salt, curry powder, coriander, cinnamon, cloves, cayenne pepper, and black pepper. Pour broth over mixture in cooker.

2 Cover and cook on low-heat setting for 7 to 8 hours or on high-heat setting for 3½ to 4 hours.

3 Reserve half of the chicken thighs (12 to 15) and half of the onion mixture (about 2 cups); store as directed below. Transfer the remaining chicken to a serving platter; cover and keep warm. For sauce, whisk yogurt into the remaining onion mixture in cooker. Serve chicken and sauce with hot cooked rice. If desired, sprinkle each serving with mint, lemon peel, and almonds.

nutrition facts per serving: 347 cal., 7 g total fat (2 g sat. fat), 123 mg chol., 645 mg sodium, 33 g carbo., 1 g dietary fiber, 35 g protein.

to store reserves: Cut chicken into ¾-inch pieces; place chicken and onion mixture in an airtight container. Seal and chill for up to 3 days. *Use in Coconut Chicken and Couscous, page 201.*

The reserved mixture from Indian-Spiced Chicken Thighs gets a new debut. Add some coconut milk and additional spice, and you'll have another meal in no time.

coconut chicken and couscous

start to finish: 20 minutes   makes: 6 servings

Reserved chicken
  and onion mixture
  from Indian-Spiced
  Chicken Thighs*
  (page 200)
1   13.5- or 14-ounce
  can unsweetened
  coconut milk
4   teaspoons cornstarch
½   teaspoon curry
  powder
¼   cup raisins
3   cups hot cooked
  couscous
Toasted shredded
  coconut (optional)

1 In a large saucepan heat reserved chicken and onion mixture over medium heat until hot. In a medium bowl stir together coconut milk, cornstarch, and curry powder; stir into chicken mixture. Stir in raisins.

2 Cook and stir over medium heat until thickened and bubbly. Cook and stir for 2 minutes more. Serve with hot cooked couscous. If desired, sprinkle each serving with toasted coconut.

nutrition facts per serving: 466 cal., 19 g total fat (12 g sat. fat), 121 mg chol., 647 mg sodium, 37 g carbo., 2 g dietary fiber, 36 g protein.

*test kitchen tip: There should be about 5½ cups reserved chicken and onion mixture.

Hoisin sauce is thick and dark with a punch of flavor. Slow cooking gives the chicken plenty of time to absorb the sauce's sweet and spicy taste.

simple hoisin chicken

prep: 15 minutes   cook: 4 to 5 hours (low) or 2½ hours (high) + 30 to 45 minutes
makes: 6 servings

Nonstick cooking
spray
12 chicken thighs (3½ to
4 pounds), skinned
2 tablespoons quick-
cooking tapioca
⅛ teaspoon salt
⅛ teaspoon ground
black pepper
½ cup bottled hoisin
sauce
1 16-ounce package
frozen broccoli
stir-fry vegetables
3 cups hot cooked rice

1 Coat the inside of a 3½- or 4-quart slow cooker with cooking spray. Place chicken in the prepared cooker. Sprinkle with tapioca, salt, and pepper. Pour hoisin sauce over chicken.

2 Cover and cook on low-heat setting for 4 to 5 hours or on high-heat setting for 2½ hours.

3 If using low-heat setting, turn to high-heat setting. Stir in frozen vegetables. Cover and cook for 30 to 45 minutes more or until vegetables are tender. Serve over hot cooked rice.

nutrition facts per serving: 345 cal., 6 g total fat (2 g sat. fat), 115 mg chol., 537 mg sodium, 37 g carbo., 3 g dietary fiber, 32 g protein.

Grits gain a whole new attitude when combined with sweet potatoes, pepper Jack cheese, and cilantro. Oh, and chicken too, of course.

sweet potato and pepper jack
grits with chicken

prep: 15 minutes   cook: 7 to 9 hours (low) or 3½ to 4½ hours (high)
stand: 5 minutes   makes: 6 to 8 servings

Disposable slow-
cooker liner
1   pound skinless,
boneless chicken
thighs, cut into
1-inch pieces
3   cups water
1   15- to 15.5-ounce
can mashed sweet
potatoes or cut
sweet potatoes*
1   12-ounce can
evaporated milk
1   cup regular (hominy)
grits
½   teaspoon salt
½   teaspoon ground
black pepper
1½ cups shredded
Monterey Jack
cheese with
jalapeño peppers
(6 ounces)
2   tablespoons butter
or margarine, cut up
¼   cup chopped fresh
cilantro

1 Line a 3½- or 4-quart slow cooker with a disposable liner. In the prepared cooker combine chicken, the water, sweet potatoes, evaporated milk, grits, salt, and pepper.

2 Cover and cook on low-heat setting for 7 to 9 hours or on high-heat setting for 3½ to 4½ hours.

3 Turn off cooker. Stir in Monterey Jack cheese and butter. Cover and let stand for 5 minutes. Stir again before serving. Sprinkle each serving with cilantro.

nutrition facts per serving: 478 cal., 21 g total fat (12 g sat. fat), 119 mg chol., 595 mg sodium, 45 g carbo., 3 g dietary fiber, 30 g protein.

*test kitchen tip: If using the cut sweet potatoes, drain and mash the potatoes before adding to the slow cooker.

Slow cooking chicken thighs with Thai ingredients—coconut milk, peanut butter, lime, and curry paste—produce a complex and richly satisfying result.

hot and spicy braised peanut chicken

prep: 30 minutes   cook: 5 to 6 hours (low) or 2½ to 3 hours (high)
stand: 5 minutes   makes: 6 servings

2   medium onions, cut
     into thin wedges
1½ cups sliced carrots
     (3 medium)
¾   cup red sweet pepper
     strips (1 small)
2   pounds skinless,
     boneless chicken
     thighs, cut into
     1-inch pieces
¾   cup chicken broth
3   tablespoons creamy
     peanut butter
2   tablespoons quick-
     cooking tapioca
½   teaspoon finely
     shredded lime peel
2   tablespoons lime
     juice
2   tablespoons soy
     sauce
1   tablespoon grated
     fresh ginger
2   to 3 teaspoons
     red curry paste
4   cloves garlic, minced
1   cup frozen peas
½   cup unsweetened
     coconut milk
3   cups hot cooked rice
     Chopped peanuts
     (optional)
     Snipped fresh cilantro
     (optional)

1 In a 3½- or 4-quart slow cooker combine onions, carrots, and sweet pepper. Top with chicken. In a medium bowl whisk together broth, peanut butter, tapioca, lime peel, lime juice, soy sauce, ginger, curry paste, and garlic until smooth. Pour over mixture in cooker.

2 Cover and cook on low-heat setting for 5 to 6 hours or on high-heat setting for 2½ to 3 hours. Stir in peas and coconut milk. Cover and let stand for 5 minutes.

3 Serve over hot cooked rice. If desired, sprinkle each serving with peanuts and cilantro.

nutrition facts per serving: 444 cal., 15 g total fat (7 g sat. fat), 126 mg chol., 708 mg sodium, 39 g carbo., 4 g dietary fiber, 37 g protein.

This sophisticated dish will appeal to those with an adventurous palate. Refrigerated polenta provides an easy go-along.

chicken with figs and blue cheese

prep: 25 minutes cook: 5 to 6 hours (low) or 2½ to 3 hours (high)
makes: 6 servings

1	cup chicken broth
¼	cup balsamic vinegar
1	tablespoon finely shredded orange peel
1	teaspoon salt
½	teaspoon ground black pepper
¼	teaspoon ground ginger
1	9-ounce package dried Mission figs, stems removed
1	large onion, thinly sliced
2½	pounds skinless, boneless chicken thighs
1	16-ounce tube refrigerated cooked polenta
⅔	cup crumbled blue cheese (about 3 ounces)

1 In a small bowl stir together broth, vinegar, orange peel, salt, pepper, and ginger; set aside. Coarsely chop figs. In a 4- to 5-quart slow cooker combine figs and onion. Top with chicken. Pour broth mixture over mixture in cooker.

2 Cover and cook on low-heat setting for 5 to 6 hours or on high-heat setting for 2½ to 3 hours.

3 Meanwhile, prepare polenta according to package directions for polenta mush. Using tongs, remove chicken from cooker. Transfer fig mixture to a serving bowl. If necessary, skim off fat from fig mixture. Serve chicken thighs and fig mixture with polenta. Sprinkle each serving with blue cheese.

nutrition facts per serving: 481 cal., 12 g total fat (5 g sat. fat), 162 mg chol., 1174 mg sodium, 47 g carbo., 7 g dietary fiber, 45 g protein.

Sauerkraut bestows its familiar tang to this dish. Serve the mixture over spaetzle or wide noodles. A side salad is all you need to complete your meal.

german-style chicken thighs

prep: 20 minutes   cook: 7 to 8 hours (low) or 3½ to 4 hours (high)
makes: 6 servings

1   27- to 28-ounce can sauerkraut, rinsed and drained
2   10.75-ounce cans condensed cream of potato soup
½   cup water
2   tablespoons Worcestershire sauce
1½ teaspoons dried thyme, crushed
¼   teaspoon salt
¼   teaspoon ground black pepper
3½ to 4 pounds chicken thighs, skinned
3   cups hot cooked spaetzle or wide noodles
    Snipped fresh parsley (optional)

1 In a 6-quart slow cooker combine drained sauerkraut, cream of potato soup, the water, Worcestershire sauce, thyme, salt, and pepper. Add chicken, stirring to coat.

2 Cover and cook on low-heat setting for 7 to 8 hours or on high-heat setting for 3½ to 4 hours.

3 Using a slotted spoon, remove chicken from cooker. Remove meat from bones; discard bones. Using two forks, pull chicken apart into shreds. Stir shredded chicken back into sauerkraut mixture.

4 Serve over hot cooked spaetzle. If desired, sprinkle with parsley.

nutrition facts per serving: 399 cal., 10 g total fat (3 g sat. fat), 156 mg chol., 1834 mg sodium, 39 g carbo., 6 g dietary fiber, 36 g protein.

This Tex-Mex take on a one-dish meal has everything—tortilla, chicken, beans, and salad—all stacked on one plate! Customize it with your favorite salsa.

chicken tostadas

prep: 25 minutes cook: 5 to 6 hours (low) or 2½ to 3 hours (high)
makes: 10 servings

3 tablespoons chili powder

3 tablespoons lime juice

2 fresh jalapeño peppers, seeded and finely chopped (see tip, page 32)

¼ teaspoon bottled hot pepper sauce

8 cloves garlic, minced

1 medium onion, sliced and separated into rings

2 pounds skinless, boneless chicken thighs

1 16-ounce can fat-free refried beans

10 tostada shells

1½ cups shredded reduced-fat cheddar cheese (6 ounces)

2 cups shredded lettuce

1¼ cups bottled salsa

¾ cup light sour cream

¾ cup sliced pitted ripe olives (optional)

1 In a 3½- to 5-quart slow cooker combine chili powder, lime juice, jalapeño peppers, hot pepper sauce, and garlic. Add onion. Top with chicken.

2 Cover and cook on low-heat setting for 5 to 6 hours or on high-heat setting for 2½ to 3 hours.

3 Using a slotted spoon, remove chicken and onion from cooker; reserve ½ cup of the cooking liquid. Using two forks, pull chicken apart into shreds. In a medium bowl combine chicken, onion, and the reserved ½ cup cooking liquid.

4 Spread refried beans on tostada shells. Top with chicken mixture and cheddar cheese. Serve with lettuce, salsa, sour cream, and, if desired, olives.

nutrition facts per serving: 317 cal., 11 g total fat (4 g sat. fat), 90 mg chol., 560 mg sodium, 23 g carbo., 5 g dietary fiber, 28 g protein.

There are two rules for dumplings: Be sure the stew is bubbling hot before dropping in the dough and don't lift the lid while the dumplings are cooking.

chicken and dumplings

prep: 25 minutes cook: 8 to 10 hours (low) or 4 to 5 hours (high) + 25 minutes
makes: 8 servings

2   pounds skinless, boneless chicken thighs
2   cups chopped carrots (4 medium)
2   cups chopped potatoes (2 large)
1½ cups chopped parsnips (3 medium)
2   bay leaves
1   teaspoon dried sage, crushed
½   teaspoon salt
¼   teaspoon ground black pepper
1   clove garlic, minced
1   14-ounce can chicken broth
1   10.75-ounce can condensed cream of chicken soup
2   tablespoons cold water
1   tablespoon cornstarch
½   cup all-purpose flour
½   cup shredded cheddar cheese (2 ounces)
⅓   cup cornmeal
1   teaspoon baking powder
¼   teaspoon salt
1   egg, lightly beaten
2   tablespoons milk
2   tablespoons butter or margarine, melted

1 Cut chicken into 1-inch pieces; set aside. In a 4- to 5-quart slow cooker combine carrots, potatoes, parsnips, bay leaves, sage, ½ teaspoon salt, pepper, and garlic. Add chicken. In a medium bowl whisk together broth and cream of chicken soup. Pour over mixture in cooker.

2 Cover and cook on low-heat setting for 8 to 10 hours or on high-heat setting for 4 to 5 hours.

3 If using low-heat setting, turn to high-heat setting. Using a wooden spoon, stir chicken mixture. Remove bay leaves. In a small bowl combine the cold water and cornstarch; stir into chicken mixture.

4 For dumplings, in a medium bowl stir together flour, cheddar cheese, cornmeal, baking powder, and ¼ teaspoon salt. In a small bowl combine egg, milk, and melted butter. Add egg mixture to flour mixture; stir just until moistened. Spoon dough formed into eight mounds on top of chicken mixture.

5 Cover and cook for 25 to 30 minutes more or until a wooden toothpick inserted into a dumpling comes out clean. (Do not lift cover during cooking.)

nutrition facts per serving: 353 cal., 13 g total fat (5 g sat. fat), 139 mg chol., 902 mg sodium, 30 g carbo., 3 g dietary fiber, 29 g protein.

Red cooking is a Chinese method of braising poultry or meat in a flavorful liquid that includes soy sauce and caramelized sugar. The food takes on a reddish-brown hue.

chinese red-cooked
chicken

prep: 25 minutes cook: 6 to 7 hours (low) or 3 to 3½ hours (high)
makes: 6 servings

2½   to 3 pounds chicken
      drumsticks and/or
      thighs, skinned
5   whole star anise
2   3-inch-long strips
      orange peel*
1   2-inch-long piece
      fresh ginger, thinly
      sliced
3   inches stick cinnamon
2   cloves garlic, smashed
1   teaspoon whole
      Szechwan
      peppercorns
2   14-ounce cans
      reduced-sodium
      chicken broth
¾   cup soy sauce
¼   cup packed brown
      sugar
1   tablespoon dry sherry
4   green onions, cut into
      2-inch pieces
1   8-ounce package
      dried Chinese
      egg noodles
1   teaspoon toasted
      sesame oil
2   tablespoons fresh
      cilantro leaves

1 Place chicken in a 3½- or 4-quart slow cooker. For the spice bag, cut an 8-inch square from a double thickness of 100-percent-cotton cheesecloth. Place star anise, orange peel, ginger, cinnamon, garlic, and peppercorns in center of the cheesecloth square. Bring up corners of the cheesecloth; tie closed with clean 100-percent-cotton kitchen string. Add spice bag to mixture in cooker. In a large bowl combine broth, soy sauce, brown sugar, sherry, and green onions. Pour over chicken.

2 Cover and cook on low-heat setting for 6 to 7 hours or on high-heat setting for 3 to 3½ hours.

3 Meanwhile, prepare noodles according to package directions. Remove chicken from cooking liquid. Strain liquid, discarding spice bag and solids; skim off fat. Serve chicken over noodles. Drizzle chicken with sesame oil and sprinkle with cilantro leaves. If desired, drizzle with cooking liquid.

nutrition facts per serving: 404 cal., 16 g total fat (3 g sat. fat), 85 mg chol., 2608 mg sodium, 36 g carbo., 2 g dietary fiber, 29 g protein.

*test kitchen tip:
Use a vegetable peeler to remove 3-inch strips of peel from an orange, avoiding the bitter white pith underneath.

When you have leftover chipotles, put them in a small freezer bag or container and freeze them for up to 2 months. Thaw in the refrigerator to use.

chipotle stewed chicken

prep: 30 minutes   cook: 8 to 9 hours (low) or 4 to 4½ hours (high)
makes: 4 servings + reserves

2   medium red sweet peppers, cut into 1-inch pieces
1   medium onion, cut into thin wedges
2   tablespoons quick-cooking tapioca
8   chicken drumsticks, skinned
8   chicken thighs, skinned
1   14.5-ounce can diced tomatoes, undrained
1   6-ounce can tomato paste
2   to 3 tablespoons finely chopped canned chipotle chile peppers in adobo sauce (see tip, page 32)
2   teaspoons sugar
1   teaspoon salt
2   16-ounce packages refrigerated mashed potatoes

1 In a 5- to 6-quart slow cooker combine red sweet peppers and onion. Sprinkle with tapioca. Top with chicken. In a medium bowl stir together tomatoes, tomato paste, chipotle peppers, sugar, and salt. Pour over mixture in cooker.

2 Cover and cook on low-heat setting for 8 to 9 hours or on high-heat setting for 4 to 4½ hours.

3 Reserve four thighs, four drumsticks, and 1 cup of sauce; store as directed below. Heat potatoes according to package directions; serve with remaining chicken and sauce.

nutrition facts per serving: 477 cal., 9 g total fat (2 g sat. fat), 136 mg chol., 1110 mg sodium, 52 g carbo., 4 g dietary fiber, 43 g protein.

to store reserves: Remove meat from drumsticks and thighs; discard bones. Using two forks, pull meat apart into shreds. Place shredded meat and sauce in separate airtight containers. Seal and chill for up to 3 days. *Use in Chicken Wraps with Lime Cream, page 211.*

Happy day! You have leftover Chipotle Stewed Chicken to use in tonight's wraps. Add mayo, sour cream, lime juice, lettuce, and tortillas and you're good to go.

chicken wraps
with lime cream

start to finish: 20 minutes makes: 4 servings

Reserved chicken and
    sauce from Chipotle
    Stewed Chicken
    (page 210)
¼ cup mayonnaise
    or salad dressing
¼ cup sour cream
1 tablespoon lime juice
¼ teaspoon salt
4 lettuce leaves
4 10-inch flour tortillas
2 tablespoons snipped
    fresh cilantro
    (optional)
Pico de gallo or lime
    wedges (optional)

1 In a large skillet heat reserved chicken and reserved sauce over medium heat until heated through.

2 Meanwhile, in a small bowl stir together mayonnaise, sour cream, lime juice, and salt. Warm tortillas according to package directions.

3 Place a lettuce leaf on each tortilla. Using a slotted spoon, spoon chicken mixture onto tortillas, just below the center. Top each with 2 tablespoons of the sour cream mixture and, if desired, sprinkle with cilantro. Fold bottom edge of a tortilla up and over filling. Fold one side in slightly, then roll up from the bottom. Repeat with remaining tortillas. If desired, serve wraps with pico de gallo or lime wedges.

nutrition facts per serving: 486 cal., 23 g total fat (6 g sat. fat), 146 mg chol., 688 mg sodium, 28 g carbo., 2 g dietary fiber, 39 g protein.

pleasing **poultry**

Cajun seasoning, smoky Polish sausage, and ham give succulent chicken thighs a lively down-by-the-bayou flavor.

creole chicken

prep: 25 minutes cook: 5 to 6 hours (low) or 2½ to 3 hours (high)
stand: 10 minutes makes: 6 servings

1 pound skinless, boneless chicken thighs, cut into ¾-inch pieces
1 14.5-ounce can diced tomatoes, undrained
1 14-ounce can chicken broth
8 ounces cooked smoked Polish sausage, coarsely chopped
1 cup diced cooked ham
¾ cup chopped onion (1 large)
1 6-ounce can tomato paste
½ cup water
1½ teaspoons Cajun seasoning
   Several dashes bottled hot pepper sauce
2 cups uncooked instant rice
1 cup chopped green sweet peppers (2 small)

1 In a 3½- or 4-quart slow cooker combine chicken, tomatoes, broth, sausage, ham, onion, tomato paste, the water, Cajun seasoning, and hot pepper sauce.

2 Cover and cook on low-heat setting for 5 to 6 hours or on high-heat setting for 2½ to 3 hours.

3 Turn off cooker. Stir in uncooked rice and sweet peppers. Cover and let stand for 10 to 15 minutes or until rice is tender and most of the liquid is absorbed.

nutrition facts per serving: 439 cal., 18 g total fat (6 g sat. fat), 99 mg chol., 1362 mg sodium, 41 g carbo., 2 g dietary fiber, 28 g protein.

Don't wait around for the holidays to enjoy this scrumptious combo. Use a hard-crusted dense sourdough loaf for the best texture.

chicken with mushroom stuffing

prep: 40 minutes   cook: 4 to 5 hours (high)   makes: 8 servings

Nonstick cooking spray

2 tablespoons finely shredded lemon peel

1 tablespoon ground sage

1 tablespoon seasoned salt

1½ teaspoons ground black pepper

8 small whole chicken legs (drumstick-thigh portion) (about 5 pounds total), skinned

¼ cup butter or margarine

4 cups quartered or sliced fresh mushrooms (such as cremini, baby portobellos, shiitakes, and/or buttons)

2 cloves garlic, thinly sliced

8 cups 1-inch pieces sourdough baguette (about 10 ounces)

1 cup coarsely shredded carrots (2 medium)

1 cup chicken broth

¼ cup chopped walnuts, toasted

3 tablespoons snipped fresh Italian (flat-leaf) parsley

1 Lightly coat a 6-quart slow cooker with cooking spray. Set aside 1 teaspoon of the lemon peel. In a small bowl stir together the remaining 5 teaspoons lemon peel, sage, seasoned salt, and pepper. Sprinkle 3 tablespoons of sage mixture evenly over chicken legs and rub in with your fingers. Place chicken in prepared slow cooker.

2 For stuffing, in a large skillet melt butter over medium heat. Cook mushrooms and garlic in hot butter for 3 to 5 minutes or just until tender. Stir in the remaining sage mixture. Transfer mushroom mixture to a large bowl. Add baguette pieces and carrots. Drizzle with broth, tossing gently to combine. Lightly pack stuffing on top of chicken.

3 Cover and cook on high-heat setting for 4 to 5 hours.

4 Using a slotted spoon, transfer stuffing and chicken to a serving platter; discard liquid in cooker. In a small bowl combine reserved 1 teaspoon lemon peel, walnuts, and parsley. Sprinkle nut mixture over chicken and stuffing.

nutrition facts per serving: 412 cal., 17 g total fat (5 g sat. fat), 146 mg chol., 1450 mg sodium, 27 g carbo., 3 g dietary fiber, 39 g protein.

What makes this better than Grandma's is the convenience of a slow cooker. Because it cooks while you're away, you can make it during the week.

better-than-grandma's
chicken and noodles

prep: 30 minutes   cook: 7 hours (low) or 3 hours (high) + 1 to 1½ hours
stand: 5 minutes   makes: 6 servings

3 medium carrots, cut into 1-inch pieces
2 medium parsnips, peeled and cut into 1-inch pieces
1 cup pearl onions* or frozen small whole onions
2 stalks celery, cut into 1-inch pieces
3 whole chicken legs (drumstick-thigh portion) (about 3 pounds total), skinned
½ teaspoon dried thyme, crushed
½ teaspoon dried sage, crushed
½ teaspoon salt
¼ teaspoon ground black pepper
2 cloves garlic, minced
2 14-ounce cans chicken broth
¼ cup dry sherry
1 12-ounce package frozen egg noodles
¾ cup frozen peas
4 or 5 fresh sage leaves (optional)

1 In a 5- to 6-quart slow cooker combine carrots, parsnips, onions, and celery. Top with chicken. Sprinkle with thyme, dried sage, salt, pepper, and garlic. Pour broth and sherry over mixture in cooker.

2 Cover and cook on low-heat setting for 7 hours or on high-heat setting for 3 hours.

3 Stir in noodles. If using low-heat setting, turn to high-heat setting. Cover and cook for 1 to 1½ hours more or until noodles are tender.

4 Remove chicken from cooker. Remove skin and meat from bones; discard skin and bones. Using two forks, pull meat apart into coarse shreds. Stir meat back into mixture in slow cooker. Add peas; cover and let stand for 5 minutes. If desired, garnish with sage leaves.

nutrition facts per serving: 372 cal., 7 g total fat (2 g sat. fat), 147 mg chol., 857 mg sodium, 46 g carbo., 5 g dietary fiber, 27 g protein.

*test kitchen tip: If using fresh onions, cook in enough boiling water to cover for 30 to 60 seconds; drain and rinse with cold water. Cut off root ends and slip off peels.

The golden red sauce and fragrant spice blend bring your taste buds to attention even before the first bite of tender chicken.

country captain

prep: 25 minutes   cook: 5 to 6 hours (low) or 2½ to 3 hours (high)
makes: 6 servings

1   medium sweet
    onion, cut into thin
    wedges
3   pounds chicken
    drumsticks and/or
    thighs, skinned
1   cup green sweet
    pepper strips
    (1 medium)
1   cup yellow sweet
    pepper strips
    (1 medium)
¼   cup dried currants
    or golden raisins
2   cloves garlic, minced
1   14-ounce can
    diced tomatoes,
    undrained
2   tablespoons quick-
    cooking tapioca,
    crushed
2   to 3 teaspoons curry
    powder
½   teaspoon salt
½   teaspoon ground
    cumin
¼   teaspoon ground
    mace
3   cups hot cooked rice
2   tablespoons chopped
    green onion (1)
2   tablespoons sliced
    almonds, toasted

1 Place onion in a 3½- or 4-quart slow cooker. Add chicken, sweet peppers, currants, and garlic. In a large bowl combine tomatoes, tapioca, curry powder, salt, cumin, and mace. Pour over mixture in cooker.

2 Cover and cook on low-heat setting for 5 to 6 hours or on high-heat setting for 2½ to 3 hours.

3 Serve over hot cooked rice. Sprinkle each serving with green onion and almonds.

nutrition facts per serving: 338 cal., 6 g total fat (1 g sat. fat), 98 mg chol., 446 mg sodium, 40 g carbo., 4 g dietary fiber, 31 g protein.

Keep fresh ginger in a resealable plastic bag in the freezer. It doesn't need to be thawed before use; simply grate what you need and return it to the freezer.

ginger-tomato chicken

prep: 20 minutes cook: 6 to 7 hours (low) or 3 to 3½ hours (high)
makes: 6 servings

2½ to 3 pounds chicken
      drumsticks and/or
      thighs, skinned
2   14.5-ounce cans
      diced tomatoes,
      undrained
2   tablespoons quick-
      cooking tapioca
1   tablespoon grated
      fresh ginger
1   tablespoon snipped
      fresh cilantro or
      parsley
2   teaspoons packed
      brown sugar
4   cloves garlic, minced
½   teaspoon salt
½   teaspoon crushed
      red pepper
3   cups hot cooked
      whole wheat
      couscous
      Snipped fresh cilantro
      or parsley

1 Place chicken in a 3½- or 4-quart slow cooker. Drain tomatoes, reserving juice from one can. For sauce, in a medium bowl combine tomatoes and the reserved juice, tapioca, ginger, 1 tablespoon cilantro, brown sugar, garlic, salt, and crushed red pepper. Pour over chicken.

2 Cover and cook on low-heat setting for 6 to 7 hours or on high-heat setting for 3 to 3½ hours. Skim off fat from sauce.

3 Serve chicken and sauce in shallow bowls with hot cooked couscous. Sprinkle with additional cilantro.

nutrition facts per serving: 281 cal., 4 g total fat (1 g sat. fat), 81 mg chol., 542 mg sodium, 35 g carbo., 6 g dietary fiber, 27 g protein.

Fresh fennel has a wonderful anise/licorice flavor. If you can't find it you can substitute 1 teaspoon fennel seeds per pound of fennel. Crush it lightly to release the flavors.

italian braised chicken with
fennel and cannellini

prep: 30 minutes   cook: 5 to 6 hours (low) or 2½ to 3 hours (high)
makes: 6 servings

2   to 2½ pounds chicken drumsticks and/or thighs, skinned
¾   teaspoon salt
¼   teaspoon ground black pepper
1   15-ounce can cannellini beans (white kidney beans), rinsed and drained
1   bulb fennel, cored and cut into thin wedges
1   medium yellow sweet pepper, cut into 1-inch pieces
1   medium onion, cut into thin wedges
3   cloves garlic, minced
1   teaspoon snipped fresh rosemary
1   teaspoon snipped fresh oregano
¼   teaspoon crushed red pepper
1   14.5-ounce can diced tomatoes, undrained
½   cup dry white wine or reduced-sodium chicken broth
¼   cup tomato paste
¼   cup shaved Parmesan cheese
1   tablespoon snipped fresh Italian (flat-leaf) parsley

1 Place chicken in a 3½- or 4-quart slow cooker. Sprinkle with ¼ teaspoon of the salt and black pepper.

2 Add drained beans, fennel, yellow sweet pepper, onion, garlic, rosemary, oregano, and crushed red pepper. In a medium bowl combine tomatoes, wine, tomato paste, and the remaining ½ teaspoon salt. Pour over mixture in cooker.

3 Cover and cook on low-heat setting for 5 to 6 hours or on high-heat setting for 2½ to 3 hours. Sprinkle each serving with Parmesan cheese and parsley.

nutrition facts per serving: 225 cal., 4 g total fat (1 g sat. fat), 68 mg chol., 777 mg sodium, 23 g carbo., 7 g dietary fiber, 25 g protein.

That's right, just three ingredients produce a richly flavored, sweet-tangy barbecue sauce for drumsticks. Choose a basic barbecue sauce with few embellishments.

super-simple barbecue chicken

prep: 10 minutes   cook: 6 to 8 hours (low) or 3 to 4 hours (high)
makes: 4 to 6 servings

2½ to 3 pounds chicken drumsticks, skinned if desired

1 cup bottled barbecue sauce

⅓ cup apricot or peach preserves

2 teaspoons yellow mustard

1 Place chicken in a 3½- or 4-quart slow cooker. For sauce, in a small bowl combine barbecue sauce, preserves, and mustard. Pour over chicken.

2 Cover and cook on low-heat setting for 6 to 8 hours or on high-heat setting for 3 to 4 hours. Transfer chicken to a serving dish; cover and keep warm.

3 If desired, transfer sauce to a medium saucepan. Bring to boiling; reduce heat. Simmer, uncovered, for about 10 minutes or to desired consistency. Serve chicken with sauce.

nutrition facts per serving: 456 cal., 17 g total fat (4 g sat. fat), 154 mg chol., 963 mg sodium, 37 g carbo., 2 g dietary fiber, 38 g protein.

If you love the flavors of Buffalo chicken wings as an appetizer, why not enjoy them as an entrée? Save some for tomorrow night's pizza!

buffalo chicken drumsticks
with blue cheese dip

prep: 25 minutes **cook:** 6 to 8 hours (low) or 3 to 4 hours (high)
makes: 4 servings + reserves

16   chicken drumsticks
      (about 4 pounds),
      skinned if desired
 1   16-ounce bottle
      Buffalo wing hot
      sauce (2 cups)
¼   cup tomato paste
 2   tablespoons white
      or cider vinegar
 2   tablespoons
      Worcestershire
      sauce
 1   8-ounce carton sour
      cream
½   cup mayonnaise
      or salad dressing
½   cup crumbled blue
      cheese (2 ounces)
¼   to ½ teaspoon cayenne
      pepper or bottled hot
      pepper sauce
      Celery sticks
      Blue cheese chunks
      (optional)

1 Place drumsticks in a 4- to 5-quart slow cooker. In a medium bowl combine Buffalo wing hot sauce, tomato paste, vinegar, and Worcestershire sauce. Pour over chicken.

2 Cover and cook on low-heat setting for 6 to 8 hours or on high-heat setting for 3 to 4 hours.

3 Meanwhile, for blue cheese dip, in a small bowl combine sour cream, mayonnaise, crumbled blue cheese, and cayenne pepper. Reserve half of the blue cheese dip (¾ cup); store as directed below. Cover and chill the remaining dip until ready to serve.

4 Using a slotted spoon, remove drumsticks from cooker. Skim off fat from cooking liquid. Reserve eight of the drumsticks and 1 cup of the cooking liquid; store as directed below. Serve remaining drumsticks with some of the remaining cooking liquid, the remaining blue cheese dip, and the celery sticks. If desired, garnish with chunks of blue cheese.

nutrition facts per serving: 454 cal., 33 g total fat (11 g sat. fat), 141 mg chol., 2084 mg sodium, 6 g carbo., 1 g dietary fiber, 31 g protein.

to store reserves: Place blue cheese dip in an airtight container. Remove skin and meat from drumsticks; discard skin and bones. Using two forks, pull meat apart into shreds (you should have 2½ to 3 cups shredded meat). Place shredded meat and the 1 cup cooking juices in a second airtight container. Seal and chill for up to 3 days. *Use in Buffalo Chicken and Blue Cheese Pizza, page 221.*

Buffalo chicken wing flavors on pizza? Excellent! It will be a welcome change from pepperoni pizza for sure.

buffalo chicken
and blue cheese pizza

prep: 15 minutes   bake: 20 minutes   oven: 400°F   makes: 4 servings

1   14-ounce Italian bread shell (Boboli)
    Reserved blue cheese dip and chicken mixture from Buffalo Chicken Drumsticks with Blue Cheese Dip* (page 220)
1½ cups shredded mozzarella cheese (6 ounces)
¼   cup sliced green onions (2)
    Bottled hot pepper sauce (optional)

1 Preheat oven to 400°F. Place bread shell on a 14-inch pizza pan or large baking sheet. Bake for 5 minutes. Spread reserved blue cheese dip over partially baked crust, leaving a ½-inch border around the edge. Sprinkle with half of the mozzarella cheese. Top with reserved chicken mixture. Sprinkle with the remaining cheese and the green onions.

2 Bake about 15 minutes more or until pizza is heated through and cheese melts. Cut into wedges. If desired, serve with hot pepper sauce.

nutrition facts per serving: 854 cal., 43 g total fat (15 g sat. fat), 219 mg chol., 2860 mg sodium, 50 g carbo., 2 g dietary fiber, 66 g protein.

*test kitchen tip: There should be ¾ cup reserved blue cheese dip and 2½ to 3 cups reserved chicken mixture.

Everyone will go for a sample of this finger-lickin' favorite. Barbecue sauce gets a boost of flavor from honey, mustard, and Worcestershire sauce.

barbecue chicken
drumsticks

prep: 15 minutes   cook: 3 to 4 hours (low) or 1½ to 2 hours (high)
broil: 15 minutes   makes: 8 servings

3   pounds chicken
      drumsticks
1½ cups bottled
      barbecue sauce
¼   cup honey
2   teaspoons yellow
      mustard
1½ teaspoons
      Worcestershire
      sauce

1 Preheat broiler. Place drumsticks on unheated rack of a broiler pan. Broil 4 to 5 inches from the heat for 15 to 20 minutes or until light brown, turning once. Place drumsticks in a 3½- or 4-quart slow cooker.

2 In a medium bowl combine barbecue sauce, honey, mustard, and Worcestershire sauce; pour over drumsticks.

3 Cover and cook on low-heat setting for 3 to 4 hours or on high-heat setting for 1½ to 2 hours.

nutrition facts per serving: 285 cal., 10g total fat (3g sat. fat), 92mg chol., 625 mg sodium, 26g carbo., 0g dietary fiber, 22g protein.

For the shredded chicken, see page 184 for Shredded Chicken Master Recipe, or purchase a deli roasted chicken and shred the meat.

easy tostadas

prep: 15 minutes   cook: 5 to 6 hours (low) or 2½ to 3 hours (high)
makes: 6 servings

12   tostada shells
4   cups shredded
       cooked chicken
2   10-ounce cans
       enchilada sauce
1   16-ounce package
       frozen sweet
       pepper and onion
       stir-fry vegetables
1   8-ounce package
       shredded Mexican-
       style four-cheese
       blend
1½   cups shredded fresh
       spinach leaves
       (optional)
       Sour cream (optional)

1 Coarsely break six of the tostada shells. In a 4- to 5-quart slow cooker combine broken tostada shells, chicken, enchilada sauce, frozen vegetables, and shredded cheese.

2 Cover and cook on low-heat setting for 5 to 6 hours or on high-heat setting for 2½ to 3 hours.

3 To serve, place the remaining six tostada shells on dinner plates. Top with chicken mixture and, if desired, spinach and sour cream.

nutrition facts per serving: 409 cal., 26 g total fat (12 g sat. fat), 100 mg chol., 1427 mg sodium, 20 g carbo., 3 g dietary fiber, 25 g protein.

Convenient hash brown potatoes with onions and peppers supply the bulk for this Mexican-style recipe. Salsa and Jack cheese with jalapeño peppers add heat.

chicken hash

prep: 20 minutes cook: 5 to 5½ hours (low) or 2½ hours (high)
makes: 6 servings

Nonstick cooking
   spray
1 28-ounce package
   frozen diced hash
   brown potatoes
   with onions and
   peppers
3 cups chopped cooked
   chicken
1 10.75-ounce can
   condensed nacho
   cheese soup
1 cup bottled salsa
2 ounces Monterey
   Jack cheese with
   jalapeño peppers,
   shredded (½ cup)
   (optional)

1 Lightly coat a 4- to 5-quart slow cooker with cooking spray. In an extra-large bowl break up frozen potatoes. Stir in chicken, soup, and salsa. Transfer to prepared cooker.

2 Cover and cook on low-heat setting for 5 to 5½ hours or on high-heat setting for 2½ hours. Stir before serving. If desired, sprinkle each serving with Monterey Jack cheese.

nutrition facts per serving: 590 cal., 28 g total fat (7 g sat. fat), 80 mg chol., 1152 mg sodium, 53 g carbo., 5 g dietary fiber, 30 g protein.

This old-fashioned favorite is a good way to make the most of leftover chicken or turkey. It gets an update with a generous amount of vegetables.

chicken à la king

prep: 25 minutes   cook: 6 to 7 hours (low) or 3 to 3½ hours (high)
stand: 10 minutes   makes: 8 to 10 servings

4   cups chopped cooked
    chicken or turkey
2   10.75-ounce cans
    condensed cream
    of chicken soup
2   4.5-ounce jars
    (drained weight)
    sliced mushrooms,
    drained
¾   cup chopped green
    sweet pepper
    (1 medium)
¾   cup chopped celery
1   5-ounce can
    evaporated milk
½   cup bottled roasted
    red sweet peppers,
    drained and
    coarsely chopped
½   cup chopped onion
    (1 medium)
3   tablespoons dry
    sherry or dry white
    wine
1   teaspoon dried basil,
    crushed
½   teaspoon ground
    black pepper
1   10-ounce package
    frozen peas
4   or 5 English muffins,
    split and toasted;
    or hot cooked rice

1 In a 4- to 5-quart slow cooker combine chicken, cream of chicken soup, mushrooms, green sweet pepper, celery, evaporated milk, roasted sweet peppers, onion, sherry, basil, and black pepper.

2 Cover and cook on low-heat setting for 6 to 7 hours or on high-heat setting for 3 to 3½ hours. Turn off cooker. Stir in peas. Cover and let stand for 10 minutes.

3 Serve chicken mixture over English muffin halves or hot cooked rice.

nutrition facts per serving: 357 cal., 12 g total fat (4 g sat. fat), 74 mg chol., 940 mg sodium, 31 g carbo., 5 g dietary fiber, 28 g protein.

Smoked chicken and cheese give this comfort food impressive flavor. Because it contains sour cream and cheese, this entrée should be cooked only on low heat.

smoky chicken-potato
casserole

prep: 15 minutes   cook: 5 to 6 hours (low)   makes: 6 servings

Nonstick cooking
   spray
1   10.75-ounce can
     condensed cream
     of chicken with
     herbs soup
1   8-ounce carton sour
     cream
6   ounces smoked
     cheddar cheese,
     shredded (1½ cups)
1   28-ounce package
     frozen diced hash
     brown potatoes
     with onions and
     peppers, thawed
3   cups chopped
     smoked or roasted
     chicken or turkey
     (about 1 pound)
   Crushed croutons
     (optional)

1 Lightly coat the inside of a 3½- or 4-quart slow cooker with cooking spray. In the prepared cooker combine cream of chicken soup, sour cream, and cheddar cheese. Stir in potatoes and chicken.

2 Cover and cook on low-heat setting for 5 to 6 hours. If desired, sprinkle each serving with croutons.

nutrition facts per serving: 399 cal., 20 g total fat (12 g sat. fat), 80 mg chol., 1313 mg sodium, 31 g carbo., 3 g dietary fiber, 25 g protein.

No doubt this will be a hit with the kids. The vegetable-studded sandwich is a pizza-flavored takeoff on ground beef sloppy joes.

sloppy chicken pizza joes

prep: 15 minutes cook: 6 to 8 hours (low) or 3 to 4 hours (high)
makes: 8 sandwiches

Nonstick cooking
  spray
3 pounds ground
    chicken or turkey
2 14-ounce jars pizza
    sauce
2 cups frozen sweet
    pepper and onion
    stir-fry vegetables,
    thawed and
    chopped
1 14.5-ounce can
    diced tomatoes,
    undrained
8 hoagie buns, split
    and toasted
8 slices mozzarella or
    provolone cheese
    (8 ounces)

1 Coat a large skillet with cooking spray. Heat over medium-high heat. Cook chicken until brown. Drain off fat. In a 3½- or 4-quart slow cooker combine chicken, pizza sauce, frozen vegetables, and tomatoes.

2 Cover and cook on low-heat setting for 6 to 8 hours or on high-heat setting for 3 to 4 hours.

3 Spoon chicken mixture onto bun bottoms. Add provolone cheese and bun tops.

nutrition facts per sandwich: 661 cal., 26 g total fat (4 g sat. fat), 135 mg chol., 1296 mg sodium, 60 g carbo., 3 g dietary fiber, 47 g protein.

Dried black beans need to be cooked first and allowed to stand for 1 hour before using. You'll love the smoky flavor the turkey sausage gives the beans.

caribbean black beans with rum

prep: 20 minutes   stand: 1 hour   cook: 11 to 12 hours (low) or 5½ to 6 hours (high)   makes: 6 servings

2¼   cups dried black
     beans (1 pound)
 6   cups water
 1   pound smoked turkey
     sausage, cut into
     1-inch pieces
 3   cups chicken broth
 1   cup water
 1   cup chopped onion
     (1 large)
 ½   cup dark rum
 2   tablespoons packed
     brown sugar
 1   tablespoon grated
     fresh ginger
 3   cloves garlic, minced
 2   teaspoons dry
     mustard
 ½   teaspoon ground
     cinnamon
 ½   teaspoon ground
     black pepper
 ¼   teaspoon ground
     cloves
     Salt

1 Rinse beans; drain. In a 4-quart Dutch oven combine beans and the 6 cups water. Bring to boiling; reduce heat. Simmer, uncovered, for 10 minutes. Cover and let stand for 1 hour. Drain and rinse beans.

2 In a 5- to 6-quart slow cooker combine beans, sausage, broth, the 1 cup water, onion, rum, brown sugar, ginger, garlic, mustard, cinnamon, pepper, and cloves.

3 Cover and cook on low-heat setting for 11 to 12 hours or on high-heat setting for 5½ to 6 hours. Season to taste with salt.

nutrition facts per serving: 458 cal., 8 g total fat (2 g sat. fat), 52 mg chol., 1249 mg sodium, 58 g carbo., 12 g dietary fiber, 29 g protein.

If you don't have time to make meatballs from scratch, use thawed frozen Italian-style cooked turkey balls instead of the homemade meatballs.

turkey sausage subs

prep: 45 minutes bake: 20 minutes cook: 3½ to 4 hours (low) or 2 to 2½ hours (high) oven: 350°F makes: 6 servings

1   egg
1   25-ounce jar mushroom and olive pasta sauce
⅓   cup roasted garlic–flavored fine dry bread crumbs
½   teaspoon salt
¼   teaspoon cayenne pepper
1½ pounds uncooked sweet Italian turkey sausage links, casings removed
1   large onion, cut into thin wedges
2   large green, yellow, and/or orange sweet peppers, cut into thin strips
6   hoagie buns, split and toasted
¾   cup shredded mozzarella cheese (3 ounces)

1 Preheat oven to 350°F. For meatballs, in a large bowl beat egg with a fork. Stir in ¼ cup of the pasta sauce, bread crumbs, salt, and cayenne pepper. Add turkey sausage; mix well. Using wet hands, shape mixture into 24 meatballs. In a 15x10x1-inch baking pan arrange meatballs in a single layer. Bake for 20 to 25 minutes or until cooked through (165°F).*

2 In a 4- to 5-quart slow cooker combine onion, sweet peppers, and the remaining pasta sauce. Gently stir in meatballs. Cover and cook on low-heat setting for 3½ to 4 hours or on high-heat setting for 2 to 2½ hours.

3 To serve, place meatballs on bun bottoms. Top with sauce and mozzarella cheese. Add bun tops.

nutrition facts per serving: 747 cal., 25 g total fat (7 g sat. fat), 117 mg chol., 2266 mg sodium, 94 g carbo., 7 g dietary fiber, 39 g protein.

*test kitchen tip: The internal color of a meatball is not a reliable doneness indicator. A turkey meatball cooked to 165°F is safe, regardless of color. To measure the doneness of a meatball, insert an instant-read thermometer into the center of the meatball.

Cornbread stuffing mix, along with butternut squash, turkey, golden raisins, celery, and onion, make up this hash. Apple jelly adds a subtle sweetness.

turkey hash

prep: 30 minutes cook: 5 to 6 hours (low) makes: 6 servings

1   tablespoon vegetable oil
1   pound ground turkey or chicken
4   cups cornbread stuffing mix
2   cups ½-inch pieces peeled butternut or acorn squash
1   cup chopped onion (1 large)
½   cup chopped celery (1 stalk)
⅓   cup golden raisins
¾   cup reduced-sodium chicken broth
¼   cup apple jelly
¼   cup butter or margarine, melted
½   teaspoon finely shredded lemon peel
1   tablespoon lemon juice
1   teaspoon dried sage, crushed
    Disposable slow-cooker liner

1 In a large skillet heat oil over medium-high heat. Cook turkey in hot oil until brown. Drain off fat.

2 In an extra-large bowl combine turkey, stuffing mix, squash, onion, celery, and raisins. In a small bowl combine broth, apple jelly, butter, lemon peel, lemon juice, and sage. Drizzle over turkey mixture; toss gently to moisten.

3 Line a 5- to 6-quart slow cooker with a disposable liner. Spoon turkey mixture into the prepared cooker. Cover and cook on low-heat setting for 5 to 6 hours.

nutrition facts per serving: 522 cal., 18 g total fat (7 g sat. fat), 80 mg chol., 852 mg sodium, 69 g carbo., 2 g dietary fiber, 21 g protein.

The crisp, dry flavor of Chablis is the perfect base for simmering turkey, and it makes a superbly rich gravy.

turkey chablis

prep: 25 minutes   cook: 9 hours (low) or 4½ hours (high)   makes: 8 servings

¾   cup dry white wine
     (such as Chablis)
     or apple juice
½   cup chopped onion
     (1 medium)
1   bay leaf
1   teaspoon dried
     rosemary, crushed
1   clove garlic, minced
¼   teaspoon ground
     black pepper
1   3-pound frozen
     boneless turkey
     roast (with gravy
     packet), thawed
     (do not remove
     cloth netting)*
⅓   cup half-and-half,
     light cream, or milk
2   tablespoons cornstarch
     Snipped fresh
     rosemary (optional)
     Dinner rolls, split
     (optional)

1 In a 4- to 5-quart slow cooker combine wine, onion, bay leaf, dried rosemary, garlic, and pepper. Add turkey.

2 Cover and cook on low-heat setting for 9 hours or on high-heat setting for 4½ hours. Remove turkey from cooker; cover and keep warm.

3 For gravy, strain cooking liquid into a 2-cup glass measuring cup. Skim off fat. Add enough water to strained liquid to equal 1⅓ cups. Pour into a small saucepan. In a small bowl combine half-and-half and cornstarch; stir into liquid in saucepan. Cook and stir over medium heat until thickened and bubbly. Cook and stir for 2 minutes more. If desired, stir in fresh rosemary.

4 Remove netting from turkey and discard. Slice turkey. If desired, arrange sliced turkey on split rolls. Spoon some of the gravy over turkey. Pass the remaining gravy.

nutrition facts per serving: 365 cal., 9 g total fat (3 g sat. fat), 176 mg chol., 193 mg sodium, 5 g carbo., 0 g dietary fiber, 58 g protein.

*test kitchen tip: Reserve giblets and/or gravy packet from turkey for another use.

If your family loves turkey, why serve it just for the holidays? Boneless turkey roasts are readily available and perfectly sized for enjoyment any time.

rosemary turkey roast with vegetables

prep: 30 minutes   cook: 9 to 10 hours (low) or 4½ to 5 hours (high)
makes: 8 servings

Nonstick cooking
    spray
1   pound carrots (6 to 8
    medium), cut into
    3-inch pieces
1   pound tiny new
    potatoes, quartered
1   large onion, cut into
    ½ -inch wedges
¼   cup water
1   teaspoon salt
1   teaspoon dried
    rosemary, crushed
¼   teaspoon garlic
    powder
¼   teaspoon dried
    thyme, crushed
¼   teaspoon ground
    black pepper
1   3-pound frozen
    boneless turkey
    roast (with gravy
    packet), thawed
    (do not remove
    cloth netting)*
    Chicken broth
¼   cup all-purpose flour
    Salt
    Ground black pepper

1 Lightly coat the inside of a 5- to 6-quart slow cooker with cooking spray. In the prepared cooker combine carrots, potatoes, onion, the water, 1 teaspoon salt, rosemary, garlic powder, thyme, and ¼ teaspoon pepper. Top with turkey.

2 Cover and cook on low-heat setting for 9 to 10 hours or on high-heat setting for 4½ to 5 hours.

3 Remove turkey from cooker; cover and keep warm. Using a slotted spoon, transfer vegetables to a serving platter; cover and keep warm.

4 For gravy, strain cooking liquid into a 2-cup glass measuring cup. Skim off fat. Add enough broth to strained liquid to equal 2 cups. Pour into a medium saucepan; stir in flour. Cook and stir over medium heat until thickened and bubbly. Cook and stir for 1 minute more. Season to taste with additional salt and pepper.

5 Remove netting from turkey and discard. Slice turkey. Serve turkey and vegetables with gravy.

nutrition facts per serving: 270 cal., 4 g total fat (1 g sat. fat), 81 mg chol., 1611 mg sodium, 29 g carbo., 3 g dietary fiber, 29 g protein.

*test kitchen tip: Reserve giblets and/or gravy packet from turkey for another use.

Traditionally made with chopped or ground lamb or mutton, shepherd's pie works equally well slow-cooked with turkey and frozen vegetables.

turkey shepherd's pie

prep: 20 minutes   cook: 6 to 7 hours (low) or 3 to 3½ hours (high) + 10 minutes
makes: 4 servings

1   10-ounce package
    frozen mixed
    vegetables
12 ounces turkey breast
    tenderloin or
    skinless, boneless
    chicken breast
    halves, cut into
    ½-inch strips
1   12-ounce jar turkey
    or chicken gravy
1   teaspoon dried
    thyme, crushed
1   24-ounce package
    refrigerated mashed
    potatoes
    Fresh thyme leaves
    (optional)

1 Place frozen vegetables in a 3½- or 4-quart slow cooker. Add turkey. In a small bowl stir together gravy and dried thyme. Pour over mixture in cooker.

2 Cover and cook on low-heat setting for 6 to 7 hours or on high-heat setting for 3 to 3½ hours.

3 If using low-heat setting, turn to high-heat setting. Spoon mashed potatoes formed into eight small mounds onto turkey mixture. Cover and cook for 10 minutes more.

4 To serve, spoon turkey mixture and potato mounds into shallow bowls. If desired, sprinkle with fresh thyme.

nutrition facts per serving: 297 cal., 5 g total fat (1 g sat. fat), 51 mg chol., 781 mg sodium, 33 g carbo., 4 g dietary fiber, 27 g protein.

Homemade dumplings can't be beat and take only minutes to stir together. The dumplings and basic turkey breast tenderloin cook to perfection in this dish.

turkey and dumplings

prep: 20 minutes   cook: 6 to 7 hours (low) or 3 to 3½ hours (high) + 45 minutes
stand: 15 minutes   makes: 6 servings

1¼   pounds turkey breast
         tenderloin, cut into
         ¾-inch pieces
1½   cups thinly sliced
         carrots (3 medium)
1½   cups thinly sliced
         celery (3 stalks)
  1   medium onion, cut
         into thin wedges
  1   14-ounce can
         reduced-sodium
         chicken broth
  1   10.75-ounce can
         condensed cream
         of chicken soup
  2   teaspoons dried sage,
         crushed
  ¼   teaspoon ground
         black pepper
  1   cup all-purpose flour
  1   teaspoon baking
         powder
  ½   teaspoon salt
  2   tablespoons
         shortening
  ½   cup milk
  ¼   cup all-purpose flour

1 In a 3½- or 4-quart slow cooker combine turkey, carrots, celery, and onion. Set aside ½ cup of the broth. In a medium bowl combine the remaining broth, cream of chicken soup, sage, and pepper. Stir into mixture in cooker.

2 Cover and cook on low-heat setting for 6 to 7 hours or on high-heat setting for 3 to 3½ hours.

3 For dumplings, in a small bowl stir together 1 cup flour, baking powder, and salt. Using a pastry blender, cut in shortening until mixture resembles coarse crumbs. Add milk all at once; stir just until moistened.

4 If using low-heat setting, turn to high-heat setting. In a small bowl combine the reserved ½ cup broth and ¼ cup flour; stir into turkey mixture. Drop dumpling dough by small spoonfuls onto turkey mixture. Cover and cook for 45 minutes more.

5 Turn off cooker. Let stand, covered, for 15 minutes before serving.

nutrition facts per serving: 327 cal., 9 g total fat (2 g sat. fat), 64 mg chol., 909 mg sodium, 31 g carbo., 2 g dietary fiber, 29 g protein.

Spike the cranberry flavor with chili sauce in this tender turkey meal.
It's a hit served with mashed sweet or regular potatoes.

turkey thighs in
spicy cranberry sauce

prep: 10 minutes cook: 9 to 10 hours (low) or 4½ to 5 hours (high)
makes: 4 to 6 servings

1   16-ounce can jellied
    cranberry sauce
½   cup bottled chili
    sauce
1   tablespoon vinegar
¼   teaspoon pumpkin
    pie spice
2½ to 3 pounds turkey
    thighs (2 or 3
    thighs), skinned

1 In a 3½- or 4-quart slow cooker combine cranberry sauce, chili sauce, vinegar, and pumpkin pie spice. Top with turkey, meaty side down.

2 Cover and cook on low-heat setting for 9 to 10 hours or on high-heat setting for 4½ to 5 hours.

3 Transfer turkey to a serving dish. Skim off fat from sauce. Serve turkey with sauce.

nutrition facts per serving: 388 cal., 5 g total fat (2 g sat. fat), 145 mg chol., 300 mg sodium, 46 g carbo., 2 g dietary fiber, 37 g protein.

For something extra special, savor this salad with friends. It is no ordinary meal! If you can't get duck hindquarters, use boneless, skinless chicken thighs.

braised duck
with pistachio salad
and squash

prep: 40 minutes cook: 7 to 8 hours (low) or 3½ to 4 hours (high)
broil: 4 minutes makes: 4 to 6 servings

3   to 3½ pounds duck
    hindquarters
½   teaspoon salt
¼   teaspoon coarsely
    ground black
    pepper
1   ½-pound butternut
    squash, peeled
    and cut into 1-inch
    pieces
1   8-ounce package
    whole fresh
    mushrooms
1   medium red onion,
    cut into wedges
¼   cup dry white wine
¼   cup chicken broth
1   tablespoon grated
    fresh ginger
1   teaspoon finely
    shredded lemon
    peel
1   tablespoon lemon
    juice
1   tablespoon honey
2   tablespoons white
    wine vinegar
1   tablespoon finely
    chopped shallot
6   cups torn mixed
    greens
2   tablespoons coarsely
    chopped pistachios

1 Sprinkle duck with salt and pepper; set aside.

2 In a 6-quart slow cooker combine squash, mushrooms, and onion. Top with duck. In a small bowl combine wine, broth, ginger, lemon peel, lemon juice, and honey. Pour over mixture in cooker.

3 Cover and cook on low-heat setting for 7 to 8 hours or on high-heat setting for 3½ to 4 hours.

4 Preheat broiler. Remove duck from the slow cooker. Place on an unheated broiler pan. Broil 4 to 5 inches from the heat for about 4 minutes or until browned and crisp, turning once.

5 Meanwhile, using a slotted spoon, remove vegetables from slow cooker to a serving bowl. Remove 3 tablespoons cooking liquid from the slow cooker, including some of the fat. Discard remaining cooking liquid. For dressing, in a screw-top jar combine reserved cooking liquid, vinegar, and shallot. Cover and shake well to combine.

6 For salad, place mixed greens in an extra-large bowl. Drizzle with dressing and sprinkle with pistachios, tossing to coat. Serve salad with duck and vegetables.

nutrition facts per serving: 681 cal., 43 g total fat (12 g sat. fat), 179 mg chol., 1382 mg sodium, 30 g carbo., 5 g dietary fiber, 42 g protein.

This company-worthy dish takes a little longer to assemble than many slow-cooker recipes, but the results are amazing.

apple-braised pheasant with watercress salad

prep: 40 minutes   cook: 6 to 7 hours (low) or 3 to 3½ hours (high)
makes: 4 servings

1½ cups coarsely chopped, peeled celeriac
1 cup coarsely chopped carrots (2 medium)
1 cup frozen small whole onions
2 cloves garlic, minced
1 2½- to 3-pound pheasant, cut into quarters and skinned
2 teaspoons snipped fresh savory or ½ teaspoon dried savory, crushed
½ teaspoon salt
¼ teaspoon ground black pepper
1 cup chicken broth
2 tablespoons Calvados or chicken broth
2 tablespoons olive oil
½ teaspoon finely shredded lemon peel
1 tablespoon lemon juice
1 tablespoon cider vinegar
½ teaspoon dry mustard
Salt
Ground black pepper
8 ounces fresh watercress, tough stems removed
3 slices bacon, crisp-cooked and crumbled
1 medium apple, cored and thinly sliced
¼ cup walnuts, toasted and coarsely chopped

1 In a 3½- or 4-quart slow cooker combine celeriac, carrots, onions, and garlic. Top with pheasant. Sprinkle with savory, ½ teaspoon salt, and ¼ teaspoon pepper. Pour broth and Calvados over mixture in cooker.

2 Cover and cook on low-heat setting for 6 to 7 hours or on high-heat setting for 3 to 3½ hours.

3 Meanwhile, for dressing, in a screw-top jar combine oil, lemon peel, lemon juice, vinegar, and dry mustard. Cover and shake well to combine. Season to taste with salt and pepper. For salad, in a serving bowl combine watercress, bacon, apple, and walnuts. Drizzle with dressing, tossing to coat.

4 Transfer pheasant and vegetables to a serving platter. Strain cooking liquid through a fine-mesh sieve. Serve pheasant and vegetables with salad. Drizzle pheasant and vegetables with some of the strained cooking liquid.

nutrition facts per serving: 528 cal., 22 g total fat (5 g sat. fat), 149 mg chol., 1148 mg sodium, 19 g carbo., 4 g dietary fiber, 57 g protein.

6

satisfying

beef

There's nothing better than beef stew that has been simmering all day. Or how about Shredded Beef French Dip sandwiches or Philadelphia Cheese Steak Wraps? We've included many classics—sloppy joes, osso buco, and beef stroganoff—and many new dishes, too—Korean Beef Short Ribs, Brisket Pie, and Chutney-Beef Paninis (made from last night's Saucy Brisket).

&veal.

Lots of sweet onions and well-seasoned juices make these sandwiches especially delicious. A packaged au jus gravy mix boosts the flavor of the cooking juices.

whip-up french dips

prep: 15 minutes   cook: 10 to 11 hours (low) or 5 to 5½ hours (high)
makes: 6 to 8 servings

1   3- to 3½-pound boneless beef bottom round roast
1   tablespoon vegetable oil
2   large sweet onions, cut into thin wedges
2   14-ounce cans seasoned beef broth with onion
1   0.6-ounce envelope dry au jus gravy mix
¼   teaspoon ground black pepper
6   to 8 hoagie buns, split and toasted if desired

1 Trim fat from meat. In a large skillet heat oil over medium-high heat. Cook meat on all sides in hot oil until brown. Drain off fat.

2 Place onions in a 5- to 6-quart slow cooker. Top with meat. In a bowl whisk together broth, gravy mix, and pepper. Pour over meat.

3 Cover and cook on low-heat setting for 10 to 11 hours or on high-heat setting for 5 to 5½ hours.

4 Transfer meat to a cutting board; slice across the grain. Return to cooker and keep warm. Using a slotted spoon, transfer meat and onions to hoagie buns. Serve with bowls of cooking liquid for dipping.

nutrition facts per serving: 611 cal., 16 g total fat (4 g sat. fat), 132 mg chol., 1504 mg sodium, 57 g carbo., 3 g dietary fiber, 60 g protein.

Keep stir-fry vegetables on hand for dishes like this one. They provide a lot of color, nutrition, and ease without all the chopping and slicing.

savory roast
with peppers and onions

prep: 15 minutes   cook: 8 to 9 hours (low) or 4 to 4½ hours (high) + 30 minutes
makes: 6 servings

Nonstick cooking spray or disposable slow-cooker liner

1 2½- to 3-pound beef chuck pot roast
1 teaspoon dried thyme, crushed
¼ teaspoon cayenne pepper
1 14.5-ounce can diced tomatoes with basil, garlic, and oregano, undrained
1 10.5-ounce can condensed French onion soup
1 tablespoon Worcestershire sauce
1 16-ounce package frozen sweet pepper and onion stir-fry vegetables
1½ cups instant white rice

1 Lightly coat a 4- to 5-quart slow cooker with cooking spray. Trim fat from meat. If necessary, cut meat to fit into slow cooker. Place meat into prepared cooker. Sprinkle meat with thyme and cayenne pepper. Add tomatoes, French onion soup, and Worcestershire sauce.

2 Cover and cook on low-heat setting for 8 to 9 hours or on high-heat setting for 4 to 4½ hours.

3 If using low-heat setting, turn to high-heat setting. Stir in stir-fry vegetables and uncooked rice. Cover and cook on high-heat setting for 30 minutes more.

nutrition facts per serving: 534 cal., 14 g total fat (4 g sat. fat), 121 mg chol., 3677 mg sodium, 52 g carbo., 6 g dietary fiber, 51 g protein.

For the dried fruit, look for a combination of these types: pears, peaches, nectarines, apricots, raisins, cherries, and/or cranberries.

pot roast with chipotle-fruit sauce

prep: 15 minutes   cook: 10 to 11 hours (low) or 5 to 5½ hours (high)
makes: 8 servings

1   3-pound boneless beef chuck pot roast
2   teaspoons garlic-pepper seasoning
1   7-ounce package dried mixed fruit
½   cup water
1   tablespoon finely chopped canned chipotle chile peppers in adobo sauce (see tip, page 32)
1   tablespoon cold water
2   teaspoons cornstarch

1 Sprinkle both sides of meat with garlic-pepper seasoning. If necessary, cut roast to fit into a 3½- or 4-quart slow cooker. Place meat in slow cooker. Add fruit, the ½ cup water, and chipotle peppers.

2 Cover and cook on low-heat setting for 10 to 11 hours or on high-heat setting for 5 to 5½ hours.

3 Transfer meat to a serving platter; thinly slice across the grain. Using a slotted spoon, transfer fruit to platter. Cover and keep warm.

4 For sauce, skim off fat from cooking liquid; pour into a medium saucepan. In a small bowl combine the 1 tablespoon cold water and cornstarch; stir into liquid in saucepan. Cook and stir over medium heat until thickened and bubbly. Cook and stir for 2 minutes more. Spoon sauce over meat and fruit.

nutrition facts per serving: 275 cal., 6 g total fat (2 g sat. fat), 101 mg chol., 378 mg sodium, 17q g carbo., 1 g dietary fiber, 37 g protein.

Here is a pot roast just the way you like it, with tender meat that falls apart with the nudge of a fork and a richly flavored sauce.

mushroom-onion
pot roast

prep: 30 minutes   cook: 10 to 12 hours (low) or 5 to 6 hours (high)
makes: 4 servings

1   3-pound boneless
      beef chuck pot roast
½   teaspoon salt
¼   teaspoon ground
      black pepper
2   tablespoons
      vegetable oil
2   large onions, halved
      and sliced ¼ inch
      thick
3   cups small button
      mushrooms, sliced
1   10.5-ounce can
      condensed beef
      consommé
½   cup dry red wine
4   cloves garlic, minced
1   teaspoon dried
      thyme, crushed
2   tablespoons
      cornstarch
2   tablespoons cold
      water
2   cups hot mashed
      potatoes

1 Trim fat from meat. Sprinkle meat with salt and pepper. In an extra-large skillet heat oil over medium-high heat. Cook meat on all sides in hot oil until brown; set aside. In a 5- to 6-quart slow cooker combine onions and mushrooms. Top with meat. In a medium bowl combine consommé, wine, garlic, and thyme. Pour over meat and vegetables.

2 Cover and cook on low-heat setting for 10 to 12 hours or high-heat setting for 5 to 6 hours.

3 Transfer meat to a serving platter. Cover and keep warm.

4 For sauce, pour cooking liquid and vegetables into a medium saucepan. In a small bowl combine cornstarch and the cold water; stir into saucepan. Cook and stir over medium heat until thickened and bubbly. Cook and stir for 2 minutes more.

5 Serve meat, vegetables, and sauce over hot mashed potatoes.

nutrition facts per serving: 523 cal., 18 g total fat (5 g sat. fat), 135 mg chol., 958 mg sodium, 30 g carbo., 3 g dietary fiber, 55 g protein.

Just a tablespoon of espresso powder contributes a subtle but interesting flavor to this beef-and-veggie stew.

espresso-braised beef

prep: 20 minutes   cook: 8 to 9 hours (low) or 4 to 4½ hours (high)
makes: 6 servings

1½ pounds boneless beef chuck
1 large onion, cut into wedges
3 medium carrots, cut into 1-inch pieces
1 medium turnip, peeled and cut into 1-inch pieces
⅔ cup dry red wine
2 tablespoons tomato paste
1 tablespoon instant espresso powder
1 teaspoon packed brown sugar
1 teaspoon dried thyme, crushed
½ teaspoon salt
¼ teaspoon ground black pepper
1 24-ounce package refrigerated mashed sweet potatoes, prepared according to package directions
Salt
Coarsely ground black pepper

1 Trim fat from meat. Cut meat into 1-inch pieces. In a 3½- or 4-quart slow cooker combine onion, carrots, and turnip. Top with meat. In a medium bowl whisk together wine, tomato paste, espresso powder, brown sugar, thyme, ½ teaspoon salt, and ¼ teaspoon pepper. Pour over mixture in cooker.

2 Cover and cook on low-heat setting for 8 to 9 hours or on high-heat setting for 4 to 4½ hours. Serve beef mixture over hot mashed sweet potatoes. Sprinkle with additional salt and coarsely ground black pepper.

nutrition facts per serving: 308 cal., 9 g total fat (4 g sat. fat), 66 mg chol., 448 mg sodium, 26 g carbo., 4 g dietary fiber, 26 g protein.

The understated combo of maple and orange deliver an appealing flavor in this fall-perfect pot roast.

maple-glazed pot roast

prep: 20 minutes   cook: 11 to 12 hours (low) or 5½ to 6 hours (high)
makes: 8 servings

1   2½ - to 3-pound boneless beef chuck pot roast
1   tablespoon vegetable oil
4   medium parsnips and/or carrots, peeled and cut into 3-inch pieces
1   medium acorn squash, seeded and cut into 1-inch-thick slices (about 1¼ pounds)
2   small onions, cut into wedges
½   cup maple syrup
3   tablespoons quick-cooking tapioca, crushed
2   tablespoons white wine vinegar
2   teaspoons finely shredded orange peel
1   teaspoon salt
¼   teaspoon ground black pepper
4   cups hot cooked noodles

1 Trim fat from meat. If necessary, cut meat to fit into a 4- to 5-quart slow cooker. In a large skillet heat oil over medium-high heat. Cook meat on all sides in hot oil until brown. Drain off fat.

2 In the cooker combine parsnips, squash, and onions. Top with meat. In a small bowl combine syrup, tapioca, vinegar, orange peel, salt, and pepper. Pour over mixture in cooker.

3 Cover and cook on low-heat setting for 11 to 12 hours or on high-heat setting for 5½ to 6 hours.

4 Transfer meat to a serving platter; slice across the grain. Using a slotted spoon, transfer vegetables to serving platter. Cover and keep warm. Skim fat from cooking liquid. Serve cooking liquid and hot cooked noodles with meat and vegetables.

nutrition facts per serving: 423 cal., 8 g total fat (2 g sat. fat), 110 mg chol., 400 mg sodium, 51 g carbo., 4 g dietary fiber, 36 g protein.

There just isn't anything better than an ultra-tender classic roast and vegetables served alongside a fluffy mound of mashed potatoes.

fork-tender pot roast

prep: 25 minutes cook: 10 to 12 hours (low) or 5 to 6 hours (high)
makes: 6 to 8 servings

1   tablespoon olive oil
1   2½ - to 3-pound
     boneless beef chuck
     pot roast
1   cup coarsely chopped
     carrots (2 medium)
2   stalks celery, cut into
     1-inch pieces
1   cup coarsely chopped
     onion (1 large)
1   clove garlic, minced
1   bay leaf
¾   cup beef broth
¼   cup dry red wine
2   tablespoons quick-
     cooking tapioca,
     crushed
1   tablespoon dried
     Italian seasoning,
     crushed
1   tablespoon tomato
     paste
1   teaspoon garlic
     powder
¾   teaspoon ground
     black pepper
½   teaspoon dry mustard
½   teaspoon paprika
⅛   teaspoon salt
     Mashed potatoes
     (optional)

1 In a large skillet heat oil over medium-high heat. Cook meat on all sides in hot oil until brown; set aside.

2 In a 3 ½ - or 4-quart slow cooker combine carrots, celery, onion, garlic, and bay leaf. Top with meat. In a medium bowl combine broth, wine, tapioca, Italian seasoning, tomato paste, garlic powder, pepper, dry mustard, paprika, and salt. Pour over meat.

3 Cover and cook on low-heat setting for 10 to 12 hours or on high-heat setting for 5 to 6 hours.

4 Transfer meat to a serving platter. Using a slotted spoon, transfer vegetables to platter. Remove and discard bay leaf from cooking liquid. Skim off fat from cooking liquid. Drizzle cooking liquid over meat and vegetables. If desired, serve with mashed potatoes.

nutrition facts per serving: 322 cal., 10 g total fat (3 g sat. fat), 83 mg chol., 349 mg sodium, 10 g carbo., 2 g dietary fiber, 43 g protein.

Pot roast heads for the untamed West when slow cooked with chili beans, corn, tomatoes, and spicy chile peppers in adobo sauce.

cowboy beef

prep: 15 minutes   cook: 10 to 12 hours (low) or 5 to 6 hours (high)
makes: 6 servings

1   2- to 2½-pound
    boneless beef chuck
    pot roast
1   15-ounce can chili
    beans in chili gravy,
    undrained
1   11-ounce can whole
    kernel corn with
    sweet peppers,
    drained
1   10-ounce can diced
    tomatoes and green
    chiles, undrained
1   to 2 teaspoons finely
    chopped canned
    chipotle chile pepper
    in adobo sauce (see
    tip, page 32)

1 Trim fat from meat. If necessary, cut meat to fit in a 3½- or 4-quart slow cooker. Place meat in cooker. In a medium bowl combine chili beans, corn, tomatoes, and chipotle pepper. Pour bean mixture over meat.

2 Cover and cook on low-heat setting for 10 to 12 hours or on high-heat setting for 5 to 6 hours.

3 Transfer meat to a cutting board and slice. Arrange slices in a shallow serving bowl. Using a slotted spoon, spoon bean mixture over meat. Drizzle with enough of the cooking liquid to moisten.

nutrition facts per serving: 307 cal., 7 g total fat (2 g sat. fat), 89 mg chol., 655 mg sodium, 23 g carbo., 5 g dietary fiber, 37 g protein.

Look for fresh fennel to add delicate flavor and a hint of licoricelike interest. If you can't find it, use three or four stalks of celery instead.

italian pot roast

prep: 20 minutes   cook: 9 to 10 hours (low) or 4½ to 5 hours (high)
makes: 4 servings + reserves

1   3-pound boneless
     beef chuck pot roast
1   teaspoon garlic salt
1   teaspoon fennel
     seeds, toasted and
     crushed
½   teaspoon ground
     black pepper
2   medium fennel bulbs,
     trimmed and cut
     into thin wedges
3   medium carrots,
     halved lengthwise
     and cut diagonally
     into 2-inch lengths
1   large onion, cut into
     thin wedges
1   26-ounce jar pasta
     sauce
2   to 3 cups hot cooked
     penne pasta
¼   cup chopped fresh
     Italian (flat-leaf)
     parsley
     Grated Parmesan
     cheese (optional)

1 Trim fat from meat. In a small bowl combine garlic salt, fennel seeds, and pepper. Sprinkle mixture evenly over meat and rub in with your fingers. In a 5- to 6-quart slow cooker combine fennel, carrots, and onion. Top with meat. Pour pasta sauce over mixture in cooker.

2 Cover and cook on low-heat setting for 9 to 10 hours or on high-heat setting for 4½ to 5 hours.

3 Reserve one-third of the meat and 2 cups of the cooking liquid; store as directed below. Toss hot cooked pasta with parsley. Serve remaining meat and cooking liquid over hot pasta mixture. If desired, sprinkle with Parmesan cheese.

nutrition facts per serving: 535 cal., 13 g total fat (4 g sat. fat), 134 mg chol., 944 mg sodium, 47 g carbo., 6 g dietary fiber, 55 g protein.

to store reserves: Chop reserved meat (about 2 cups). Place meat and reserved cooking liquid in separate airtight containers. Seal and chill for up to 3 days. *Use in Beef and Olive Calzones, page 249.*

Sit back and relax. You have dinner all figured out for tonight. Use the leftovers from Italian Pot Roast and make these easy cheesy calzones.

beef and olive calzones

prep: 20 minutes   bake: 18 minutes   cool: 5 minutes   oven: 400°F
makes: 4 servings

Nonstick cooking
   spray
1 10- to 13.8-ounce
   package refrigerated
   pizza dough
   Reserved beef and
   cooking liquid from
   Italian Pot Roast*
   (page 248)
1 cup finely shredded
   Italian cheese blend
   (4 ounces)
¼ cup sliced pitted
   black olives

*test kitchen tip: There should be about 2 cups reserved beef and 2 cups reserved cooking liquid.

1 Preheat oven to 400°F. Line a baking sheet with foil; lightly coat foil with cooking spray. Unroll pizza dough on prepared baking sheet. Cut dough in half crosswise and lengthwise to make four rectangles; set aside.

2 In a blender or food processor puree reserved cooking liquid. In a medium bowl combine ⅓ cup of the pureed cooking liquid, reserved beef, ½ cup of the Italian cheese blend, and olives. Place about ½ cup of the beef mixture in the center of each dough rectangle. For each calzone, fold a short edge of a dough rectangle over filling to opposite edge, stretching slightly if necessary. Seal edges with the tines of a fork. Arrange calzones so they are evenly spaced on the baking sheet. Sprinkle with the remaining ½ cup cheese.

3 Prick tops of calzones to allow steam to escape. Bake, uncovered, for 18 to 20 minutes or until golden. Cool for 5 minutes before serving. Meanwhile, in a small saucepan heat the remaining pureed cooking liquid; serve with calzones.

nutrition facts per serving: 165 cal., 17 g total fat (6 g sat. fat), 87 mg chol., 951 mg sodium, 40 g carbo., 4 g dietary fiber, 37 g protein.

Unless you grow your own basil, having a large amount of the herb isn't always possible. You may stir in spinach or escarole and garnish with shredded basil.

country italian beef

prep: 25 minutes   cook: 8 to 10 hours (low) or 4 to 5 hours (high)
makes: 6 to 8 servings

2 pounds boneless beef
    chuck pot roast
8 ounces tiny new
    potatoes, halved
    or quartered
2 medium carrots or
    parsnips, peeled
    and cut into 1- to
    2-inch pieces
1 cup chopped onion
    (1 large)
1 medium fennel bulb,
    trimmed and cut
    into ½-inch wedges
1 teaspoon dried
    rosemary, crushed
1 14-ounce can beef
    broth
1 cup dry red wine
    or beef broth
1 6-ounce can tomato
    paste
2 tablespoons quick-
    cooking tapioca
4 cloves garlic, minced
½ teaspoon ground
    black pepper
1 to 2 cups fresh basil
    leaves, spinach
    leaves, or torn
    escarole

1 Trim fat from meat. Cut meat into 2-inch pieces; set aside. In a 4- to 5-quart slow cooker combine potatoes, carrots, onion, and fennel. Top with meat. Sprinkle with rosemary.

2 In a medium bowl whisk together broth, wine, tomato paste, tapioca, garlic, and pepper. Pour over mixture in cooker.

3 Cover and cook on low-heat setting for 8 to 10 hours or on high-heat setting for 4 to 5 hours. Just before serving, stir in basil.

nutrition facts per serving: 319 cal., 6 g total fat (2 g sat. fat), 89 mg chol., 596 mg sodium, 23 g carbo., 4 g dietary fiber, 36 g protein.

Maque choux (MOCK-shoo) is a Cajun dish of corn smothered with green pepper, onion, and tomatoes. Like most versions, this one has some heat.

cajun pot roast
with maque choux

prep: 20 minutes   cook: 8 to 10 hours (low) or 4 to 5 hours (high)
makes: 6 servings

1   2- to 2½ -pound
    boneless beef chuck
    roast
1   tablespoon Cajun
    seasoning
1   10-ounce package
    frozen whole kernel
    corn
1¼ cups chopped green
    sweet pepper
    (1 large)
½   cup chopped onion
    (1 medium)
1   teaspoon sugar
½   teaspoon bottled
    hot pepper sauce
⅛   teaspoon ground
    black pepper
1   14.5-ounce can
    diced tomatoes,
    undrained

1 Trim fat from meat. Sprinkle Cajun seasoning evenly over all sides of the meat and rub in with your fingers. If necessary, cut meat to fit into a 3½- to 4½-quart slow cooker.

2 Place meat in slow cooker. Add corn, green sweet pepper, onion, sugar, hot pepper sauce, and black pepper. Pour tomatoes over mixture in cooker.

3 Cover and cook on low-heat setting for 8 to 10 hours or on high-heat setting for 4 to 5 hours.

4 Transfer meat to serving platter. Using a slotted spoon, transfer vegetables to a serving bowl. Discard cooking liquid. Serve vegetables with meat.

nutrition facts per serving: 255 cal., 5 g total fat (2 g sat. fat), 90 mg chol., 311 mg sodium, 17 g carbo., 2 g dietary fiber, 34 g protein.

This classic French dish consists of fork-tender beef and a rich,
seasoned wine gravy. It's a dish that never loses its crowd appeal.

boeuf à la
bourguignonne

prep: 45 minutes   cook: 10 to 12 hours (low) or 5 to 6 hours (high)
makes: 6 servings

3   slices bacon, coarsely
     chopped
2   pounds boneless beef
     chuck roast
1½ cups chopped onions
     (3 medium)
2   cloves garlic, minced
4   stems fresh Italian
     (flat-leaf) parsley
3   sprigs fresh thyme
1   sprig fresh rosemary
2   bay leaves
¼   teaspoon whole black
     peppercorns
4   medium carrots, cut
     into ¾-inch pieces
2   cups frozen small
     whole onions
3   tablespoons quick-
     cooking tapioca,
     crushed
1   cup Burgundy wine
½   cup beef broth
¼   cup brandy
1   tablespoon tomato
     paste
1   tablespoon olive oil
1   cup quartered fresh
     cremini mushrooms
     Mashed potatoes
     Snipped fresh Italian
     (flat-leaf) parsley

1 In a large skillet cook bacon until crisp.
Drain on paper towels. Reserve bacon
drippings in skillet. Cover and chill cooked
bacon until serving time. Trim fat from meat.
Cut meat into 1-inch cubes. Heat bacon
drippings over medium heat. Cook half of the
meat in hot drippings until browned; remove
from skillet. Add remaining meat, chopped
onions, and garlic to skillet. Cook until meat
is brown and onions are tender. Remove from
heat; combine all meat in skillet.

2 For a spice bag, cut an 8-inch square from
a double thickness of 100-percent-cotton
cheesecloth. Place parsley, thyme, rosemary,
bay leaves, and peppercorns in the center
of the cheesecloth square. Bring up corners
of the cheesecloth; tie closed with clean
100-percent-cotton kitchen string. Set aside.

3 In a 3½- or 4-quart slow cooker combine
carrots and whole onions. Sprinkle with
tapioca. Spoon meat mixture over mixture in
cooker. Add spice bag. In a small bowl whisk
together wine, broth, brandy, and tomato
paste. Pour over mixture in cooker.

4 Cover and cook on low-heat setting
for 10 to 12 hours or on high-heat setting
for 5 to 6 hours. Remove spice bag and discard.

5 In a large skillet heat oil over medium-high
heat. Cook mushrooms in hot oil until
brown. Serve beef with mashed potatoes. Top
each serving with mushrooms, bacon, and
snipped parsley.

nutrition facts per serving: 616 cal., 30 g total fat
(12 g sat. fat), 127 mg chol., 556 mg sodium, 37 g carbo.,
5 g dietary fiber, 36 g protein.

Hold on to this recipe. It is needed in the following six recipes, pages 255 to 260. It makes a total of 6 cups, enough meat for three of the six recipes.

shredded beef
master recipe

prep: 30 minutes cook: 11 to 12 hours (low) or 5½ to 6 hours (high)
makes: 3 (2-cup) portions

1 3- to 3½ - pound
   boneless beef chuck
   pot roast
2 large onions, cut into
   thin wedges
2 cloves garlic, minced
1 14-ounce can beef
   broth
1 tablespoon
   Worcestershire
   sauce
2 teaspoons dry
   mustard
1 teaspoon dried
   thyme, crushed
½ teaspoon salt
¼ teaspoon cayenne
   pepper

1 Trim fat from meat. If necessary, cut meat to fit into a 4- to 5-quart slow cooker. Combine onions and garlic in the cooker. Top with meat. In a medium bowl combine broth, Worcestershire sauce, dry mustard, thyme, salt, and cayenne pepper. Pour over meat.

2 Cover and cook on low-heat setting for 11 to 12 hours or on high-heat setting for 5½ to 6 hours.

3 Remove meat from cooker. Using two forks, pull meat apart into shreds. Skim fat from cooking liquid. Remove onions from cooker and add to meat. Drizzle with enough of the cooking liquid to moisten.

4 Place 2-cup portions of meat mixture in separate airtight containers. Seal and chill for up to 3 days. (Or freeze for up to 3 months. Thaw overnight in the refrigerator before using.)

nutrition facts per cup: 326 cal., 10 g total fat (4 g sat. fat), 100 mg chol., 404 mg sodium, 5 g carbo., 1 g dietary fiber, 51 g protein.

Shredded Beef Master Recipe, onion, canned tomatoes, and spices easily come together for a south-of-the border sandwich.

southwestern shredded beef sandwiches

start to finish: 25 minutes makes: 4 servings

1   tablespoon vegetable
    oil
1   cup chopped onion
    (1 large)
2   cups Shredded Beef
    Master Recipe
    (page 254)
1   10-ounce can diced
    tomatoes and green
    chiles, undrained
1   teaspoon ground
    cumin
1   teaspoon chili
    powder
1   tablespoon snipped
    fresh cilantro
½   cup shredded cheddar
    or Monterey Jack
    cheese (2 ounces)
4   onion rolls, split and
    toasted if desired
1   cup coarsely
    shredded lettuce

1 In a large saucepan heat oil over medium-high heat. Cook onion in hot oil for about 4 minutes or until tender. Add shredded beef, tomatoes, cumin, and chili powder. Bring to boiling; reduce heat. Simmer, uncovered, for about 5 minutes or until heated through and desired consistency. Stir in cilantro.

2 Sprinkle some cheddar cheese over bottoms of onion rolls. Spoon about ½ cup of the meat mixture over cheese on each bun. Sprinkle with remaining cheese and the shredded lettuce. Add roll tops.

nutrition facts per serving: 114 cal., 4 g total fat (1 g sat. fat), 16 mg chol., 230 mg sodium, 10 g carbo., 1 g dietary fiber, 9 g protein.

Do you have 10 minutes? How about 15? That's how long it will take to make and cook this recipe. Use 2 cups Shredded Beef Master Recipe for this entrée.

shredded beef french dips

start to finish: 25 minutes   makes: 4 servings

2 tablespoons butter
   or margarine
1 medium sweet
   onion, cut into thin
   wedges
1 cup thin red or yellow
   sweet pepper strips
   (1 medium)
2 cloves garlic, minced
2 cups Shredded Beef
   Master Recipe
   (page 254)
1 14-ounce can
   seasoned beef broth
   with onion
1 teaspoon dried Italian
   seasoning, crushed
¼ teaspoon ground
   black pepper
4 French rolls, split
   and toasted

1 In a large saucepan heat butter over medium heat. Cook onion, red sweet pepper, and garlic in hot butter for about 10 minutes or until tender. Stir in shredded beef, broth, Italian seasoning, and black pepper. Bring to boiling; reduce heat. Simmer for 5 minutes.

2 Using a slotted spoon, divide meat and vegetables among French rolls. Serve with bowls of cooking liquid for dipping.

nutrition facts per serving: 367 cal., 13 g total fat (6 g sat. fat), 65 mg chol., 850 mg sodium, 31 g carbo., 3 g dietary fiber, 31 g protein.

Lo mein is a popular dish in Asian restaurants. But you won't have to leave the house for this 20-minute dish. And, you'll save serious cash to boot.

shredded beef lo mein

start to finish: 20 minutes   makes: 4 to 6 servings

12 ounces dried lo mein noodles, Chinese egg noodles, or fettuccine
 1 tablespoon vegetable oil
 1 large onion, sliced
 1 16-ounce package frozen broccoli, carrots, red peppers, celery, water chestnuts, and mushrooms stir-fry vegetables
 2 cups Shredded Beef Master Recipe (page 254)
 1 12.1-ounce jar stir-fry sauce
 1 4-ounce can (drained weight) sliced mushrooms, drained
 ⅓ cup coarsely chopped cashews
 2 green onions, cut into thin strips

1 Prepare noodles according to package directions; set aside.

2 In a large skillet or wok heat oil over medium-high heat. Cook and stir onion in hot oil for 2 minutes. Add frozen stir-fry vegetables; cook and stir for about 5 minutes more or until crisp-tender. Add shredded beef, stir-fry sauce, and mushrooms. Heat until bubbly.

3 Serve with noodles. Top with cashews and green onions.

nutrition facts per serving: 726 cal., 17 g total fat (4 g sat. fat), 124 mg chol., 2295 mg sodium, 93 g carbo., 7 g dietary fiber, 48 g protein.

Philadelphia is famous for its beef sandwiches. It might not be reasonable to fly off for a sammy. So, try this version at home to satisfy your Philly fetish.

philly shredded beef sandwiches

start to finish: 25 minutes   makes: 4 servings

1   tablespoon olive oil
1   large onion, cut into thin wedges
2   cloves garlic, minced
2   cups Shredded Beef Master Recipe (page 254)
⅓   cup beef broth
5   bottled pepperoncini salad peppers, stems removed and thinly sliced
1   teaspoon dried oregano, crushed
1   teaspoon paprika
½   teaspoon ground black pepper
¼   teaspoon salt
¼   teaspoon celery seeds
4   slices Monterey Jack cheese
8   slices sourdough bread, toasted
2   tablespoons mayonnaise

1 In a large skillet heat oil over medium-high heat. Cook onion and garlic in hot oil for about 5 minutes or until tender. Add shredded beef, broth, pepperoncini peppers, oregano, paprika, black pepper, salt, and celery seeds. Bring to boiling; reduce heat. Simmer, uncovered, for about 5 minutes or until heated through and liquid nearly evaporates.

2 Place Monterey Jack cheese slices on half of the bread slices. Spread mayonnaise on one side of the remaining bread slices. Spoon meat mixture over cheese slices. Top with remaining bread slices, mayonnaise side down.

nutrition facts per serving: 518 cal., 23 g total fat (9 g sat. fat), 78 mg chol., 1212 mg sodium, 37 g carbo., 3 g dietary fiber, 39 g protein.

This sassy beef mixture with tomatoes, chiles, and sweet peppers is great served over rice. Or tuck it and some cheese into a warmed flour tortilla. Yum.

ropa vieja

start to finish: 25 minutes   makes: 4 servings

1 In a large skillet heat oil over medium-high heat. Cook onion, sweet peppers, and garlic in hot oil for about 5 minutes or until crisp-tender. Add shredded beef, tomatoes, vinegar, cumin, salt, and black pepper. Bring to boiling; reduce heat. Simmer, uncovered, for about 5 minutes or until heated through. Serve over rice.

- 1 tablespoon vegetable oil
- 1 large onion, cut into thin wedges
- 1 cup thin green sweet pepper strips (1 medium)
- 1 cup thin red sweet pepper strips (1 medium)
- 3 cloves garlic, minced
- 2 cups Shredded Beef Master Recipe (page 254)
- 1 14.5-ounce can diced tomatoes and green chiles, undrained
- 1 tablespoon red wine vinegar
- 1 teaspoon ground cumin
- ¼ teaspoon salt
- ¼ teaspoon ground black pepper
- Hot cooked rice

nutrition facts per serving: 359 cal., 9 g total fat (2 g sat. fat), 50 mg chol., 1103 mg sodium, 38 g carbo., 4 g dietary fiber, 30 g protein.

This dish has all the favorites of Mexican fare wrapped up in a flour tortilla. The cucumber-jicama salsa adds a new twist.

shredded **beef, bean,** and **corn** tacos

start to finish: 25 minutes   makes: 6 servings

1	tablespoon olive oil
1	small red onion, cut into thin wedges
2	cloves garlic, minced
2	cups Shredded Beef Master Recipe (page 254)
1	14.5-ounce can Mexican-style stewed tomatoes, undrained and cut up
1	cup frozen whole kernel corn
1	cup canned black beans, rinsed and drained
2	teaspoons chili powder
½	cup seeded and chopped cucumber (1 small)
½	cup peeled and chopped jicama
1	tablespoon snipped fresh cilantro
6	7- to 8-inch flour tortillas, warmed*
½	cup sour cream and/or purchased guacamole

1 In a large skillet heat oil over medium heat. Cook onion and garlic in hot oil for about 4 minutes or until tender. Stir in shredded beef, tomatoes, corn, beans, and chili powder. Bring to boiling; reduce heat. Simmer, uncovered, for about 5 minutes or until heated through and desired consistency is reached.

2 Meanwhile, in a small bowl combine cucumber, jicama, and cilantro. Divide meat and vegetables among tortillas. Serve with cucumber mixture and sour cream and/or guacamole.

nutrition facts per serving: 367 cal., 13 g total fat (4 g sat. fat), 40 mg chol., 521 mg sodium, 37 g carbo., 4 g dietary fiber, 26 g protein.

*test kitchen tip: To warm tortillas, wrap in foil and place in a 350°F oven for 10 minutes.

Set out bowls of the succulent Asian-seasoned beef mixture and a platter of lettuce leaves so diners can create their own works of wraps.

asian beef-lettuce wraps

prep: 20 minutes cook: 8 to 10 hours (low) or 4 to 5 hours (high) + 15 minutes
makes: 12 servings

1   3-pound boneless
      beef chuck pot roast
1½ cups diced jicama
      or chopped celery
½   cup chopped green
      onions (4)
¼   cup rice vinegar
¼   cup reduced-sodium
      soy sauce
2   tablespoons hoisin
      sauce
1   tablespoon finely
      chopped fresh
      ginger
½   teaspoon salt
½   teaspoon chili oil
¼   teaspoon ground
      black pepper
2   tablespoons
      cornstarch
2   tablespoons cold
      water
24 Bibb or Boston
      lettuce leaves

1 Trim fat from meat. If necessary, cut meat to fit in a 3½- or 4-quart slow cooker. Place meat in cooker. In a medium bowl combine jicama, green onions, vinegar, soy sauce, hoisin sauce, ginger, salt, chili oil, and pepper. Pour over meat.

2 Cover and cook on low-heat setting for 8 to 10 hours or on high-heat setting for 4 to 5 hours.

3 If using low-heat setting, turn to high-heat setting. In a small bowl combine cornstarch and the cold water. Stir cornstarch mixture into liquid around the meat. Cover and cook for about 15 minutes more or until thickened.

4 Remove meat from cooker. Using two forks, pull meat apart into shreds. Return meat to cooker; stir. Spoon meat mixture onto lettuce leaves. Fold bottom edge of each lettuce leaf up and over filling. Fold in opposite sides; roll up from bottom.

nutrition facts per serving: 168 cal., 4 g total fat (1 g sat. fat), 67 mg chol., 401 mg sodium, 5 g carbo., 0 g dietary fiber, 25 g protein.

The cheesesteak sandwich is said to have originated in Philadelphia in the 1930s. We updated the classic by bundling the meat and cheese in flour tortillas.

philadelphia
cheesesteak wraps

prep: 20 minutes   cook: 10 to 12 hours (low) or 5 to 6 hours (high)
makes: 6 servings

1   tablespoon cooking
    oil
1   pound beef flank
    steak
1   cup red sweet pepper
    strips
1   cup thin onion
    wedges
1½ teaspoons dried
    Italian seasoning,
    crushed
1   14-ounce can beef
    broth
½   cup mayonnaise
4   teaspoons prepared
    horseradish
6   10-inch flour tortillas
3   slices provolone
    cheese slices,
    halved

1 In a large skillet, heat oil over medium-high heat. Cook meat on both sides in hot oil until brown. Place pepper strips, onion wedges, and Italian seasoning in a 4- to 5-quart slow cooker. Top with flank steak. Pour beef broth over mixture in cooker.

2 Cover and cook on low-heat setting for 10 to 12 hours or on high-heat setting for 5 to 6 hours.

3 Remove meat from slow cooker and slice. In a small bowl combine mayonnaise and prepared horseradish. Place sliced meat along the center of each tortilla. Using a slotted spoon, divide pepper and onion mixture over beef. Top with half a slice of provolone cheese. Roll tortilla tightly.

nutrition facts per serving: 484 cal., 30 g total fat (8 g sat. fat), 48 mg chol., 627 mg sodium, 27 g carbo., 2 g dietary fiber, 25 g protein.

Queso fresco (KAY-so FRES-ko) means "fresh cheese" in Spanish. It tastes similar to feta. Although optional, it adds a great flavor to this recipe.

spicy steak and beans

prep: 25 minutes   cook: 7 to 8 hours (low) or 3½ to 4 hours (high) + 30 minutes
makes: 6 servings

1½   pounds beef flank
       steak
  1   10-ounce can diced
       tomatoes and green
       chiles, undrained
  ½   cup chopped onion
       (1 medium)
  2   cloves garlic, minced
  1   tablespoon snipped
       fresh oregano or
       1 teaspoon dried
       oregano, crushed
  1   teaspoon chili
       powder
  1   teaspoon ground
       cumin
  ¼   teaspoon salt
  ¼   teaspoon ground
       black pepper
  1   cup thin green, red,
       and/or yellow sweet
       pepper strips
       (2 small)
  1   15-ounce can pinto
       beans, rinsed and
       drained
  2   cups hot cooked
       brown rice
       Crumbled queso
       fresco or feta
       cheese (optional)

1 Trim fat from meat. Place meat in a 3½- or 4-quart slow cooker. In a bowl stir together tomatoes, onion, garlic, dried oregano (if using), chili powder, cumin, salt, and black pepper. Pour over meat.

2 Cover and cook on low-heat setting for 7 to 8 hours or on high-heat setting for 3½ to 4 hours.

3 If using low-heat setting, turn to high-heat setting. Stir in sweet peppers and beans. Cover and cook for 30 minutes more. Remove meat to a cutting board; cool slightly. Using two forks, pull meat apart into shreds or thinly slice meat across the grain. Stir fresh oregano (if using) into bean mixture.

4 Spoon rice into soup bowls. Top rice with meat. Spoon bean mixture over meat. If desired, sprinkle with queso fresco.

nutrition facts per serving: 262 cal., 8 g total fat (3 g sat. fat), 45 mg chol., 452 mg sodium, 17 g carbo., 4 g dietary fiber, 29 g protein.

This recipe makes enough for two sandwiches and requires a 1½-quart slow cooker. For four servings, double the ingredients and use a 3½-quart cooker.

italian beef sandwiches

prep: 15 minutes   cook: 7 to 8 hours (low), 3½ to 4 hours (high), or 6 to 7 hours (no heat setting)   makes: 2 sandwiches

- 6 ounces beef flank steak
- ½ teaspoon dried oregano, crushed
- 1 clove garlic, minced Dash crushed red pepper
- ½ cup low-sodium tomato juice
- ¼ cup bottled roasted red sweet pepper strips (optional)
- 2 4-inch-long pieces French bread, split and toasted
- ¼ cup shredded provolone cheese (1 ounce)

1 Trim fat from meat. If necessary, cut meat to fit into a 1½-quart slow cooker. Place meat in cooker. Sprinkle meat with oregano, garlic, and crushed red pepper. Pour tomato juice over meat.

2 Cover and cook on low-heat setting for 7 to 8 hours or on high-heat setting for 3½ to 4 hours. (If no heat setting is available, cook for 6 to 7 hours.)

3 Remove meat from cooker. Reserve cooking liquid. Using two forks, pull meat apart into shreds. If desired, combine roasted pepper strips with meat. Divide meat among bottoms of French bread pieces. Drizzle enough of the cooking liquid over meat to moisten. Sprinkle meat with provolone cheese. Cover with tops of French bread pieces.

nutrition facts per sandwich: 302 cal., 11 g total fat (5 g sat. fat), 44 mg chol., 442 mg sodium, 23 g carbo., 2 g dietary fiber, 26 g protein.

Stuffed with veggies and Parmesan cheese, these beef bundles cook up moist and tender in meatless spaghetti sauce from a jar.

italian steak rolls

prep: 35 minutes cook: 8 to 10 hours (low) or 4 to 5 hours (high)
makes: 6 servings

½ cup shredded carrot
⅓ cup chopped zucchini
⅓ cup chopped red or
    green sweet pepper
¼ cup sliced green
    onions (2)
2 tablespoons grated
    Parmesan cheese
1 tablespoon snipped
    fresh parsley
1 clove garlic, minced
¼ teaspoon ground
    black pepper
6 tenderized beef
    round steaks (about
    2 pounds total)*
2 cups purchased
    meatless spaghetti
    sauce

1 For vegetable filling, in a small bowl combine carrot, zucchini, red sweet pepper, green onions, Parmesan cheese, parsley, garlic, and black pepper. Spoon ¼ cup of the vegetable filling onto each piece of meat. Roll up meat around the filling; secure with clean 100-percent-cotton kitchen string or wooden toothpicks.

2 Place meat rolls in a 3½- or 4-quart slow cooker. Pour spaghetti sauce over meat rolls.

3 Cover and cook on low-heat setting for 8 to 10 hours or on high-heat setting for 4 to 5 hours.

4 Discard string or toothpicks. Serve cooking liquid with meat rolls.

nutrition facts per serving: 261 cal., 9 g total fat (3 g sat. fat), 73 mg chol., 523 mg sodium, 7 g carbo., 2 g dietary fiber, 36 g protein.

*test kitchen tip: If you can't find tenderized round steak, ask a butcher to tenderize 2 pounds boneless beef round steak and cut it into six pieces. Or cut 2 pounds boneless beef round steak into six serving-size pieces; place each steak piece between two pieces of plastic wrap. Using a meat mallet, pound the steak pieces until ¼ to ½ inch thick.

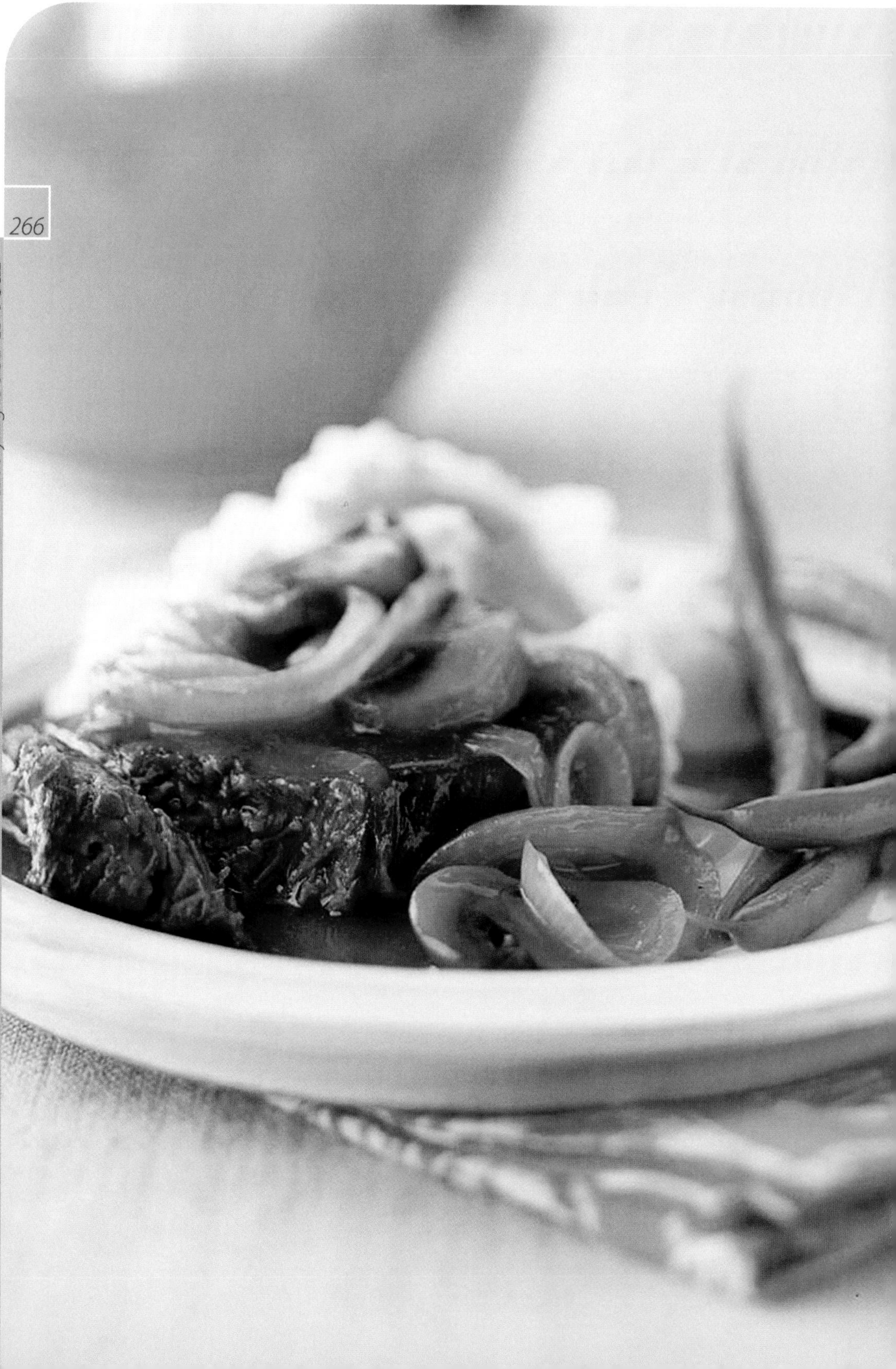

Add a jar of beef gravy to this slow-cooker meat recipe and you get a smooth sauce that's the perfect consistency for topping mashed potatoes or noodles.

mushroom-and-onion-sauced
round steak

prep: 20 minutes   cook: 8 to 10 hours (low) or 4 to 5 hours (high)
makes: 8 servings

2 pounds boneless beef
   round steak, cut
   ¾ inch thick
1 tablespoon vegetable
   oil
2 medium onions,
   sliced
3 cups sliced fresh
   mushrooms
1 12-ounce jar beef
   gravy
1 1.1-ounce package
   dry mushroom
   gravy mix
   Mashed potatoes or
   hot cooked noodles
   (optional)

1 Trim fat from meat. Cut meat into eight serving-size pieces. In a large skillet heat oil over medium-high heat. Cook meat, half at a time, in hot oil until brown. Drain off fat. Place onions in a 3½- or 4-quart slow cooker. Top with meat and mushrooms. In a small bowl combine beef gravy and mushroom gravy mix. Pour over mixture in cooker.

2 Cover and cook on low-heat setting for 8 to 10 hours or on high-heat setting for 4 to 5 hours. If desired, serve over mashed potatoes or noodles.

nutrition facts per serving: 194 cal., 7 g total fat (2 g sat. fat), 57 mg chol., 479 mg sodium, 7 g carbo., 1 g dietary fiber, 24 g protein.

For a whole new dish, vary the stewed tomatoes—Cajun-, Mexican-, or Italian-style—each time you make this simple standby.

pepper steak

prep: 15 minutes cook: 10 to 12 hours (low) or 5 to 6 hours (high)
makes: 8 servings

2	pounds boneless beef round steak, cut ¾ to 1 inch thick
	Salt
	Ground black pepper
1	14.5-ounce can Cajun-, Mexican-, or Italian-style stewed tomatoes, undrained
⅓	cup tomato paste with Italian seasoning
½	teaspoon bottled hot pepper sauce
1	16-ounce package frozen sweet pepper and onion stir-fry vegetables
	Hot cooked whole wheat pasta (optional)

1 Trim fat from meat. Cut meat into eight serving-size pieces. Sprinkle lightly with salt and pepper. Place meat in a 3½- or 4-quart slow cooker. In a medium bowl combine tomatoes, tomato paste, and hot pepper sauce. Pour over meat. Top with stir-fry vegetables.

2 Cover and cook on low-heat setting for 10 to 12 hours or on high-heat setting for 5 to 6 hours. If desired, serve with hot cooked pasta.

nutrition facts per serving: 196 cal., 5 g total fat (2 g sat. fat), 54 mg chol., 411 mg sodium, 9 g carbo., 1 g dietary fiber, 27 g protein.

Browning the steak pieces adds a step and a few minutes of prep time but yields appetizing color and richer flavor.

italian round steak dinner

prep: 20 minutes cook: 9 to 10 hours (low) or 4½ to 5 hours (high)
makes: 8 servings

2¼ pounds boneless
    beef round steak
    Salt
    Ground black pepper
1 tablespoon vegetable
    oil
1 large fennel bulb,
    trimmed and cut
    into thin wedges
1 large onion, halved
    and thinly sliced
1 cup packaged fresh
    carrots cut in bite-
    size strips
1 28-ounce can
    crushed tomatoes,
    undrained
1 15-ounce can tomato
    sauce
½ cup beef broth
2 teaspoons dried
    Italian seasoning,
    crushed
⅛ teaspoon crushed
    red pepper
6 cups hot cooked
    pasta
¼ cup finely shredded
    Parmesan cheese

1 Cut meat into eight serving-size pieces; sprinkle lightly with salt and black pepper. In a large skillet heat oil over medium-high heat. Cook meat, half at a time, in hot oil until brown.

2 In a 4- or 4½-quart slow cooker combine fennel, onion, and carrots. Top vegetables with meat. In a large bowl combine tomatoes, tomato sauce, broth, Italian seasoning, and crushed red pepper. Pour over mixture in cooker.

3 Cover and cook on low-heat setting for 9 to 10 hours or on high-heat setting for 4½ to 5 hours.

4 Divide hot cooked pasta among eight dinner plates; top each with a meat portion and some of the cooking liquid. Sprinkle with Parmesan cheese.

nutrition facts per serving: 434 cal., 9 g total fat (3 g sat. fat), 72 mg chol., 764 mg sodium, 47 g carbo., 6 g dietary fiber, 38 g protein.

If you don't have time to make mashed potatoes from scratch, stop by the supermarket and pick up some refrigerated mashed potatoes; just heat and serve.

country swiss steak

prep: 20 minutes cook: 10 to 12 hours (low) or 5 to 6 hours (high)
makes: 4 servings

1   pound boneless beef
    round steak, cut
    ¾ to 1 inch thick
1   tablespoon vegetable
    oil
1   small onion, sliced
    and separated into
    rings
2   tablespoons quick-
    cooking tapioca
1   teaspoon dried
    thyme, crushed
¼   teaspoon salt
¼   teaspoon ground
    black pepper
1   14-ounce can chunky
    tomatoes with
    garlic and spices,
    undrained
4   cups hot mashed
    potatoes
    Fresh thyme sprigs
    (optional)

1 Trim fat from meat. Cut meat into four serving-size pieces. In a large skillet heat oil over medium heat. Cook meat in hot oil, turning to brown evenly. Drain off fat.

2 Place onion in a 3½- or 4-quart slow cooker. Sprinkle with tapioca, dried thyme, salt, and pepper. Pour tomatoes over onion. Top with meat.

3 Cover and cook on low-heat setting for 10 to 12 hours or on high-heat setting for 5 to 6 hours.

4 Serve with hot mashed potatoes. If desired, garnish with thyme.

nutrition facts per serving: 481 cal., 16 g total fat (5 g sat. fat), 89 mg chol., 1405 mg sodium, 50 g carbo., 4 g dietary fiber, 31 g protein.

Proportioned for a small cooker and two or three servings, these beef strips get their devilish kick from horseradish mustard.

deviled steak strips

prep: 20 minutes cook: 6 to 8 hours (low), 3 to 4 hours (high), or 5 to 6 hours (no heat setting) makes: 2 or 3 servings

12 ounces boneless
    beef round steak
1   8-ounce can tomato
    sauce
½   cup chopped onion
    (1 medium)
1   4-ounce can (drained
    weight) sliced
    mushrooms,
    drained
¼   cup water
1   tablespoon
    horseradish
    mustard
1   tablespoon quick-
    cooking tapioca*
1   teaspoon instant beef
    bouillon granules
⅛   teaspoon ground
    black pepper
1   to 1½ cups hot
    mashed potatoes
    Sour cream (optional)
    Snipped fresh chives
    (optional)

1 Trim fat from meat. Thinly slice meat across the grain into bite-size strips. In a 1½-quart slow cooker combine tomato sauce, onion, mushrooms, the water, horseradish mustard, tapioca, bouillon granules, and pepper. Stir meat strips into mixture in cooker.

2 Cover and cook on low-heat setting for 6 to 8 hours or on high-heat setting for 3 to 4 hours. (If no heat setting is available, cook for 5 to 6 hours.)

3 Serve over mashed potatoes. If desired, top with sour cream and chives.

nutrition facts per serving: 407 cal., 9 g total fat (3 g sat. fat), 83 mg chol., 1627 mg sodium, 36 g carbo., 5 g dietary fiber, 43 g protein.

*test kitchen tip: For a smoother sauce, grind the tapioca in a coffee grinder or blender.

Adding cabbage, mushrooms, and sauce just before the meat is finished cooking ensures that each part of the meal is just the right doneness at serving time.

russian braised brisket

prep: 20 minutes   cook: 10 hours (low) or 5 hours (high) + 30 to 60 minutes
makes: 6 servings

1   2- to 3-pound beef
      brisket
     Salt
     Ground black pepper
1   tablespoon vegetable
      oil
1   large onion, cut into
      wedges
2   medium parsnips, cut
      into 2-inch pieces
2   medium carrots, cut
      into 2-inch pieces
½   teaspoon dill seeds
½   teaspoon caraway
      seeds
¼   teaspoon salt
1½ cups beef broth
¼   cup vodka (optional)
1   8-ounce carton sour
      cream
⅓   cup all-purpose flour
¼   cup water
2   teaspoons dried dill
2   teaspoons
      horseradish
      mustard
2   cups finely shredded
      cabbage
1   cup sliced fresh
      mushrooms

1 Trim fat from meat. Cut meat to fit into a 3½- or 4-quart slow cooker. Sprinkle meat with salt and pepper. In a large skillet heat oil over medium-high heat. Cook meat on all sides in hot oil until brown.

2 In the slow cooker combine onion, parsnips, and carrots. Sprinkle with dill seeds, caraway seeds, and ¼ teaspoon salt. Top with meat. Pour broth and vodka, if desired, over mixture in cooker.

3 Cover and cook on low-heat setting for 10 hours or on high-heat setting for 5 hours.

4 If using low-heat setting, turn to high-heat setting. In a medium bowl stir together sour cream, flour, the water, dill, and mustard until smooth. Stir about 1 cup of the hot cooking liquid into the sour cream mixture. Add to cooker, stirring to combine. Stir in cabbage and mushrooms. Cover and cook for 30 to 60 minutes more or until vegetables are tender and liquid is thickened and bubbly.

5 Transfer meat to a serving platter; slice thinly across the grain. Using a slotted spoon, transfer vegetables to platter. Serve cooking liquid with meat and vegetables.

nutrition facts per serving: 379 cal., 17 g total fat (7 g sat. fat), 79 mg chol., 589 mg sodium, 20 g carbo., 4 g dietary fiber, 37 g protein.

This easy-to-fix steak tastes sassy and lively, just like the classic cocktail. Hot-style tomato juice is the base for the sauce.

bloody mary steak

prep: 20 minutes   cook: 8 to 9 hours (low) or 4 to 4½ hours (high)
makes: 6 servings

1   2-pound beef round
    steak, cut ¾ inch
    thick
    Nonstick cooking
    spray
¾   cup hot-style tomato
    juice
¼   cup water
2   cloves garlic, minced
2   tablespoons cold
    water
4   teaspoons cornstarch
2   teaspoons prepared
    horseradish
    Salt
    Ground black pepper

1 Trim fat from meat. Cut meat into six serving-size pieces. Lightly coat a large skillet with cooking spray. Heat skillet over medium-high heat. Add meat pieces; cook until brown, turning once. Place meat in a 2½- to 3½-quart slow cooker. Add tomato juice, the ¼ cup water, and garlic.

2 Cover and cook on low-heat setting for 8 to 9 hours or on high-heat setting for 4 to 4½ hours.

3 Transfer meat to a serving platter. Reserve cooking liquid. If desired, slice meat. Cover and keep warm.

4 For gravy, strain cooking liquid into a 2-cup glass measuring cup. Skim off fat. Add water if necessary to make 1½ cups liquid. Pour into a small saucepan. In a small bowl combine the 2 tablespoons cold water and the cornstarch; stir into liquid in saucepan. Cook and stir over medium heat until thickened and bubbly. Cook and stir for 2 minutes more. Stir in horseradish. Season to taste with salt and pepper. Serve meat with gravy.

nutrition facts per serving: 196 cal., 4 g total fat (1 g sat. fat), 85 mg chol., 292 mg sodium, 3 g carbo., 0 g dietary fiber, 35 g protein.

Brisket benefits from the long cooking time, so simmer it on low heat if your slow cooker has a high/low option. It will reward you with ultra-tenderness.

tangy barbecue
beef sandwiches

prep: 25 minutes   cook: 10 to 12 hours (low)   stand: 15 minutes
makes: 8 sandwiches

2	tablespoons chili powder
1	teaspoon celery seeds
½	teaspoon salt
½	teaspoon ground black pepper
1	3-pound fresh beef brisket
2	medium onions, thinly sliced
1	cup bottled smoke-flavor barbecue sauce
½	cup beer or ginger ale
8	kaiser or Portuguese rolls, split and toasted
	Bottled hot pepper sauce (optional)
	Mango slices

1 In a small bowl combine chili powder, celery seeds, salt, and pepper. Trim fat from meat. Sprinkle chili mixture evenly over meat and rub in with your fingers. If necessary, cut meat to fit into a 3½- to 6-quart slow cooker; set aside.

2 Place half of the onions in the cooker. Top with meat and remaining onions. In a small bowl stir together barbecue sauce and beer. Pour over meat and onions.

3 Cover and cook on low-heat setting for 10 to 12 hours. Remove meat from cooker. Let stand for 15 minutes. Using two forks, pull meat apart into shreds. Return meat to cooker; heat through.

4 Using a slotted spoon, spoon meat mixture over roll bottoms. If desired, season to taste with hot pepper sauce. Top with mango slices; add roll tops.

nutrition facts per sandwich: 434 cal., 10 g total fat (3 g sat. fat), 72 mg chol., 992 mg sodium, 52 g carbo., 3 g dietary fiber, 31 g protein.

Hoisin sauce and salsa might sound like an odd couple to season pot roast, but they harmonize perfectly in this meat-and-potato dish.

hoisin beef brisket

prep: 20 minutes   cook: 10 to 11 hours (low) or 5 to 5½ hours (high)
makes: 8 servings

3   medium baking potatoes, peeled and cut into 1-inch cubes

2   medium sweet potatoes, peeled and cut into 1-inch cubes

1   3- to 3½ -pound fresh beef brisket

½   cup bottled hoisin sauce

½   cup bottled salsa

2   tablespoons quick-cooking tapioca

2   cloves garlic, minced

1 In a 5- to 6-quart slow cooker combine baking potatoes and sweet potatoes. Trim fat from meat; top potatoes with meat. In a small bowl combine hoisin sauce, salsa, tapioca, and garlic. Pour over meat, spreading evenly.

2 Cover and cook on low-heat setting for 10 to 11 hours or on high-heat setting for 5 to 5½ hours.

3 Transfer meat to a serving platter; slice across the grain. Using a slotted spoon, transfer potatoes to platter. Serve cooking liquid with meat and potatoes.

nutrition facts per serving: 344 cal., 11 g total fat (3 g sat. fat), 103 mg chol., 382 mg sodium, 22 g carbo., 2 g dietary fiber, 38 g protein.

Long and slow—that's what this dish takes to make it meltingly tender. Add the vegetables after 5 hours of cooking time and cook for an additional 3 hours.

corned beef and cabbage

prep: 15 minutes cook: 8 hours (low) makes: 10 servings

8 whole cloves
1 medium onion, halved
1 lean center-cut corned beef brisket (about 2 pounds)
3 large carrots, quartered lengthwise and cut into 2-inch pieces
8 ounces tiny new potatoes, halved
8 ounces boiling onions, peeled
1 small head cabbage, outer leaves removed, cut into 6 wedges

1 Stick cloves in halved onion. In a 3½- or 4-quart slow cooker combine onion and meat. Add enough water to cover ingredients plus 3 more inches. Cover and cook on low-heat setting for 5 hours.

2 Add carrots, potatoes, boiling onions, and cabbage to slow cooker. Cover and cook for 3 hours more.

3 Transfer meat to serving platter; slice. Using a slotted spoon, remove vegetables from cooker. Reserve cooking liquid. Arrange vegetables around sliced meat. Serve with cooking liquid.

nutrition facts per serving: 238 cal., 14 g total fat (4 g sat. fat), 49 mg chol., 1026 mg sodium, 13 g carbo., 3 g dietary fiber, 15 g protein.

This is slow cooking at its best. Everything—main dish and sides— cook together for a meal you'll anticipate all day. Beer adds an interesting flavor note.

braised corned beef dinner

prep: 15 minutes   cook: 10 to 11 hours (low) or 5 to 5½ hours (high)
makes: 4 servings

4   medium red-skinned potatoes, quartered
4   carrots, cut into 1½-inch pieces
2   medium onions, cut into thin wedges
2   teaspoons dried thyme, crushed
1   bay leaf
1   3-pound corned beef brisket, juices and spices reserved
1   12-ounce bottle light beer

1 In a 5- to 6-quart slow cooker combine potatoes, carrots, onions, thyme, and bay leaf. Trim fat from meat. Top vegetables with meat. Pour reserved juices and spices from brisket and the beer over mixture in cooker.

2 Cover and cook on low-heat setting for 10 to 11 hours or on high-heat setting for 5 to 5½ hours.

3 Remove bay leaf and discard. Transfer meat to a serving platter; thinly slice across the grain. Using a slotted spoon, transfer vegetables to a serving bowl. Reserve cooking liquid. Serve cooking liquid with meat and vegetables.

nutrition facts per serving: 478 cal., 21 g total fat (6 g sat. fat), 86 mg chol., 1195 mg sodium, 37 g carbo., 5 g dietary fiber, 29 g protein.

Classic corned beef and cabbage is truly an all-time favorite. For those die-hard fans, here is a gem that is topped with a pickled beet relish.

new england boiled
dinner with beet relish

prep: 30 minutes   cook: 8 to 10 hours (low) or 4 to 5 hours (high) + 30 to 60 minutes
makes: 6 to 8 servings

3   medium potatoes, peeled and cut into 2-inch pieces
4   medium carrots, cut into 2-inch lengths
1   large onion, quartered
1   2- to 3-pound corned beef brisket with spice packet
1   teaspoon snipped fresh thyme
½   teaspoon dill seeds
⅛   teaspoon ground nutmeg
1   14-ounce can beef broth
1   small head cabbage, cut into 8 wedges
    Beet Relish

1 In a 3½- or 4-quart slow cooker combine potatoes, carrots, and onion. Trim fat from meat. Sprinkle spices from packet, thyme, dill seeds, and nutmeg evenly over the meat and rub in with your fingers. If necessary, cut meat to fit into the slow cooker. Top vegetables with meat. Pour broth over mixture in cooker.

2 Cover and cook on low-heat setting for 8 to 10 hours or on high-heat setting for 4 to 5 hours.

3 If using low-heat setting, turn to high-heat setting. Add cabbage wedges, tucking them down into the cooking liquid. Cover and cook for 30 to 60 minutes more or until cabbage is tender.

4 Transfer meat to a serving platter; thinly slice meat across the grain. Using a slotted spoon, transfer vegetables to platter. Serve with Beet Relish.

nutrition facts per serving: 576 cal., 34 g total fat (10 g sat. fat), 148 mg chol., 2246 mg sodium, 36 g carbo., 8 g dietary fiber, 32 g protein.

beet relish: In a medium bowl combine one 15- to 16-ounce jar sliced pickled beets, drained and chopped, and ⅓ cup finely chopped red onion. For dressing, in a screw-top jar, combine 2 tablespoons olive oil; 2 tablespoons cider vinegar; 2 teaspoons coarse-grain brown mustard; 1 clove garlic, minced; and dash cayenne pepper. Cover; shake well to combine. Pour over beets; toss to coat. Chill, covered, until ready to serve.

A long-smoked beef brisket is heavenly. But during the week, who has time? You do! Just put it in your slow cooker with smoky barbecue sauce.

saucy brisket

prep: 15 minutes   cook: 12 to 14 hours (low) or 6 to 7 hours (high)
makes: 6 servings + reserves

1   4- to 4½-pound fresh
    beef brisket
    Cracked black pepper
1   16-ounce package
    peeled fresh baby
    carrots
2   stalks celery, cut into
    ½-inch slices
1½ cups smoke-flavor
    barbecue sauce
2   tablespoons quick-
    cooking tapioca,
    crushed
2   tablespoons Dijon-
    style mustard
1   tablespoon
    Worcestershire
    sauce
4   cups hot cooked
    noodles or mashed
    potatoes

1 Trim fat from meat. If necessary, cut meat to fit into a 5- to 6-quart slow cooker. Sprinkle meat with pepper. In the slow cooker combine carrots and celery. Top vegetables with meat. In a small bowl combine barbecue sauce, tapioca, mustard, and Worcestershire sauce. Pour over mixture in cooker.

2 Cover and cook on low-heat setting for 12 to 14 hours or on high-heat setting for 6 to 7 hours.

3 Transfer meat to cutting board; cut meat in half. Reserve half of the meat; store as directed below. Thinly slice remaining meat across the grain; transfer to a bowl. Using a slotted spoon, transfer vegetables to bowl. Skim fat from cooking liquid. Serve cooking liquid with meat and vegetables over hot cooked noodles.

nutrition facts per serving: 411 cal., 21 g total fat (9 g sat. fat), 84 mg chol., 583 mg sodium, 23 g carbo., 2 g dietary fiber, 32 g protein.

to store reserves: Place reserved meat in an airtight container. Seal and chill for up to 3 days. ***Use in Chutney-Beef Panini, page 281.***

Leftovers from Saucy Brisket are masterful in a sandwich topped with purchased mango chutney and provolone cheese.

chutney-beef panini

prep: 10 minutes cook: 5 minutes makes: 6 sandwiches

½ cup mango chutney
12 slices whole wheat bread
Reserved brisket from Saucy Brisket (page 280)
6 slices provolone cheese
Olive oil or melted butter

1 Finely chop chutney. Spread chutney evenly on one side of each bread slice. Thinly slice meat; arrange on six of the bread slices. Top with provolone cheese. Cover with remaining bread slices, chutney sides down. Lightly brush bread with olive oil.

2 Preheat an indoor grill, griddle, or skillet over medium heat or heat according to manufacturer's directions. Place sandwiches, a few at a time, on the hot grill, griddle, or skillet. If using a covered indoor grill, close lid and grill for 5 to 6 minutes or until bread is toasted and cheese melts. (If using an uncovered indoor grill, griddle, or skillet, place a heavy plate on top of the sandwiches. Cook for 2 to 3 minutes or until bottoms are toasted. Carefully remove plate, turn sandwiches over, and top again with the plate. Cook for 2 to 3 minutes more or until bread is toasted and cheese melts.)

nutrition facts per sandwich: 411 cal., 21 g total fat (4 g sat. fat), 84 mg chol., 583 mg sodium, 23 g carbo., 2 g dietary fiber, 32 g protein.

*Got the weeknight "what's for dinner" blues? You'll sing
another tune when you come home to a tender brisket with
a wine-enhanced sauce.*

wine-braised beef brisket

prep: 30 minutes   cook: 10 to 12 hours (low) or 5 to 6 hours (high)
makes: 6 servings + reserves

1   4-pound fresh beef
    brisket
4   medium carrots, cut
    diagonally into
    2-inch pieces
1   cup finely chopped
    onion (1 large)
1   cup dry red wine
½   of a 6-ounce can
    (⅓ cup) tomato
    paste
2   tablespoons quick-
    cooking tapioca
1   tablespoon
    Worcestershire
    sauce
2   teaspoons garlic salt
2   teaspoons liquid
    smoke
1½ teaspoons chili
    powder
3   cups hot mashed
    potatoes

1 Trim fat from meat. If necessary, cut meat
to fit into a 4- to 5-quart slow cooker. In
the cooker combine carrots and onion. Top
with meat. In a medium bowl stir together
wine, tomato paste, tapioca, Worcestershire
sauce, garlic salt, liquid smoke, and chili
powder. Pour over mixture in cooker.

2 Cover and cook on low-heat setting
for 10 to 12 hours or on high-heat setting
for 5 to 6 hours.

3 Transfer meat to a cutting board; cut meat
in half. Using a slotted spoon, remove
vegetables from cooker. Reserve cooking
liquid. Reserve half of the meat (about 1 pound),
1 cup of the vegetables, and 1 cup of the
cooking liquid; store as directed below.

4 Slice the remaining meat. Serve meat, the
remaining vegetables, and the remaining
cooking liquid with hot mashed potatoes.

nutrition facts per serving: 355 cal., 11 g total fat
(4 g sat. fat), 96 mg chol., 641 mg sodium, 25 g carbo.,
3 g dietary fiber, 33 g protein.

to store reserves: Chop meat (about
4 cups). Place meat in an airtight container.
Place vegetables and cooking liquid in a
second airtight container. Seal and chill for
up to 3 days. *Use in Brisket Pie, page 283.*

Transform Wine-Braised Beef Brisket into a hearty and moist casserole of chopped beef and veggies topped with golden biscuits.

brisket pie

prep: 25 minutes   bake: 30 minutes   stand: 10 minutes   oven: 350°F
makes: 6 servings

Reserved beef and
   vegetable mixture
   from Wine-Braised
   Beef Brisket*
   (page 282)
1   cup frozen whole
      kernel corn
2   cups shredded
      cheddar cheese
      (8 ounces)
½   cup chopped green
      sweet pepper
      (1 small)
2   eggs, lightly beaten
1   cup milk
2   cups packaged
      biscuit mix
¼   teaspoon onion salt

1 Preheat oven to 350°F. In a large saucepan combine the reserved chopped meat and vegetable mixture, corn, ¾ cup of the cheddar cheese, and the green sweet pepper. Bring to boiling, stirring occasionally. Transfer to a 2-quart rectangular baking dish.

2 In a small bowl combine eggs and milk. In a medium bowl stir together biscuit mix and onion salt. Stir in 1 cup of the remaining cheese. Add egg mixture to biscuit mixture, stirring just until moistened. Spoon batter over hot meat mixture in baking dish.

3 Bake for about 30 minutes or until top is lightly browned. Sprinkle with the remaining ¼ cup cheese. Let stand for 10 minutes before serving.

nutrition facts per serving: 653 cal., 32 g total fat (14 g sat. fat), 207 mg chol., 1164 mg sodium, 42 g carbo., 2 g dietary fiber, 48 g protein.

*test kitchen tip: There should be about 4 cups reserved chopped meat and 1 cup reserved vegetables mixed with 1 cup reserved cooking liquid.

Two simple ingredients—beer and chili sauce—do great things to the beef brisket and sliced onions.

beer brisket

prep: 15 minutes   cook: 10 to 12 hours (low) or 5 to 6 hours (high)
makes: 9 to 12 servings

1   3- to 4-pound fresh
    beef brisket
2   large onions, sliced
1   12-ounce bottle
    or can beer
½   cup bottled chili
    sauce
2   teaspoons dried steak
    seasoning
9   to 12 kaiser rolls,
    split and toasted
    (optional)

1 Trim fat from meat. If necessary, cut meat to fit in a 3½- or 4-quart slow cooker. Place onions in cooker. Top with meat. In a medium bowl stir together beer, chili sauce, and steak seasoning. Pour over onions and meat.

2 Cover and cook on low-heat setting for 10 to 12 hours or on high-heat setting for 5 to 6 hours.

3 Transfer meat to a serving platter; thinly slice across the grain. Using a slotted spoon, place the onions over the meat. Drizzle with some of the cooking liquid. If desired, serve sliced meat and onions on kaiser rolls.

nutrition facts per serving: 265 cal., 10 g total fat (4 g sat. fat), 94 mg chol., 378 mg sodium, 8 g carbo., 2 g dietary fiber, 31 g protein.

Gremolata, a sprightly relish made of orange peel, garlic, and parsley, adds freshness to the tender, savory short ribs.

spanish braised short ribs with orange gremolata

prep: 20 minutes   cook: 7 to 8 hours (low) or 3½ to 4 hours (high)
makes: 4 servings

2 pounds beef short ribs or meaty oxtails
Salt
Ground black pepper
1 large onion, cut into wedges
2 medium carrots, cut into 2-inch pieces
4 ounces cooked smoked chorizo sausage, casing removed, chopped
1 14.5-ounce can diced tomatoes, undrained
¼ cup white wine
¼ cup orange juice
2 teaspoons sherry vinegar
1 teaspoon paprika
2 bay leaves
3 tablespoons snipped fresh parsley
6 cloves garlic, minced
1 tablespoon finely shredded orange peel

1 Sprinkle meat with salt and pepper. In a 3½- or 4-quart slow cooker combine onion, carrots, chorizo, and ribs. Add tomatoes, wine, orange juice, vinegar, paprika, and bay leaves.

2 Cover and cook on low-heat setting for 7 to 8 hours or on high-heat setting for 3½ to 4 hours. Discard bay leaves. Skim off fat.

3 For gremolata, in a small bowl combine parsley, garlic, and orange peel.

4 To serve, spoon meat, vegetables, and cooking liquid into shallow bowls. Top with gremolata.

nutrition facts per serving: 360 cal., 20 g total fat (7 g sat. fat), 293 mg chol., 775 mg sodium, 15 g carbo., 4 g dietary fiber, 27 g protein.

Lemon peel brightens this creamy leek and beef dish. Dried herbs are called for, but it deserves fresh rosemary and thyme, if you have them.

satisfying **beef & veal**

short ribs with leeks

prep: 30 minutes   cook: 7 to 8 hours (low) or 3½ to 4 hours (high)
makes: 6 servings

8   ounces fresh
    mushrooms, halved
4   medium carrots, cut
    into 1-inch pieces
4   medium leeks, cut
    into 1-inch slices
2   pounds boneless beef
    short ribs
2   teaspoons finely
    shredded lemon
    peel
½   teaspoon ground
    black pepper
½   teaspoon dried
    rosemary, crushed
½   teaspoon dried
    thyme, crushed
¼   teaspoon salt
¾   cup beef broth
⅓   cup sour cream
1   tablespoon
    all-purpose flour

1 In a 3½- or 4-quart slow cooker combine mushrooms, carrots, and leeks. Top with meat. Sprinkle with lemon peel, pepper, rosemary, thyme, and salt. Pour broth over mixture in cooker.

2 Cover and cook on low-heat setting for 7 to 8 hours or on high-heat setting for 3½ to 4 hours.

3 Using a slotted spoon, transfer meat and vegetables to a serving dish. Reserve cooking liquid. Cover and keep warm.

4 For sauce, skim off fat from cooking liquid. Measure 1 cup cooking liquid; pour into a small saucepan. In a small bowl combine sour cream and flour; whisk into liquid in saucepan. Cook and stir over medium heat until slightly thickened and bubbly. Cook and stir for 1 minute more. Ladle sauce over meat and vegetables.

nutrition facts per serving: 173 cal., 8 g total fat (4 g sat. fat), 33 mg chol., 252 mg sodium, 10 g carbo., 2 g dietary fiber, 15 g protein.

Who would have known that beer, molasses, and balsamic vinegar are flavors that would make meat taste amazing? Try it for yourself.

beer-braised beef short ribs

prep: 15 minutes cook: 11 to 12 hours (low) or 5½ to 6 hours (high)
makes: 4 to 6 servings

5   pounds beef short
     ribs
1   14-ounce can beef
     broth
1   12-ounce can dark
     beer
1   medium onion, cut
     into thin wedges
¼   cup molasses
2   tablespoons balsamic
     vinegar
1   teaspoon dried
     thyme, crushed
1   teaspoon bottled hot
     pepper sauce
½   teaspoon salt
     Mashed potatoes
       or hot buttered
       noodles (optional)
     Fresh thyme leaves
       (optional)

1 Place ribs in a 5- to 6-quart slow cooker. Add broth, beer, onion, molasses, vinegar, dried thyme, hot pepper sauce, and salt.

2 Cover and cook on low-heat setting for 11 to 12 hours or on high-heat setting for 5½ to 6 hours.

3 Using a slotted spoon, transfer ribs to a serving platter. Cover and keep warm. Skim off fat from cooking liquid. Serve cooking liquid with ribs for dipping. If desired, serve ribs with mashed potatoes and garnish with fresh thyme leaves.

nutrition facts per serving: 481 cal., 19 g total fat (8 g sat. fat), 132 mg chol., 821 mg sodium, 22 g carbo., 0 g dietary fiber, 46 g protein.

To make the polenta ahead, before adding the cheese, cover the cooled polenta and hold at room temperature for a couple of hours or chill for several hours. Reheat and add the cheese.

short ribs over
gorgonzola polenta

prep: 20 minutes + 30 minutes (for polenta)   cook: 9 to 10 hours (low) or 4½ to 5 hours (high)   makes: 6 servings

2½   to 3 pounds boneless beef short ribs
2   large onions, cut into thin wedges
1   cup thinly sliced carrots (2 medium)
1   medium fennel bulb, cored and cut into thin wedges
1   14.5-ounce can diced tomatoes, undrained
1   cup dry red wine
2   tablespoons quick-cooking tapioca, crushed
2   tablespoons tomato paste
1   teaspoon dried rosemary, crushed
1   teaspoon salt
½   teaspoon ground black pepper
4   cloves garlic, minced
Gorgonzola Polenta

1 Trim fat from meat. In a 5- to 6-quart slow cooker combine onions, carrots, and fennel. Top with meat.

2 In a small bowl combine tomatoes, wine, tapioca, tomato paste, rosemary, salt, pepper, and garlic. Pour over mixture in cooker.

3 Cover and cook on low-heat setting for 9 to 10 hours or on high-heat setting for 4½ to 5 hours.

4 Meanwhile, prepare Gorgonzola Polenta. To serve, spoon polenta into shallow bowls. Spoon meat and vegetable mixture over polenta.

nutrition facts per serving: 489 cal., 18 g total fat (8 g sat. fat), 113 mg chol., 1121 mg sodium, 32 g carbo., 4 g dietary fiber, 41 g protein.

gorgonzola polenta: In a large saucepan bring 2½ cups water to boiling. Meanwhile, in a bowl stir together 1 cup coarse-ground yellow cornmeal, 1 cup cold water, and ½ teaspoon salt. Slowly add cornmeal mixture to boiling water, stirring constantly. Cook and stir until mixture returns to boiling. Reduce heat to medium low. Cook for 25 to 30 minutes or until very thick, stirring frequently and adjusting heat as necessary to maintain a very slow boil. Stir in ⅓ cup crumbled Gorgonzola cheese or other blue cheese.

Quick-cooking polenta is a faster option than regular polenta or yellow cornmeal. It also is a speedier side-dish alternative to mashed potatoes.

short ribs arrabbiata over polenta

prep: 40 minutes   cook: 6 to 7 hours (low) or 3 to 3½ hours (high)
makes: 8 servings

4	slices pancetta or bacon, chopped
3	pounds boneless beef short ribs
1½	teaspoons salt
½	teaspoon ground black pepper
1	cup chopped onion (1 large)
3	cloves garlic, minced
1	28-ounce can Italian-style whole peeled tomatoes in puree, undrained and cut up
¼	cup dry red wine
1	teaspoon dried basil, crushed
1	teaspoon dried oregano, crushed
¼	to ½ teaspoon crushed red pepper
3¾	cups water
1	cup quick-cooking polenta or cornmeal
¾	cup finely shredded Romano cheese
2	tablespoons snipped fresh basil or parsley

1 In a large skillet cook pancetta until crisp. Using a slotted spoon, remove from skillet. Reserve drippings in skillet. Sprinkle meat with ½ teaspoon of the salt and black pepper. Cook meat on all sides in hot drippings until brown; remove from skillet. Cook onion and garlic in hot drippings until tender. Drain off fat.

2 In a 3½- or 4-quart slow cooker combine pancetta, onion, garlic, and meat. Add tomatoes, wine, dried basil, oregano, ½ teaspoon of the salt, and crushed red pepper.

3 Cover and cook on low-heat setting for 6 to 7 hours or on high-heat setting for 3 to 3½ hours.

4 In a large saucepan bring the water and the remaining ½ teaspoon salt to boiling. Stir in polenta; reduce heat. Cook and stir until thickened and bubbly. Stir in ½ cup of the Romano cheese and fresh basil.

5 To serve, spoon polenta into eight shallow bowls. Divide meat mixture among bowls. Sprinkle with remaining cheese.

nutrition facts per serving: 882 cal., 68 g total fat (30 g sat. fat), 148 mg chol., 1050 mg sodium, 39 g carbo., 5 g dietary fiber, 34 g protein.

Fluffy couscous provides a soothing counterpoint to the spicy short ribs, and will soak up the cooking liquid.

moroccan-style
short ribs

prep: 30 minutes   cook: 9 to 10 hours (low) or 4½ to 5 hours (high)
makes: 8 servings

1 tablespoon dried thyme, crushed
1 teaspoon salt
1 teaspoon ground black pepper
1 teaspoon ground ginger
½ teaspoon ground cinnamon
3½ pounds beef short ribs
2 tablespoons olive oil
3 cups beef broth
1 16-ounce can garbanzo beans (chickpeas), rinsed and drained
1 14.5-ounce can diced tomatoes, undrained
1 large onion, cut into thin wedges
1 medium fennel bulb, cored and cut into thin wedges
1 cup chopped carrots (2 medium)
4 cloves garlic, minced
1 10-ounce package quick-cooking couscous

1 In a small bowl stir together thyme, salt, pepper, ginger, and cinnamon. Sprinkle evenly over meat and rub in with your fingers. In a large skillet heat oil over medium-high heat. Cook meat, half at a time, in hot oil until brown. Drain off fat. In a 6- or 7-quart slow cooker combine broth, beans, tomatoes, onion, fennel, carrots, and garlic. Top with meat.

2 Cover and cook on low-heat setting for 9 to 10 hours or on high-heat setting for 4½ to 5 hours.

3 Using a slotted spoon, transfer meat and vegetables to a serving dish. If desired, drizzle with enough of the cooking liquid to moisten.

4 Meanwhile, prepare couscous according to package directions. Serve couscous with meat and vegetables.

nutrition facts per serving: 512 cal., 11 g total fat (3 g sat. fat), 46 mg chol., 989 mg sodium, 71 g carbo., 7 g dietary fiber, 29 g protein.

Because gochujang, *or chile bean paste, contains a hefty amount of chile peppers, wear plastic or rubber gloves when rubbing it onto the ribs.*

korean beef short ribs

prep: 20 minutes   cook: 6 to 7 hours (low) or 3 to 3½ hours (high)
makes: 6 to 8 servings

1 tablespoon vegetable oil
3 pounds boneless beef short ribs
2 teaspoons gochujang (chile bean paste)
4 cloves garlic
2 teaspoons grated fresh ginger
½ teaspoon paprika
¼ teaspoon ground black pepper
1 cup reduced-sodium beef broth
¼ cup reduced-sodium soy sauce
2 tablespoons vermouth or apple juice
1 tablespoon rice vinegar
1 tablespoon packed brown sugar
1 teaspoon toasted sesame oil
   Finely shredded napa cabbage
2 tablespoons shredded carrot
2 tablespoons sliced green onion (1)
½ teaspoon sesame seeds, toasted

1 In a large skillet heat oil over medium-high heat. Cook meat, half at a time, in hot oil until brown. In a small bowl combine gochujang, garlic, ginger, paprika, and pepper. Wearing plastic gloves, rub mixture into meat.

2 Place meat in a 3½- or 4-quart slow cooker. In a small bowl combine broth, soy sauce, vermouth, vinegar, brown sugar, and sesame oil. Pour over meat.

3 Cover and cook on low-heat setting for 6 to 7 hours or on high-heat setting for 3 to 3 ½ hours.

4 Line a serving platter with napa cabbage. Place meat on cabbage. Skim fat from cooking liquid. Stir carrot, onion, and sesame seeds into cooking liquid. Serve with meat.

nutrition facts per serving: 457 cal., 26 g total fat (10 g sat. fat), 134 mg chol., 695 mg sodium, 5 g carbo., 1 g dietary fiber, 45 g protein.

Aside from a streamlined prep time—thanks to convenience products—this is a traditional take on the classic. Fans of this dish wouldn't want it any other way.

swedish meatballs

prep: 20 minutes cook: 5 to 6 hours (low) or 2½ to 3 hours (high)
makes: 10 servings

2   12-ounce jars beef gravy
3   4.5-ounce jars (drained weight) sliced mushrooms, drained
1   large onion, cut into wedges
1   tablespoon Worcestershire sauce
¼   teaspoon ground allspice
2   16-ounce packages frozen cooked plain meatballs, thawed
1   8-ounce carton sour cream
6   cups hot cooked noodles
    Snipped fresh parsley (optional)

1 In a 4½- or 5-quart slow cooker combine gravy, mushrooms, onion, Worcestershire sauce, and allspice. Stir in meatballs.

2 Cover and cook on low-heat setting for 5 to 6 hours or on high-heat setting for 2½ to 3 hours.

3 In a small bowl gradually stir about ½ cup of the hot gravy mixture into sour cream. Add sour cream mixture to cooker, stirring gently until combined. Serve meatball mixture over hot cooked noodles. If desired, sprinkle with parsley.

nutrition facts per serving: 503 cal., 31 g total fat (14 g sat. fat), 76 mg chol., 1240 mg sodium, 37 g carbo., 4 g dietary fiber, 20 g protein.

292

satisfying **beef & veal**

Please the kids at the potluck with this entrée. Macaroni and cheese with taco flavorings combines two of their favorite foods into one delish dish.

tex-mex mac and cheese

prep: 20 minutes   cook: 5½ to 6 hours (low)   makes: 10 servings

2 pounds lean ground beef
1 cup chopped onion (1 large)
3 cups shredded Mexican-blend cheese (12 ounces)
1 16-ounce jar salsa
1 15-ounce jar cheese dip
1 4-ounce can diced green chile peppers, undrained
1 2.25-ounce can sliced pitted black olives, drained
12 ounces dried elbow macaroni

1 In a large skillet cook ground beef and onion until meat is brown and onion is tender. Drain off fat. Place meat mixture in a 4½- to 6-quart slow cooker. Add Mexican-blend cheese, salsa, cheese dip, chile peppers, and olives; stir to combine.

2 Cover and cook on low-heat setting for 5½ to 6 hours (do not use high-heat setting).

3 Meanwhile, cook macaroni according to package directions; drain. Stir macaroni into mixture in cooker.

nutrition facts per serving: 577 cal., 32 g total fat (17 g sat. fat), 113 mg chol., 1337 mg sodium, 36 g carbo., 2 g dietary fiber, 35 g protein.

Working parents, have your teens dump and pour this easy meal into the slow cooker when they get home from school. When set to high, it will cook in just 2½ to 3 hours.

saucy ravioli with meatballs

prep: 20 minutes   cook: 4½ to 5 hours (low) or 2½ to 3 hours (high)
stand: 15 minutes   makes: 10 to 12 servings

Nonstick cooking
  spray
2 26-ounce jars
     spaghetti sauce
     with mushrooms
     and onions
2 24-ounce packages
     frozen ravioli
1 12-ounce package
     frozen cooked
     Italian meatballs,
     thawed
2 cups shredded
     mozzarella cheese
     (8 ounces)
½ cup finely shredded
     Parmesan cheese
   Snipped fresh basil
     (optional)

1 Lightly coat a 5½- or 6-quart slow cooker with cooking spray. Add 1 cup of the spaghetti sauce to prepared cooker. Add one package of the ravioli and the meatballs. Sprinkle with 1 cup of the mozzarella cheese. Top with the remaining spaghetti sauce from the first jar. Add the remaining package of ravioli and the remaining 1 cup mozzarella cheese. Pour spaghetti sauce from second jar over mixture in cooker.

2 Cover and cook on low-heat setting for 4½ to 5 hours or on high-heat setting for 2½ to 3 hours.

3 Turn off cooker. Sprinkle ravioli mixture with Parmesan cheese. Cover and let stand for 15 minutes before serving. If desired, sprinkle each serving with basil.

nutrition facts per serving: 510 cal., 18 g total fat (8 g sat. fat), 78 mg chol., 1551 mg sodium, 67 g carbo., 5 g dietary fiber, 26 g protein.

Although this classic sauce originally cooked for hours on the stove in a past life, it is perfect for today's slow cooker. No pot watching is required, and it tastes like those sauces eaten in authentic Italian restaurants.

spaghetti sauce italiano

prep: 25 minutes   cook: 9 to 10 hours (low) or 4½ to 5 hours (high)
makes: 8 servings

1   pound lean ground
    beef
8   ounces bulk Italian
    sausage
1   28-ounce can
    diced tomatoes,
    undrained
2   6-ounce cans tomato
    paste
3   cups sliced fresh
    mushrooms
    (8 ounces)
1   cup chopped onion
    (1 large)
¾   cup chopped green
    sweet pepper
    (1 medium)
½   cup dry red wine
    or water
⅓   cup water
1   2.25-ounce can sliced
    pitted black olives,
    drained
2   teaspoons sugar
1½ teaspoons
    Worcestershire
    sauce
½   teaspoon salt
½   teaspoon chili powder
⅛   teaspoon ground
    black pepper
2   cloves garlic, minced
8   cups hot cooked
    spaghetti (1 pound)
    Finely shredded
    Parmesan cheese
    (optional)

1 In a large skillet cook ground beef and sausage over medium heat until brown. Drain off fat.

2 Place meat mixture to a 3½- or 4-quart slow cooker. Stir in tomatoes, tomato paste, mushrooms, onion, green sweet pepper, wine, the water, olives, sugar, Worcestershire sauce, salt, chili powder, black pepper, and garlic.

3 Cover and cook on low-heat setting for 9 to 10 hours or on high-heat setting for 4½ to 5 hours.

4 Serve meat mixture over hot cooked spaghetti. If desired, sprinkle each serving with Parmesan cheese.

nutrition facts per serving: 543 cal., 20 g total fat (7 g sat. fat), 60 mg chol., 1010 mg sodium, 62 g carbo., 7 g dietary fiber, 27 g protein.

This makes a bunch, so reserve 5 cups of the meat mixture; you'll want to use it in Spicy Beef Taco Salad, page 297, an encore meal.

spicy beef sloppy joes

prep: 20 minutes cook: 8 to 10 hours (low) or 4 to 5 hours (high)
makes: 6 servings + reserved meat mixture

2   pounds lean ground
     beef
2   16-ounce jars salsa
3   cups sliced fresh
     mushrooms
     (8 ounces)
1½ cups shredded
     carrots (3 medium)
1½ cups finely chopped
     red and/or green
     sweet peppers
     (2 medium)
⅓   cup tomato paste
2   teaspoons dried basil,
     crushed
1   teaspoon dried
     oregano, crushed
½   teaspoon salt
¼   teaspoon cayenne
     pepper
4   cloves garlic, minced
6   kaiser rolls, split and
     toasted

1 In a large skillet cook ground beef over medium heat until brown. Drain off fat. In a 5- to 6-quart slow cooker combine meat, salsa, mushrooms, carrots, sweet peppers, tomato paste, basil, oregano, salt, cayenne pepper, and garlic.

2 Cover and cook on low-heat setting for 8 to 10 hours or on high heat setting for 4 to 5 hours.

3 Reserve 5 cups of the meat mixture; store as directed below. Serve remaining meat mixture in kaiser rolls.

nutrition facts per serving: 294 cal., 8 g total fat (3 g sat. fat), 36 mg chol., 756 mg sodium, 37 g carbo., 3 g dietary fiber, 18 g protein.

to store reserves: Place reserved meat mixture into an airtight container. Seal and chill for up to 3 days. (Or freeze for up to 3 months. Thaw overnight in refrigerator before using.) *Use in Spicy Beef Taco Salad, page 297.*

With an array of flavors, textures, and colors, taco salads are terrific one-dish meals. This one also sneaks some fiber-packed black beans into your diet.

spicy beef taco salad

start to finish: 25 minutes makes: 6 servings

Reserved meat
   mixture from Spicy
   Beef Sloppy Joes
   (page 296)
1 15-ounce can black
   beans, rinsed and
   drained
1 2.25-ounce can sliced
   pitted black olives,
   drained
1 teaspoon Mexican or
   taco seasoning
9 cups torn iceberg
   lettuce
1 cup shredded cheddar
   cheese (4 ounces)
   Corn chips
1 cup chopped tomatoes
   (2 medium) (optional)
⅓ cup sour cream
   (optional)

1 In a large saucepan stir together reserved meat mixture, black beans, olives, and Mexican seasoning. Heat to boiling; reduce heat. Cover and simmer for 10 minutes.

2 Place lettuce in shallow bowls. Add meat mixture. Top with cheddar cheese and corn chips. If desired, serve with tomatoes and sour cream.

nutrition facts per serving: 495 cal., 26 g total fat (10 g sat. fat), 84 mg chol., 1181 mg sodium, 41 g carbo., 9 g dietary fiber, 32 g protein.

These sandwiches are a little messy to eat—they don't get their name by being tidy. But the spicy sweet flavor is worth every sauce-stained napkin.

rockin' sloppy joes

prep: 30 minutes   cook: 6 to 8 hours (low) or 3 to 4 hours (high)
makes: 8 servings

1½ pounds ground beef
1 cup chopped onion
   (1 large)
2 cloves garlic, minced
1¼ cups chopped red
   sweet pepper
   (1 large)
1 cup shredded carrots
   (2 medium)
1 4-ounce can diced
   green chile peppers,
   undrained
1 5.5-ounce can hot-
   style vegetable
   juice or vegetable
   juice
½ cup ketchup
1 tablespoon packed
   brown sugar
1 tablespoon yellow
   mustard
2 teaspoons chili
   powder
1 teaspoon cider
   vinegar
8 hamburger buns,
   split and toasted
   Purchased deli
   coleslaw (optional)

1 In a large skillet cook ground beef, onion, and garlic over medium heat until meat is brown and onion is tender. Drain off fat.

2 In a 3½- or 4-quart slow cooker combine meat mixture, red sweet pepper, carrots, chile peppers, vegetable juice, ketchup, brown sugar, mustard, chili powder, and vinegar.

3 Cover and cook on low-heat setting for 6 to 8 hours or on high-heat setting for 3 to 4 hours.

4 Serve meat mixture on toasted buns. If desired, top meat mixture with coleslaw.

nutrition facts per serving: 354 cal., 15 g total fat (6 g sat. fat), 58 mg chol., 572 mg sodium, 33 g carbo., 3 g dietary fiber, 21 g protein.

To trim preparation time, substitute an 18-ounce package of frozen cooked meatballs (about 32 meatballs) for the homemade ones, if you like.

meatball sandwiches

prep: 30 minutes bake: 25 minutes cook: 3 to 4 hours (low) or 1½ to 2 hours (high) oven: 350°F makes: 8 servings

1   egg, lightly beaten
⅓   cup fine dry bread crumbs
⅔   cup finely chopped onions (2 small)
½   teaspoon salt
½   teaspoon dried oregano, crushed
½   teaspoon ground black pepper
1½   pounds lean ground beef
1   15-ounce can tomato sauce
½   cup chopped green sweet pepper (1 small)
2   tablespoons packed brown sugar
1   tablespoon yellow mustard
1   teaspoon chili powder
¼   teaspoon garlic salt
⅛   teaspoon bottled hot pepper sauce
8   hoagie buns, split and toasted
2   cups shredded mozzarella cheese (8 ounces)

1 In a large bowl combine egg, bread crumbs, ⅓ cup of the onions, salt, oregano, and ¼ teaspoon of the black pepper. Add ground beef; mix well. Shape meat mixture into 32 balls. Arrange meatballs in a single layer in an ungreased 15x10x1-inch baking pan. Bake, uncovered, in a 350°F oven for 25 minutes. Drain off fat.

2 For sauce, in a 3½- or 4-quart slow cooker combine tomato sauce, remaining ⅓ cup of the onions, green sweet pepper, brown sugar, mustard, chili powder, garlic salt, remaining ¼ teaspoon of the black pepper, and hot pepper sauce. Add cooked meatballs, stirring gently to coat with sauce.

3 Cover and cook on low-heat setting for 3 to 4 hours or on high-heat setting for 1½ to 2 hours.

4 Place four meatballs in each bun. Top with some of the sauce and some of the cheese.

nutrition facts per serving: 724 cal., 28 g total fat (11 g sat. fat), 99 mg chol., 1504 mg sodium, 84 g carbo., 5 g dietary fiber, 36 g protein.

satisfying **beef & veal**

Celebrate a family fiesta two nights in a row with a wonderful taco dish the first night and a bowl of hearty posole the next (see recipe, page 302).

zesty beef medley

prep: 25 minutes cook: 6 to 8 hours (low) or 3 to 3½ hours (high)
makes: 6 servings

2 pounds lean ground beef

1 cup finely chopped onions (2 medium)

1½ cups chopped green sweet peppers (2 medium)

2 16-ounce jars medium or hot salsa

2 15- to 16-ounce can black beans, rinsed and drained

12 taco shells

½ cup sliced green onions (4)

1 small tomato, chopped
Mixed salad greens, torn

1 In an extra-large skillet cook ground beef over medium-high heat until brown. Drain off fat. Place meat in a 5- to 6-quart slow cooker. Stir in onions, green sweet peppers, salsa, and black beans.

2 Cover and cook on low-heat setting for 6 to 8 hours or on high-heat setting for 3 to 3½ hours.

3 Reserve half of the meat mixture; store as directed below. Spoon remaining meat mixture into taco shells. Sprinkle with green onions and tomato. If desired, sprinkle each serving with salad greens.

nutrition facts per serving: 398 cal., 16 g total fat (6 g sat. fat), 54 mg chol., 1146 mg sodium, 23 g carbo., 2 g dietary fiber, 32 g protein.

to store reserves: Place reserved meat mixture in an airtight container. Seal and chill for up to 3 days. *Use in Easy Posole, page 302.*

Zesty Beef Medley (page 301) gets a second go-round tonight with added hominy and hash brown potatoes. Crown with a few toppings for a tasty meal.

easy posole

start to finish: 20 minutes makes: 6 servings

Reserved beef mixture from Zesty Beef Medley (page 301)
2 14-ounce cans reduced-sodium chicken broth
1 14.5-ounce can golden hominy, rinsed and drained
1½ cups frozen hash brown potatoes
Sour cream (optional)
Fresh cilantro sprigs (optional)
Chopped jarred roasted red sweet peppers (optional)

1 In a large saucepan combine reserved beef mixture, broth, hominy, and potatoes. Bring to boiling; reduce heat. Simmer, uncovered, for 10 minutes. Ladle soup into bowls. If desired, top with sour cream, cilantro, and/or roasted peppers.

nutrition facts per serving: 230 cal., 6 g total fat (3 g sat. fat), 68 mg chol., 856 mg sodium, 33 g carbo., 6 g dietary fiber, 11 g protein.

This flavorful Southwestern main dish eats like a casserole but comes straight from your convenient slow cooker. Polenta in a tube is a time-saver.

green chile tamale pie

prep: 30 minutes   cook: 6 to 8 hours (low) or 3 to 4 hours (high)
stand: 5 minutes   makes: 8 to 10 servings

1   pound ground beef
1   pound bulk pork
    sausage
1   cup chopped onion
    (1 large)
3   cloves garlic, minced
1   15-ounce can pinto
    beans or black
    beans, rinsed and
    drained
1   cup frozen whole
    kernel corn
1   4-ounce can diced
    green chile peppers
1   teaspoon ground
    cumin
1   16-ounce tube
    refrigerated cooked
    polenta, cut into
    ¼-inch slices
1   8-ounce package
    shredded Monterey
    Jack cheese
1   8-ounce carton sour
    cream
1   tablespoon snipped
    fresh cilantro
½   teaspoon finely
    shredded lime peel

1 In an extra-large skillet combine ground beef, sausage, onion, and garlic. Cook over medium heat until meat is brown and onion is tender. Drain off fat. In a large bowl combine meat mixture, pinto beans, corn, chile peppers, and cumin.

2 In a 5- to 6-quart slow cooker layer half of the meat mixture, half of the polenta slices, and half of the Monterey Jack cheese. Top with remaining meat mixture and remaining polenta slices.

3 Cover and cook on low-heat setting for 6 to 8 hours or on high-heat setting for 3 to 4 hours. Turn off cooker. Top meat mixture in cooker with remaining cheese. Let stand for 5 minutes or until cheese melts.

4 In a small bowl stir together sour cream, cilantro, and lime peel. Serve with pie.

nutrition facts per serving: 427 cal., 24 g total fat (13 g sat. fat), 79 mg chol., 660 mg sodium, 30 g carbo., 5 g dietary fiber, 25 g protein.

This is a bona fide kid pleaser, but we bet the adults will like it too. Just four ingredients go into the cooker and then go straight to a bun.

easy cheesy sloppy joes

prep: 20 minutes   cook: 4½ to 5 hours (low) or 2 to 2½ hours (high)
makes: 16 servings

2½ pounds lean ground
     beef
1   cup chopped onion
     (1 large)
2   10.75-ounce cans
     condensed nacho
     cheese soup
¾   cup ketchup
16 hamburger buns,
     split and toasted

1 In a 12-inch skillet cook ground beef and onion over medium heat until meat is brown and onion is tender. Drain off fat.

2 In a 3½- or 4-quart slow cooker combine meat mixture, nacho cheese soup, and ketchup.

3 Cover and cook on low-heat setting for 4½ to 5 hours or on high-heat setting for 2 to 2½ hours. Serve meat mixture on toasted buns.

nutrition facts per serving: 389 cal., 22 g total fat (9 g sat. fat), 63 mg chol., 680 mg sodium, 29 g carbo., 2 g dietary fiber, 17 g protein.

Sesame-ginger stir-fry sauce infuses just the right amount of nutty zing. Add crushed red pepper if you want extra heat.

sesame-ginger beef and noodles

prep: 10 minutes cook: 9 to 10 hours (low) or 4½ to 5 hours (high)
stand: 10 minutes makes: 4 to 6 servings

1   16-ounce package
     frozen stir-fry
     vegetables
2   pounds beef stew
     meat
1   12-ounce bottle
     sesame-ginger
     stir-fry sauce
½   cup water
¼   teaspoon crushed red
     pepper (optional)
1   3-ounce package
     ramen noodles,
     broken

1 Place frozen vegetables in a 3½- or 4-quart slow cooker. Top with meat. In a medium bowl combine stir-fry sauce, the water, and, if desired, crushed red pepper. Pour over mixture in cooker.

2 Cover and cook on low-heat setting for 9 to 10 hours or on high-heat setting for 4½ to 5 hours.

3 Stir in noodles. (Save spice packet from ramen noodles for another use.) Cover and let stand for 10 minutes. Stir before serving.

nutrition facts per serving: 494 cal., 11 g total fat (2 g sat. fat), 135 mg chol., 1889 mg sodium, 37 g carbo., 2 g dietary fiber, 53 g protein.

Gremolata, traditionally a blend of fresh parsley, lemon peel, and garlic, brightens the flavors and appearance of this hearty stew.

mediterranean beef ragout

prep: 25 minutes   cook: 7 to 9 hours (low) or 3½ to 4½ hours (high) + 30 minutes
makes: 6 servings

1 tablespoon olive oil
1½ pounds beef stew
   meat
2 medium onions, cut
   into thin wedges
3 medium carrots,
   cut diagonally into
   ½-inch slices
2 cloves garlic, minced
1 teaspoon dried
   thyme, crushed
¼ teaspoon salt
¼ teaspoon ground
   black pepper
1 14.5-ounce can
   diced tomatoes,
   undrained
½ cup beef broth
1 medium zucchini,
   halved lengthwise
   and cut into ¼-inch
   slices
6 ounces fresh green
   beans, cut into
   2-inch pieces
   Hot cooked whole
   wheat couscous
   or brown rice
   (optional)
   Gremolata

1 In a large skillet heat oil over medium-high heat. Cook meat, half at a time, in hot oil until brown. Drain off fat. Place meat in a 3½- or 4-quart slow cooker. Add onions and carrots. Sprinkle with garlic, thyme, salt, and pepper. Pour tomatoes and broth over mixture in cooker.

2 Cover and cook on low-heat setting for 7 to 9 hours or on high-heat setting for 3½ to 4½ hours.

3 If using low-heat setting, turn cooker to high-heat setting. Stir in zucchini and green beans. Cover and cook for 30 minutes more. If desired, serve over hot cooked couscous. Top each serving with Gremolata.

nutrition facts per serving: 260 cal., 11 g total fat (3 g sat. fat), 55 mg chol., 405 mg sodium, 14 g carbo., 4 g dietary fiber, 28 g protein.

gremolata: In a small bowl combine ¼ cup snipped fresh parsley, 1 tablespoon finely shredded lemon peel, and 2 cloves garlic, minced.

Beef Stroganoff usually calls for more expensive meat, such as tenderloin or sirloin steak. This recipe calls for stew meat, which is much less expensive.

classic beef stroganoff

prep: 30 minutes   cook: 8 to 10 hours (low) or 4 to 5 hours (high) + 30 minutes
makes: 6 servings

1½	pounds beef stew meat
1	tablespoon vegetable oil
2	cups sliced fresh mushrooms
½	cup sliced green onions (4) or chopped onion (1 medium)
2	cloves garlic, minced
½	teaspoon dried oregano, crushed
½	teaspoon salt
¼	teaspoon dried thyme, crushed
¼	teaspoon ground black pepper
1	bay leaf
1½	cups reduced-sodium beef broth
⅓	cup dry sherry
1	8-ounce carton light sour cream
¼	cup cold water
2	tablespoons cornstarch
	Snipped fresh parsley (optional)

1 Trim fat from meat. Cut meat into 1-inch pieces. In a large skillet heat oil over medium heat. Cook meat, half at a time, in hot oil until brown. Drain off fat; set aside.

2 In a 3½- or 4-quart slow cooker combine mushrooms, green onions, garlic, oregano, salt, thyme, pepper, and bay leaf. Top with meat. Pour broth and sherry over mixture in cooker.

3 Cover and cook on low-heat setting for 8 to 10 hours or on high-heat setting for 4 to 5 hours.

4 Remove bay leaf and discard. If using low-heat setting, turn to high-heat setting. In a medium bowl combine sour cream, the cold water, and cornstarch. Stir about 1 cup of the hot cooking liquid into sour cream mixture. Stir sour cream mixture into cooker. Cover and cook for about 30 minutes more or until thickened. If desired, sprinkle each serving with parsley.

nutrition facts per serving: 248 cal., 9 g total fat (4 g sat. fat), 79 mg chol., 408 mg sodium, 8 g carbo., 1 g dietary fiber, 28 g protein.

308

Like the traditional Italian meal, this tender veal dish features the flavors of red wine and garlic. Optional Gremolata gives it a fresh taste.

veal osso buco

prep: 20 minutes   cook: 8 to 9 hours (low) or 4 to 4½ hours (high)
makes: 4 to 6 servings

2½   to 3 pounds veal
    shank crosscuts
    (4 to 6)
    Salt (optional)
    Ground black pepper
    (optional)
¼   cup all-purpose flour
2   tablespoons cooking
    oil
2   14.5-ounce cans diced
    tomatoes with basil,
    garlic, and oregano
½   cup dry red wine
    Gremolata (optional)
    Hot cooked rice
    (optional)

1 If desired, season meat with salt and pepper. Place flour in a shallow dish. Dredge meat in flour to coat. In a large skillet heat oil over medium-high heat. Cook meat, half at a time, in hot oil until brown, turning once. Drain off fat. Place meat in a 3½- or 4-quart slow cooker. Pour tomatoes and wine over veal.

2 Cover and cook on low-heat setting for 8 to 9 hours or on high-heat setting for 4 to 4½ hours.

3 Using a slotted spoon, transfer meat and tomatoes to a serving dish. If desired, sprinkle with Gremolata and serve with hot cooked rice.

nutrition facts per serving: 397 cal., 9 g total fat (2 g sat. fat), 163 mg chol., 1249 mg sodium, 25 g carbo., 2 g dietary fiber, 46 g protein.

gremolata: In a small bowl stir together ½ cup snipped fresh parsley, 2 teaspoons finely shredded lemon peel, and 2 cloves garlic, minced.

Pronounced AW-soh BOO-koh, this artfully seasoned veal dish is one for which Italian cooks are noted. Serve it with ruffled mafalda or campanelle pasta.

rosemary osso buco

prep: 35 minutes   cook: 8 to 9 hours (low) or 4 to 4½ hours (high)
makes: 4 to 6 servings

¼   cup all-purpose flour
2½ to 3 pounds veal
      shank crosscuts
      (4 to 6)
2   tablespoons olive oil
1   1-pound butternut
      squash, peeled,
      seeded, and cut into
      2-inch pieces
8   ounces tiny new
      potatoes, halved
1   large onion, cut into
      wedges
1   6-ounce jar whole
      mushrooms,
      drained
8   cloves garlic, halved
1   teaspoon dried
      rosemary, crushed
½   teaspoon salt
½   teaspoon dried
      thyme, crushed
½   teaspoon finely
      shredded lemon
      peel
¼   teaspoon ground
      black pepper
1   cup chicken broth
¼   cup Madeira
1   tablespoon lemon
      juice
8   ounces cooked
      mafalda pasta
      Fresh Italian (flat-
      leaf) parsley sprigs
      (optional)

1 Place flour in a shallow dish. Dredge meat in flour to coat. In a large skillet heat oil over medium-high heat. Cook meat, half at a time, in hot oil until brown, turning once.

2 In a 4- to 5-quart slow cooker combine squash, potatoes, onion, mushrooms, and garlic. Top with meat. Sprinkle with rosemary, salt, thyme, lemon peel, and pepper. Pour chicken broth, Madeira, and lemon juice over mixture in cooker.

3 Cover and cook on low-heat setting for 8 to 9 hours or on high-heat setting for 4 to 4½ hours.

4 To serve, place pasta in shallow bowls. Using a slotted spoon, divide meat and vegetables among bowls. Strain cooking liquid and spoon over the top. If desired, garnish with parsley sprigs.

nutrition facts per serving: 662 cal., 13 g total fat (2 g sat. fat), 149 mg chol., 896 mg sodium, 80 g carbo., 8 g dietary fiber, 51 g protein.

Slow cookers are great time-savers
when you make extra food for
another meal. Slow cook a batch
of the Pulled Pork Master Recipe
and you will have enough meat for
three dinners (with six tasty recipes
to choose from). You can also create
dishes you never thought possible,
such as Chile Verde, Carnitas, or
Chipotle Pork Tamale Pie, for the
Mexican food lover in you.

perfect

pork

7

&lamb

Although brown rice is suggested as a side dish, this green salsa and pork mixture could also be just as happy wrapped up in a tortilla.

braised pork with
salsa verde

prep: 20 minutes   cook: 6 to 6½ hours (low) or 3 hours (high)   makes: 6 servings

1   large onion, cut into
    thin wedges
1½ pounds boneless pork
    loin, cut into
    1½-inch pieces
1⅓ cups coarsely
    chopped tomatoes
    (2 large)
1   16-ounce jar green
    salsa (salsa verde)
½   cup reduced-sodium
    chicken broth
2   cloves garlic, minced
1   teaspoon ground
    cumin
¼   teaspoon ground
    black pepper
3   cups hot cooked
    brown rice
    Snipped fresh cilantro

1 Place onion and pork in a 3½- or 4-quart slow cooker. Top with tomatoes, salsa, broth, garlic, cumin, and pepper.

2 Cover and cook on low-heat setting for 6 to 6½ hours or on high-heat setting for 3 hours. Serve with brown rice and top each serving with cilantro.

nutrition facts per serving: 297 cal., 6 g total fat (1 g sat. fat), 78 mg chol., 231 mg sodium, 31 g carbo., 3 g dietary fiber, 29 g protein.

Three herbs, apricots, and Dijon-style mustard all come together splendidly in this pork roast recipe. The sauce is thickened before serving it over the sliced meat.

herbed apricot
pork loin roast

prep: 20 minutes   cook: 6 to 7 hours (low) or 3 to 3½ hours (high)
stand: 15 minutes   makes: 8 servings

1	3-pound boneless pork top loin roast (double loin, tied)
	Salt
	Ground black pepper
1	10-ounce jar apricot spreadable fruit
⅓	cup finely chopped onion
2	tablespoons Dijon-style mustard
1	tablespoon brandy
1	teaspoon finely shredded lemon peel
1	teaspoon snipped fresh rosemary
1	teaspoon snipped fresh sage
1	teaspoon snipped fresh thyme
¼	teaspoon ground black pepper
4	teaspoons cornstarch
2	tablespoons water
	Fresh apricots, halved and pitted (optional)
	Fresh thyme, sage, and/or rosemary (optional)

1 Sprinkle meat with salt and pepper. In a medium bowl combine spreadable fruit, onion, mustard, brandy, lemon peel, rosemary, sage, thyme, and ¼ teaspoon pepper.

2 Place meat in a 4- to 5-quart slow cooker. Pour fruit mixture over roast.

3 Cover and cook on low-heat setting for 6 to 7 hours or on high-heat setting for 3 to 3½ hours.

4 Transfer meat to a serving platter. Cover loosely with foil and let stand for 15 minutes before carving.

5 For sauce, pour cooking liquid into a medium saucepan. Skim off fat. In a small bowl combine cornstarch and the water; stir into liquid in saucepan. Cook and stir until thickened and bubbly. Cook and stir for 2 minutes more. Serve sauce with meat. If desired, garnish with fresh apricots and herbs.

nutrition facts per serving: 314 cal., 7 g total fat (2 g sat. fat), 107 mg chol., 247 mg sodium, 21 g carbo., 0 g dietary fiber, 38 g protein.

Pork and apples, a classic pairing, cook up beautifully in the slow cooker. Save part of the meat if you want to use it in the Pork and Berry Salad, page 315.

cider-braised
pork roast and apples

prep: 30 minutes   cook: 8 to 10 hours (low) or 4 to 5 hours (high)
makes: 6 servings + reserves

1   3-pound boneless pork top loin roast
½   teaspoon salt
½   teaspoon dried thyme, crushed
½   teaspoon dried sage, crushed
¼   teaspoon ground black pepper
2   tablespoons cooking oil
4   red, yellow, and/or green apples, cored and each cut into 6 wedges
⅓   cup chopped shallots
1   tablespoon bottled minced garlic or 6 cloves garlic, minced
3   tablespoons quick-cooking tapioca
¾   cup chicken broth
¾   cup apple cider or juice
3   cups hot cooked rice

1 Trim fat from meat. In a small bowl combine salt, thyme, sage, and pepper. Sprinkle spice mixture over meat; rub in with your fingers. In a large skillet heat the oil over medium heat. Cook the meat on all sides in hot oil until brown.

2 In a 6- to 7-quart slow cooker place apples, shallots, and garlic; sprinkle with tapioca. Top with meat. Pour broth and apple cider over mixture in cooker.

3 Cover and cook on low-heat setting for 8 to 10 hours or high-heat setting for 4 to 5 hours.

4 Reserve one-third of the meat; store as directed below. Slice remaining pork. Serve with apples and hot cooked rice. Spoon some of the cooking liquid over.

nutrition facts per serving: 407 cal., 12 g total fat (3 g sat. fat), 67 mg chol., 303 mg sodium, 43 g carbo., 2 g dietary fiber, 30 g protein.

to store reserves: Place meat in an airtight container. Seal and chill for up to 3 days. (Or freeze for up to 3 months. Thaw in refrigerator overnight before using.) ***Use in Pork and Berry Salad, page 315.***

Partnered with sweet berries, leftover pork hits a home run in this main-dish salad. Slice the meat or chop it, you choose. Either way, it tastes the same.

pork and berry salad

start to finish: 20 minutes   makes: 6 servings

Reserved meat from
Cider-Braised Pork
Roast and Apples
(see recipe, page
314)
6 cups torn mixed
greens
3 cups mixed berries,
such as sliced
strawberries,
blueberries, and/or
raspberries
½ cup bottled balsamic
vinaigrette or your
favorite vinaigrette

1 Chop or slice meat. Arrange greens on individual plates. Top with meat and berries. Drizzle with vinaigrette.

nutrition facts per serving: 236 cal., 11 g total fat (2 g sat. fat), 66 mg chol., 371 mg sodium, 9 g carbo., 2 g dietary fiber, 24 g protein.

perfect **pork & lamb**

If you don't have arrowroot on hand for thickening, use 3 tablespoons cornstarch combined with 3 tablespoons water instead.

herbed pork pot roast

prep: 15 minutes   cook: 8 to 10 hours (low) or 4 to 5 hours (high)
makes: 8 to 10 servings

1   2½ - to 3-pound
    boneless pork
    sirloin or shoulder
    roast
½   cup chopped onion
    (1 medium)
½   cup port wine
    or apple juice
1   8-ounce can tomato
    sauce
3   tablespoons quick-
    cooking tapioca
1   tablespoon
    Worcestershire
    sauce
1   teaspoon dried
    thyme, crushed
1   teaspoon dried
    oregano, crushed
2   cloves garlic, minced
    Hot cooked whole
    wheat pasta
    (optional)

1 Trim fat from meat. If necessary, cut meat to fit into a 3½ - or 4-quart slow cooker. Place meat in cooker. In a small bowl combine onion, port, tomato sauce, tapioca, Worcestershire sauce, thyme, oregano, and garlic. Pour over meat.

2 Cover and cook on low-heat setting for 8 to 10 hours or on high-heat setting for 4 to 5 hours. Transfer meat to a serving platter. Skim off fat from gravy. Pass gravy with meat. If desired, serve with hot cooked pasta.

nutrition facts per serving: 230 cal., 5 g total fat (2 g sat. fat), 84 mg chol., 247 mg sodium, 9 g carbo., 1 g dietary fiber, 31 g protein.

This classic is often breaded and fried. With only 10 grams of fat in a serving, this homemade rendition saves you calories and fat but doesn't skimp on flavor.

sweet-and-sour pork

prep: 30 minutes cook: 7 to 8 hours (low) or 3½ to 4 hours (high)
makes: 6 servings

1   20-ounce can
    pineapple chunks
    in juice
1   cup bias-sliced
    carrots (2 medium)
1   large onion, cut into
    thin wedges
1   8-ounce can sliced
    water chestnuts,
    drained
1   medium red sweet
    pepper, cut into
    1-inch pieces
½   cup bias-sliced celery
    (1 stalk)
2   pounds boneless pork
    shoulder, cut into
    1-inch pieces
3   tablespoons packed
    brown sugar
2   tablespoons rice
    vinegar
2   tablespoons tomato
    paste
2   tablespoons quick-
    cooking tapioca,
    crushed
1   tablespoon soy sauce
1   tablespoon sherry
    (optional)
2   cloves garlic, minced
½   teaspoon salt
½   teaspoon sesame oil
    Hot cooked rice
    Chopped green onion

1 Drain pineapple chunks, reserving the juice; set pineapple chunks aside.

2 In a 3½- or 4-quart slow cooker combine carrots, onion, water chestnuts, red sweet pepper, and celery. Top with pork. In a medium bowl whisk together reserved pineapple juice, brown sugar, rice vinegar, tomato paste, tapioca, soy sauce, sherry (if desired), garlic, salt, and sesame oil. Pour over mixture in cooker.

3 Cover and cook on low-heat setting for 7 to 8 hours or on high-heat setting for 3½ to 4 hours. Stir in pineapple chunks. Serve over hot cooked rice. Sprinkle with green onion.

nutrition facts per serving: 456 cal., 10 g total fat (3 g sat. fat), 98 mg chol., 866 mg sodium, 56 g carbo., 3 g dietary fiber, 33 g protein.

This 6-cup pork recipe is very versatile and is the foundation for the next six recipes. Each recipe calls for 2-cup portions, so you'll have enough meat for three of the six recipes.

pulled pork master recipe

prep: 30 minutes   cook: 10 to 11 hours (low) or 5 to 6 hours (high)
cool: 20 minutes   makes: 6 cups

3   to 3½ pounds
     boneless pork
     shoulder
1   cup chopped sweet
     onion (1 large)
6   cloves garlic, minced
1   12-ounce bottle chili
     sauce
2   tablespoons packed
     brown sugar
2   tablespoons cider
     vinegar
1   tablespoon
     Worcestershire
     sauce
1   tablespoon chili
     powder
½   teaspoon salt
½   teaspoon ground
     black pepper

1 Trim fat from meat. If necessary, cut pork to fit into a 4- to 5-quart slow cooker. Place pork, onion, and garlic in slow cooker. In a medium bowl combine chili sauce, brown sugar, vinegar, Worcestershire sauce, chili powder, salt, and pepper. Pour over meat in cooker.

2 Cover and cook on low-heat setting for 10 to 11 hours or on high-heat setting for 5 to 6 hours. Remove pork from cooker, reserving juices. Using two forks, pull pork apart into shreds, discarding any fat. Skim off fat from cooking liquid. Drizzle pork with enough of the cooking liquid to moisten. Place 2-cup portions of pork in airtight containers and refrigerate for up to 3 days or freeze for up to 3 months.

nutrition facts per serving: 396 cal., 13 g total fat (5 g sat. fat), 147 mg chol., 1069 mg sodium, 20 g carbo., 1 g dietary fiber, 46 g protein.

Mmmm. Apricots augment a hot-style barbecue sauce for this sweet-and-spicy finger-licking pork sandwich.

apricot pulled pork hoagies

start to finish: 30 minutes   cool: 20 minutes   makes: 4 servings

1 tablespoon cooking oil
1 cup chopped sweet onion (1 large)
2 cups Pulled Pork Master Recipe (see recipe, page 318)
½ cup apricot spreadable fruit
½ cup bottled hot-style barbecue sauce
2 tablespoons snipped dried apricots
4 hoagie rolls, split and toasted

1 In a large skillet heat oil over medium heat. Cook onion in hot oil for about 4 minutes or until tender. Stir in shredded pork, spreadable fruit, barbecue sauce, and dried apricots. Bring to boiling; reduce heat. Simmer, uncovered, for about 5 minutes or until desired consistency is reached, stirring occasionally.

2 Divide meat mixture evenly among hoagie rolls.

nutrition facts per serving: 641 cal., 14 g total fat (3 g sat. fat), 73 mg chol., 1386 mg sodium, 96 g carbo., 4 g dietary fiber, 32 g protein.

Prepare the Pulled Pork Master Recipe on page 318 and use it in this tasty Asian-inspired wrap. If you like, use preshredded coleslaw mix or broccoli slaw in place of the cabbage.

asian pork wraps

start to finish: 20 minutes   makes: 8 servings

1 tablespoon olive oil

1 16-ounce package frozen stir-fry vegetables

2 cups Pulled Pork Master Recipe (see recipe, page 318)

½ cup hoisin sauce

1 teaspoon ground ginger

½ teaspoon garlic powder

8 10-inch flour tortillas, warmed*

2 cups shredded or coarsely chopped napa cabbage or bok choy

1 In a large skillet heat oil over medium-high heat. Cook vegetables in hot oil for 4 to 5 minutes or until nearly tender. Drain any excess liquid from the pan. Add shredded pork, hoisin sauce, ginger, and garlic powder. Cook and stir until heated through.

2 Arrange meat and vegetable mixture along center of each tortilla. Top with shredded cabbage. Fold bottom edges of tortillas up and over the filling. Fold opposite sides in, just until they meet. Roll up from bottom. If desired, secure with wooden toothpicks.

nutrition facts per serving: 306 cal., 9 g total fat (2 g sat. fat), 37 mg chol., mg sodium, 38 g carbo., 3 g dietary fiber, 17 g protein.

*test kitchen tip: To warm tortillas, wrap in foil and heat in a 350°F oven for 10 minutes.

The Pulled Pork Master Recipe morphs into yet another delicious weeknight meal. Peach preserves add a pleasant sweetness to the dish.

peachy pulled pork stir-fry

start to finish: 40 minutes makes: 4 servings

½ cup chicken broth
¼ cup peach preserves
1 tablespoon Asian sweet chili sauce
1 tablespoon soy sauce
2 teaspoons cornstarch
¼ teaspoon sesame oil
1 tablespoon cooking oil
1 small onion, cut into thin wedges
1 tablespoon grated fresh ginger
3 cloves garlic, minced
½ cup thinly bias-sliced carrot (1 medium)
1 medium yellow or red sweet pepper, cut into thin strips
1 cup small broccoli florets
2 cups Pulled Pork Master Recipe (see recipe, page 318)
Hot cooked rice
Cashews (optional)

1 In a small bowl whisk together chicken broth, peach preserves, sweet chili sauce, soy sauce, cornstarch, and sesame oil; set aside.

2 In a large skillet or wok heat oil over medium-high heat. Cook and stir onion, ginger, and garlic in hot oil for 2 minutes. Add carrot; cook and stir for 2 minutes more. Add yellow sweet pepper and broccoli; cook and stir for 2 minutes more. Add shredded pork and the broth mixture. Cook and stir until heated through and sauce is thickened and bubbly.

3 Serve over rice. If desired, top with cashews.

nutrition facts per serving: 443 cal., 11 g total fat (3 g sat. fat), 74 mg chol., 1287 mg sodium, 58 g carbo., 3 g dietary fiber, 27 g protein.

The word mole *comes from* molli, *the Aztec word meaning "sauce."*
Moles highlight a variety of chile peppers and other ingredients that
often, but not always, include chocolate.

mole pork and green olive
quesadillas

prep: 1 hour cook: 4 minutes per batch cool: 20 minutes oven: 300°F
makes: 6 servings

2   tablespoons olive oil
1   cup chopped onion
    (1 large)
3   cloves garlic, minced
2   teaspoons chili
    powder
½   teaspoon ground
    cumin
¼   teaspoon ground
    cinnamon
¼   teaspoon dried
    oregano, crushed
2   teaspoons all-purpose
    flour
⅓   cup chicken broth
2   tablespoons
    semisweet
    chocolate pieces
2   cups Pulled Pork
    Master Recipe (see
    recipe, page 318)
6   8-inch flour tortillas
    Nonstick cooking
    spray
1½ cups shredded
    Monterey Jack
    cheese (6 ounces)
⅔   cup pimiento-stuffed
    green olives, sliced
½   cup thinly sliced red
    onion (1 medium)

1 In a large skillet heat oil over medium heat. Cook chopped onion and garlic in hot oil for about 4 minutes or until tender. Stir in chili powder, cumin, cinnamon, and oregano. Cook and stir for 1 minute more. Stir in flour. Add chicken broth and stir. Cook until thickened and bubbly, stirring constantly. Add chocolate and stir until melted. Stir in shredded pork and heat through.

2 Coat one side of each tortilla with cooking spray. Place tortillas, sprayed sides down, on cutting board or waxed paper. Sprinkle ¼ cup Monterey Jack cheese over half of each tortilla. Top evenly with pork mixture, green olives, and red onion slices. Fold tortillas in half, pressing gently.

3 Heat a large nonstick skillet over medium heat. Cook quesadillas, two at a time, in hot skillet for 4 to 6 minutes or until light brown, turning once. Remove quesadillas from skillet; place on a baking sheet. Keep warm in a 300°F oven. Repeat with remaining quesadillas. To serve, cut each quesadilla into three wedges.

nutrition facts per serving: 294 cal., 21 g total fat (7 g sat. fat), 66 mg chol., 861 mg sodium, 30 g carbo., 3 g dietary fiber, 23 g protein.

Use your leftover pork to make this Thai-inspired entrée. Coconut milk, soy sauce, fresh basil, and cilantro are just some of the delicious ingredients.

shredded pork big bowl

start to finish: 30 minutes makes: 6 servings

1 tablespoon cooking oil

1 tablespoon minced garlic

1 tablespoon grated fresh ginger

1 teaspoon ground cumin

¼ teaspoon cayenne pepper

2 14-ounce cans chicken broth

1 14-ounce can unsweetened coconut milk

2 cups purchased shredded carrots

2 cups small broccoli florets

1 medium red sweet pepper, cut into bite-size strips

2 3-ounce packages ramen noodles, coarsely broken

2 cups Pulled Pork Master Recipe (see recipe, page 318)

2 cups snow pea pods, halved crosswise

2 tablespoons soy sauce

1 tablespoon lime juice

½ cup slivered fresh basil

2 tablespoons snipped fresh cilantro

1 In a 4-quart Dutch oven heat oil over medium heat. Cook garlic, ginger, cumin, and cayenne pepper in hot oil for 30 seconds. Stir in broth, coconut milk, carrots, broccoli, sweet pepper, and noodles (discard seasoning packets). Bring to boiling; reduce heat. Simmer, covered, for 3 minutes. Stir in shredded pork, pea pods, soy sauce, and lime juice. Heat through. Stir in basil and cilantro. Serve in soup bowls.

nutrition facts per serving: 460 cal., 24 g total fat (15 g sat. fat), 50 mg chol., 1349 mg sodium, 37 g carbo., 4 g dietary fiber, 23 g protein.

Use the brand of taco seasoning mix you like best and add it to the pork leftovers. Green chile peppers create additional heat.

shredded pork and green chile
roll-ups

start to finish: 15 minutes makes: 4 servings

1	tablespoon cooking oil
1	large onion, thinly sliced and separated into rings
2	cups Pulled Pork Master Recipe (see recipe, page 318)
1	4-ounce can diced green chile peppers, drained
½	cup water
1	1.25-ounce envelope taco seasoning mix
4	10-inch flour tortillas, warmed*
½	cup chopped tomato (1 medium)
1	cup shredded cheddar cheese (4 ounces)
½	cup sour cream
2	tablespoons snipped fresh cilantro

1 In a large skillet heat oil over medium heat. Cook onion in hot oil for about 5 minutes or until tender, stirring occasionally. Stir in shredded pork, green chiles, the water, and taco seasoning. Cook and stir for 3 to 4 minutes or until mixture is simmering and most of the liquid is absorbed.

2 Spoon pork mixture onto tortillas. Top with tomato, cheddar cheese, sour cream, and cilantro. Roll up tortillas. Cut in half to serve.

nutrition facts per serving: 578 cal., 30 g total fat (13 g sat. fat), 114 mg chol., 1880 mg sodium, 43 g carbo., 3 g dietary fiber, 37 g protein.

*test kitchen tip: To warm tortillas, wrap in foil and place in a 350°F oven for 10 minutes.

Pork shoulder roast cooks to melt-in-your-mouth tenderness in the slow cooker. Hispanic ingredients flavor the meat for a unique main-dish salad.

shredded pork salad

prep: 15 minutes   cook: 8 to 10 hours (low) or 4 to 5 hours (high)
makes: 8 servings

1   2-pound boneless
     pork shoulder roast
1   cup water
2   large onions,
     quartered
3   fresh jalapeño
     peppers, cut up
     (see tip, page 32)
8   cloves garlic, minced
2   teaspoons ground
     coriander
2   teaspoons ground
     cumin
2   teaspoons dried
     oregano, crushed
½   teaspoon salt
½   teaspoon ground
     black pepper
4   cups Bibb lettuce
     leaves or shredded
     lettuce
½   cup finely shredded
     reduced-fat
     Monterey Jack
     cheese (2 ounces)
     (optional)
    Bottled salsa
     (optional)
    Reduced-fat sour
     cream (optional)

1 Trim fat from meat. If necessary, cut meat to fit into a 3½- or 4-quart slow cooker. Place meat in the cooker. Add the water, onions, jalapeño peppers, garlic, coriander, cumin, oregano, salt, and black pepper.

2 Cover and cook on low-heat setting for 8 to 10 hours or on high-heat setting for 4 to 5 hours.

3 Remove meat from cooker. Discard cooking liquid. Using two forks, pull meat apart into shreds. To serve, place lettuce on a serving platter. Spoon meat over lettuce. If desired, top with Monterey Jack cheese, salsa, and sour cream.

nutrition facts per serving: 198 cal., 9 g total fat (3 g sat. fat), 77 mg chol., 229 mg sodium, 5 g carbo., 1 g dietary fiber, 23 g protein.

Choose your purchased barbecue sauce according to your family's desires. Spicy or not, you decide. Dr. Pepper soda adds sweetness, so choose accordingly.

spicy pulled pork

prep: 15 minutes   cook: 8 to 10 hours (low) or 4 to 5 hours (high)
makes: 8 to 10 servings

2   to 2½ pounds
      boneless pork
      shoulder
    Salt
    Ground black pepper
1   large sweet onion,
      cut into thin
      wedges
1   18- to 20-ounce bottle
      hot-style barbecue
      sauce (about 1¾
      cups)
1   cup Dr. Pepper soda
16 to 20 baguette slices,
      toasted
    Sliced pickles
      (optional)

1 Trim fat from meat. If necessary, cut meat to fit into a 3½- or 4-quart slow cooker. Sprinkle meat with salt and pepper.

2 Place onion in the slow cooker. Top with meat. In a medium bowl combine barbecue sauce and Dr. Pepper. Pour over meat.

3 Cover and cook on low-heat setting for 8 to 10 hours or on high-heat setting for 4 to 5 hours.

4 Transfer meat to a cutting board. Using two forks, pull meat apart into shreds. Return to cooker and stir; keep warm.

5 Using a slotted spoon, divide meat mixture among half of the baguette slices. Top with remaining slices and secure with wooden picks. If desired, serve sandwiches with sliced pickles.

nutrition facts per serving: 393 cal., 10 g total fat (3 g sat. fat), 76 mg chol., 1422 mg sodium, 46 g carbo., 1 g dietary fiber, 27 g protein.

Look for sauerkraut with caraway seeds next to the plain sauerkraut in your supermarket's canned vegetable aisle. You'll love the flavor they add.

sauerkraut and pork
shoulder roast

prep: 20 minutes   cook: 7 to 9 hours (low) or 3½ to 4½ hours (high)
makes: 6 servings

1   2½-pound boneless
    pork shoulder
    or beef sirloin roast
    Salt
    Ground black pepper
2   tablespoons Dijon-
    style mustard
1   14.5-ounce can
    sauerkraut with
    caraway seeds,
    drained
2   medium cooking
    apples, cored and
    cut into 1-inch
    pieces
1   cup regular or
    nonalcoholic beer

1 Trim fat from meat. If necessary, cut meat to fit into a 3½- or 4-quart slow cooker. Lightly sprinkle meat with salt and pepper. Spread mustard over meat; set aside.

2 Place sauerkraut and apple pieces in the slow cooker. Top with meat. Pour beer over mixture in cooker.

3 Cover and cook on low-heat setting for 7 to 9 hours or on high-heat setting for 3½ to 4½ hours. Remove meat from cooker. Break meat into serving-size pieces. Using a slotted spoon, serve sauerkraut-apple mixture with the meat.

nutrition facts per serving: 341 cal., 11 g total fat (4 g sat. fat), 122 mg chol., 2018 mg sodium, 17 g carbo., 1 g dietary fiber, 38 g protein.

Your favorite teriyaki glaze provides most of the flavor for this recipe. You can use vermicelli or angel hair pasta instead of Chinese noodles, if you like.

pork lo mein

prep: 20 minutes   cook: 6½ to 7 hours (low) or 3½ to 4 hours (high) + 10 minutes
makes: 6 servings

1½	pounds boneless pork shoulder
2	medium onions, cut into wedges
2	cups frozen sliced carrots
1	12-ounce jar teriyaki glaze
1	cup thinly bias-sliced celery
1	8-ounce can sliced water chestnuts, drained
1	5-ounce can sliced bamboo shoots, drained
1	teaspoon grated fresh ginger
1	6-ounce package frozen snow pea pods
1	cup broccoli florets
9	ounces dried curly thin egg noodles
¼	cup cashews

1 Trim fat from pork. Cut pork into ¾-inch pieces. In a 3½- or 4-quart slow cooker, combine pork, onions, frozen carrots, teriyaki glaze, celery, water chestnuts, bamboo shoots, and ginger.

2 Cover and cook on low-heat setting for 6½ to 7 hours or on high-heat setting for 3½ to 4 hours.

3 If using low-heat setting, turn to high-heat setting. Stir in pea pods and broccoli. Cover and cook for 10 to 15 minutes more or until pea pods are crisp-tender.

4 Meanwhile, cook noodles according to package directions; drain. Serve pork mixture over noodles. Sprinkle each serving with cashews.

nutrition facts per serving: 509 cal., 12 g total fat (3 g sat. fat), 73 mg chol., 2274 mg sodium, 66 g carbo., 6 g dietary fiber, 33 g protein.

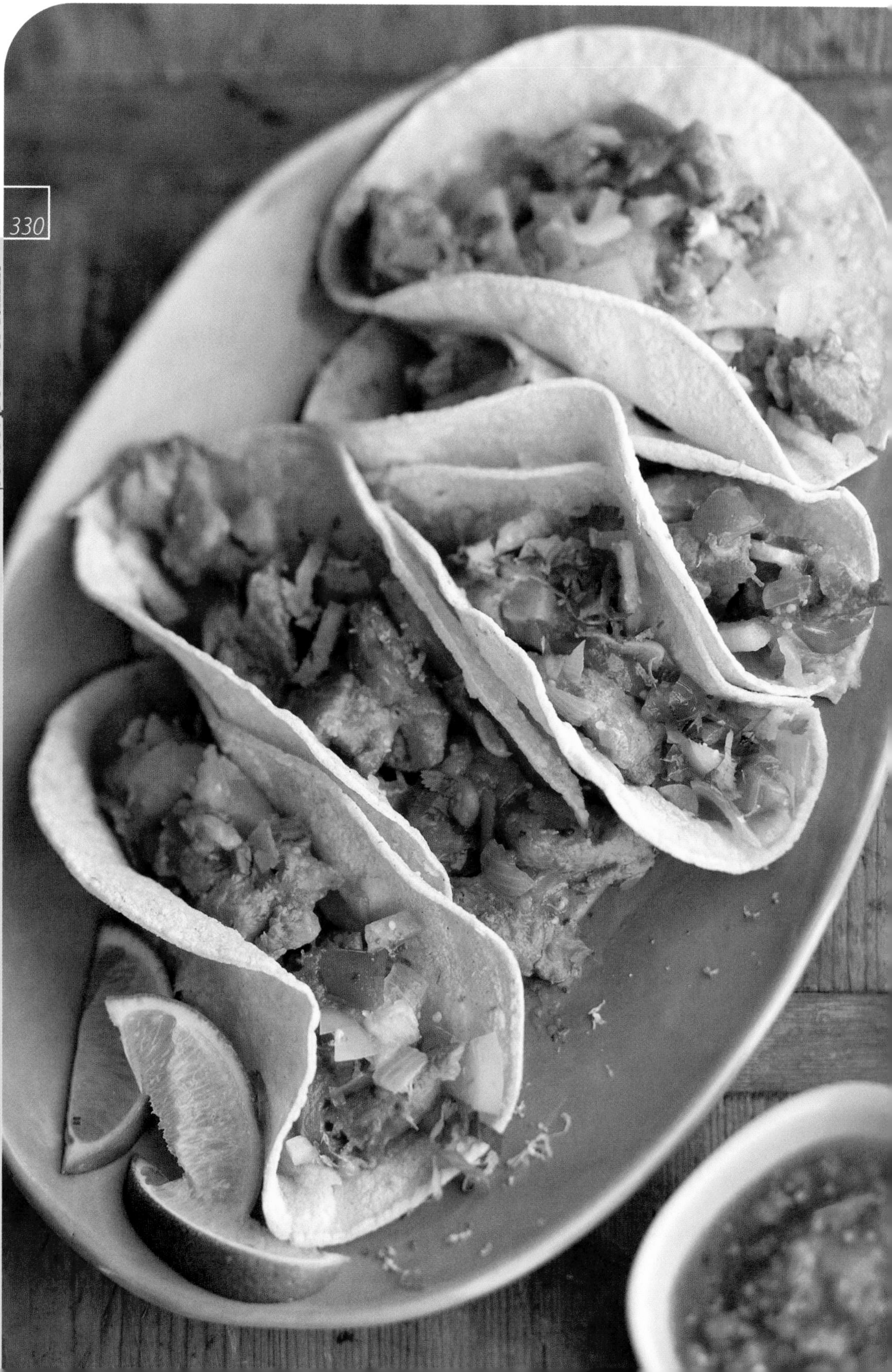

Pork shoulder simmers up beautifully in the slow cooker and lends itself to classic shredded pork dishes of Mexico.

chile verde

prep: 40 minutes   cook: 6 to 8 hours (low) or 3 to 4 hours (high) + 15 minutes
makes: 6 servings

1 teaspoon ground cumin
½ teaspoon salt
¼ teaspoon ground black pepper
1½ pounds boneless pork shoulder, cut into 1-inch pieces
Nonstick cooking spray
1 tablespoon olive oil
1 pound fresh tomatillos, husks removed, chopped (about 4 cups)
1 cup chopped onion (1 large)
3 teaspoons finely shredded lime peel
2 tablespoons lime juice
4 cloves garlic, minced
¾ cup chopped yellow or red sweet pepper (1 medium)
12 6-inch corn tortillas
2 tablespoons snipped fresh cilantro
Purchased green salsa (optional)

1 In a small bowl combine cumin, salt, and pepper. Set aside. Trim fat from meat. Cut meat into 1-inch pieces. Sprinkle cumin mixture over meat. Coat a large skillet with cooking spray. Cook half of the meat in hot skillet over medium heat until brown. Remove meat from skillet. Add oil to skillet and heat. Brown remaining meat in hot oil. Drain off fat. Place meat in a 3½- to 4½-quart slow cooker. Add tomatillos, onion, 2 teaspoons of the lime peel, the lime juice, and garlic. Stir to combine.

2 Cover and cook on low-heat setting for 6 to 8 hours or on high-heat setting for 3 to 4 hours.

3 If using low-heat setting, turn to high-heat setting. Add yellow sweet pepper to cooker. Cover and cook for 15 minutes more. Fill corn tortillas with meat mixture; sprinkle with cilantro and remaining 1 teaspoon lime peel. If desired, serve with green salsa.

nutrition facts per serving: 333 cal., 11 g total fat (3 g sat. fat), 73 mg chol., 314 mg sodium, 32 g carbo., 4 g dietary fiber, 27 g protein.

Purchased broths conveniently now come seasoned, such as with roasted garlic, saving you time from roasting garlic yourself.

home-style pork pot roast

prep: 20 minutes   cook: 10 to 12 hours (low) or 5 to 6 hours (high)
makes: 6 servings

1   3- to 3½-pound
    boneless pork
    shoulder roast
1   tablespoon cooking
    oil
3   tablespoons Dijon-
    style mustard
1   teaspoon dried
    thyme, crushed
½   teaspoon dried
    rosemary, crushed
½   teaspoon salt
¼   teaspoon ground
    black pepper
12 ounces round red
    potatoes, cut into
    1-inch pieces
3   medium parsnips, cut
    into 1-inch pieces
3   medium carrots, cut
    into 1-inch pieces
1   large onion, cut into
    wedges
¾   cup canned seasoned
    chicken broth with
    roasted garlic
3   tablespoons quick-
    cooking tapioca

1 Trim fat from meat. If necessary, cut meat to fit into a 4- to 6-quart slow cooker. In a large skillet heat oil over medium-high heat. Cook meat on all sides in hot oil until brown. Brush meat with mustard. Sprinkle with thyme, rosemary, salt, and pepper.

2 Place potatoes, parsnips, carrots, and onion in the slow cooker. Pour broth over vegetables. Sprinkle with tapioca. Top with meat.

3 Cover and cook on low-heat setting for 10 to 12 hours or on high-heat setting for 5 to 6 hours.

4 Transfer meat and vegetables to a serving platter. Strain cooking juices. Skim off fat. Drizzle some of the cooking juices over meat. Serve with remaining juices.

nutrition facts per serving: 451 cal., 15 g total fat (5 g sat. fat), 136 mg chol., 671 mg sodium, 29 g carbo., 5 g dietary fiber, 45 g protein.

Onion soup mix has long been a favorite ingredient for time-pressed cooks. Combined with cranberry-orange relish and mustard, the three bring a windfall of flavor to pork roast.

cranberry-mustard
pork roast

prep: 20 minutes   cook: 5 to 6 hours (low) or 2½ to 3 hours (high)
makes: 8 servings

1   2½- to 3-pound pork shoulder roast
1   tablespoon cooking oil
1   10-ounce package frozen cranberry-orange sauce, thawed
1   envelope (½ of a 2.2-ounce package) dry onion soup mix
2   tablespoons Dijon-style mustard
2   tablespoons water

1 Trim fat from meat. If necessary, cut meat to fit in a 3½- or 4-quart slow cooker. In a large skillet heat oil over medium heat. Cook meat on all sides in hot oil. Drain off fat. Place meat in slow cooker. In a medium bowl combine cranberry-orange sauce, soup mix, mustard, and the water. Pour over meat.

2 Cover and cook on low-heat setting for 5 to 6 hours or on high-heat setting for 2½ to 3 hours.

3 Transfer meat to a cutting board; slice meat. Arrange meat on a serving platter. Skim off fat from cooking liquid. Serve cooking liquid with meat.

nutrition facts per serving: 293 cal., 9 g total fat (3 g sat. fat), 89 mg chol., 480 mg sodium, 18 g carbo., 2 g dietary fiber, 30 g protein.

The chipotle chiles in adobo sauce create a smoky flavor in these multilayered shredded pork tostadas. Reserve some pork for Chipotle Pork Tamale Casserole, page 335.

adobo pork tostadas

prep: 30 minutes   cook: 10 to 12 hours (low) or 5 to 6 hours (high)
makes: 4 servings + reserves

1   3- to 3½-pound boneless pork shoulder roast
1   15-ounce can tomato sauce
½   cup chicken broth
2   tablespoons finely chopped canned chipotle chile peppers in adobo sauce
1   tablespoon bottled minced garlic (6 cloves)
½   teaspoon salt
½   teaspoon ground cumin
½   teaspoon ground coriander
¼   teaspoon ground black pepper
1   cup canned refried beans
8   tostada shells
1   cup shredded lettuce
1   cup chopped tomatoes (2 medium)
1   medium avocado, pitted, peeled, and sliced
1   cup shredded Monterey Jack cheese or queso fresco (4 ounces)
½   cup sour cream

1 Trim fat from meat. Cut meat into chunks. Place meat in a 4- to 5-quart slow cooker. In a medium bowl stir together tomato sauce, broth, chipotle pepper, garlic, salt, cumin, coriander, and black pepper. Pour sauce over meat.

2 Cover and cook on low-heat setting for 10 to 12 hours or on high-heat setting for 5 to 6 hours.

3 Remove meat from cooker. Using two forks, pull meat apart into shreds. Reserve half of the meat (about 3 cups) and 2 cups of the sauce; store as directed below. In a medium bowl combine the remaining meat and ½ cup of the sauce. Discard any remaining sauce.

4 Spread refried beans over tostada shells. Top with meat mixture. Divide lettuce, tomatoes, and avocado among tostadas. Top with cheese and sour cream.

nutrition facts per serving: 720 cal., 38 g total fat (14 g sat. fat), 151 mg chol., 1378 mg sodium, 44 g carbo., 9 g dietary fiber, 49 g protein.

to store reserves: Place meat and sauce in separate airtight containers. Seal and chill for up to 3 days. (Or freeze for up to 3 months. Thaw in refrigerator overnight before using.) *Use in Chipotle Pork Tamale Casserole, page 335.*

Refrigerated polenta is a time-saving product you just slice to use. Tonight's meal is in the bag because last night's dinner is encoring in this casserole.

chipotle pork
tamale casserole

prep: 15 minutes bake: 35 minutes oven: 375°F makes: 4 servings

1   16-ounce tube
     refrigerated cooked
     polenta, sliced
     ½ inch thick
     Reserved meat and
     sauce from Adobo
     Pork Tostadas* (see
     recipe, page 334)
1   cup shredded
     cheddar cheese
     (4 ounces)
½   cup chopped tomato
     (1 medium)
¼   cup sliced green
     onions (2)

1 Preheat oven to 375°F. In an ungreased 2-quart square baking dish, arrange polenta slices, overlapping if necessary. Top with the reserved meat. Remove any fat from surface of the reserved sauce. Spoon ½ cup of the reserved sauce over meat.

2 Bake, covered, for 30 minutes. Sprinkle with cheddar cheese. Bake, uncovered, for about 5 minutes more or until cheese is melted.

3 Meanwhile, heat the remaining 1½ cups reserved sauce. Sprinkle tomato and green onions over casserole. Serve with warm sauce.

nutrition facts per serving: 488 cal., 21 g total fat (10 g sat. fat), 143 mg chol., 1215 mg sodium, 27 g carbo., 4 g dietary fiber, 44 g protein.

*test kitchen tip: There should be about 3 cups reserved shredded meat and 2 cups reserved sauce.

336

With a bouquet garni, removing seasonings from dishes like this is a cinch—no fishing around for small pieces. If you don't have cheesecloth, use a coffee filter.

carnitas

prep: 10 minutes   cook: 10 to 12 hours (low) or 4½ to 5 hours (high)
makes: 6 servings

1   2-pound boneless
    pork shoulder roast,
    cut into 2-inch
    pieces
    Salt
    Ground black pepper
1   tablespoon whole
    black peppercorns
2   teaspoons cumin
    seeds
4   cloves garlic, minced
1   teaspoon dried
    oregano, crushed
3   bay leaves
2   14-ounce cans
    chicken broth
2   teaspoons finely
    shredded lime peel
2   tablespoons lime
    juice
12 6-inch crisp corn
    tortillas
    Sour cream
    Bottled salsa

1 Sprinkle pork generously with salt and pepper. Place in a 3½- or 4-quart slow cooker.

2 To make a bouquet garni, cut a 6-inch square from a double thickness of 100-percent-cotton cheesecloth. Place peppercorns, cumin seeds, garlic, oregano, and bay leaves in center of cheesecloth square. Bring up corners of cheesecloth and tie with clean 100-precent-cotton kitchen string. Add to slow cooker. Pour broth over meat.

3 Cover and cook on low-heat setting for 10 to 12 hours or on high-heat setting for 4½ to 5 hours.

4 Using a slotted spoon, remove meat from slow cooker. Discard bouquet garni and cooking liquid. Using two forks, pull meat apart into shreds; discard any fat. Sprinkle meat with lime peel and lime juice; toss to mix. Serve with tortillas, sour cream, and salsa.

nutrition facts per serving: 399 cal., 18 g total fat (6 g sat. fat), 106 mg chol., 1079 mg sodium, 24 g carbo., 3 g dietary fiber, 34 g protein.

A surprise ingredient—cola—adds sweetness to this saucy pulled pork sandwich. The recipe makes a lot, so be sure to invite over some hungry neighbors.

barbecue pulled pork

prep: 15 minutes cook: 12 to 13 hours (low) or 6 to 6½ hours (high)
makes: 16 servings

1   4-pound boneless
     pork shoulder roast
1   large sweet onion,
     cut into thin
     wedges
1   12-ounce bottle chili
     sauce
1   cup cola
½   cup ketchup
2   tablespoons yellow
     mustard
1   tablespoon chili
     powder
1   tablespoon cider
     vinegar
2   teaspoons ground
     cumin
3   cloves garlic, minced
1   teaspoon paprika
½   teaspoon salt
½   teaspoon ground
     black pepper
¼   teaspoon crushed
     red pepper
16 hamburger buns,
     split and toasted,
     or thickly sliced
     toasted bread
     Purchased coleslaw
     (optional)

1 Trim fat from meat. If necessary, cut meat to fit into a 5- to 6-quart slow cooker. Place onion in slow cooker. Top with meat. In a medium bowl, combine chili sauce, cola, ketchup, mustard, chili powder, vinegar, cumin, garlic, paprika, salt, black pepper, and crushed red pepper; pour over meat.

2 Cover and cook on low-heat setting for 12 to 13 hours or on high-heat setting for 6 to 6½ hours.

3 Transfer meat to a cutting board; thinly slice meat or pull apart with two forks. Using a slotted spoon, remove onion from cooker. Combine meat and onion.

4 Drizzle with enough of the cooking liquid to moisten. (If necessary, return pork mixture to cooker. Cover and cook on high-heat setting for 15 minutes more to heat through.) Serve pork mixture on toasted buns. If desired, top each sandwich with coleslaw.

nutrition facts per serving: 322 cal., 9 g total fat (3 g sat. fat), 73 mg chol., 769 mg sodium, 31 g carbo., 3 g dietary fiber, 27 g protein.

Succulent pork shoulder gets simmered in a tomato-based sauce spiked with deeply flavored balsamic vinegar. The results are down home yet a little gourmet.

balsamic-sauced
pork roast

prep: 25 minutes cook: 12 to 14 hours (low) or 6 to 7 hours (high)
makes: 6 servings + reserves

1   4-pound boneless
    pork shoulder roast
2   teaspoons dried
    Italian seasoning
1   teaspoon seasoned
    salt
¼   teaspoon ground
    black pepper
2   large onions, halved
    and thinly sliced
4   cloves garlic, minced
¼   cup quick-cooking
    tapioca
2   14.5-ounce cans
    Italian-style
    stewed tomatoes,
    undrained
¼   cup balsamic vinegar
3   cups hot cooked
    noodles (about
    8 ounces dry)

1 Trim fat from meat. If necessary, cut meat to fit into a 5- to 6-quart slow cooker. Sprinkle meat with Italian seasoning, salt, and pepper. Place onions and garlic in slow cooker. Sprinkle with tapioca. Top with meat. In a small bowl combine tomatoes and vinegar. Pour over mixture in cooker.

2 Cover and cook on low-heat setting for 12 to 14 hours or on high-heat setting for 6 to 7 hours.

3 Remove meat from cooker. Reserve one-third of the meat (about 14 ounces); store as directed below. Skim off fat from cooking liquid. Reserve 1½ cups cooking juices; store as directed below.

4 Cut remaining meat into six slices. Serve sliced meat and juices over hot cooked noodles.

nutrition facts per serving: 455 cal., 13 g total fat (4 g sat. fat), 157 mg chol., 662 mg sodium, 37 g carbo., 1 g dietary fiber, 45 g protein.

to store reserves: Place meat and cooking juices in separate airtight containers. Seal and chill for up to 3 days. (Or freeze for up to 3 months. Thaw in refrigerator overnight before using.)
Use in Pork and Noodles, page 339.

Breathe a sigh of relief. Dinner for tonight is under control. Use leftover Balsamic-Sauced Pork Roast and just three additional ingredients for a new meal.

pork and noodles

start to finish: 25 minutes   makes: 6 (1⅓-cup) servings

Reserved meat
   and juices from
   Balsamic-Sauced
   Pork Roast* (see
   recipe, page 338)
3 cups hot cooked
   noodles
1 12-ounce jar
   mushroom gravy
1 16-ounce bag frozen
   cut green beans,
   thawed

1 Cube the reserved meat. In a large saucepan combine meat, reserved juices, noodles, gravy, and beans. Cook over medium heat just until mixture comes to a boil, stirring occasionally. Cover and cook for 3 to 5 minutes or until beans are crisp-tender.

nutrition facts per serving: 331 cal., 8 g total fat (2 g sat. fat), 92 mg chol., 674 mg sodium, 37 g carbo., 3 g dietary fiber, 27 g protein.

*test kitchen tip: There should be about 14 ounces reserved meat and 1½ cups reserved cooking juices.

Tender red beans go from bland to sassy when spiced with cumin. Don't have Spanish rice? Make regular rice and stir in some of your favorite salsa.

red beans over spanish rice

prep: 25 minutes   stand: 1 hour   cook: 10 to 11 hours (low) or 5 to 5½ hours (high)
makes: 6 to 8 servings

2   cups dried red beans or dried red kidney beans
5   cups cold water
1   tablespoon cooking oil
12 ounces boneless pork shoulder, cut into 1-inch pieces
    Nonstick cooking spray
2½ cups chopped onions (2 large)
1   tablespoon bottled minced garlic or 6 cloves garlic, minced
1   tablespoon ground cumin
4   cups water
1   6.75-ounce package Spanish rice mix
    Fresh jalapeño peppers, sliced (see tip, page 32), and/ or lime wedges (optional)

1 Rinse dried red beans; drain. In a large saucepan combine beans and the 5 cups cold water. Bring to boiling; reduce heat. Simmer, uncovered, for 10 minutes. Remove from heat. Cover and let stand for 1 hour. (Or omit simmering; soak beans in 5 cups cold water for 6 to 8 hours or overnight in a covered saucepan.) Rinse and drain beans.

2 In a large skillet heat oil over medium-high heat. Cook pork, half at a time, in hot oil until brown. Drain off fat. Lightly coat a 3½- or 4-quart slow cooker with nonstick cooking spray. In prepared slow cooker combine beans, pork, onions, garlic, and cumin. Stir in the 4 cups water.

3 Cover and cook on low-heat setting for 10 to 11 hours or on high-heat setting for 5 to 5½ hours.

4 Meanwhile, prepare the rice mix according to package directions. Using a slotted spoon, remove bean mixture from cooker. Serve beans over cooked rice. If desired, spoon some of the cooking liquid from the cooker over each serving. If desired, garnish with jalapeño pepper slices and/or lime wedges.

nutrition facts per serving: 344 cal., 1 g total fat (0 g sat. fat), 0 mg chol., 450 mg sodium, 68 g carbo., 17 g dietary fiber, 19 g protein.

Pork shoulder roast, a not-so-tender cut often overlooked by food shoppers, cooks to perfection in a slow cooker. Serve with hot rice.

apricot-glazed
pork roast

prep: 15 minutes   cook: 10 to 12 hours (low) or 5 to 6 hours (high)
makes: 6 to 8 servings

1   3- to 3½-pound
     boneless pork
     shoulder roast
1   18-ounce jar apricot
     preserves
1   cup chopped onion
     (1 large)
¼   cup chicken broth
2   tablespoons Dijon-
     style mustard
     Hot cooked rice
     (optional)

1 Trim fat from meat. If necessary, cut meat to fit into a 3½- to 6-quart slow cooker. Place meat in cooker. In a small bowl combine preserves, onion, broth, and mustard. Pour over meat.

2 Cover and cook on low-heat setting for 10 to 12 hours or on high-heat setting for 5 to 6 hours. Transfer meat to a serving platter. Skim off fat from sauce. Spoon some of the sauce over the roast; discard any remaining sauce. Serve with hot cooked rice.

nutrition facts per serving: 456 cal., 10 g total fat (3 g sat. fat), 93 mg chol., 184 mg sodium, 61 g carbo., 2 g dietary fiber, 29 g protein.

The sass in these chops comes from the chipotle chile peppers. Satisfy your heat preference by using more or less of the chopped chile peppers.

sassy pork chops

prep: 25 minutes   cook: 6 to 7 hours (low) or 3 to 3½ hours (high)
makes: 8 servings

2   medium red, green, and/or yellow sweet peppers, cut into strips
1   cup thinly sliced celery (2 stalks)
½   cup chopped onion (1 medium)
8   pork loin chops (with bone), cut ¾ inch thick
½   teaspoon garlic salt
¼   teaspoon ground black pepper
2   tablespoons cooking oil
¼   cup reduced-sodium chicken broth
¼   cup orange juice
1   tablespoon chopped chipotle chile peppers in adobo sauce (see tip, page 32)
½   teaspoon dried oregano, crushed

1 Place sweet peppers, celery, and onion in a 4- to 5-quart slow cooker; set aside. Season chops with garlic salt and black pepper. In a 12-inch skillet heat oil over medium heat. Cook chops, half at a time, in hot oil until brown on both sides. Place chops in cooker. In a small bowl combine broth, orange juice, chipotle peppers, and oregano. Pour over mixture in cooker.

2 Cover and cook on low-heat setting for 6 to 7 hours or on high-heat setting for 3 to 3½ hours. Using a slotted spoon, transfer chops and vegetables to a serving platter. Discard cooking liquid.

nutrition facts per serving: 215 cal., 7 g total fat (1g sat. fat), 78 mg chol., 363 mg sodium, 4 g carbo., 1 g dietary fiber, 33 g protein.

Pork and fruit have an affinity for each other. Choose a mix of dried fruit that your family loves for this recipe, such as peaches, apricots, cranberries, and raisins.

fruited pork chops

prep: 15 minutes   cook: 4 to 4½ hours (low) or 2 to 2½ hours (high)
makes: 6 servings

6   boneless pork loin chops, cut 1 inch thick
1   teaspoon dried thyme, crushed
2   7-ounce packages mixed dried fruit
1   medium red and/or yellow sweet pepper, seeded and sliced
1   cup bottled barbecue sauce
    Fresh thyme sprigs (optional)

1 Trim fat from meat. Place meat in a 3½- or 4-quart slow cooker. Sprinkle with thyme. Add dried fruit and sweet pepper. Pour barbecue sauce over mixture in cooker.

2 Cover and cook on low-heat setting for 4 to 4½ hours or on high-heat setting for 2 to 2½ hours

3 Transfer meat to a serving platter. Skim off fat from sauce. Spoon some of the sauce over chops. Pass remaining sauce. If desired, garnish with fresh thyme sprigs.

nutrition facts per serving: 450 cal., 11 g total fat (4 g sat. fat), 92 mg chol., 421 mg sodium, 49 g carbo., 3 g dietary fiber, 40 g protein.

Just before serving, boost the flavor of the cooking liquid with two stir-ins: Dijon-style mustard and caraway seeds. Reserve four chops for the gratin on page 345.

sage-scented pork chops

prep: 30 minutes   cook: 4 to 5 hours (low) or 2 to 2½ hours (high)
makes: 6 servings + reserves

10   boneless pork loin chops, cut ¾ inch thick (about 3½ pounds)
2   teaspoons dried sage, crushed
1   teaspoon ground black pepper
½   teaspoon salt
2   tablespoons cooking oil
1   medium onion, thinly sliced
½   cup chicken broth
⅓   cup dry white wine or apple juice
3   tablespoons quick-cooking tapioca, crushed
½   of a medium head green cabbage, cut into ½-inch strips
1   tablespoon Dijon-style mustard
1   teaspoon caraway seeds

1 Trim fat from meat. In a small bowl stir together sage, pepper, and salt. Sprinkle mixture evenly over one side of meat and rub in with your fingers. In an extra-large skillet heat the oil over medium heat. Cook meat, half at a time, in hot oil until brown on both sides. Drain off fat. Set aside.

2 In a 6- to 7-quart slow cooker place onion, broth, wine, and tapioca. Top with meat. Top with cabbage.

3 Cover and cook on low-heat setting for 4 to 5 hours or on high-heat setting for 2 to 2½ hours.

4 Reserve four chops; store as directed below. Transfer the remaining chops to a serving platter; cover and keep warm. Using a slotted spoon, transfer cabbage and onion to a serving bowl. Stir mustard and caraway seeds into cooking liquid. Serve meat, cabbage, and onion with reserved liquid.

nutrition facts per serving: 300 cal., 12 g total fat (4 g sat. fat), 87 mg chol., 351 mg sodium, 9 g carbo., 1 g dietary fiber, 37 g protein.

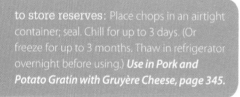

to store reserves: Place chops in an airtight container; seal. Chill for up to 3 days. (Or freeze for up to 3 months. Thaw in refrigerator overnight before using.) *Use in Pork and Potato Gratin with Gruyère Cheese, page 345.*

If you like scalloped ham and potatoes, give this casserole a try. Instead of ham, rich bits of Sage-Scented Pork Chops give the classic a nice change of flavor.

pork and potato gratin
with gruyère cheese

prep: 30 minutes bake: 45 minutes stand: 10 minutes oven: 375°F
makes: 6 servings

3	tablespoons butter
½	cup chopped onion (1 medium)
3	tablespoons all-purpose flour
¾	teaspoon salt
½	teaspoon ground black pepper
¼	teaspoon ground nutmeg
1¾	cups milk
1¼	cups shredded Gruyère cheese (5 ounces)
2	pounds round red or white potatoes, peeled and thinly sliced (5 to 6 potatoes) (do not use russet potatoes)
	Reserved Sage-Scented Pork Chops,* chopped (see recipe, page 344)

1 For sauce, in a medium saucepan melt butter over medium heat. Cook onion in hot butter until tender. Stir in flour, salt, pepper, and nutmeg. Cook and stir for 1 minute. Add milk. Cook and stir until thickened and bubbly. Add Gruyère cheese. Cook and stir until melted.

2 Spread half of the potatoes in a greased 2½- or 3-quart rectangular baking dish or au gratin dish. Top with reserved meat. Cover with half of the sauce. Repeat potato and sauce layers.

3 Bake, covered, in a 375°F oven for about 45 minutes or until potatoes are tender. Let stand for 10 minutes before serving.

nutrition facts per serving: 488 cal., 24 g total fat (12 g sat. fat), 109 mg chol., 618 mg sodium, 29 g carbo., 2 g dietary fiber, 37 g protein.

*test kitchen tip: There should be about 3 cups reserved chopped meat.

Now this is down-home cooking at its finest. The cranberry, sage, and apple in the stuffing and sauce provide harvest flavor any time of year.

cranberry pork chops with
cornbread stuffing

prep: 25 minutes   cook: 5 to 6 hours (low) or 2½ to 3 hours (high)
makes: 4 servings

Disposable slow-
   cooker liner
4   pork rib chops
    (with bone), cut
    ¾ inch thick (about
    2 pounds)
    Salt
    Ground black pepper
1   tablespoon cooking
    oil
1   16-ounce can whole
    cranberry sauce
1   tablespoon Dijon-
    style mustard
2   teaspoons snipped
    fresh sage
4   cups cornbread
    stuffing mix
½   cup chopped sweet
    onion (1 small)
½   cup chopped celery
    (1 stalk)
½   cup cored and
    chopped Granny
    Smith apple
1   teaspoon finely
    shredded orange
    peel
½   cup reduced-sodium
    chicken broth
¼   cup butter, melted
    Fresh sage leaves
    (optional)

1 Line a 3½- or 4-quart slow cooker with disposable slow-cooker liner; set aside. Sprinkle meat with salt and pepper. In a large skillet heat oil over medium heat. Cook pork chops in hot oil until brown on both sides.

2 In a medium bowl combine cranberry sauce, mustard, and sage; set aside.

3 In the prepared slow cooker combine stuffing mix, onion, celery, apple, and orange peel. Add broth and butter, stirring to combine. Place chops on top of mixture in cooker. Pour cranberry mixture over mixture in cooker.

4 Cover and cook on low-heat setting for 5 to 6 hours or on high-heat setting for 2½ to 3 hours. Transfer chops and sauce to serving platter. Stir stuffing gently before serving. If desired, sprinkle each serving with fresh sage leaves.

nutrition facts per serving: 835 cal., 36 g total fat (13 g sat. fat), 116 mg chol., 1517 mg sodium, 90 g carbo., 4 g dietary fiber, 37 g protein.

Choucroute garnie *is a French term that refers to sauerkraut garnished with meat—in this case, smoked pork and sausage—and sometimes potatoes.*

choucroute garnie

prep: 10 minutes   cook: 8 to 9 hours (low) or 4 to 4½ hours (high)
makes: 8 servings

1   14- to 15-ounce can
    Bavarian-style
    sauerkraut (with
    caraway seeds),
    rinsed and drained
1   pound Yukon gold
    potatoes, quartered
1   pound cooked
    smoked boneless
    pork chops, halved
    crosswise
1   pound cooked
    bratwurst, halved
    crosswise, or
    cooked smoked
    Polish sausage, cut
    into 3-inch lengths
1   12-ounce bottle or
    can beer

1 Place sauerkraut and potatoes in a 4½- to 6-quart slow cooker. Top with pork chops and bratwurst. Pour beer over mixture in cooker.

2 Cover and cook on low-heat setting for 8 to 9 hours or on high-heat setting for 4 to 4½ hours.

nutrition facts per serving: 311 cal., 17 g total fat (6 g sat. fat), 64 mg chol., 2158 mg sodium, 16 g carbo., 1 g dietary fiber, 19 g protein.

Be sure to use seedless raspberry preserves for these spicy, vinegar-sauced country-style pork ribs. Simple, yet delightful.

pork ribs in
raspberry-chipotle sauce

prep: 15 minutes   cook: 8 to 10 hours (low) or 4 to 5 hours (high)
makes: 4 to 6 servings

2   medium onions, sliced and separated into rings
3   pounds country-style pork ribs
1   18-ounce jar seedless raspberry preserves
1   canned chipotle chile pepper in adobo sauce
⅓   cup apple cider or juice
2   tablespoons balsamic vinegar

1 Place onions in a 4- to 5-quart slow cooker. Top with meat. In a blender combine preserves, chipotle pepper, apple cider, and vinegar. Cover and blend until smooth. Reserve 1¼ cups raspberry mixture for sauce; cover and chill until needed. Pour remaining raspberry mixture over ribs in cooker.

2 Cover and cook on low-heat setting for 8 to 10 hours or on high-heat setting for 4 to 5 hours.

3 For sauce, in a medium saucepan bring reserved raspberry mixture to boiling; reduce heat. Simmer, uncovered, for 5 minutes. Using tongs, transfer ribs and onions to a serving platter. Discard cooking liquid. Spoon some of the sauce over ribs and onions. Pass remaining sauce.

nutrition facts per serving: 689 cal., 15 g total fat (5 g sat. fat), 121 mg chol., 211 mg sodium, 97 g carbo., 2 g dietary fiber, 38 g protein.

Tomato paste, molasses, vinegar, and dry mustard each play a part in developing the great flavor of these ribs. Rosemary and thyme add earthy notes.

country-style pork ribs

prep: 15 minutes   cook: 10 to 12 hours (low) or 5 to 6 hours (high)
makes: 4 to 6 servings

1	large onion, sliced
2½	to 3 pounds country-style pork ribs
½	of a 6-ounce can (⅓ cup) tomato paste
¼	cup molasses
3	tablespoons vinegar
1	teaspoon dry mustard
¼	teaspoon salt
¼	teaspoon ground black pepper
⅛	teaspoon dried thyme, crushed
⅛	teaspoon dried rosemary, crushed
1½	cups vegetable juice

1 Place onion in a 3½- to 6-quart slow cooker. Top with meat. In a medium bowl combine tomato paste, molasses, vinegar, mustard, salt, pepper, thyme, and rosemary. Pour over meat. Reserve 1 cup tomato juice for sauce; cover and refrigerate. Pour remaining ½ cup juice over mixture in cooker.

2 Cover and cook on low-heat setting for 10 to 12 hours or on high-heat setting for 5 to 6 hours.

3 For sauce, in a small saucepan heat reserved juice to boiling; reduce heat. Simmer, uncovered, for 10 minutes.

4 Using a slotted spoon, transfer meat to a serving platter. Discard cooking liquid. Serve sauce with meat.

nutrition facts per serving: 354 cal., 13 g total fat (4 g sat. fat), 101 mg chol., 518 mg sodium, 26 g carbo., 2 g dietary fiber, 33 g protein.

The pleasure of eating ribs that fall off the bone starts with a simple blend of seasonings, barbecue sauce, and a container of honey mustard.

honey mustard
barbecue pork ribs

prep: 15 minutes cook: 8 to 10 hours (low) or 4 to 5 hours (high)
makes: 6 to 8 servings

3½   pounds country-style pork ribs
1   cup bottled barbecue sauce
1   8-ounce jar honey mustard
2   teaspoons zesty herb grill seasoning blend

1 Place meat in a 3½- or 4-quart slow cooker. In a small bowl combine barbecue sauce, honey mustard, and seasoning blend. Pour over meat in cooker, stirring to coat.

2 Cover and cook on low-heat setting for 8 to 10 hours or on high-heat setting for 4 to 5 hours.

3 Transfer meat to a serving platter. Strain sauce into a bowl; skim off fat. Drizzle some of the sauce over the meat and pass remaining sauce.

nutrition facts per serving: 322 cal., 12 g total fat (4 g sat. fat), 94 mg chol., 497 mg sodium, 18 g carbo., 1 g dietary fiber, 29 g protein.

Too cold outside to grill? Turn to these ribs in a flavorful barbecue sauce. Save half of the ribs and sauce for Shredded Pork Sandwiches on page 352.

barbecued
country-style ribs

prep: 30 minutes   cook: 10 to 11 hours (low) or 5 to 5½ hours (high)
makes: 4 servings + reserves

4½   to 5 pounds boneless country-style pork ribs
1½   cups bottled barbecue sauce
½   cup chopped onion (1 medium)
½   cup chopped celery (1 stalk)
2   tablespoons yellow mustard
1   tablespoon packed brown sugar
1   tablespoon Worcestershire sauce
2   cloves garlic, minced
1   teaspoon dried thyme, crushed
2   cups hot cooked noodles (optional)
     Fresh thyme sprigs (optional)

1 Trim fat from meat. Place meat in a 4- to 5-quart slow cooker. In a medium bowl combine barbecue sauce, onion, celery, mustard, brown sugar, Worcestershire sauce, garlic, and thyme. Pour over meat.

2 Cover and cook on low-heat setting for 10 to 11 hours or on high-heat setting for 5 to 5½ hours.

3 Using a slotted spoon, remove meat from cooking liquid. Strain sauce into a bowl. If necessary, skim off fat. Serve half of the ribs and half of the sauce with hot cooked noodles and thyme springs if desired.

4 Using two forks, pull remaining meat apart into shreds, trimming fat as necessary; store as directed below.

nutrition facts per serving: 554 cal., 22 g total fat (7 g sat. fat), 189 mg chol., 632 mg sodium, 30 g carbo., 2 g dietary fiber, 54 g protein.

to store reserves: Place shredded pork (about 3 cups) and 1 cup sauce in an airtight container; stir to combine. Place remaining sauce (about 2 cups) in a second airtight container. Seal and chill for up to 3 days. (Or freeze for up to 3 months. Thaw in refrigerator overnight before using.) *Use in Shredded Pork Sandwiches with Vinegar Slaw, page 352.*

Although you can use our recipe to make homemade slaw, if you don't have the time or the ingredients to make it, pick some up from your favorite deli.

shredded pork sandwiches with vinegar slaw

prep: 25 minutes   chill: 2 hours   makes: 4 servings

2   cups packaged shredded cabbage with carrot (coleslaw mix)
¼   cup cider vinegar
3   tablespoons honey
¼   teaspoon salt
⅛   teaspoon ground black pepper
    Reserved meat and sauce from Barbecued Country-Style Ribs* (see recipe, page 351)
4   kaiser rolls or hoagie buns, split and toasted
    Bottled hot pepper sauce (optional)

1 In a medium bowl combine coleslaw mix, vinegar, honey, salt, and pepper, tossing to combine. Cover and chill for 2 to 24 hours, stirring occasionally.

2 In a medium saucepan heat reserved meat mixture, covered, over medium heat for about 10 minutes or until heated through, stirring occasionally. If desired, drizzle enough of the reserved sauce over to moisten meat. In a small saucepan heat any remaining reserved sauce over medium-low heat until heated through.

3 To serve, strain cabbage mixture, discarding liquid. Divide meat mixture among roll bottoms. Top with cabbage and roll tops. Pass reserved sauce and, if desired, bottled hot pepper sauce.

nutrition facts per serving: 673 cal., 23 g total fat (7 g sat. fat), 162 mg chol., 1089 mg sodium, 56 g carbo., 3 g dietary fiber, 57 g protein.

✳test kitchen tip: There should be 3 cups reserved shredded pork mixed with 1 cup sauce and about 2 cups additional reserved sauce.

When food lovers use terms like rustic *and* country French, *this is no doubt the type of nourishing fare that they are speaking about.*

pork ribs and beans

prep: 20 minutes   cook: 8 to 9 hours (low) or 4 to 4½ hours (high)
makes: 6 servings

2½ pounds boneless country-style pork ribs
¾ teaspoon dried rosemary, crushed
¼ teaspoon salt
¼ teaspoon ground black pepper
1 medium onion, chopped
1 15- or 19-ounce can cannellini beans (white kidney beans), rinsed and drained
1 15-ounce can black beans, rinsed and drained
1 14.5-ounce can diced tomatoes with basil, garlic, and oregano, undrained
¼ cup dry red wine
¼ cup shredded Parmesan cheese (optional)

1 Trim fat from meat. Sprinkle with rosemary, salt, and pepper. Place meat in a 4- to 5-quart slow cooker. Add onion, cannellini and black beans, and tomatoes to meat. Pour wine over mixture in cooker.

2 Cover and cook on low-heat setting for 8 to 9 hours or on high-heat setting for 4 to 4½ hours.

3 Using a slotted spoon, transfer meat and bean mixture to a serving platter. Spoon some of the cooking liquid over meat and beans. If desired, sprinkle individual servings with Parmesan cheese.

nutrition facts per serving: 289 cal., 9 g total fat (3 g sat. fat), 67 mg chol., 759 mg sodium, 27 g carbo., 7 g dietary fiber, 30 g protein.

Chipotle peppers, smoked jalapeños, offer considerable heat as well as a subtle smokiness. The adobo sauce also contains chiles as well as herbs and vinegar.

cranberry-chipotle
country-style ribs

prep: 15 minutes   cook: 7 to 8 hours (low) or 3½ to 4 hours (high)
makes: 6 to 8 servings

2½   to 3 pounds boneless
        country-style pork
        ribs
        Salt
        Ground black pepper
1   16-ounce can whole
        cranberry sauce
1   large onion, chopped
3   chipotle chile peppers
        in adobo sauce,
        finely chopped (see
        tip, page 32)
3   cloves garlic, minced

1 Trim fat from meat. Sprinkle with salt and pepper.

2 Place meat in a 3½- or 4-quart slow cooker. In a medium bowl combine cranberry sauce, onion, chipotle peppers, and garlic. Pour over meat.

3 Cover and cook on low-heat setting for 7 to 8 hours or on high-heat setting for 3½ to 4 hours. Transfer meat to a serving platter. Stir sauce. Drizzle some of the sauce over the ribs. If desired, serve with remaining sauce.

nutrition facts per serving: 395 cal., 10 g total fat (4 g sat. fat), 139 mg chol., 247 mg sodium, 32 g carbo., 2 g dietary fiber, 40 g protein.

At first, the sauce might seem thin, but it will thicken nicely when stirred into the pasta. Save 2 cups of the ham and cheese sauce for the recipe on page 357.

ham and four-cheese
linguine

prep: 25 minutes   cook: 2 to 2½ hours (low)   makes: 4 servings + reserves

1   cup shredded
     Emmentaler cheese
     (4 ounces)
1   cup shredded
     Gruyère cheese
     (4 ounces)
1   cup crumbled blue
     cheese (4 ounces)
¾   cup finely shredded
     Parmesan cheese
     (3 ounces)
2   tablespoons all-
     purpose flour
1   pound cooked ham,
     coarsely chopped
2   cups whipping cream
12 ounces dried linguine
     Milk (optional)
     Finely shredded
     Parmesan cheese
     (optional)
     Toasted pine nuts
     (optional)

1 In a 3½- or 4-quart slow cooker combine Emmentaler, Gruyère, blue, and ¾ cup Parmesan cheeses. Add flour, tossing well to coat the cheeses. Stir in ham and cream.

2 Cover and cook on low-heat setting for 2 to 2½ hours (do not use high-heat setting). Reserve 2 cups of the ham and cheese sauce; store as directed below.

3 Meanwhile, cook linguine according to package directions; drain. Add cooked pasta to remaining sauce in cooker; toss to combine. If necessary, stir in a little milk to thin. If desired, sprinkle each serving with shredded Parmesan and pine nuts.

nutrition facts per serving: 914 cal., 51 g total fat (30 g sat. fat), 191 mg chol., 1397 mg sodium, 71 g carbo., 3 g dietary fiber, 41 g protein.

to store reserves: Place ham and cheese sauce in an airtight container. Seal and chill for up to 3 days. *Use in Ham, Cheese, and Broccoli Baked Potatoes, page 357.*

Add broccoli to last night's dinner and serve it over baked potatoes for an easy meal for you and a fun dish for the kids.

ham, cheese, and broccoli
baked potatoes

prep: 10 minutes   bake: 40 minutes   oven: 425°F   makes: 4 servings

4   large baking potatoes
     (8 to 10 ounces
     each)
     Reserved sauce from
     Ham and Four-
     Cheese Linguine*
     (see recipe, page
     356)
2   cups frozen broccoli
     florets, thawed

1 Preheat oven to 425°F. Scrub potatoes thoroughly with a brush; pat dry. Prick potatoes with a fork. Bake potatoes for 40 to 45 minutes or until tender. Meanwhile, in a small saucepan heat reserved ham and cheese sauce until melted and smooth. Stir in broccoli; heat through.

2 Roll baked potatoes under your hand. Using a knife, cut an X in the top of each potato. Press in and up on ends of potatoes. Spoon ham sauce evenly over potatoes.

nutrition facts per serving: 540 cal., 34 g total fat (20 g sat. fat), 127 mg chol., 956 mg sodium, 36 g carbo., 5 g dietary fiber, 25 g protein.

*test kitchen tip: There should be 2 cups reserved ham and cheese sauce.

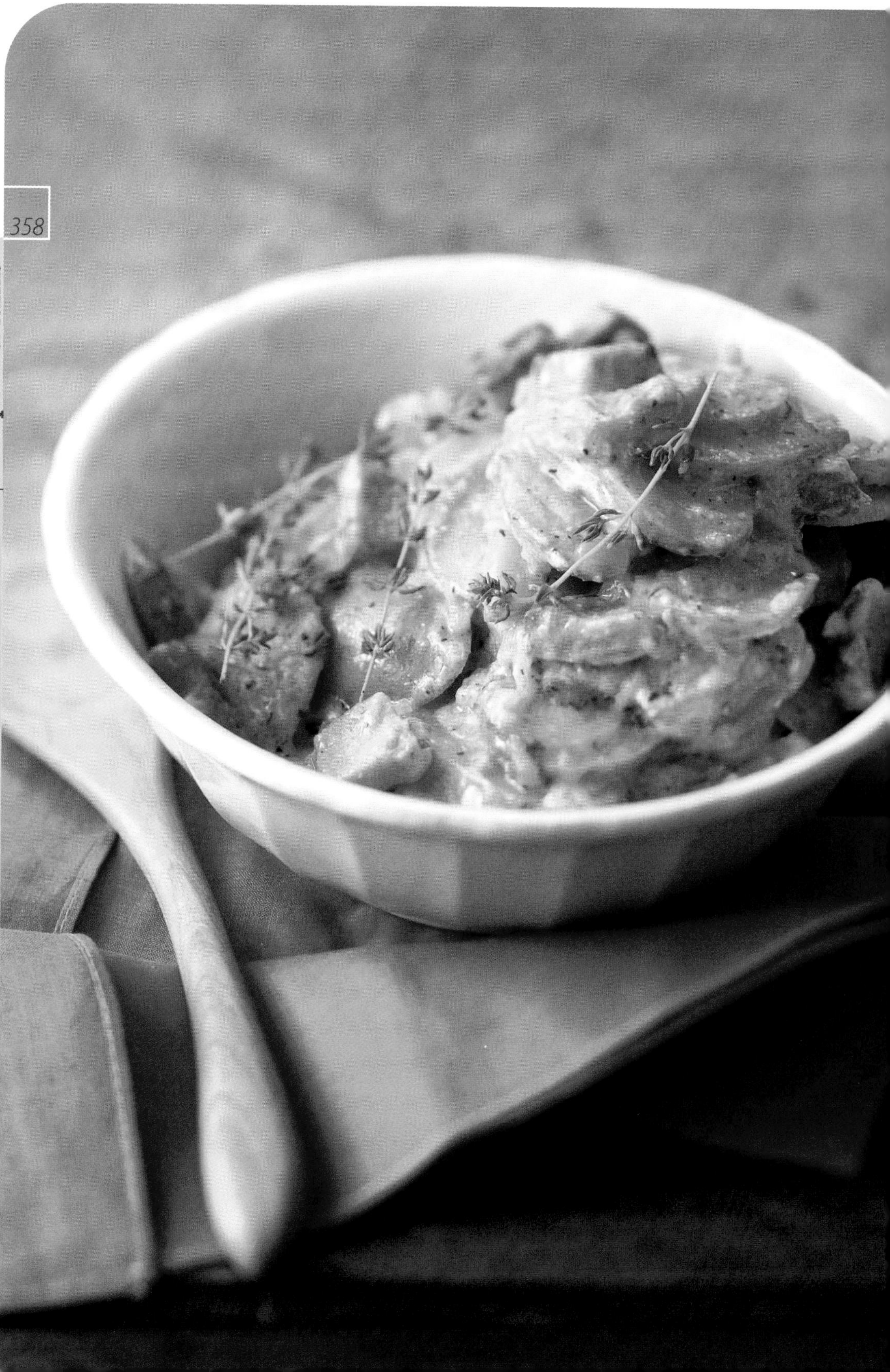

As a one-dish meal, this potato combo serves four. As a potato side dish, plan on eight servings. At potlucks, it will disappear in a flash, so make more!

creamy ham and potatoes

prep: 15 minutes   cook: 6 to 8 hours (low) or 3 to 4 hours (high)
makes: 4 servings

1½ pounds Yukon gold potatoes
8 ounces sliced cooked ham, coarsely chopped
1 cup shredded Gruyère cheese or Swiss cheese (4 ounces)
½ cup chopped onion (1 medium)
1 3-ounce package cream cheese, cut into cubes
1 10-ounce package refrigerated Alfredo pasta sauce
2 tablespoons Dijon-style mustard
1 teaspoon dried thyme, crushed
2 cloves garlic, minced
   Fresh thyme sprigs (optional)

1 Scrub potatoes thoroughly with a brush; pat dry. Halve lengthwise and slice ¼ inch thick. In a 3½- or 4-quart slow cooker combine potatoes, ham, Gruyère cheese, onion, and cream cheese. In a small bowl combine pasta sauce, mustard, thyme, and garlic. Pour sauce over mixture in cooker.

2 Cover and cook on low-heat setting for 6 to 8 hours or on high-heat setting for 3 to 4 hours. Stir before serving. If desired, garnish with fresh thyme.

nutrition facts per serving: 602 cal., 36 g total fat (20 g sat. fat), 128 mg chol., 1597 mg sodium, 42 g carbo., 5 g dietary fiber, 27 g protein.

Pineapple chunks stirred in at the end of cooking provide texture and sweetness to this barbecue-sauced brats and pepper dish. Serve over hot rice.

sweet-and-sour bratwurst

prep: 20 minutes   cook: 6 to 7 hours (low) or 3 to 3½ hours (high)
makes: 6 servings

1½ pounds smoked
      bratwurst links, cut
      into 1-inch pieces
1   16-ounce package
      frozen pepper
      and onion stir-fry
      vegetables
2   tablespoons quick-
      cooking tapioca
1   18-ounce bottle
      barbecue sauce
      (1¾ cups)
1   tablespoon spicy
      brown mustard
1   tablespoon cider
      vinegar
1   tablespoon
      Worcestershire
      sauce
¼   teaspoon celery
      seeds
1   20-ounce can
      pineapple chunks,
      drained
      Hot cooked rice

1 In a 4- to 5-quart slow cooker combine bratwurst and frozen stir-fry vegetables. Sprinkle with tapioca. In a medium bowl combine barbecue sauce, mustard, vinegar, Worcestershire sauce, and celery seeds. Pour over mixture in cooker.

2 Cover and cook on low-heat setting for 6 to 7 hours or on high-heat setting for 3 to 3½ hours. Stir in pineapple. Serve over hot cooked rice.

nutrition facts per serving: 627 cal., 30 g total fat (7 g sat. fat), 88 mg chol., 1988 mg sodium, 70 g carbo., 3 g dietary fiber, 17 g protein.

Traditional risotto takes a long time to prepare and a lot of attention from the cook. This mimics the creaminess and appeal of risotto, but without all the fuss.

barley "risotto" with ham

prep: 25 minutes   cook: 5 to 5½ hours (low)   stand: 5 minutes
makes: 6 servings

2 cups pearled barley
   (not quick-cooking)
4 14-ounce cans
   chicken broth
4 ounces cooked ham,
   chopped
½ cup coarsely
   shredded carrot
   (1 medium)
½ teaspoon finely
   shredded lemon
   peel
1 tablespoon lemon
   juice
1 teaspoon dried
   thyme, crushed
2 cloves garlic, minced
¼ teaspoon ground
   black pepper
1 cup frozen peas*
½ cup shredded Swiss
   cheese (2 ounces)
½ cup milk
2 tablespoons butter

1 In a 3½- or 4-quart slow cooker combine barley, broth, ham, carrot, lemon peel, lemon juice, thyme, garlic, and pepper.

2 Cover and cook on low-heat setting for 5 to 5½ hours (do not use high-heat setting). Stir in peas, Swiss cheese, milk, and butter. Cover and let stand for 5 minutes before serving.

nutrition facts per serving: 363 cal., 10 g total fat (5 g sat. fat), 33 mg chol., 1467 mg sodium, 52 g carbo., 12 g dietary fiber, 18 g protein.

✳test kitchen tip: If desired, substitute 1 cup 1-inch pieces fresh asparagus for the peas. Cover and let stand for 15 minutes before serving.

Fruity cola and horseradish make an unexpected pair in this robust entrée. If you are taking this to a party, tote the sauce separately from the ham. Reheat to serve.

cherry cola ham

prep: 20 minutes   cook: 8 to 9 hours (low)   makes: 20 to 24 servings

1   cup packed brown sugar
⅔   cup cherry-flavor cola
2   tablespoons lemon juice
1   tablespoon dry mustard
1   5- to 5½-pound cooked boneless ham
¼   cup cold water
2   tablespoons cornstarch
1   tablespoon prepared horseradish
    Fresh sage leaves (optional)

1 In a 5½- or 6-quart slow cooker combine brown sugar, cola, lemon juice, and mustard. Add ham, turning to coat. Cover and cook on low-heat setting for 8 to 9 hours (do not use high-heat setting).

2 Transfer ham to a platter; cover to keep warm. In a small saucepan stir together the water and cornstarch. Add cooking liquid from cooker. Cook and stir over medium heat until thickened and bubbly. Cook and stir for 2 minutes more. Stir in horseradish. Slice ham and serve with sauce. If desired, garnish with sage leaves.

nutrition facts per serving: 201 cal., 7 g total fat (2 g sat. fat), 81 mg chol., 1379 mg sodium, 13 g carbo., 0 g dietary fiber, 20 g protein.

Too few cooks take advantage of hominy, a Southern favorite that dates back to Colonial times. It retains shape, color, and flavor through hours of slow cooking.

sausage-hominy supper

prep: 15 minutes   cook: 6 to 8 hours (low) or 3 to 4 hours (high)
makes: 8 servings

2   pounds cooked smoked sausage, cut into 1-inch pieces

3   15-ounce cans golden hominy, drained

1½   cups chopped onions (3 medium)

1   15-ounce can tomato sauce

1   cup coarsely chopped green sweet pepper

¾   cup tomato juice

½   teaspoon dried oregano, crushed

1   cup shredded mozzarella cheese (4 ounces)

1 In a 4½- to 6-quart slow cooker combine sausage, hominy, onions, tomato sauce, green sweet pepper, tomato juice, and oregano.

2 Cover and cook on low-heat setting for 6 to 8 hours or on high-heat setting for 3 to 4 hours.

3 Sprinkle each serving with shredded mozzarella cheese.

nutrition facts per serving: 572 cal., 30 g total fat (18 g sat. fat), 58 mg chol., mg sodium, 36 g carbo., 6 g dietary fiber, 21 g protein.

*American cooks have taken pizza in a dozen delicious directions.
Here's a new way to enjoy it—as a saucy mixture spooned over
toasted slices of French bread.*

pizza in a pot

prep: 15 minutes   cook: 6 to 8 hours (low) or 3 to 4 hours (high)   broil: 2 minutes
makes: 10 servings

1½   pounds bulk Italian
      sausage or lean
      ground beef

1   medium onion, cut
      into thin wedges

1   15-ounce can pizza
      sauce with cheese

1   14.5-ounce can
      Italian-style
      stewed tomatoes,
      undrained

2   cups frozen (yellow,
      green, and red)
      pepper and onion
      stir-fry vegetables

1   4.5-ounce jar
      (drained weight)
      sliced mushrooms,
      drained, or one
      2.25-ounce can
      sliced pitted black
      olives, drained

1   16-ounce loaf Italian
      bread or French
      baguette, halved
      lengthwise

1   8-ounce package
      (2 cups) shredded
      pizza cheese

1 In a large skillet cook sausage and onion over medium heat until meat is brown and onion is tender. Drain off fat. Place cooked meat mixture in a 3½- or 4-quart slow cooker. Stir in pizza sauce, tomatoes, stir-fry vegetables, and mushrooms.

2 Cover and cook on low-heat setting for 6 to 8 hours or on high-heat setting for 3 to 4 hours.

3 Arrange bread, cut side up, on a large baking sheet. Broil 3 to 4 inches from the heat for 1 to 2 minutes or until golden. Spoon meat mixture on top of bread slices. Sprinkle with pizza cheese. Broil for 1 to 2 minutes more or until cheese melts. Cut into 10 pieces.

nutrition facts per serving: 473 cal., 28 g total fat (11 g sat. fat), 68 mg chol., 1371 mg sodium, 33 g carbo., 3 g dietary fiber, 21 g protein.

This no-fuss sauce—just for two—picks up its traditional flavor from Italian sausage, garlic, and Italian-seasoned canned tomatoes.

penne italiano

prep: 20 minutes   cook: 8 to 9 hours (low) or 4 to 4½ hours (high)
makes: 2 servings

6 ounces bulk Italian sausage and/or lean ground beef
1 small clove garlic, minced
1 14.5-ounce can diced tomatoes with basil, garlic, and oregano, undrained
1 8-ounce can tomato sauce
¼ cup chopped green sweet pepper
1 tablespoon quick-cooking tapioca
⅛ teaspoon crushed red pepper (optional)
1 cup hot cooked penne or spaghetti
   Shards of Parmesan cheese (optional)

1 In a medium skillet cook sausage and garlic over medium until meat is brown. Drain off fat.

2 Meanwhile, in a 1½-quart slow cooker combine tomatoes, tomato sauce, green sweet pepper, tapioca, and, if desired, crushed red pepper. Stir in meat mixture.

3 Cover and cook on low-heat setting for 8 to 9 hours or on high-heat setting for 4 to 4½ hours. Serve over hot cooked pasta. If desired, top with Parmesan cheese.

nutrition facts per serving: 525 cal., 27 g total fat (10 g sat. fat), 65 mg chol., 2204 mg sodium, 50 g carbo., 3 g dietary fiber, 20 g protein.

Lasagna in a slow cooker? You bet. Sweet Italian sausage is layered with no-boil lasagna noodles, ricotta, Italian cheeses, and pasta sauce. How easy is that?

lasagna

prep: 20 minutes   cook: 4 to 6 hours (low) or 2 to 3 hours (high)
stand: 15 minutes   makes: 8 to 10 servings

Nonstick cooking
   spray
1   pound bulk sweet
   Italian sausage
1   26-ounce jar chunky
   tomato, basil, and
   cheese pasta sauce
¾   cup water
12   no-boil lasagna
   noodles
1   15-ounce container
   ricotta cheese
1   8-ounce package
   shredded Italian-
   blend cheese

1 Lightly coat a 3½- or 4-quart slow cooker with cooking spray; set aside. In a large skillet cook sausage over medium heat until brown. Drain off fat. Stir in pasta sauce and the water.

2 Place ½ cup of the meat mixture in the bottom of the prepared cooker. Layer four of the noodles (break noodles to fit) on top the meat mixture. Top with one-third of the ricotta cheese, one-third of the remaining meat mixture, and one-third of the shredded Italian-blend cheese. Repeat layers twice starting with noodles and ending with meat mixture. Set aside remaining Italian-blend cheese.

3 Cover and cook on low-heat setting for 4 to 6 hours or on high-heat setting for 2 to 3 hours. Uncover and sprinkle with remaining Italian-blend cheese. Let stand for about 15 minutes before serving.

nutrition facts per serving: 497 cal., 30 g total fat (14 g sat. fat), 87 mg chol., 909 mg sodium, 26 g carbo., 1 g dietary fiber, 26 g protein.

Grinders are great street food. Enjoy them at home—piping hot and saucy, with lots of napkins at hand—for a much better price than you'd pay at the fair.

italian sausage grinders

prep: 25 minutes   cook: 8 to 10 hours (low) or 4 to 5 hours (high)   broil: 2 to 3 minutes

makes: 4 sandwiches

- 1 pound bulk hot or sweet Italian sausage
- 1 15 ounce can fire-roasted diced tomatoes, undrained
- 1 15 ounce can crushed tomatoes, undrained
- 2 cloves garlic, minced
- 1 teaspoon balsamic vinegar
- 1 teaspoon dried basil
- ½ teaspoon dried oregano
- ¼ teaspoon salt
- ¼ teaspoon crushed red pepper
- 2 tablespoons olive oil
- 1 small yellow onion, sliced
- 1 small green sweet pepper, seeded and cut into strips
- 4 French-style rolls or hoagie buns, split
- 4 slices provolone cheese

1 In a large saucepan cook sausage over medium heat until no longer pink. Drain off fat.

2 Meanwhile in a 3½- to 4-quart slow cooker stir together diced tomatoes, crushed tomatoes, garlic, vinegar, basil, oregano, salt, and crushed red pepper. Stir in cooked sausage.

3 Cover and cook on low heat setting for 8 to 10 hours or on high heat setting for 4 to 5 hours.

4 Meanwhile, in a large skillet heat oil over medium heat. Cook onion and sweet pepper in hot oil until tender. Set aside and keep warm.

5 Preheat broiler. Place rolls on a baking sheet. Spoon sausage mixture on roll bottoms. Top with the onion mixture and cheese. Broil 4 to 5 inches from the heat for 2 to 3 minutes or until cheese is melted.

nutrition facts per sandwich: 663 cal., 42 g total fat (16 g sat. fat), 96 mg chol., 1820 mg sodium, 35 g carbo., 4 g dietary fiber, 29 g protein.

variation: If desired, omit onion, green pepper, and olive oil. Top meat mixture evenly with ½ cup bottled roasted red sweet peppers, drained, and ½ cup bottled sliced banana or pepperoncini peppers, drained.

"Comfort food German-style" describes this hearty dish brimming with authentic German flavor. Serve it over spaetzle, a dumpling-like noodle.

german sausages and
sauerkraut in beer

prep: 20 minutes   cook: 7 to 9 hours (low) or 3½ to 4½ hours (high)
makes: 6 servings

1   large sweet onion,
    cut into thin
    wedges (1 cup)
8   ounces tiny new
    potatoes, halved
3   medium carrots, cut
    into ½-inch pieces
1   pound smoked
    cooked bratwurst,
    knockwurst, and/
    or kielbasa, cut into
    2-inch pieces
1   12-ounce bottle
    Oktoberfest beer or
    other amber lager
    beer or nonalcoholic
    beer
1   cup chicken broth
½   teaspoon paprika
½   teaspoon caraway
    seeds
½   teaspoon cracked
    black pepper
1   14- to 16-ounce can
    sauerkraut, rinsed
    and drained
    Hot cooked spaetzle
    or noodles
    Coarse-grain mustard
    (optional)

1 In a 4-quart slow cooker place onion, potatoes, and carrots. Top with sausages. Add beer, broth, paprika, caraway seeds, and pepper. Top with sauerkraut.

2 Cover and cook on low-heat setting for 7 to 9 hours or on high-heat setting for 3½ to 4½ hours.

3 Using a slotted spoon, transfer sausages and vegetables to a serving dish. Serve over spaetzle or noodles drizzled with cooking liquid. If desired, serve with mustard.

nutrition facts per serving: 550 cal., 22 g total fat (5 g sat. fat), 103 mg chol., 1837 mg sodium, 62 g carbo., 7 g dietary fiber, 21 g protein.

Red beans and rice is a familiar dish in Louisiana. Spicy andouille and pork hocks make this a hearty version. Serve with a salad for a complete meal.

red beans and rice
with andouille

prep: 30 minutes stand: 1 hour cook: 9 to 10 hours (low) or 4½ to 5 hours (high) + 30 minutes makes: 6 (1⅓-cup) servings

1 cup dried red kidney beans
6 cups water
1 smoked pork hock
12 ounces andouille sausage or cooked kielbasa, cut into ½-inch pieces
2½ cups reduced-sodium chicken broth
½ cup chopped onion (1 medium)
½ cup chopped celery (1 stalk)
1 tablespoon tomato paste
2 cloves garlic, minced
½ teaspoon dried thyme, crushed
½ teaspoon dried oregano, crushed
⅛ to ¼ teaspoon cayenne pepper
1 8.8-ounce package cooked long grain rice
½ cup chopped red or yellow sweet pepper (1 small)

1 Rinse dried kidney beans; drain. In a large saucepan combine kidney beans and the water. Bring to boiling; reduce heat. Simmer, uncovered, for 10 minutes. Remove from heat. Cover and let stand for 1 hour. Drain and rinse beans.

2 In a 3½- or 4-quart slow cooker combine beans, pork hock, andouille sausage, broth, onion, celery, tomato paste, garlic, thyme, oregano, and cayenne pepper.

3 Cover and cook on low-heat setting for 9 to 10 hours or on high-heat setting for 4½ to 5 hours.

4 Remove pork hock. When cool enough to handle, cut meat off bone; cut meat into bite-size pieces. Discard bone. Stir meat, rice, and sweet pepper into bean mixture in slow cooker. If using low-heat setting, turn to high-heat setting. Cover and cook for 30 minutes more.

nutrition facts per serving: 300 cal., 6 g total fat (1 g sat. fat), 64 mg chol., 882 mg sodium, 37 g carbo., 6 g dietary fiber, 25 g protein.

Creamy yogurt-dill sauce tops tender lamb chops and new potatoes.
Use Greek yogurt for an extra-creamy sauce.

braised lamb
with dill sauce

prep: 40 minutes   cook: 7 to 8 hours (low) or 3½ to 4 hours (high)
makes: 3 servings

¾   pound tiny new
      potatoes
3   medium carrots, cut
      into 1-inch pieces
2   teaspoons vegetable
      oil
6   lamb rib chops, cut
      1 inch thick
¾   cup water
2   teaspoons snipped
      fresh dill or ½
      teaspoon dried dill
½   teaspoon salt
¼   teaspoon ground
      black pepper
½   cup plain low-fat
      yogurt
4   teaspoons all-purpose
      flour
      Salt
      Ground black pepper
      Fresh dill (optional)

1 Remove a narrow strip of peel from center of each potato. In a 3½- or 4-quart slow cooker combine potatoes and carrots. In a large skillet heat oil over medium-high heat. Cook chops, a few at a time, in hot oil until brown. Drain off fat. Top vegetables with meat. Add the water; sprinkle with 1 teaspoon of the fresh or ¼ teaspoon of the dried dill, ½ teaspoon salt, and ¼ teaspoon pepper.

2 Cover and cook on low-heat setting for 7 to 8 hours or on high-heat setting for 3½ to 4 hours.

3 Transfer chops and vegetables to a serving platter; cover and keep warm.

4 For sauce, strain cooking liquid into a glass measuring cup. Skim off fat. Measure and reserve ½ cup cooking liquid. In a small heavy saucepan combine yogurt and flour. Stir in reserved cooking liquid and the remaining 1 teaspoon fresh or ¼ teaspoon dried dill. Cook and stir over medium heat until thickened and bubbly. Cook and stir for 1 minute more. Season to taste with salt and pepper.

5 Serve chops and vegetables with sauce. If desired, garnish with fresh dill.

nutrition facts per serving: 288 cal., 10 g total fat (3 g sat. fat), 55 mg chol., 510 mg sodium, 29 g carbo., 3 g dietary fiber, 21 g protein.

*This main dish comes with a side-dish bonus: a crisp, refreshing
slaw that contrasts with the complex flavors of the lamb.*

spiced lamb with curried slaw

prep: 30 minutes   cook: 10 to 12 hours (low) or 5 to 6 hours (high)   makes: 6 servings

1   2½- to 3-pound
    boneless lamb
    shoulder roast
1   medium onion, cut
    into thin wedges
¼   teaspoon ground
    black pepper
¼   cup reduced-sodium
    beef broth
¼   cup reduced-sugar
    apricot jam
¼   cup reduced-sodium
    soy sauce
1   teaspoon curry
    powder
1   teaspoon finely
    shredded lemon
    peel
½   teaspoon ground
    cinnamon
¼   teaspoon cayenne
    pepper
½   cup low-fat
    mayonnaise
3   tablespoons fat-free
    half-and-half
½   teaspoon curry
    powder
5   cups shredded
    cabbage or one
    10-ounce package
    shredded cabbage
    with carrot
    (coleslaw mix)

1 Trim fat from meat. If necessary, cut meat
to fit into a 3½- or 4-quart slow cooker.
Place onion in cooker. Top with meat. Sprinkle
with black pepper. In a small bowl combine
broth, jam, soy sauce, 1 teaspoon curry powder,
lemon peel, cinnamon, and cayenne pepper.
Pour over meat in cooker.

2 Cover and cook on low-heat setting
for 10 to 12 hours or on high-heat setting
for 5 to 6 hours.

3 For curried slaw, in a large bowl combine
mayonnaise, half-and-half, and ½ teaspoon
curry powder. Add cabbage; stir until coated.
Cover and chill for up to 12 hours.

4 Remove meat and onion from cooker.
Using two forks, pull meat apart into
shreds. Transfer meat and onion to a serving
bowl. Skim off fat from cooking liquid. Drizzle
meat with enough of the cooking liquid to
moisten. Serve with curried slaw.

nutrition facts per serving: 316 cal., 11 g total fat
(3 g sat. fat), 119 mg chol., 724 mg sodium, 14 g carbo.,
2 g dietary fiber, 40 g protein.

Tagine (tah-JEAN) is the name of Moroccan stews as well as of the ceramic vessel in which they are cooked. A slow cooker mimics the tagine cooker.

moroccan lamb tagine

prep: 40 minutes   cook: 8 to 10 hours (low) or 4 to 5 hours (high)
makes: 6 servings

½   teaspoon ground
       ginger
½   teaspoon ground
       cumin
½   teaspoon salt
¼   teaspoon ground
       turmeric
¼   teaspoon ground
       cinnamon
1½ to 2 pounds boneless
       lamb shoulder or
       lamb stew meat, cut
       into 1-inch pieces
1½ cups peeled, coarsely
       chopped sweet potato
1   medium roma tomato,
       chopped
2   medium carrots, cut
       into 1-inch pieces
½   cup chopped onion
       (1 medium)
⅓   cup pitted dates,
       quartered
¼   cup green olives, halved
2   tablespoons quick-
       cooking tapioca
½   teaspoon finely
       shredded lemon peel
1   tablespoon lemon juice
1   tablespoon honey
2   cloves garlic, minced
1   14-ounce can chicken
       broth
1   teaspoon orange-
       flower water
     Hot cooked couscous
     Toasted sliced almonds

1 In a large bowl combine ginger, cumin, salt, turmeric, and cinnamon. Add lamb, tossing to coat.

2 Place lamb, sweet potato, tomato, carrots, onion, dates, olives, tapioca, lemon peel, lemon juice, honey, and garlic in a 3½- or 4-quart slow cooker. Pour broth over mixture in cooker.

3 Cover and cook on low-heat setting for 8 to 10 hours or on high-heat setting for 4 to 5 hours. Stir in orange-flower water.

4 Serve over couscous topped with toasted sliced almonds.

nutrition facts per serving: 368 cal., 8 g total fat (2 g sat. fat), 70 mg chol., 674 mg sodium, 45 g carbo., 5 g dietary fiber, 28 g protein.

Slow cooking works perfectly for curry, giving the sweet and spicy flavors time to meld to great depth and complexity.

apple-raisin lamb curry

prep: 50 minutes cook: 8 to 10 hours (low) or 4 to 5 hours (high)
stand: 5 minutes makes: 6 servings

1½ pounds boneless lamb shoulder
2 cups coarsely chopped round red-skinned potatoes
2 cups chopped carrots (4 medium)
⅔ cup coarsely chopped Granny Smith apple (1 medium)
½ cup chopped onion (1 medium)
½ cup raisins
2 cloves garlic, minced
1 serrano chile pepper, seeded and finely chopped (see tip, page 32)
1 cup chicken broth
1 tablespoon honey
2 to 3 teaspoons curry powder
1 teaspoon grated fresh ginger
½ teaspoon salt
¼ teaspoon ground cardamom
½ cup frozen peas
½ cup unsweetened coconut milk
2 tablespoons snipped fresh cilantro
   Hot cooked rice
   Sliced almonds, toasted
6 fresh cilantro sprigs (optional)

1 Trim fat from meat. Cut meat into ¾- to 1-inch pieces. In a 3½- or 4-quart slow cooker combine potatoes, carrots, apple, onion, raisins, garlic, and serrano pepper. Top with meat. In a medium bowl combine broth, honey, curry powder, ginger, salt, and cardamom. Pour over mixture in cooker.

2 Cover and cook on low-heat setting for 8 to 10 hours or on high-heat setting for 4 to 5 hours. Stir in peas, coconut milk, and snipped cilantro. Let stand for 5 minutes.

3 Serve with rice. Top each serving with almonds and, if desired, a cilantro sprig.

nutrition facts per serving: 423 cal., 11 g total fat (5 g sat. fat), 72 mg chol., 786 mg sodium, 54 g carbo., 5 g dietary fiber, 29 g protein.

Mediterranean flavors come alive in this robust dish that showcases chunks of lamb tossed with orzo. Serve over fresh spinach and sprinkle with feta.

greek lamb
with spinach and orzo

prep: 25 minutes   cook: 8 to 10 hours (low) or 4 to 5 hours (high)
makes: 8 servings

1 tablespoon dried oregano, crushed
1 tablespoon finely shredded lemon peel
4 cloves garlic, minced
½ teaspoon salt
3 pounds lamb stew meat
¼ cup lemon juice
12 ounces dried orzo
1 10-ounce bag prewashed fresh spinach, chopped
1 cup crumbled feta cheese (4 ounces)
  Lemon wedges

1 In a small bowl stir together oregano, lemon peel, garlic, and salt. Sprinkle evenly over meat and rub in with your fingers. Place meat in a 3½- or 4-quart slow cooker. Sprinkle with lemon juice.

2 Cover and cook on low-heat setting for 8 to 10 hours or on high-heat setting for 4 to 5 hours.

3 Prepare orzo according to package directions. Stir cooked orzo into meat mixture in cooker.

4 Place spinach on a large serving platter. Spoon meat mixture over spinach. Sprinkle with feta cheese. Serve with lemon wedges.

nutrition facts per serving: 437 cal., 13 g total fat (5 g sat. fat), 123 mg chol., 445 mg sodium, 35 g carbo., 2 g dietary fiber, 43 g protein.

*Olives, lemon, and Greek herbs—rosemary, marjoram, and thyme—
season tender chops. Seek out arugula for this dish. It adds a
peppery bite that is irresistible.*

greek braised lamb chops

prep: 35 minutes   cook: 5 to 6 hours (low) or 2½ to 3 hours (high)
makes: 6 servings

1   teaspoon salt
½   teaspoon dried
      rosemary, crushed
½   teaspoon dried
      marjoram, crushed
¼   teaspoon dried
      thyme, crushed
½   teaspoon finely
      shredded lemon
      peel
¼   teaspoon ground
      black pepper
⅛   teaspoon crushed
      red pepper
6   lamb loin chops
      (about 1¾ pounds),
      cut 1½ inches thick
1   15-ounce can
      cannellini beans
      (white kidney
      beans), rinsed and
      drained
1   14.5-ounce can
      diced tomatoes,
      undrained
1   large onion, cut into
      thin wedges
⅓   cup Kalamata olives,
      halved
1   tablespoon lemon juice
2   cloves garlic, minced
1   tablespoon olive oil
6   cups arugula,
      coarsely chopped
1   teaspoon lemon juice
      Salt
      Ground black pepper
      Herbed Goat Cheese

1 In a small bowl combine ½ teaspoon of the salt, the rosemary, marjoram, thyme, lemon peel, ¼ teaspoon black pepper, and crushed red pepper. Sprinkle herb mixture on meat and rub in with your fingers.

2 Place meat in a 3½- or 4-quart slow cooker. Add cannellini beans, tomatoes, onion, olives, lemon juice, garlic, and the remaining ½ teaspoon salt.

3 Cover and cook on low-heat setting for 5 to 6 hours or on high-heat setting for 2½ to 3 hours.

4 When ready to serve, in an extra-large skillet heat oil over medium-high heat. Cook arugula briefly to wilt. Add lemon juice and season to taste with salt and pepper. Serve meat and bean mixture with arugula. Top with Herbed Goat Cheese.

nutrition facts per serving: 463 cal., 10 g total fat
(4 g sat. fat), 75 mg chol., 839 mg sodium, 60 g carbo.,
7 g dietary fiber, 37 g protein.

herbed goat cheese: In a small bowl
combine 2 ounces goat cheese and
2 teaspoons snipped fresh mint.

Lamb shanks make perfect partners for slow cookers because they require long, slow, moist cooking.

lamb shanks with
herbed potatoes

prep: 35 minutes   cook: 10 to 11 hours (low) or 5 to 5½ hours (high)
makes: 4 servings

1   tablespoon Dijon-
    style mustard
1   tablespoon olive oil
½   teaspoon salt
¼   teaspoon ground
    black pepper
3   to 4 meaty lamb
    shanks (4 to 5
    pounds)
1½ pounds round red-
    skinned potatoes
    or Yukon gold
    potatoes, cut into
    2-inch pieces
8   cloves garlic, peeled
1   teaspoon snipped
    fresh thyme
1   teaspoon snipped
    fresh rosemary
1   teaspoon snipped
    fresh sage
⅓   cup chicken broth
    Salt
    Ground black pepper
½   cup chopped tomato
1   tablespoon snipped
    fresh parsley

1 In a small bowl combine mustard, oil, ½ teaspoon salt, and ¼ teaspoon pepper. Brush over meat and potatoes.

2 In a 5- to 6 quart slow cooker combine potatoes and garlic. Sprinkle with thyme, rosemary, and sage. Top with meat. Pour broth over meat and potatoes.

3 Cover and cook on low-heat setting for 10 to 11 hours or on high-heat setting for 5 to 5½ hours.

4 Transfer meat to a bowl. Using a slotted spoon, transfer potatoes to bowl. Skim off fat from cooking liquid. Season to taste with salt and pepper. Serve cooking liquid with meat and potatoes Sprinkle servings with tomato and parsley.

nutrition facts per serving: 650 cal., 26 g total fat (11 g sat. fat), 227 mg chol., 83 mg sodium, 32 g carbo., 3 g dietary fiber, 69 g protein.

Lamb foreshanks are smaller than hind shanks, making them a great size for the slow cooker. You may need to ask the butcher to order them.

lamb shanks with polenta

prep: 15 minutes   cook: 11 to 12 hours (low) or 5½ to 6 hours (high)
makes: 4 to 6 servings

1   pound boiling onions, peeled
½   cup pitted Greek black olives
4   meaty lamb shanks (about 4 pounds) or meaty veal shank crosscuts (about 3 pounds)
4   cloves garlic, minced
2   teaspoons dried rosemary, crushed
½   teaspoon salt
¼   teaspoon ground black pepper
1   cup chicken broth
1¼   cups quick-cooking polenta
    Snipped fresh Italian (flat-leaf) parsley (optional)

1 In a 5- to 6-quart slow cooker combine onions and olives. Top with meat. Sprinkle with garlic, rosemary, salt, and pepper. Pour broth over mixture in cooker.

2 Cover and cook on low-heat setting for 11 to 12 hours or on high-heat setting for 5½ to 6 hours.

3 Meanwhile, prepare polenta according to package directions. Using a slotted spoon, transfer meat, onions, and olives to a serving platter. If you wish to serve cooking liquid with meat, skim off fat. Strain cooking liquid. Serve meat mixture with polenta and, if desired, cooking liquid. If desired, garnish with parsley.

nutrition facts per serving: 701 cal., 21 g total fat (7 g sat. fat), 136 mg chol., 768 mg sodium, 79 g carbo., 12 g dietary fiber, 46 g protein.

Lamb shanks are a flavorful but underutilized cut of lamb. Infused with orange and spices, this is the perfect warming supper to showcase the lamb.

spicy lamb shanks

prep: 25 minutes cook: 8 to 9 hours (low) or 4 to 4½ hours (high) + 10 minutes
makes: 4 to 6 servings

2	large oranges
5	medium carrots, cut into 2-inch pieces
1½	cups frozen small whole onions
4	large cloves garlic, thinly sliced
4	meaty lamb shanks (about 4 pounds), cut into 3- to 4-inch pieces
6	inches stick cinnamon, broken into 1-inch pieces
1¼	cups reduced-sodium beef broth
1½	teaspoons ground cardamom
1	teaspoon ground cumin
½	teaspoon ground turmeric
½	teaspoon ground black pepper
2	tablespoons cold water
4	teaspoons cornstarch
⅓	cup pitted Kalamata or other black olives, halved (optional)
1	tablespoon snipped fresh cilantro (optional)

1 Using a vegetable peeler, remove the orange part of the peel from one of the oranges. Cut peel into thin strips (to yield about ¼ cup). Squeeze juice from both oranges to make about ⅔ cup; set aside.

2 In a 5- to 6-quart slow cooker combine carrots, onions, and garlic. Add orange peel strips, meat, and stick cinnamon. In a small bowl combine orange juice, broth, cardamom, cumin, turmeric, and pepper. Pour over mixture in cooker.

3 Cover and cook on low-heat setting for 8 to 9 hours or on high-heat setting for 4 to 4½ hours. Remove stick cinnamon.

4 Using a slotted spoon, transfer meat and vegetables to a serving platter; cover and keep warm.

5 For sauce, pour cooking liquid into a glass measuring cup. Skim off fat. Measure 1½ cups of the cooking liquid; pour into a small saucepan. In a small bowl stir together the water and cornstarch; stir into liquid in saucepan. Cook and stir over medium heat until thickened and bubbly. Cook and stir for 2 minutes more. Serve sauce with meat and vegetables. If desired, sprinkle with olives and cilantro.

nutrition facts per serving: 207 cal., 4 g total fat (1 g sat. fat), 85 mg chol., 428 mg sodium, 15 g carbo., 3 g dietary fiber, 28 g protein.

For health or economic reasons, at times you just want a meal without meat. No problem. Grab your slow cooker and serve up some Garbanzo Bean Stew, Falafel-Style Patties with Tahini, or Bean-and-Rice-Stuffed Peppers. You can serve creative and delicious meals without any meat. It will do your heart and wallet some good and you won't even miss the meat!

mouthwatering

meat-less

8

meals

Sometimes it's nice to take a break from eating meat, not only for your health but also for your pocketbook. Beans are a protein-packed alternative that will fill you up.

white beans
with dried tomatoes

prep: 15 minutes cook: 6 to 8 hours (low) or 3½ to 4 hours (high) + 15 minutes
makes: 6 servings

3 15- to 19-ounce cans
   cannellini beans
   (white kidney
   beans), rinsed and
   drained
1 14-ounce can
   vegetable broth
3 cloves garlic, minced
1 7-ounce jar dried
   tomatoes in oil,
   drained and
   chopped
1 cup shaved Asiago
   or Parmesan cheese
   (4 ounces)
⅓ cup pine nuts, toasted
   (optional)

1 In a 3½- or 4-quart slow cooker combine beans, broth, and garlic.

2 Cover and cook on low-heat setting for 6 to 8 hours or on high-heat setting for 3½ to 4 hours. If using low-heat setting, turn to high-heat setting. Stir in tomatoes. Cover and cook for 15 minutes more or until tomatoes are heated through.

3 To serve, top each serving with Asiago cheese. If desired, top with pine nuts.

nutrition facts per serving: 283 cal., 12 g total fat (5 g sat. fat), 20 mg chol., 884 mg sodium, 38 g carbo., 12 g dietary fiber, 18 g protein.

This slow-cooker version of the popular barbecue multibean bake gets a spice nudge from chili beans and a jalapeño pepper.

cowboy rice and beans

prep: 10 minutes cook: 5 to 6 hours (low) or 2½ to 3 hours (high) + 30 minutes
makes: 12 servings

2   15-ounce cans chili
    beans in chili gravy
1   15.5- to 16-ounce can
    butter beans, rinsed
    and drained
1   15-ounce can black
    beans, rinsed and
    drained
1   cup chopped onion
    (1 large)
1   cup chopped green
    sweet pepper
    (1 medium)
1   cup chopped red
    sweet pepper,
    (1 medium)
1   fresh jalapeño
    pepper, seeded and
    finely chopped (see
    tip, page 32)
1   18-ounce bottle
    barbecue sauce
1   cup vegetable broth
1   cup instant brown
    rice

1 In a 5- to 6-quart slow cooker combine chili beans, butter beans, black beans, onion, green sweet pepper, red sweet pepper, and jalapeño. Pour barbecue sauce and broth over mixture in cooker.

2 Cover and cook on low-heat setting for 5 to 6 hours or on high-heat setting for 2½ to 3 hours.

3 If using low-heat setting, turn to high-heat setting. Stir in uncooked rice. Cover and cook for about 30 minutes more or until rice is tender.

nutrition facts per serving: 365 cal., 3 g total fat (0 g sat. fat), 0 mg chol., 1676 mg sodium, 68 g carbo., 17 g dietary fiber, 19 g protein.

*Be sure to reserve 4 cups of this stew for
Falafel-Style Patties with Tahini, page 385.
Garbanzo beans and potatoes make a
hearty combination for a meatless dinner.*

garbanzo bean stew

prep: 25 minutes cook: 9 to 10 hours (low) or 4½ to 5 hours (high)
makes: 4 servings + reserves

3   15-ounce cans
    garbanzo beans
    (chickpeas), rinsed
    and drained
1   pound red potatoes,
    cut into ¾-inch
    pieces
1   14.5-ounce can
    diced tomatoes,
    undrained
¾   cup chopped red
    sweet pepper
    (1 medium)
½   cup chopped onion
    (1 medium)
3   cloves garlic, minced
2   teaspoons cumin
    seeds, toasted
½   teaspoon paprika
¼   teaspoon cayenne
    pepper
2   14-ounce cans
    vegetable broth

1 In a 5- to 6-quart slow cooker combine
garbanzo beans, potatoes, tomatoes, red
sweet pepper, onion, garlic, 1 teaspoon of the
cumin seeds, paprika, and cayenne pepper.
Pour broth over mixture in cooker.

2 Cover and cook on low-heat setting for
9 to 10 hours or on high-heat setting for
4½ to 5 hours. Reserve 4 cups of the stew;
store as directed below. Sprinkle servings of
remaining stew with remaining cumin seeds.

nutrition facts per serving: 245 cal., 3 g total fat
(0 g sat. fat), 0 mg chol., 1251 mg sodium, 46 g carbo.,
8 g dietary fiber, 10 g protein.

to store reserves: Place stew in an airtight
container. Seal and chill for up to 3 days. *Use
in Falafel-Style Patties with Tahini Sauce,
page 385.*

Plan to serve these delectable patties when you need an easy meal. Make the sauce in the morning or when you are home for lunch and stash it in the fridge until dinnertime.

falafel-style patties
with tahini sauce

prep: 30 minutes cook: 8 minutes makes: 4 servings

Reserved Garbanzo
   Bean Stew* (see
   recipe, page 384)
½ cup soft bread crumbs
2 tablespoons olive oil
⅓ cup plain low-fat
   yogurt
1 tablespoon tahini
2 teaspoons lemon juice
¼ cup chopped seeded
   cucumber
   Salt
   Ground black pepper
2 pita bread rounds,
   halved crosswise
½ cup chopped tomato
   (1 medium)
1 cup arugula leaves or
   shredded lettuce

1 Drain liquid from reserved stew; discard liquid. In a medium bowl mash stew with a potato masher. Stir in bread crumbs. Shape bean mixture into eight patties, ½ to ¾ inch thick.

2 In a large nonstick skillet heat oil over medium-high heat. Cook patties, four at a time, in hot oil for 2 minutes per side or until golden brown. Drain patties on paper towels.

3 Meanwhile, in a small bowl combine yogurt, tahini, and lemon juice. Stir in cucumber and season to taste with salt and pepper. Serve patties with tahini sauce, pita bread, chopped tomato, and shredded arugula.

nutrition facts per serving: 364 cal., 11 g total fat (2 g sat. fat), 1 mg chol., 1126 mg sodium, 54 g carbo., 7 g dietary fiber, 12 g protein.

*test kitchen tip: There should be 4 cups reserved stew.

When you combine lentils and bulgur, two hearty ingredients, you won't even miss the meat. Feta cheese sprinkled over the top adds a profusion of flavor.

lentil and bulgur pilaf with feta

prep: 15 minutes   cook: 3 hours (high)   stand: 10 minutes   makes: 6 servings

2	14-ounce cans vegetable or chicken broth
2	cups sliced carrots (4 medium)
2	cups frozen whole kernel corn
1	cup bulgur
½	cup brown lentils, rinsed and drained
1	teaspoon dried oregano, crushed
1	teaspoon ground cumin
¼	teaspoon ground coriander
¼	teaspoon ground black pepper
4	cloves garlic, minced
2	cups chopped tomatoes (4 medium)
¾	cup crumbled feta cheese (3 ounces)

1 In a 3½- or 4-quart slow cooker combine broth, carrots, corn, bulgur, lentils, oregano, cumin, coriander, pepper, and garlic. Cover and cook on high-heat setting for 3 hours (do not use low-heat setting).

2 Stir in tomatoes. Turn off cooker. Cover and let stand for 10 minutes. Sprinkle each serving with feta cheese.

nutrition facts per serving: 266 cal., 5 g total fat (3 g sat. fat), 17 mg chol., 799 mg sodium, 47 g carbo., 12 g dietary fiber, 12 g protein.

Greek seasoning—a blend of onion, garlic, marjoram, basil, oregano, and mint—imparts a zesty flavor to this lentil dish.

greek-seasoned lentils

prep: 15 minutes cook: 6 to 7 hours (low) or 3 to 3½ hours (high)
makes: 6 to 8 servings

Nonstick cooking
   spray
2 cups brown lentils,
   rinsed and drained
2 cups purchased
   shredded carrots
1 cup chopped onion
   (1 large)
3 14-ounce cans
   vegetable broth
2 teaspoons dried
   Greek seasoning

1 Lightly coat the inside of a 3½- to 5-quart slow cooker with cooking spray. In the prepared slow cooker combine lentils, carrots, onion, broth, and Greek seasoning.

2 Cover and cook on low-heat setting for 6 to 7 hours or on high-heat setting for 3 to 3½ hours. Use a slotted spoon to serve lentils.

nutrition facts per serving: 260 cal., 2 g total fat (0 g sat. fat), 0 mg chol., 874 mg sodium, 45 g carbo., 21 g dietary fiber, 20 g protein.

Wheat berries, barley, and wild rice really boost the chew-factor of this pilaf. Green soybeans add a huge dose of protein and nutrition.

multigrain pilaf

prep: 25 minutes   cook: 6 to 8 hours (low) or 3 to 4 hours (high)
makes: 6 servings

⅔ cup wheat berries
½ cup regular barley
    (not quick-cooking)
½ cup wild rice
2 14-ounce cans
    vegetable or
    chicken broth
2 cups frozen
    green soybeans
    (edamame) or baby
    lima beans
¾ cup chopped red
    sweet pepper
    (1 medium)
½ cup finely chopped
    onion (1 medium)
1 tablespoon butter
¾ teaspoon dried sage,
    crushed
½ teaspoon salt
¼ teaspoon coarsely
    ground black
    pepper
4 cloves garlic, minced
    Grated Parmesan
    cheese (optional)

1 Rinse and drain wheat berries, barley, and wild rice. In a 3½- or 4-quart slow cooker combine wheat berries, barley, wild rice, broth, soybeans, red sweet pepper, onion, butter, sage, salt, black pepper, and garlic.

2 Cover and cook on low-heat setting for 6 to 8 hours or on high-heat setting for 3 to 4 hours. Stir before serving. If desired, sprinkle each serving with Parmesan cheese.

nutrition facts per serving: 342 cal., 9 g total fat (2 g sat. fat), 5 mg chol., 814 mg sodium, 50 g carbo., 10 g dietary fiber, 20 g protein.

A curry flavor packet from couscous is the major player in this dish. Toasted almonds create some welcome crunch.

curried
couscous with vegetables

prep: 15 minutes cook: 4 to 6 hours (low) or 2 to 3 hours (high)
stand: 5 minutes makes: 8 servings

1 large onion, cut into thin wedges

2 cups coarsely chopped yellow summer squash and/or zucchini (2 medium)

2 14.5-ounce cans diced tomatoes with jalapeño peppers, undrained

2 cups water

2 5.7-ounce packages curry-flavor couscous mix

1 cup chopped toasted slivered almonds

½ cup raisins (optional)
Fresh cilantro sprigs (optional)

1 In a 3½- or 4-quart slow cooker combine onion, summer squash, tomatoes, the water, and seasoning packets from couscous mixes.

2 Cover and cook on low-heat setting for 4 to 6 hours or on high-heat setting for 2 to 3 hours. Stir in couscous. Turn off cooker. Cover and let stand for 5 minutes. Fluff couscous mixture with a fork.

3 To serve, sprinkle each serving with almonds and, if desired, raisins. If desired, garnish with cilantro sprigs.

nutrition facts per serving: 280 cal., 9 g total fat (1 g sat. fat), 0 mg chol., 842 mg sodium, 43 g carbo., 6 g dietary fiber, 10 g protein.

Although this meatless dish tastes great with its vegetables, barley, and feta cheese, it also makes a huge contribution to your daily fiber needs at 14 grams.

greek beans and barley

prep: 20 minutes cook: 6 to 8 hours (low) or 3 to 4 hours (high)
stand: 10 minutes makes: 6 to 8 servings

Nonstick cooking
  spray
1⅔ cups regular barley
  (not quick-cooking),
  rinsed and drained
1 28-ounce can diced
  tomatoes, undrained
2 medium zucchini,
  halved lengthwise
  and cut into 1-inch
  pieces
2 medium yellow
  summer squash,
  halved lengthwise
  and cut into 1-inch
  pieces
2 tablespoons tomato
  paste
3 cloves garlic, minced
1 teaspoon dried
  oregano, crushed
½ teaspoon coarsely
  ground black
  pepper
1 cup chicken broth
1½ cups frozen Italian
  green beans
¼ cup crumbled feta
  cheese (1 ounce)

1 Lightly coat the inside of a 3½- or 4-quart slow cooker with cooking spray. In the prepared cooker combine barley, tomatoes, zucchini, summer squash, tomato paste, garlic, oregano, and pepper. Pour broth over mixture in cooker.

2 Cover and cook on low-heat setting for 6 to 8 hours or on high-heat setting for 3 to 4 hours. Stir in green beans. Cover and let stand for 10 minutes. Top each serving with feta cheese.

nutrition facts per serving: 270 cal., 3 g total fat (1 g sat. fat), 6 mg chol., 552 mg sodium, 54 g carbo., 14 g dietary fiber, 11 g protein.

Stuffed peppers make a delightful meatless meal for a change.
A can of chili beans with gravy, rice, tomato sauce, and
cheese create the stuffing.

bean-and-rice-
stuffed peppers

prep: 15 minutes   cook: 6 to 6½ hours (low) or 3 to 3½ hours (high)
makes: 4 servings

4 medium green, red,
    and/or yellow sweet
    peppers
1 15-ounce can chili
    beans with chili
    gravy
1 cup cooked converted
    rice
1 cup shredded
    Monterey Jack
    cheese (4 ounces)
1 15-ounce can tomato
    sauce

1 Remove tops, membranes, and seeds from peppers. In a medium bowl stir together chili beans, rice, and ½ cup of the Monterey Jack cheese; spoon into peppers. Pour tomato sauce into the bottom of a 5- to 6-quart slow cooker. Place peppers, open top side up, in slow cooker.

2 Cover and cook on low-heat setting for 6 to 6½ hours or on high-heat setting for 3 to 3½ hours.

3 Transfer peppers to serving plate. Spoon tomato sauce over peppers. Sprinkle with remaining cheese.

nutrition facts per serving: 332 cal., 12 g total fat (5 g sat. fat), 25 mg chol., 918 mg sodium, 42 g carbo., 10 g dietary fiber, 16 g protein.

Ready-to-use coconut milk, made from pressed coconuts, is easily found in Asian markets and many supermarkets. It adds a wonderful flavor to this dish.

thai-style vegetable rice

prep: 20 minutes cook: 4½ to 5 hours (low) or 2 to 2½ hours (high) + 10 minutes makes: 2 servings

1¼ cups reduced-sodium chicken broth
1 cup frozen green soybeans (edamame)
1 small sweet potato, peeled and cut into 1-inch pieces (1 cup)
½ cup thinly sliced carrot (1 medium)
½ teaspoon curry powder
¼ teaspoon ground cumin
⅛ teaspoon ground ginger
1 clove garlic, minced
1 cup instant brown rice
¼ cup unsweetened light coconut milk
1 tablespoon snipped fresh cilantro
2 tablespoons chopped cashews

1 In a 1½-quart slow cooker combine broth, soybeans, sweet potato, carrot, curry powder, cumin, ginger, and garlic.

2 Cover and cook on low-heat setting for 4½ to 5 hours or on high-heat setting for 2 to 2½ hours.

3 If using low-heat setting, turn to high-heat setting. Stir in uncooked rice. Cover and cook for 10 to 15 minutes more or until rice is tender and most of the liquid is absorbed. Stir in coconut milk and cilantro. Sprinkle each serving with cashews.

nutrition facts per serving: 345 cal., 9 g total fat (2 g sat. fat), 0 mg chol., 406 mg sodium, 52 g carbo., 12 g dietary fiber, 15 g protein.

Chocolate is often added to savory Mexican foods, as it is here.
A couple of cans of chili beans are the base for this spicy meal.

chili beans and potatoes

prep: 15 minutes cook: 8 to 9 hours (low) or 4 to 4½ hours (high)
makes: 6 servings

2 pounds round red or
   russet potatoes, cut
   into 1-inch pieces
2 15-ounce cans chili
   beans in chili gravy
1 10-ounce package
   frozen whole kernel
   corn
1 tablespoon chili
   powder
½ teaspoon unsweetened
   cocoa powder
½ cup vegetable broth
   or chicken broth
   Shredded cheddar
   cheese
   Sour cream

1 In a 4- to 5-quart slow cooker combine potatoes, chili beans, corn, chili powder, cocoa powder, and broth.

2 Cover and cook on low-heat setting for 8 to 9 hours or on high-heat setting for 4 to 4½ hours. Garnish individual servings with cheddar cheese and sour cream.

nutrition facts per serving: 362 cal., 9 g total fat (5 g sat. fat), 19 mg chol., 724 mg sodium, 60 g carbo., 9 g dietary fiber, 14 g protein.

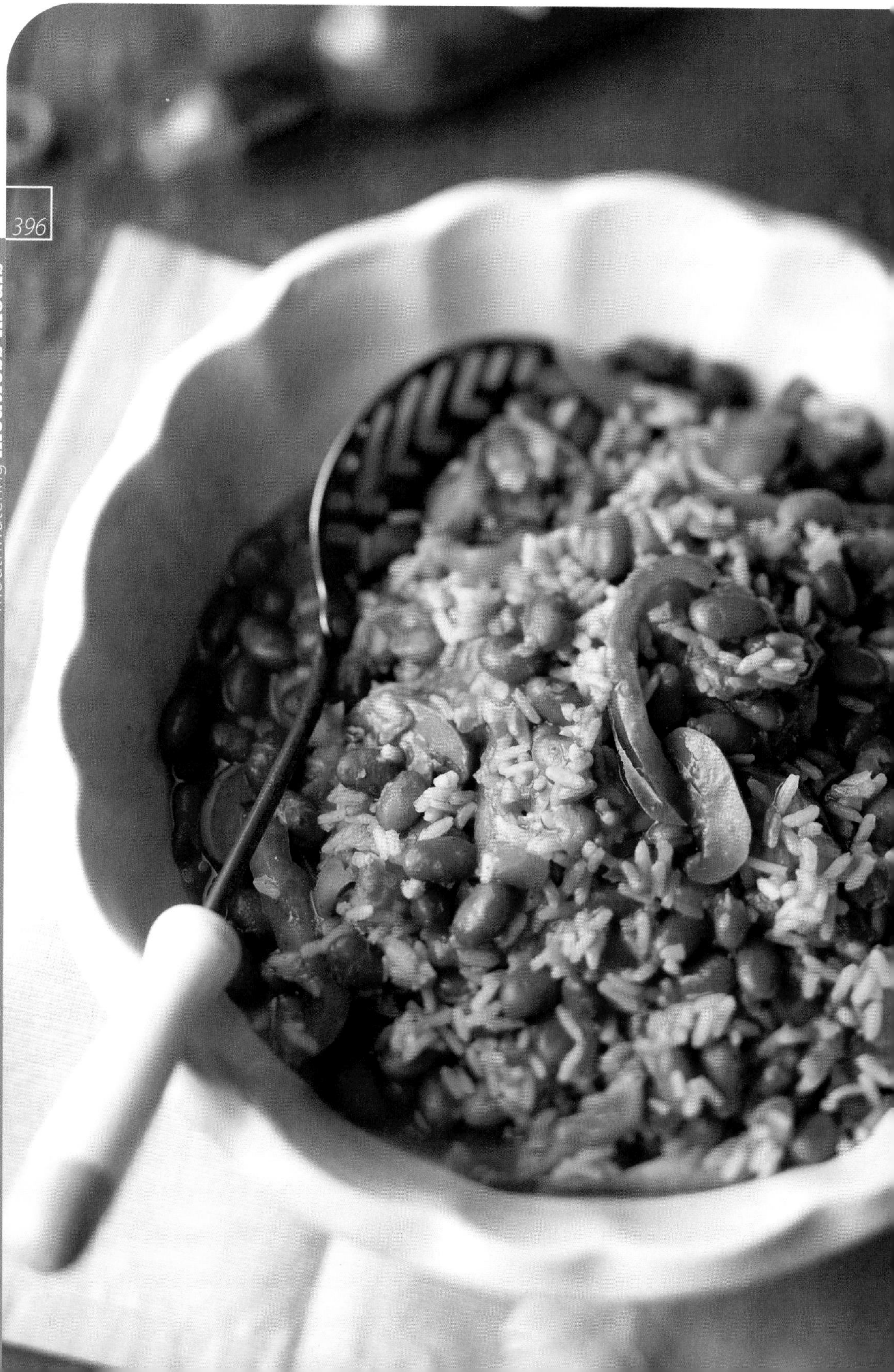

Creole seasoning supplies the spice for this delicious bean and rice dish. Let everyone boost the heat, if they choose, with bottled hot pepper sauce.

red beans creole

prep: 25 minutes stand: 1 hour cook: 11 to 13 hours (low) or 5½ to 6½ hours (high) + 30 minutes makes: 4 or 5 servings

3½ cups dried red beans (1½ pounds), rinsed and drained
5 cups water
3 cups chopped onions (3 large)
2 4-ounce cans (drained weight) sliced mushrooms, drained
6 cloves garlic, minced
2 tablespoons Creole seasoning
1 14.5-ounce can diced tomatoes with basil, garlic, and oregano, undrained
2 cups instant brown rice
2 medium green sweet peppers, cut into strips
   Bottled hot pepper sauce (optional)

1 Place beans in a large saucepan. Add enough water to cover beans by 2 inches. Bring to boiling; reduce heat. Simmer, uncovered, for 10 minutes. Remove from heat. Cover and let stand for 1 hour. Drain and rinse beans.

2 In a 3½- or 4-quart slow cooker combine beans, the 5 cups water, onions, mushrooms, garlic, and Creole seasoning.

3 Cover and cook on low-heat setting for 11 to 13 hours or on high-heat setting for 5½ to 6½ hours.

4 If using low-heat setting, turn to high-heat setting. Stir in tomatoes, uncooked rice, and green sweet peppers. Cover and cook for 30 minutes more. If desired, pass bottled hot pepper sauce.

nutrition facts per serving: 415 cal., 2 g total fat (0 g sat. fat), 0 mg chol., 541 mg sodium, 81 g carbo., 16 g dietary fiber, 23 g protein.

Rev up a simple combo of hominy and black beans with a taco seasoning mix. Spoon the mixture into taco shells and cap with your choice of toppings.

taco-style black beans and hominy

prep: 15 minutes cook: 7 to 8 hours (low) or 3½ to 4 hours (high)
makes: 9 servings

Nonstick cooking
  spray
2 15-ounce cans black
  beans, rinsed and
  drained
2 15.5-ounce cans
  golden hominy,
  drained
1¼ cups water
1 10.75-ounce can
  condensed cream
  of mushroom soup
½ of a 1.25-ounce
  package
  (1½ tablespoons)
  taco seasoning mix
18 taco shells
  Sliced green onions,
  chopped tomatoes,
  and/or shredded
  lettuce (optional)

1 Coat the inside of a 3½- or 4-quart slow cooker with nonstick cooking spray. In the prepared cooker combine beans, hominy, the water, cream of mushroom soup, and taco seasoning.

2 Cover and cook on low-heat setting for 7 to 8 hours or on high-heat setting for 3½ to 4 hours.

3 Spoon into taco shells. If desired, sprinkle with sliced green onions, chopped tomatoes, and/or shredded lettuce.

nutrition facts per serving: 317 cal., 10 g total fat (2 g sat. fat), 0 mg chol., 1001 mg sodium, 52 g carbo., 11 g dietary fiber, 12 g protein.

Barley, wheat berries, and corn create a satisfying trio of flavors and textures in this healthy gratin. Don't forget the Parmesan cheese.

corn and grain gratin

prep: 25 minutes cook: 5 to 5½ hours (low) or 2½ to 3 hours (high)
makes: 6 servings

1 cup regular barley (not quick-cooking)
⅔ cup wheat berries
2 14-ounce cans chicken broth
1 cup frozen whole kernel corn
1 4-ounce can (drained weight) sliced mushrooms, drained
½ cup thinly sliced carrot (1 medium)
½ cup chopped bottled roasted red sweet peppers
½ cup finely chopped onion (1 medium)
½ cup dry white wine or chicken broth
½ cup water
2 cloves garlic, minced
¼ teaspoon ground black pepper
¼ cup finely shredded Parmesan cheese

1 Rinse and drain barley and wheat berries. In a 3½- or 4-quart slow cooker combine barley, wheat berries, broth, corn, mushrooms, carrot, roasted red sweet peppers, onion, wine, the water, garlic, and pepper.

2 Cover and cook on low-heat setting for 5 to 5½ hours or on high-heat setting for 2½ to 3 hours. Stir before serving. Sprinkle each serving with Parmesan cheese.

nutrition facts per serving: 246 cal., 3 g total fat (1 g sat. fat), 4 mg chol., 669 mg sodium, 49 g carbo., 10 g dietary fiber, 10 g protein.

Purchased marinara sauce gets a flavor boost from brown sugar, raisins, and lemon juice. The sauce is cooked along with the bean-filled cabbage rolls.

sweet-and-sour
cabbage rolls

prep: 1 hour cook: 7 to 9 hours (low) or 3½ to 4½ hours (high)
makes: 4 servings

1 large head green cabbage
1 15-ounce can black beans or red kidney beans, rinsed and drained
1 cup cooked brown rice
½ cup chopped onion (1 medium)
½ cup chopped celery (2 stalks)
½ cup chopped carrot (1 medium)
1 clove garlic, minced
3½ cups marinara sauce or meatless spaghetti sauce
⅓ cup raisins
3 tablespoons lemon juice
1 tablespoon brown sugar

1 Remove eight large outer leaves from head of cabbage. In a large pot, cook cabbage leaves in boiling water for 4 to 5 minutes or just until leaves are limp. Drain cabbage leaves. Trim the thick rib in center of each leaf. Set leaves aside. Shred 4 cups of remaining cabbage; place shredded cabbage in a 3½- to 6-quart slow cooker.

2 In a medium bowl combine beans, rice, onion, celery, carrot, garlic, and ½ cup of the marinara sauce. Divide bean mixture evenly among the cabbage leaves, using about ⅓ cup on each leaf. Fold sides of each leaf over filling and roll up.

3 In a large bowl combine remaining marinara sauce, raisins, lemon juice, and brown sugar. Pour about half of the sauce mixture over shredded cabbage in cooker. Stir to mix. Place cabbage rolls on shredded cabbage mixture. Top with remaining sauce mixture.

4 Cover and cook on low-heat setting for 7 to 9 hours or on high-heat setting for 3½ to 4½ hours. Carefully remove the cooked cabbage rolls and serve with the shredded cabbage.

nutrition facts per serving: 406 cal., 12 g total fat (3 g sat. fat), 0 mg chol., 1368 mg sodium, 69 g carbo., 15 g dietary fiber, 14 g protein.

Tofu (fresh bean curd) provides the low-fat protein source for this one-dish meal. It's a great way to add soy to your diet.

cheesy multigrain
spaghetti casserole

prep: 25 minutes   cook: 7 to 8 hours (low) or 3½ to 4 hours (high)
makes: 6 servings

2½   cups water
1   10.75-ounce can
      reduced-fat and
      reduced-sodium
      condensed cream of
      mushroom soup
1   14.5-ounce can
      no-salt-added
      diced tomatoes,
      undrained
1   cup sliced celery
      (2 stalks)
1   cup sliced carrots
      (2 medium)
1   cup chopped onion
      (1 large)
2   cloves garlic, minced
1½   teaspoons dried
      Italian seasoning,
      crushed
¼   teaspoon salt
¼   teaspoon ground
      black pepper
1   16-ounce package
      extra-firm tofu,
      drained if necessary,
      cubed
8   ounces dried
      multigrain spaghetti,
      broken, cooked
      according to
      package directions
½   cup shredded
      reduced-fat cheddar
      cheese (2 ounces)

1 In a 3½- or 4-quart slow cooker whisk together the water and cream of mushroom soup. Stir in tomatoes, celery, carrots, onion, garlic, Italian seasoning, salt, and pepper.

2 Cover and cook on low-heat setting for 7 to 8 hours or high-heat setting for 3½ to 4 hours.

3 Gently stir in tofu cubes and spaghetti. Sprinkle each serving with cheddar cheese.

nutrition facts per serving: 263 cal., 5 g total fat (2 g sat. fat), 7 mg chol., 480 mg sodium, 40 g carbo., 5 g dietary fiber, 16 g protein.

Eggplant stars as the robust beefy hero in many meatless dishes.
Reserve 5 cups of the sauce for Double-Sauced Vegetable Lasagna,
page 403.

zesty vegetable pasta sauce

prep: 30 minutes cook: 10 to 12 hours (low) or 5 to 6 hours (high)
makes: 6 servings + reserves

2 small eggplant,
   peeled if desired,
   cut into 1-inch
   cubes (6 cups)
1 cup chopped onions
   (2 medium)
2 cups chopped red
   or orange sweet
   peppers (3 medium)
8 cloves garlic, minced
   (4 teaspoons)
4 14.5-ounce cans
   Italian-style stewed
   tomatoes, undrained
   and cut up
1 6-ounce can Italian-
   style tomato paste
2 tablespoons packed
   brown sugar
2 tablespoons dried
   Italian seasoning,
   crushed
¼ to ½ teaspoon
   crushed red pepper
12 ounces dried extra-
   wide egg noodles
⅓ cup sliced pitted
   Kalamata olives or
   sliced pitted black
   olives
   Finely shredded or
   grated Parmesan
   or Romano cheese
   (optional)
   Fresh oregano sprigs

1 In a 5- to 7-quart slow cooker combine
eggplant, onions, red sweet peppers,
garlic, tomatoes, tomato paste, brown sugar,
Italian seasoning, and crushed red pepper.

2 Cover and cook on low-heat setting for
10 to 12 hours or on high-heat setting
for 5 to 6 hours.

3 Meanwhile, cook noodles according to
package directions; drain and keep warm.
Reserve 5 cups sauce; store as directed below.
Stir olives into remaining sauce. Serve with
hot cooked noodles and, if desired, Parmesan
cheese. Garnish with oregano sprigs.

nutrition facts per serving: 339 cal., 4 g total fat
(0 g sat. fat), 0 mg chol., 548 mg sodium, 65 g carbo.,
g dietary fiber, 10 g protein.

to store reserves: Place sauce in an airtight
container. Seal and chill for up to 3 days. *Use in*
Double-Sauced Vegetable Lasagna, page 403.

Here is an unexpected bonus—this recipe makes 12 servings. Unless you have a crowd to serve, that means you'll have another night's meal all ready to go.

double-sauced
vegetable lasagna

prep: 35 minutes   bake: 50 minutes   oven: 350°F   makes: 12 servings

1   16-ounce jar Alfredo sauce

1   10-ounce package frozen cut asparagus or chopped broccoli, thawed and well drained

2   cups shredded mozzarella cheese (8 ounces)

1   cup finely shredded Parmesan cheese (4 ounces)

Reserved Zesty Vegetable Pasta Sauce* (see recipe, page 402)

1   9-ounce package no-boil lasagna noodles

1 Preheat oven to 350°F. In a large bowl combine Alfredo sauce and asparagus; set aside. In a medium bowl combine mozzarella and ¾ cup of the Parmesan cheese. Spread 1 cup of the reserved pasta sauce in the bottom of a greased 3-quart rectangular baking dish. Top with four lasagna noodles, overlapping and breaking noodles as necessary to fit the dish. Spread half of the asparagus mixture over the noodles. Sprinkle with ½ cup of the cheese mixture. Top with four more noodles. Spread 1 cup of the reserved sauce over the noodles. Sprinkle with ½ cup cheese mixture. Top with four more noodles. Spread the remaining asparagus mixture over the noodles. Sprinkle with ½ cup of the cheese mixture. Top with the remaining lasagna noodles, reserved sauce, and cheese mixture.

2 Bake, covered, for 40 minutes. Uncover and bake for 10 to 15 minutes more or until lasagna is heated through. Sprinkle with remaining ¼ cup Parmesan cheese.

nutrition facts per serving: 270 cal., 14 g total fat (7 g sat. fat), 72 mg chol., 749 mg sodium, 28 g carbo., 3 g dietary fiber, 13 g protein.

*test kitchen tip: There should be 5 cups reserved sauce.

This recipe makes enough classic marinara sauce for 12 servings. If you don't need that much sauce, follow the directions below for storage.

marinara sauce

prep: 30 minutes   cook: 10 to 12 hours (low) or 5 to 6 hours (high)
makes: 12 servings

2   28-ounce cans Italian-style whole peeled tomatoes in puree, cut up and undrained
3   cups shredded carrots* (6 medium)
2   cups thinly sliced celery (4 stalks)
2   cups chopped red and/or green sweet peppers (3 medium)
1½ cups finely chopped onions (3 medium)
2   6-ounce cans tomato paste
½   cup water
½   cup dry red wine
4   teaspoons bottled minced garlic or 8 cloves garlic, minced
5   teaspoons dried Italian seasoning, crushed
1   tablespoon sugar
2   teaspoons salt
¼   to ½ teaspoon ground black pepper
12 ounces dried penne pasta
⅓   cup grated Parmesan cheese

1 In a 6- to 7-quart slow cooker combine tomatoes, carrots, celery, sweet peppers, onions, tomato paste, the water, wine, garlic, Italian seasoning, sugar, salt, and black pepper.

2 Cover and cook on low-heat setting for 10 to 12 hours or on high-heat setting for 5 to 6 hours.

3 Meanwhile, cook pasta according to package directions; drain and keep warm. Serve sauce over hot cooked pasta; sprinkle with Parmesan cheese.

nutrition facts per serving: 327 cal., 3 g total fat (1 g sat. fat), 4 mg chol., 844 mg sodium, 62 g carbo., 5 g dietary fiber, 13 g protein.

*test kitchen tip: For quicker preparation, use purchased shredded carrots.

to store reserves: Place sauce in an airtight container. Seal and chill for up to 3 days or freeze for up to 1 month.

*Herb-infused tomatoes tango with garlic, artichokes, and cream—
a dance that renders a pasta sauce with Mediterranean flair.
Garnish with cheese and olives.*

garlic-artichoke pasta

prep: 15 minutes   cook: 6 to 8 hours (low) or 3 to 4 hours (high)
stand: 5 minutes   makes: 6 servings

Nonstick cooking
   spray
3 14.5-ounce cans diced
   tomatoes with basil,
   oregano, and garlic,
   undrained
2 14-ounce cans
   artichoke hearts,
   drained and
   quartered
6 cloves garlic, minced
½ cup whipping cream
12 ounces dried linguine,
   fettuccine, or other
   favorite pasta
Sliced pimiento-
   stuffed green
   olives and/or sliced
   pitted black olives
   (optional)
Crumbled feta cheese
   or finely shredded
   Parmesan cheese
   (optional)

1 Coat the inside of a 3½- or 4-quart slow cooker with cooking spray. Drain two of the cans of diced tomatoes (do not drain remaining can). In the prepared cooker stir together drained and undrained tomatoes, artichoke hearts, and garlic.

2 Cover and cook on low-heat setting for 6 to 8 hours or on high-heat setting for 3 to 4 hours. Stir in whipping cream; let stand for about 5 minutes to heat through.

3 Meanwhile, cook pasta according to package directions; drain. Serve sauce over hot cooked pasta. If desired, top with olives and/or feta cheese.

nutrition facts per serving: 403 cal., 8 g total fat (5 g sat. fat), 27 mg chol., 1513 mg sodium, 68 g carbo., g dietary fiber, 13 g protein.

savory

side

During summer months when the weather is hot and you'd like to keep things cool, the slow cooker is a lifesaver. Or during the holidays when you have a full oven or stovetop, try using your slow cooker to ease the load. Smoky Green Bean Casserole, Easy Cheesy Potatoes, Orange-Sage Sweet Potatoes with Bacon, and Creamy Corn with Roasted Red Peppers are just a sampling of tasty sides to choose from.

dishes

If you like, turn this creamy vegetable-and-rice side dish into a main dish by stirring in chopped cooked chicken or ham.

california vegetables casserole

prep: 15 minutes   cook: 4 to 5 hours (low) or 2 to 2½ hours (high)
makes: 8 servings

1   16-ounce package
    loose-pack frozen
    California-blend
    vegetables
    (cauliflower,
    broccoli, and
    carrots)
1   10.75-ounce can
    condensed cream of
    mushroom soup
1   cup instant white rice
1   cup milk
½   of a 15-ounce jar
    (about ¾ cup)
    cheese dip
⅓   cup chopped onion
    (1 small)
¼   cup water
2   tablespoons butter,
    cut into small
    pieces

1 Place vegetables in a 3½- or 4-quart slow cooker. In a medium bowl combine cream of mushroom soup, rice, milk, cheese dip, onion, the water, and butter. Pour over vegetables in cooker.

2 Cover and cook on low-heat setting for 4 to 5 hours or on high-heat setting for 2 to 2½ hours or until vegetables and rice are tender. Stir before serving.

nutrition facts per serving: 209 cal., 12 g total fat (7 g sat. fat), 36 mg chol., 717 mg sodium, 21 g carbo., 2 g dietary fiber, 6 g protein.

This isn't your grandma's green bean casserole. Updated with roasted peppers, water chestnuts, and smoked Gouda, this appeals even to those with an epicurean palate.

smoky green bean casserole

prep: 20 minutes cook: 3½ to 4½ hours (low) or 2 to 2½ hours (high)
makes: 12 servings

4   14.5-ounce cans
    cut green beans,
    drained
1   cup bottled roasted
    red sweet peppers,
    drained and cut into
    strips
1   8-ounce can sliced
    water chestnuts,
    drained
1   10.75-ounce can
    condensed cream
    of mushroom soup
1   cup shredded smoked
    Gouda or cheddar
    cheese (4 ounces)
¼   cup milk
2   tablespoons coarse-
    grain mustard
1⅓ cups canned French-
    fried onions

1 In a large bowl combine green beans, red sweet peppers, and water chestnuts. In a medium bowl combine cream of mushroom soup, Gouda cheese, milk, and mustard. Pour over mixture in large bowl, gently stirring to combine. Spoon half of the bean mixture into a 4- to 5-quart slow cooker. Top with half of the onions. Repeat layers.

2 Cover and cook on low-heat setting for 3½ to 4½ hours or on high-heat setting for 2 to 2½ hours.

nutrition facts per serving: 139 cal., 8 g total fat (2 g sat. fat), 9 mg chol., 622 mg sodium, 15 g carbo., 2 g dietary fiber, 4 g protein.

Cheesy and delicious, here's a side dish everyone will love. Served simply with beef or pork, it will take center stage. A side of rice will help sop up the sauce.

cauliflower and broccoli in
swiss cheese sauce

prep: 25 minutes cook: 6 to 7 hours (low) or 3 to 3½ hours (high)
makes: 10 servings

4 cups broccoli florets*
4 cups cauliflower
   florets*
1 14- to 16-ounce jar
   Alfredo pasta sauce
6 ounces process
   Swiss cheese, torn
   (1½ cups)
1 cup chopped onion
   (1 large)
1 teaspoon dried
   thyme, oregano,
   or basil, crushed
¼ teaspoon ground
   black pepper
½ cup ranch-flavor
   sliced almonds
   (optional)

1 In a 3½- or 4-quart slow cooker combine broccoli, cauliflower, pasta sauce, Swiss cheese, onion, thyme, and pepper.

2 Cover and cook on low-heat setting for 6 to 7 hours or on high-heat setting for 3 to 3½ hours.

3 Stir gently before serving. If desired, sprinkle with almonds.

nutrition facts per serving: 177 cal., 12 g total fat (7 g sat. fat), 37 mg chol., 573 mg sodium, 10 g carbo., 2 g dietary fiber, 8 g protein.

*test kitchen tip: If you like, substitute one-and-a-half 16-ounce packages (about 8 cups) frozen broccoli and cauliflower florets for the fresh. Prepare as directed.

412

This saucy side dish is perfect for your next potluck—or at holiday time when your oven is busy with turkey.

alfredo green beans

prep: 15 minutes   cook: 5 to 6 hours (low) or 2½ to 3 hours (high)
makes: 8 servings

Nonstick cooking
spray
2   9-ounce packages
or one 20-ounce
package frozen cut
green beans (about
5 cups)
1½ cups chopped red
sweet peppers
(2 medium)
1   10-ounce container
refrigerated light
Alfredo sauce
1   cup chopped onion
(1 large)
1   8-ounce can sliced
water chestnuts,
drained
¼ teaspoon garlic salt
½ cup Parmesan-
flavored croutons,
slightly crushed
(optional)

1 Lightly coat the inside of a 3½- or
4-quart slow cooker with cooking spray.
In a large bowl combine green beans, red
sweet peppers, Alfredo sauce, onion, water
chestnuts, and garlic salt. Spoon bean mixture
into prepared slow cooker.

2 Cover and cook on low-heat setting
for 5 to 6 hours or on high-heat setting
for 2½ to 3 hours. Serve with a slotted
spoon. If desired, sprinkle each serving
with crushed croutons.

nutrition facts per serving: 117 cal., 5 g total fat
(3 g sat. fat), 16 mg chol., 358 mg sodium, 14 g carbo.,
3 g dietary fiber, 4 g protein.

It's holiday time and it's your turn to bring the stuffing. Cook and tote it in your slow cooker. This savory herb-onion stuffing gets a sweet note from raisins.

raisin-and-herb-seasoned
stuffing

prep: 20 minutes   cook: 5 to 6 hours (low) or 2½ to 3 hours (high)
makes: 8 to 10 servings

Nonstick cooking
 spray
1 16-ounce package
   herb-seasoned
   stuffing mix
1 cup golden and/or
   dark raisins
½ cup chopped onion
1½ cups water
1 10.75-ounce can
   condensed golden
   mushroom soup
1 8-ounce carton sour
   cream

1 Lightly coat a 3½- or 4-quart slow cooker with cooking spray. Combine stuffing mix, raisins, and onion in prepared slow cooker. In a medium bowl, combine the water, golden mushroom soup, and sour cream. Pour over mixture in cooker, gently stirring to combine.

2 Cover and cook on low-heat setting for 5 to 6 hours or on high-heat setting for 2½ to 3 hours.

nutrition facts per serving: 377 cal., 9 g total fat (4 g sat. fat), 14 mg chol., 1105 mg sodium, 65 g carbo., 6 g dietary fiber, 9 g protein.

Dump some cornmeal, cheese, corn, and chiles (oh, and broth, too), into your slow cooker and you'll end up with polenta. So easy.

southwestern polenta
with corn and chiles

prep: 20 minutes   cook: 7 to 9 hours (low) or 3½ to 4½ hours (high)
stand: 30 minutes makes: 12 servings

Disposable slow
  cooker liner
Nonstick cooking
  spray
2 14-ounce cans
   chicken broth
1½ cups shredded
    Monterey Jack
    cheese (6 ounces)
1 cup evaporated milk
1 cup coarse yellow
   cornmeal
1 cup frozen whole
   kernel corn
1 4-ounce can diced
   green chiles
1 teaspoon dried
   oregano, crushed
2 cloves garlic, minced
½ teaspoon salt

1 Line a 3½- or 4-quart slow cooker with a disposable slow cooker liner. Coat liner with cooking spray. In a large bowl combine broth, Monterey Jack cheese, evaporated milk, cornmeal, corn, green chiles, oregano, garlic, and salt. Transfer cornmeal mixture to prepared slow cooker.

2 Cover and cook on low-heat setting for 7 to 9 hours or on high-heat setting for 3½ to 4½ hours, stirring once halfway through cooking time. Turn off cooker. Let stand for 30 minutes, stirring occasionally, before serving.

nutrition facts per serving: 137 cal., 7 g total fat (4 g sat. fat), 19 mg chol., 491 mg sodium, 14 g carbo., 1 g dietary fiber, 6 g protein.

Try this fluffy corn side dish instead of dressing with chicken or turkey. A corn muffin mix makes it über convenient.

corny spoon bread

prep: 15 minutes   cook: 4 hours (low)   stand: 30 minutes
makes: 8 to 10 servings

Nonstick cooking
 spray
4 eggs, lightly beaten
2 8.5-ounce packages
 corn muffin mix
1 14.75-ounce can
 cream-style corn
¾ cup milk
¾ cup chopped red
 sweet pepper
 (1 medium)
1 4-ounce can diced
 green chiles
½ cup shredded
 Mexican cheese
 blend (2 ounces)

1 Lightly coat the inside of a 3½- or 4-quart slow cooker with cooking spray. In a large bowl stir together eggs, corn muffin mix, cream-style corn, milk, red sweet pepper, and green chiles. Spoon egg mixture into prepared slow cooker.

2 Cover and cook on low-heat setting for about 4 hours (do not use high-heat setting) or until a toothpick inserted near the center comes out clean. Turn off cooker. Sprinkle top of spoon bread with Mexican cheese blend. Let stand, covered, for 30 to 45 minutes before serving.

nutrition facts per serving: 360 cal., 12 g total fat (2 g sat. fat), 114 mg chol., 713 mg sodium, 54 g carbo., 1 g dietary fiber, 11 g protein.

Succotash is a dish consisting primarily of corn and lima beans or other shell beans. Tomatoes are often added, as in this version.

succotash

prep: 20 minutes   cook: 7 to 9 hours (low) or 3½ to 4½ hours (high)
makes: 12 servings

1   28-ounce can
      diced tomatoes,
      undrained
1   16-ounce package
      frozen lima beans
1   16-ounce package
      frozen whole kernel
      corn
3   cups coarsely
      chopped round
      red potatoes
      (12 ounces)
½   cup sliced green
      onions (4)
½   cup chicken broth
1   teaspoon salt
1   teaspoon dried
      thyme, crushed
¼   teaspoon ground
      black pepper

1 In a 4- to 5-quart slow cooker combine tomatoes, lima beans, corn, potatoes, and green onions. Add broth, salt, thyme, and pepper.

2 Cover and cook on low-heat setting for 7 to 9 hours or on high-heat setting for 3½ to 4½ hours.

nutrition facts per serving: 120 cal., 1 g total fat (0 g sat. fat), 0 mg chol., 388 mg sodium, 26 g carbo., 5 g dietary fiber, 5 g protein.

Succotash gets a creamy flavor boost with cream cheese with chive and onion and cream of celery soup.

cheesy succotash

prep: 15 minutes   cook: 7 to 8 hours (low) or 3½ to 4 hours (high)
makes: 12 servings

2   16-ounce packages
      frozen whole kernel
      corn
1   16-ounce package
      frozen lima beans
1   cup frozen small
      whole onions
1   10.75-ounce can
      condensed cream
      of celery soup
1   8-ounce tub cream
      cheese spread with
      chive and onion
¼   cup water

1 In a 4- or 4½-quart slow cooker combine corn, lima beans, and onions. In a medium bowl, combine cream of celery soup, cream cheese, and the water. Stir into mixture in cooker.

2 Cover and cook on low-heat setting for 7 to 8 hours or on high-heat setting for 3½ to 4 hours. Stir before serving.

nutrition facts per serving: 211 cal., 8 g total fat (5 g sat. fat), 19 mg chol., 296 mg sodium, 29 g carbo., 4 g dietary fiber, 6 g protein.

This creamed corn casserole is better than any creamed corn in a can. Tangy cream cheese surely makes it a potluck favorite.

creamed corn casserole

prep: 15 minutes   cook: 8 to 10 hours (low) or 4 to 5 hours (high)
makes: 12 servings

Nonstick cooking
  spray
2 16-ounce packages
  frozen whole kernel
  corn
2 cups chopped red
  and/or green sweet
  peppers (2 large)
1 cup chopped onion
  (1 large)
¼ teaspoon ground
  black pepper
1 10.75-ounce can
  condensed cream
  of celery soup
1 8-ounce tub cream
  cheese spread with
  chive and onion
  or cream cheese
  spread with garden
  vegetables
¼ cup milk

1 Lightly coat a 3½- or 4-quart slow cooker with cooking spray. Combine corn, sweet peppers, onion, and black pepper in prepared slow cooker. In a medium bowl whisk together soup, cream cheese, and milk. Pour over mixture in cooker.

2 Cover and cook on low-heat setting for 8 to 10 hours or on high-heat setting for 4 to 5 hours. Stir before serving.

nutrition facts per serving: 166 cal., 8 g total fat (5 g sat. fat), 21 mg chol., 280 mg sodium, 22 g carbo., 4 g dietary fiber, 4 g protein.

Wild rice is a long-cooking rice and something you probably rarely make. But when you put it in a slow cooker, it just seems easier, doesn't it?

wild rice with pecans and cherries

prep: 20 minutes cook: 5 to 6 hours (low) or 4½ to 5 hours (no heat setting)
stand: 10 minutes

makes: 6 to 8 servings

2⅓	cups chicken broth
¾	cup wild rice, rinsed and drained
½	cup coarsely shredded carrot (1 medium)
1	2.5-ounce jar (drained weight) sliced mushrooms, drained
1	tablespoon butter or margarine
1	teaspoon dried marjoram, crushed
⅛	teaspoon salt
⅛	teaspoon ground black pepper
⅓	cup dried tart cherries
⅓	cup sliced green onions (3)
¼	cup broken pecans, toasted (see tip, page 18)

1 In a 1½- or 2-quart slow cooker combine broth, wild rice, carrot, mushrooms, butter, marjoram, salt, and pepper.

2 Cover and cook on low-heat setting for 5 to 6 hours (do not use high-heat setting). If no heat setting is available, cook for 4½ to 5 hours.

3 Turn off cooker. Stir in dried cherries and green onions. Let stand, covered, for 10 minutes. Before serving, sprinkle with pecans.

nutrition facts per serving: 166 cal., 6 g total fat (2 g sat. fat), 6 mg chol., 491 mg sodium, 26 g carbo., 3 g dietary fiber, 4 g protein.

Sour cream and cream of mushroom soup give this rice its creamy consistency. Dried apricots add a bit of sweetness. It's great with pork chops.

creamy wild rice pilaf

prep: 20 minutes cook: 7 to 8 hours (low) or 3½ to 4 hours (high)
makes: 12 servings

1 cup wild rice, rinsed and drained
1 cup regular brown rice
1 cup shredded carrots (2 medium)
1 cup sliced fresh mushrooms
½ cup thinly sliced celery (1 stalk)
⅓ cup chopped onion (1 small)
¼ cup snipped dried apricots
1 10.75-ounce can condensed cream of mushroom with roasted garlic or condensed golden mushroom soup
1 teaspoon dried thyme, crushed
1 teaspoon poultry seasoning
¾ teaspoon salt
½ teaspoon ground black pepper
5½ cups water
½ cup sour cream

1 In a 3½- or 4-quart slow cooker combine wild rice, brown rice, carrots, mushrooms, celery, onion, apricots, cream of mushroom soup, thyme, poultry seasoning, salt, and pepper. Stir in the water.

2 Cover and cook on low-heat setting for 7 to 8 hours or on high-heat setting for 3½ to 4 hours. Stir in sour cream.

nutrition facts per serving: 165 cal., 4 g total fat (2 g sat. fat), 4 mg chol., 339 mg sodium, 28 g carbo., 2 g dietary fiber, 4 g protein.

Topped with pistachios, this barley and wild rice side dish just got a whole lot better. Fresh rosemary also catapults the flavor factor.

barley–wild rice pilaf
with pistachios

prep: 20 minutes cook: 5 to 6 hours (low) or 2½ to 3 hours (high)
stand: 10 minutes makes: 12 servings

¾ cup regular barley
   (not quick-cooking)
¾ cup wild rice
2 14.5-ounce cans diced
   tomatoes with basil,
   garlic, and oregano,
   undrained
1 cup finely chopped
   celery (2 stalks)
½ cup finely chopped
   onion (1 medium)
4 cloves garlic, minced
1 teaspoon chopped
   fresh rosemary
½ teaspoon cracked
   black pepper
¼ teaspoon salt
2 14-ounce cans
   chicken broth
¼ cup coarsely chopped
   pistachios

1 Rinse and drain barley and wild rice. In a 3½- or 4-quart slow cooker combine barley, wild rice, tomatoes, celery, onion, garlic, rosemary, pepper, and salt. Pour broth over mixture in cooker.

2 Cover and cook on low-heat setting for 5 to 6 hours or on high-heat setting for 2½ to 3 hours. Turn off cooker. Let stand, covered, for 10 minutes before serving. Sprinkle with pistachios.

nutrition facts per serving: 128 cal., 2 g total fat (0 g sat. fat), 1 mg chol., 675 mg sodium, 24 g carbo., 3 g dietary fiber, 5 g protein.

An appetizing side dish, this savory gratin also is terrific as a main dish for six. Serve with roast pork or grilled fish.

barley-squash gratin

prep: 15 minutes   cook: 6 to 7 hours (low) or 3 to 3½ hours (high)
stand: 10 minutes   makes: 12 servings

1 In a 3½- or 4-quart slow cooker combine squash, spinach, onion, barley, broth, the water, garlic, salt, and pepper.

2 Cover and cook on low-heat setting for 6 to 7 hours or on high-heat setting for 3 to 3½ hours.

3 Turn off cooker. Sprinkle with Parmesan cheese. Let stand, covered, for 10 minutes before serving.

- 1 2-pound butternut squash, peeled, seeded, and cubed (about 5 cups)
- 1 10-ounce package frozen chopped spinach, thawed and well drained
- 1 medium onion, cut into wedges
- 1 cup regular barley (not quick-cooking)
- 1 14-ounce can vegetable broth
- ½ cup water
- 3 cloves garlic, minced
- ¾ teaspoon salt
- ¼ teaspoon ground black pepper
- ½ cup shredded Parmesan cheese (2 ounces)

nutrition facts per serving: 196 cal., 3 g total fat (1 g sat. fat), 5 mg chol., 737 mg sodium, 36 g carbo., 8 g dietary fiber, 9 g protein.

Wild rice and brown rice come together as a tomato-studded side for a crowd. Steak, chicken, or pork are hearty go-alongs.

herbed wild rice

prep: 25 minutes   cook: 6 to 7 hours (low) or 3 to 3½ hours (high)
makes: 12 to 14 servings

2 cups fresh button mushrooms, quartered
1 cup sliced carrots (2 medium)
1½ cups chopped onions (3 medium)
1 cup uncooked wild rice, rinsed and drained
1 cup uncooked brown rice, rinsed and drained
1 teaspoon dried basil, crushed
½ teaspoon dried thyme, crushed
½ teaspoon dried rosemary, crushed
¼ teaspoon ground black pepper
4 cloves garlic, minced
1 tablespoon butter
1 14.5-ounce can diced tomatoes, undrained
2 14-ounce cans vegetable or chicken broth

1 In a 3½- or 4-quart slow cooker combine mushrooms, carrots, onions, wild rice, brown rice, basil, thyme, rosemary, pepper, garlic, and butter. Pour tomatoes and broth over mixture in cooker.

2 Cover and cook on low-heat setting for 6 to 7 hours or on high-heat setting for 3 to 3½ hours. Stir before serving.

nutrition facts per serving: 143 cal., 2 g total fat (1 g sat. fat), 3 mg chol., 333 mg sodium, 28 g carbo., 2 g dietary fiber, 4 g protein.

Hollandaise mix creates a creamy sauce for corn. Roasted red sweet peppers add a wonderful flavor and color.

creamy corn and roasted red peppers

prep: 15 minutes   cook: 6 to 8 hours (low) or 3 to 4 hours (high)
makes: 8 servings

3   10-ounce packages frozen whole kernel corn or white whole kernel corn (shoepeg) in light or regular butter sauce

1   12-ounce bottle roasted red sweet peppers, drained and chopped (about 1 cup)

1   green onion, thinly sliced

2   cups milk

2   0.88- to 1.5-ounce envelopes hollandaise sauce mix

1 In a 3½-quart slow cooker combine corn, sweet peppers, and green onion. In a small bowl whisk together milk and hollandaise sauce mix. Add sauce to mixture in cooker, stirring to combine (frozen chunks of corn may remain).

2 Cover and cook on low-heat setting for 6 to 8 hours or on high-heat setting for 3 to 4 hours. Stir before serving.

nutrition facts per serving: 155 cal., 2 g total fat (1 g sat. fat), 5 mg chol., 249 mg sodium, 32 g carbo., 2 g dietary fiber, 5 g protein.

Put on your tropical shirt and wear your flip-flops for this island-style side dish with beef, beans, pineapple, and barbecue sauce.

hawaiian pineapple baked beans

prep: 15 minutes   cook: 7 to 9 hours (low) or 3½ to 4½ hours (high)
makes: 16 servings

8   ounces ground beef
1   cup chopped onion
    (1 large)
2   15- or 16-ounce cans
    pork and beans in
    tomato sauce
2   15-ounce cans chili
    beans with chili
    gravy
1   20-ounce can
    pineapple tidbits in
    juice, drained
1   cup ketchup
1   cup bottled hot-style
    barbecue sauce

1 In a large skillet cook ground beef and onion until meat is brown and onion is tender. Drain off fat. In a 5- to 6-quart slow cooker combine ground beef mixture, pork and beans, chili beans, pineapple, ketchup, and barbecue sauce, stirring to combine.

2 Cover and cook on low-heat setting for 7 to 9 hours or on high-heat setting for 3½ to 4½ hours.

nutrition facts per serving: 189 cal., 3 g total fat (1 g sat. fat), 13 mg chol., 762 mg sodium, 35 g carbo., 6 g dietary fiber, 9 g protein.

Potluck offerings don't come any easier than these well-seasoned beans. Hot barbecue sauce makes you take notice.

western beans

prep: 15 minutes   cook: 4 to 5 hours (low) or 2 to 2½ hours (high)
makes: 12 servings

3   28-ounce cans
      vegetarian baked
      beans, drained
¾   cup bottled hot-style
      barbecue sauce
½   cup chopped onion
      (1 medium)
⅓   cup packed brown
      sugar
1   tablespoon dry
      mustard

1 In a 3½- to 5-quart slow cooker combine baked beans, barbecue sauce, onion, brown sugar, and mustard.

2 Cover and cook on low-heat setting for 4 to 5 hours or on high-heat setting for 2 to 2½ hours.

nutrition facts per serving: 238 cal., 1 g total fat (0 g sat. fat), 0 mg chol., mg sodium, 53 g carbo., 10 g dietary fiber, 10 g protein.

This recipe is just right for two people and a 1½-quart slow cooker. If you are hankering for more or need more, double the ingredients and cook in a 3½-quart cooker.

hot kielbasa and potato salad

prep: 20 minutes   cook: 6 to 8 hours (low) or 3½ to 4 hours (high)
makes: 2 servings

5   whole tiny new
      potatoes (about
      6 ounces)
½   pound cooked turkey
      kielbasa or smoked
      sausage, cut into
      ¾-inch pieces
1   rib celery, chopped
      (½ cup)
1   small onion, chopped
      (⅓ cup)
¾   cup water
¼   cup cider vinegar
2   tablespoons sugar
1   tablespoon quick-
      cooking tapioca
¼   teaspoon celery
      seeds
¼   teaspoon ground
      black pepper
3   cups fresh baby
      spinach leaves

1 Cut potatoes into halves or quarters. Place in a 3½- or 4-quart slow cooker. Add sausage, celery, and onion. In a medium bowl combine the water, vinegar, sugar, tapioca, celery seeds, and pepper. Pour over mixture in cooker.

2 Cover and cook on low-heat setting for 6 to 8 hours or on high-heat setting for 4 to 4½ hours.

3 To serve, divide spinach among four individual salad plates. Drizzle 2 tablespoons of the cooking juices over the spinach on each plate. Using a slotted spoon, arrange potatoes and sausage on top of spinach.

nutrition facts per serving: 332 cal., 9 g total fat (0 g sat. fat), 0 mg chol., 1122 mg sodium, 40 g carbo., 3 g dietary fiber, 24 g protein.

These are no ordinary spuds. Hash browns get all dressed up with bacon, leeks, and three kinds of cheese. It can't get any better than that.

easy cheesy potatoes

prep: 20 minutes   **cook:** 5 to 6 hours (low)   **makes:** 12 servings

1   28-ounce package frozen diced hash brown potatoes with peppers and onions, thawed
1   10.75-ounce can condensed cream of chicken with herbs soup
1   cup finely shredded smoked Gouda cheese (4 ounces)
1   cup finely shredded provolone cheese (4 ounces)
1   8-ounce package cream cheese, cut into cubes
¾   cup milk
¼   cup sliced leek or thinly sliced green onion
½   teaspoon ground black pepper
4   strips bacon, crisp-cooked and crumbled

1 In 3½- or 4-quart slow cooker combine potatoes, cream of chicken soup, Gouda cheese, provolone cheese, cream cheese, milk, leek, and pepper.

2 Cover and cook on low-heat setting for 5 to 6 hours (do not use high-heat setting). Sprinkle with bacon.

nutrition facts per serving: 218 cal., 14 g total fat (8 g sat. fat), 41 mg chol., 564 mg sodium, 16 g carbo., 2 g dietary fiber, 9 g protein.

Spiff up refrigerated mashed potatoes with cream cheese and sour cream dip for a side dish that tastes as if it were a secret family recipe.

super-creamy mashed potatoes

prep: 10 minutes cook: 3½ to 4 hours (low) makes: 12 to 14 servings

Nonstick cooking
   spray
3 20-ounce packages
   refrigerated mashed
   potatoes
1 8-ounce package
   cream cheese,
   cut into cubes
1 8-ounce container
   sour cream and
   onion or chive dip
¼ teaspoon garlic
   powder

1 Coat the inside of a 4- or 4½-quart slow cooker with nonstick cooking spray. Place two-thirds (2 packages) of the potatoes in prepared slow cooker. Top with cream cheese and sour cream dip. Sprinkle with garlic powder. Top with remaining package of mashed potatoes.

2 Cover and cook on low-heat setting for 3½ to 4 hours (do not use high-heat setting). Stir before serving.

nutrition facts per serving: 214 cal., 11 g total fat (6 g sat. fat), 21 mg chol., 409 mg sodium, 22 g carbo., 1 g dietary fiber, 5 g protein.

When your oven is busy with a huge holiday bird, you can "roast" these rosemary and garlic potatoes in your slow cooker.

crock-roasted
new potatoes

prep: 20 minutes   cook: 3 to 4 hours (high)   makes: 12 servings

3 pounds tiny new potatoes, halved
8 cloves garlic, peeled
2 tablespoons olive oil
1 tablespoon snipped fresh rosemary or 1 teaspoon dried rosemary, crushed
1 teaspoon kosher salt or salt
½ teaspoon coarsely ground black pepper

1 In a large bowl toss potatoes and garlic with oil to coat. Sprinkle with rosemary, salt, and pepper. Place potato mixture in a 3½- or 4-quart slow cooker.

2 Cover and cook on high-heat setting for 3 to 4 hours (do not use low-heat setting) or until potatoes are tender when pierced with a fork.

nutrition facts per serving: 103 cal., 2 g total fat (0 g sat. fat), 0 mg chol., 168 mg sodium, 19 g carbo., 2 g dietary fiber, 2 g protein.

Potatoes and green beans achieve elegance in a mustard-dill sauce that owes its satiny texture to a can of cream of celery soup.

saucy green beans and potatoes

prep: 20 minutes   cook: 6 to 8 hours (low) or 3 to 4 hours (high)
makes: 12 servings

2   pounds new potatoes, large ones halved

1   pound fresh green beans, trimmed and halved crosswise

1   10.75-ounce can condensed cream of celery soup

¾   cup water

¼   cup Dijon-style mustard

¾   teaspoon dried dill weed

1 Place potatoes and green beans in a 3½- or 4-quart slow cooker. In a medium bowl combine cream of celery soup, the water, mustard, and dill weed. Pour over mixture in cooker, stirring gently to combine.

2 Cover and cook on low-heat setting for 6 to 8 hours or on high-heat setting for 3 to 4 hours. Stir gently before serving.

nutrition facts per serving: 95 cal., 2 g total fat (1 g sat. fat), 1 mg chol., 313 mg sodium, 17 g carbo., 3 g dietary fiber, 3 g protein.

For a change from mashed potatoes, add some turnips. Your fellow diners will love this dish with its mellow turnip flavor.

mashed potatoes
with turnips

prep: 35 minutes cook: 6 to 7 hours (low) or 3 to 4 hours (high)
makes: 8 to 12 servings

3   pounds baking
     potatoes, peeled
     and cut into 1-inch
     cubes (7 cups)
1½   pounds turnips,
     peeled and cut into
     1-inch cubes
     (4½ cups)
3   14-ounce cans
     reduced-sodium
     chicken broth
¾   cup whipping cream
¼   cup butter
½   teaspoon white wine
     vinegar
½   teaspoon ground
     black pepper
     Salt

1 In a 4- to 5-quart slow cooker combine potatoes, turnips, and broth.

2 Cover and cook on low-heat setting for 6 to 7 hours or on high-heat setting for 3 to 4 hours.

3 Drain vegetables, reserving some of the cooking liquid.* In a large bowl mash vegetables with a potato masher or pass vegetables through a food mill or potato ricer into the bowl.

4 In a small saucepan combine whipping cream and butter. Heat until cream is hot and butter melts. Add to potato mixture along with the vinegar and pepper; mix well. Season to taste with salt.

nutrition facts per serving: 186 cal., 10 g total fat (6 g sat. fat), 31 mg chol., 401 mg sodium, 23 g carbo., 2 g dietary fiber, 4 g protein.

*make-ahead tip: If desired, return mashed potato mixture to slow cooker; keep warm on low or warm setting for up to 2 hours. If mixture has thickened, stir in some of the reserved cooking liquid to reach desired consistency.

Will you ever make an impression on guests when you serve this dish. The beets turn it into a crimson beauty in a bowl.

crock-roasted
root vegetables

prep: 30 minutes   cook: 3 to 4 hours (high)   makes: 12 servings

1   pound butternut
    squash, peeled,
    seeded, and cut into
    2-inch pieces
8   ounces tiny new red
    potatoes, halved
8   ounces beets, peeled
    and cut into 1-inch
    pieces
8   ounces turnips or
    rutabagas, peeled
    and cut into 1-inch
    pieces
1   cup packaged peeled
    fresh baby carrots,
    halved lengthwise
1   small red onion, cut
    into ½-inch wedges
8   cloves garlic, peeled
2   tablespoons olive oil
½   teaspoon salt
½   teaspoon ground
    black pepper
    Snipped fresh Italian
    (flat-leaf) parsley
    (optional)

1 In an extra-large bowl combine squash, potatoes, beets, turnips, carrots, onion, and garlic. Drizzle with oil and toss to coat. Sprinkle with salt and pepper. Place mixture in a 4- to 5-quart slow cooker.

2 Cover and cook on high-heat setting for 3 to 4 hours (do not use low-heat setting) or until vegetables are tender when pierced with a fork. If desired, sprinkle with parsley.

nutrition facts per serving: 71 cal., 2 g total fat (0 g sat. fat), 0 mg chol., 130 mg sodium, 12 g carbo., 2 g dietary fiber, 1 g protein.

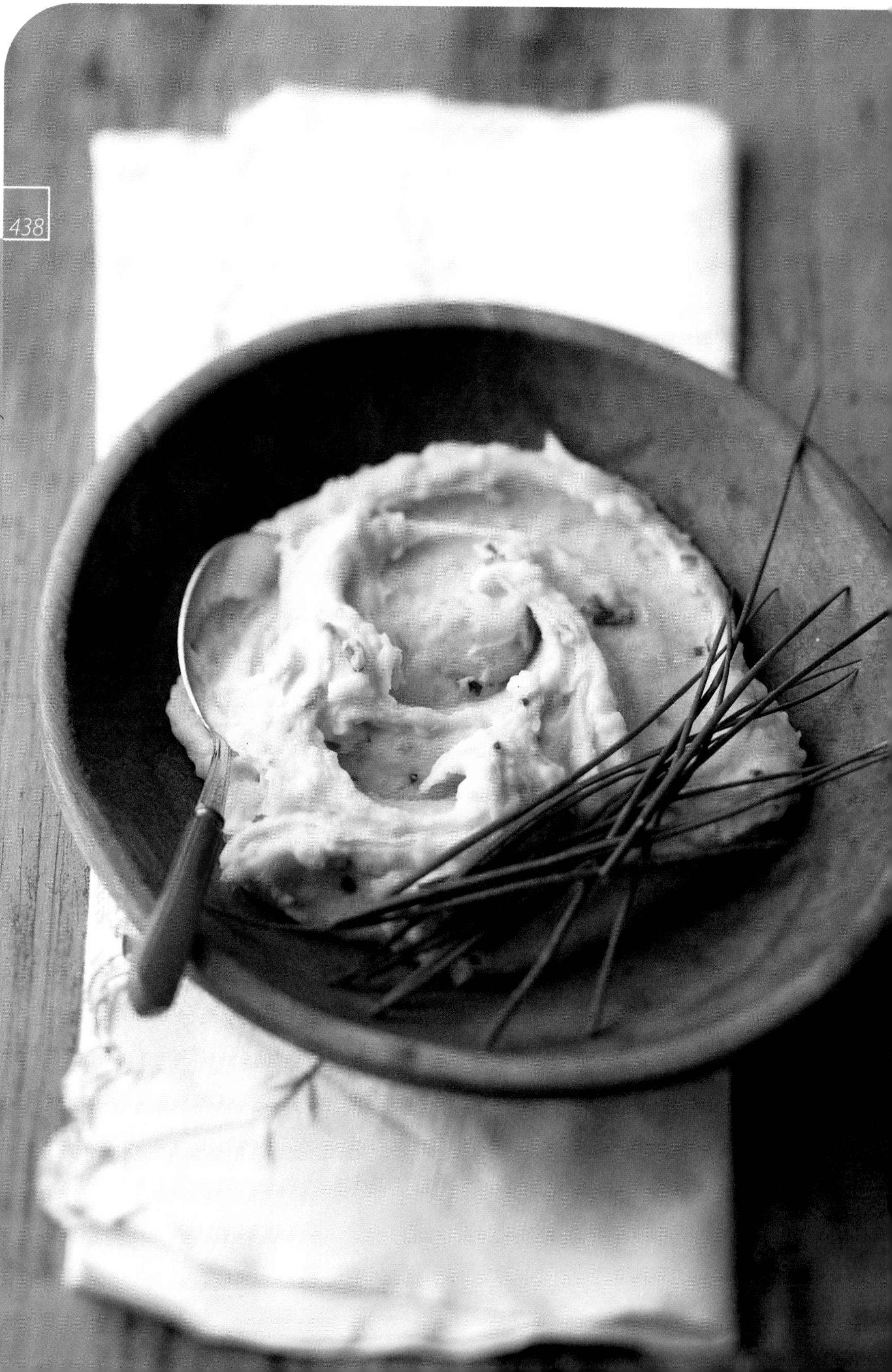

The slow cooker is a great way to make mashed potatoes for a crowd. It keeps them warm for a long time and it frees up your stovetop for cooking other dishes.

rustic garlic mashed potatoes

prep: 25 minutes cook: 6 to 8 hours (low) or 3 to 4 hours (high)
makes: 12 servings

3   pounds russet potatoes, peeled and cut into 2-inch pieces
6   cloves garlic, halved
1   bay leaf
2   14-ounce cans seasoned chicken broth with roasted garlic
1   cup whole milk
¼   cup butter
1   teaspoon salt
    Freshly ground black pepper
    Bay leaves (optional)

1 In a 3½- or 4-quart slow cooker combine potatoes, garlic, and 1 bay leaf. Pour broth over potatoes in cooker.

2 Cover and cook on low-heat setting for 6 to 8 hours or on high-heat setting for 3 to 4 hours.

3 Drain potatoes in a colander over a bowl to catch cooking juices. Remove bay leaf and discard. Return potatoes to slow cooker. Mash to desired consistency with a potato masher.

4 In a small saucepan heat milk and butter until steaming and butter is almost melted. Add milk mixture, salt, and enough of reserved cooking juices to the potato mixture to reach desired consistency. Transfer potatoes to a serving bowl. Sprinkle with pepper. If desired, garnish with bay leaves. Reserve remaining cooking juices.*

nutrition facts per serving: 135 cal., 5 g total fat (3 g sat. fat), 13 mg chol., 496 mg sodium, 21 g carbo., 1 g dietary fiber, 3 g protein.

✳make-ahead tip: If desired, return mashed potato mixture to slow cooker; keep warm on low or warm setting for up to 2 hours. If mixture has thickened, stir in some of the reserved cooking juices to reach desired consistency.

Root vegetables and balsamic vinegar are two popular ingredients on trendy bistro menus. Create your own bistro darling at home with this dish.

balsamic root vegetables

prep: 15 minutes   cook: 9 to 11 hours (low) or 4½ to 5½ hours (high)
makes: 8 servings

3 medium potatoes, peeled and cut into 1-inch pieces
3 medium parsnips, peeled and cut into 1-inch pieces
1 16-ounce package peeled fresh baby carrots
½ of a 16-ounce package (2 cups) frozen small whole onions
1 cup chicken broth
¼ cup balsamic vinegar
2 tablespoons packed brown sugar
¼ teaspoon salt
¼ teaspoon ground black pepper
2 cloves garlic, minced

1 In a 3½- or 4-quart slow cooker combine potatoes, parsnips, carrots, onions, broth, vinegar, brown sugar, salt, pepper, and garlic.

2 Cover and cook on low-heat setting for 9 to 11 hours or on high-heat setting for 4½ to 5½ hours.

nutrition facts per serving: 136 cal., 1 g total fat (0 g sat. fat), 0 mg chol., 235 mg sodium, 32 g carbo., 6 g dietary fiber, 3 g protein.

If cranberry sauce at Thanksgiving has grown a little tired, jazz it up by combining some with a few root vegetables, ginger, and orange. Very tasty idea.

glazed carrots and parsnips

prep: 20 minutes cook: 7 to 8 hours (low) or 3½ to 4 hours (high)
makes: 10 servings

1½ pounds carrots,
      peeled and bias-
      sliced 1 inch thick
1½ pounds parsnips,
      peeled and bias-
      sliced 1 inch thick
  2 teaspoons ground
      ginger
  ½ cup water
  ½ of a 16-ounce can
      jellied cranberry
      sauce
  ½ teaspoon finely
      shredded orange
      peel
  1 tablespoon orange
      juice
  1 tablespoon butter,
      melted
  ⅛ teaspoon salt

1 In a 3½- or 4-quart slow cooker combine carrots and parsnips. Sprinkle with ginger. Pour the water over mixture in cooker.

2 Cover and cook on low-heat setting for 7 to 8 hours on high-heat setting for 3½ to 4 hours.

3 Using a slotted spoon, remove carrots and parsnips from slow cooker. For sauce, add cranberry sauce, orange peel, orange juice, melted butter, and salt to cooking liquid in cooker. Whisk until smooth. Return carrots and parsnips to slow cooker, stirring gently to coat.

nutrition facts per serving: 115 cal., 2 g total fat (1 g sat. fat), 3 mg chol., 92 mg sodium, 25 g carbo., 5 g dietary fiber, 1 g protein.

Kohlrabi, a member of the cabbage family, got its name from a German word meaning "cabbage-turnip." It has a mild turnip flavor.

creamy kohlrabi in a crock

prep: 25 minutes   cook: 5 to 6 hours (low) or 2½ to 3 hours (high)
makes: 10 to 12 servings

3   pounds kohlrabi, peeled, halved, and sliced ½ inch thick
1   17-ounce jar Alfredo pasta sauce
½   teaspoon finely shredded lemon peel
2   tablespoons lemon juice
1   teaspoon dried thyme, crushed
¼   teaspoon salt
¼   teaspoon ground black pepper
    Snipped fresh thyme (optional)
    Cracked black pepper (optional)

1 Place kohlrabi in a 3½- or 4-quart slow cooker. In a medium bowl combine Alfredo sauce, lemon peel, lemon juice, dried thyme, salt, and pepper. Pour over kohlrabi in cooker.

2 Cover and cook on low-heat setting for 5 to 6 hours or on high-heat setting for 2½ to 3 hours. If desired, garnish with snipped fresh thyme and/or cracked black pepper.

nutrition facts per serving: 191 cal., 15 g total fat (0.0 g sat. fat), 24 mg chol., 261 mg sodium, 12 g carbo., 5 g dietary fiber, 5 g protein.

Orange juice, maple syrup, and apricots provide a wonderful combination of flavors to the humble sweet potato and carrot.

maple-orange sweet potatoes and carrots

prep: 20 minutes   cook: 8 to 9 hours (low) or 4 to 4½ hours (high)
makes: 10 servings

Nonstick cooking
   spray
1 16-ounce package
   peeled fresh baby
   carrots
2 pounds yellow and/
   or orange sweet
   potatoes, peeled
   and cut into
   1½-inch pieces
1 cup snipped dried
   apricots
½ cup maple syrup
¼ cup water
¼ cup frozen orange
   juice concentrate,
   thawed
2 tablespoons butter,
   melted
½ teaspoon salt
¼ teaspoon ground
   white pepper
¼ teaspoon ground
   cinnamon

1 Lightly coat a 3½- or 4-quart slow cooker with cooking spray. Place carrots in prepared slow cooker. Top with sweet potatoes and apricots. In a large bowl combine maple syrup, the water, orange juice concentrate, melted butter, salt, white pepper, and cinnamon. Pour over mixture in cooker.

2 Cover and cook on low-heat setting for 8 to 9 hours or on high-heat setting for 4 to 4½ hours. Serve with a slotted spoon.

nutrition facts per serving: 194 cal., 3 g total fat (2 g sat. fat), 7 mg chol., 168 mg sodium, 42 g carbo., 5 g dietary fiber, 2 g protein.

Take a break from the usual candied sweet potatoes and serve this herb-accented dish instead. Crispy bacon is a nice addition.

orange-sage
sweet potatoes with bacon

prep: 15 minutes   cook: 5 to 6 hours (low) or 2½ to 3 hours (high)
makes: 10 to 12 servings

4   pounds sweet
      potatoes, peeled
      and cut into ¼-inch-
      thick slices (about
      10 cups)
½   cup frozen orange
      juice concentrate,
      thawed
3   tablespoons packed
      brown sugar
1½ teaspoons salt
½   teaspoon dried leaf
      sage, crushed
½   teaspoon dried
      thyme, crushed
2   tablespoons butter,
      cut up
4   slices bacon,
      crisp-cooked and
      crumbled

1 Place sweet potato slices in a 5- to 6-quart slow cooker. In a small bowl stir together orange juice concentrate, brown sugar, salt, sage, and thyme. Pour over sweet potato slices, tossing to coat. Dot with butter.

2 Cover and cook on low-heat setting for 5 to 6 hours or on high-heat setting for 2½ to 3 hours. Stir before serving. Sprinkle with crumbled bacon.

nutrition facts per serving: 189 cal., 4 g total fat (2 g sat. fat), 10 mg chol., 509 mg sodium, 36 g carbo., 4 g dietary fiber, 4 g protein.

Sweet potatoes and apples make great partners. A few dried cherries offer tiny bursts of tart flavor. Did we mention the apple butter and cream? Oh my.

apple-buttered
sweet potatoes

prep: 15 minutes   cook: 6 to 7 hours (low) or 3 to 3½ hours (high)
makes: 10 servings

3 pounds sweet potatoes, peeled and cut into 1-inch pieces (about 8 cups)
2 medium Granny Smith or other tart cooking apples, peeled and cut into wedges (2 cups)
½ cup dried cherries or dried cranberries (optional)
1 cup whipping cream
1 cup apple butter
1½ teaspoons pumpkin pie spice

1 In a 3½- or 4-quart slow cooker combine sweet potatoes, apples, and, if desired, cherries. In a medium bowl combine whipping cream, apple butter, and pumpkin pie spice. Pour over mixture in cooker, stirring gently to combine.

2 Cover and cook on low-heat setting for 6 to 7 hours or on high-heat setting for 3 to 3½ hours.

nutrition facts per serving: 351 cal., 9 g total fat (6 g sat. fat), 33 mg chol., 25 mg sodium, 65 g carbo., 5 g dietary fiber, 2 g protein.

Everyone loves dessert. And you'll have a hard time deciding which dessert to choose when you see the variety you can make in your slow cooker. Mixed Berry Cobbler, anyone? How about Cranberry Bread Pudding with a homemade caramel sauce to drizzle over the top? If chocolate is your passion, try Brownie Pudding Cake or Candy Bar Fondue. You won't be disappointed!

delectable

dess

10

erts

These velvety and lemony-sauced pears make a captivating finish to any meal. If you like, spoon the mixture over toasted pound cake slices for a company dessert.

pears in lemon cream sauce

prep: 20 minutes   **cook:** 1½ to 2 hours (high)   **makes:** 6 servings

6	medium ripe yet firm pears
1	teaspoon finely shredded lemon peel
2	tablespoons lemon juice
⅓	cup packed brown sugar
¼	teaspoon ground nutmeg
½	of an 8-ounce package cream cheese, cut into cubes and softened
¼	cup whipping cream
3	tablespoons broken pecans, toasted
6	sugar cookies (optional)

1 If desired, peel pears; halve pears lengthwise and remove cores. Place pears in a medium bowl. Add lemon peel and lemon juice; toss gently to coat. Add brown sugar and nutmeg; toss gently to combine. Transfer pear mixture to a 3½- or 4-quart slow cooker.

2 Cover and cook on high-heat setting for 1½ to 2 hours (do not use low-heat setting). Using a slotted spoon, transfer pears to dessert dishes. Reserve cooking liquid.

3 For sauce, add cream cheese and whipping cream to liquid in cooker. Cook and stir with a wire whisk until cream cheese is melted. Spoon the sauce over pears. Sprinkle with pecans. If desired, garnish with sugar cookies.

nutrition facts per serving: 273 cal., 13 g total fat (7 g sat. fat), 34 mg chol., 65 mg sodium, 40 g carbo., 4 g dietary fiber, 3 g protein.

Warm pears drizzled with caramel and sprinkled with cashews—now that's a dessert lover's delight. Don't skip the vanilla ice cream.

caramel-spiced pears

prep: 20 minutes   **cook:** 3½ to 4 hours (low) or 1½ to 2 hours (high)
makes: 8 servings

8   pears (7 to 8 ounces each)
1   teaspoon ground cinnamon
¼   teaspoon ground cloves
¾   cup apple juice or apple cider
2   tablespoons lemon juice
1   12-ounce jar caramel ice cream topping
½   cup chopped lightly salted cashews or honey-roasted cashews

1 If desired, peel pears; halve pears lengthwise and remove cores. Place pears in a 4- to 6-quart slow cooker. Sprinkle evenly with cinnamon and cloves. Pour apple juice and lemon juice over pears.

2 Cover and cook on low-heat setting for 3½ to 4 hours or on high-heat setting for 1½ to 2 hours. Using a slotted spoon, transfer pears to serving dishes. Drizzle with caramel topping; sprinkle with cashews.

nutrition facts per serving: 286 cal., 4 g total fat (1 g sat. fat), 0 mg chol., 130 mg sodium, 63 g carbo., 7 g dietary fiber, 2 g protein.

Make this apricot-studded rice pudding and be sure to turn the slow cooker off just before serving your dinner. Dessert will be ready to eat just after you've finished your meal.

fruity rice pudding

prep: 15 minutes **cook:** 2 hours (low) **stand:** 30 minutes **makes:** 8 servings

Nonstick cooking
   spray
2 5.5-ounce packages
   rice pudding mix
   with raisins and
   spice
3 cups whole milk
½ cup snipped dried
   apricots or snipped
   dried cherries
2 tablespoons butter,
   softened
⅓ cup pecans or
   almonds, toasted*

1 Lightly coat the inside of a 3½- or 4-quart slow cooker with cooking spray. In the prepared cooker combine the rice mixes, milk, apricots, and butter.

2 Cover and cook on low-heat setting for 2 hours or until rice is tender (do not use high-heat setting). Turn off cooker. Stir pudding. Let stand, uncovered, for about 30 minutes.

3 To serve, stir well and spoon into dessert dishes. Top with toasted nuts.

nutrition facts per serving: 280 cal., 10 g total fat (4 g sat. fat), 21 mg chol., 214 mg sodium, 44 g carbo., 2 g dietary fiber, 6 g protein.

*test kitchen tip: To toast nuts, spread nuts in a single layer in a shallow baking pan. Bake in a 350°F oven for 5 to 10 minutes or until light golden brown, watching carefully and stirring once or twice so the nuts don't burn.

If you have the time, be sure to make your own crunchy granola using the recipe below. Enjoy any leftovers for breakfast splashed with some milk.

almond granola–topped
dates and applesauce

prep: 25 minutes **cook:** 5 to 6 hours (low) or 2½ to 3 hours (high)
makes: 10 servings

3½ to 4 pounds cooking
apples (such as
Granny Smith),
peeled, cored, and
cut into chunks
¼ cup orange juice
¼ cup apple juice or
apple cider
½ cup packed brown
sugar
1½ teaspoons apple pie
spice
1 8-ounce package
chopped dates or
1 cup dried cherries
or raisins
⅔ cup Almond Granola
or purchased
granola cereal

1 Place apples in a 4- to 6-quart slow cooker. Add orange juice, apple juice, brown sugar, and apple pie spice; toss to coat. Cover and cook on low-heat setting for 5 to 6 hours or on high-heat setting for 2½ to 3 hours (apples should be very tender).

2 Using a potato masher or an immersion blender mash or blend apple mixture to desired consistency. Stir in dates. Serve warm topped with Almond Granola.

nutrition facts per serving: 223 cal., 2 g total fat (0 g sat. fat), 1 mg chol., 9 mg sodium, 54 g carbo., 6 g dietary fiber, 2 g protein.

almond granola: Preheat oven to 300°F. In a large bowl combine 2 cups regular rolled oats, 1½ cups sliced almonds, ¼ cup toasted wheat germ, and 1 teaspoon ground cinnamon. In a small bowl stir together ½ cup honey and 2 tablespoons butter, melted; stir honey mixture into oat mixture. Spread evenly in a greased 15x10x1-inch baking pan. Bake, uncovered, for 30 to 35 minutes or until lightly browned, stirring once. Transfer and spread on a large piece of foil to cool. Store in an airtight container at room temperature for up to 1 week or place in a freezer container and freeze for up to 3 months. Makes 5 cups.

Figs or raisins, brown sugar, and cinnamon are perfect mates for the stuffing in these apples. If you like, sprinkle each serving with chopped toasted pecans.

stuffed apples

prep: 20 minutes **cook:** 5 hours (low) or 2½ hours (high) **makes:** 4 servings

4	medium tart baking apples (such as Granny Smith)
⅓	cup snipped dried figs or raisins
¼	cup packed brown sugar
½	teaspoon apple pie spice or ground cinnamon
¼	cup apple juice
1	tablespoon butter or margarine, cut into 4 pieces

1 Core apples; peel a strip from the top of each apple. Place apples, top sides up, in a 3½- or 4-quart slow cooker.

2 In a small bowl combine figs, brown sugar, and apple pie spice. Spoon mixture into centers of apples, patting in with a knife or narrow metal spatula. Pour apple juice around apples in cooker. Top each apple with a piece of butter.

3 Cover and cook on low-heat setting for 5 hours or on high-heat setting for 2½ hours.

4 Using a large spoon, transfer apples to dessert dishes. Spoon the cooking liquid from cooker over apples. Serve warm.

nutrition facts per serving: 200 cal., 3 g total fat (2 g sat. fat), 8 mg chol., 31 mg sodium, 45 g carbo., 5 g dietary fiber, 1 g protein.

How easy it is to serve a warm and comforting dessert for a winter meal—especially when it cooks all afternoon. A muffin mix makes it possible.

mixed berry cobbler

prep: 15 minutes   **cook:** 3 hours (low) + 1 hour (high)   **stand:** 30 minutes
makes: 8 to 10 servings

Nonstick cooking
   spray
1   12- to 14-ounce
   package frozen
   mixed berries
1   21-ounce can
   blueberry pie filling
¼   cup sugar
1   6.5-ounce package
   blueberry or triple-
   berry muffin mix
⅓   cup water
2   tablespoons cooking
   oil
Frozen whipped
   dessert topping,
   thawed, or vanilla
   ice cream (optional)

1 Lightly coat the inside of a 3½- or 4-quart slow cooker with nonstick cooking spray. In the prepared cooker combine frozen mixed berries, pie filling, and sugar.

2 Cover and cook on low-heat setting (do not use high-heat setting) for 3 hours.

3 Turn to high-heat setting. In a medium bowl combine muffin mix, the water, and oil; stir just until combined. Spoon muffin mixture over mixture in cooker. Cover and cook for about 1 hour more or until a toothpick inserted into center of muffin mixture comes out clean.

4 Turn off cooker. Let stand, uncovered, for 30 to 45 minutes.

5 To serve, spoon warm cobbler into dessert dishes. If desired, top with whipped dessert topping.

nutrition facts per serving: 257 cal., 7 g total fat (1 g sat. fat), 1 mg chol., 155 mg sodium, 50 g carbo., 4 g dietary fiber, 1 g protein.

Serve this warm fruit compote as a dessert soup or over ice cream to make an amazing sundae. It's simply delicious.

spiced peach compote

prep: 10 minutes **cook:** 5 to 6 hours (low) or 2½ to 3 hours (high)
makes: 8 servings

2 29-ounce cans sliced
    peaches in juice
½ cup dried tart
    cherries
½ cup dried apricots
½ cup dried figs, stems
    removed
½ cup orange juice
3 2-inch-long cinnamon
    sticks
    Vanilla ice cream
    (optional)

1 Drain one of the cans of sliced peaches. In a 3½- or 4-quart slow cooker combine drained peaches, peaches with juice, cherries, apricots, figs, orange juice, and cinnamon sticks.

2 Cover and cook on low-heat setting for 5 to 6 hours or on high-heat setting for 2½ to 3 hours. Discard cinnamon sticks. If desired, using a slotted spoon, serve warm fruit mixture over ice cream.

nutrition facts per serving: 246 cal., 0 g total fat (0 g sat. fat), 0 mg chol., 20 mg sodium, 60 g carbo., 4 g dietary fiber, 3 g protein.

If you've never eaten bread pudding, this cranberry-jeweled recipe will convince you of its appeal. The homemade caramel sauce is a must!

cranberry bread pudding

prep: 25 minutes **cook:** 4 hours (low) or 2 hours (high) **makes:** 6 servings

1½   cups half-and-half or light cream
½   of a 6-ounce package white baking bars or squares, coarsely chopped
⅓   cup snipped dried cranberries or dried cherries
2   eggs, beaten
½   cup sugar
½   teaspoon ground ginger
3   cups dry ½-inch bread cubes (about 4½ slices)
¼   cup coarsely chopped pecans or hazelnuts
Whipped cream (optional)
Grated white baking bar (optional)
Ground ginger (optional)

1 In a small saucepan heat half-and-half over medium heat until very warm but not boiling. Remove from heat; add chopped white baking bar and cranberries. Stir until baking bar is melted.

2 In a bowl combine eggs, sugar, and ½ teaspoon ginger. Whisk in the cream mixture. Gently stir in bread cubes and nuts. Pour mixture into a 1-quart soufflé dish (dish will be full). Cover the dish tightly with foil.

3 Pour 1 cup warm water into a 3½- to 5-quart slow cooker. Tear off an 18x12-inch piece of heavy foil. Divide in half lengthwise. Fold each piece into thirds lengthwise. Crisscross the strips and place the soufflé dish in the center of the foil cross. Bringing up foil strips, lift the ends of the strips to transfer the dish and foil to the cooker. (Leave foil strips under dish.)

4 Cover and cook on low-heat setting for 4 hours or on high-heat setting for 2 hours. Using the foil strips, carefully lift dish out of cooker. Serve pudding warm or chilled. If desired, serve with whipped cream and sprinkle with grated white baking bar and additional ground ginger.

nutrition facts per serving: 360 cal., 17 g total fat (8 g sat. fat), 98 mg chol., 177 mg sodium, 45 g carbo., 1 g dietary fiber, 7 g protein.

Triangles of refrigerated crescent rolls are baked ahead of time to place on top of each serving of this luscious apple and cherry cobbler.

apple-cherry cobbler

prep: 15 minutes **cook:** 5 to 6 hours (low) or 2½ to 3 hours (high)
makes: 6 to 8 servings

½   cup sugar
4   teaspoons quick-cooking tapioca
1   teaspoon apple pie spice
1½ pounds cooking apples, peeled, cored, and cut into ½-inch-thick slices (4½ cups)
1   16-ounce can pitted tart red cherries, undrained
½   cup dried cherries
    Spiced Triangles
    Ice cream (such as butter pecan or cinnamon) (optional)

1 In a 3½- or 4-quart slow cooker combine sugar, tapioca, and apple pie spice. Stir in apple slices, canned cherries, and dried cherries.

2 Cover and cook on low-heat setting for 5 to 6 hours or on high-setting for 2½ to 3 hours.

3 To serve, spoon the apple mixture into dessert dishes. Top with Spiced Triangles and, if desired, ice cream.

nutrition facts per serving: 414 cal., 10 g total fat (4 g sat. fat), 5 mg chol., 317 mg sodium, 79 g carbo., 5 g dietary fiber, 7 g protein.

spiced triangles: Preheat oven to 375°F. In a small bowl combine 1 tablespoon sugar and ½ teaspoon apple pie spice. Unroll one 8-ounce package (8) refrigerated crescent rolls. Separate triangles. Brush 1 tablespoon melted butter or margarine over dough triangles; lightly sprinkle with sugar mixture. Cut each triangle into three smaller triangles. Place on an ungreased baking sheet. Bake for 8 to 10 minutes or until bottoms are lightly browned. Transfer triangles to a wire rack and let cool. Makes 24 triangles.

A sweet and spicy classic gets an update. The crystallized ginger and dried cherries give this homey dessert a sophisticated flair.

cherry gingerbread

prep: 20 minutes **cook:** 1¾ hours (high) **cool:** 30 minutes **makes:** 6 servings

¾ cup all-purpose flour
¼ teaspoon baking powder
¼ teaspoon baking soda
¼ teaspoon ground cinnamon
   Dash salt
   Dash ground allspice
¼ cup shortening
2 tablespoons packed brown sugar
1 egg
3 tablespoons molasses
¼ cup boiling water
2 tablespoons snipped dried cherries or mixed dried fruit bits
2 teaspoons finely chopped crystallized ginger
¾ cup whipped cream (optional)
1 teaspoon finely shredded lemon peel (optional)

1 Generously grease the bottom and halfway up the sides of a 1-pint straight-sided wide-mouth canning jar. Flour the jar; set aside.

2 In a bowl stir together flour, baking powder, baking soda, cinnamon, salt, and allspice. In a mixing bowl beat shortening and brown sugar with an electric mixer on medium speed until combined. Add egg and molasses. Beat for 1 minute more. Alternately add flour mixture and the boiling water, beating on low speed after each addition. Stir in cherries and ginger. Pour into prepared canning jar. Cover jar tightly with greased foil, greased side down. Place in a 3½- or 4-quart slow cooker. Pour 1 cup water around jar.

3 Cover and cook on high-heat setting for 1¾ hours or until a toothpick inserted near the center comes out clean (do not use low-heat setting).

4 Remove jar from slow cooker; cool for 10 minutes. Using a small spatula, loosen bread from sides of jar; remove from jar. Cool for 20 minutes on a wire rack. To serve, cut bread into 12 slices and place 2 slices on each dessert plate. If desired, in small bowl combine the whipped cream and lemon peel; top each serving with whipped cream mixture.

nutrition facts per serving: 189 cal., 10 g total fat (2 g sat. fat), 36 mg chol., 104 mg sodium, 24 g carbo., 1 g dietary fiber, 3 g protein.

If you love pudding and adore spice cake, this is the dessert for you.
Don't be alarmed—a pudding is nestled underneath the cake!

gingerbread pudding cake

prep: 15 minutes **cook:** 2 hours (high) **stand:** 45 minutes **makes:** 8 servings

Nonstick cooking
spray
1 14.5-ounce package
gingerbread mix
½ cup milk
½ cup raisins
2¼ cups water
¾ cup packed brown
sugar
¾ cup butter
Vanilla ice cream
(optional)

1 Lightly coat the inside of a 3½- or 4-quart slow cooker with cooking spray; set aside. In a medium bowl stir together the gingerbread mix and milk until moistened. Stir in raisins (batter will be thick). Spread gingerbread batter evenly in the bottom of the prepared cooker.

2 In a medium saucepan combine the water, brown sugar, and butter; bring to boiling. Carefully pour sugar mixture over batter in cooker.

3 Cover and cook on high-heat setting for 2 hours (do not use low-heat setting; center may appear moist but will set up as it stands). Turn off cooker. Let stand, uncovered, for 45 minutes before serving.

4 To serve, spoon warm cake into dessert dishes. If desired, serve with vanilla ice cream.

nutrition facts per serving: 501 cal., 24 g total fat (13 g sat. fat), 50 mg chol., 548 mg sodium, 70 g carbo., 1 g dietary fiber, 4 g protein.

Who could resist this dessert? The cake bakes up perfectly in the slow cooker while an orange-flavored pudding develops below it. Brilliant!

orange pudding
caramel cake

prep: 25 minutes cook: 4½ to 5 hours (low) stand: 45 minutes
makes: 6 to 8 servings

Nonstick cooking
    spray or disposable
    slow-cooker liner
1 cup all-purpose flour
⅓ cup granulated sugar
1 teaspoon baking
    powder
½ teaspoon ground
    cinnamon
¼ teaspoon salt
½ cup milk
2 tablespoons butter,
    melted
½ cup chopped pecans
¼ cup dried currants
    or raisins
¾ cup water
½ teaspoon finely
    shredded orange
    peel
¾ cup orange juice
⅔ cup packed brown
    sugar
1 tablespoon butter
    Caramel ice cream
    topping
    Chopped pecans

1 Lightly coat the inside of a 3½- or 4-quart slow cooker with nonstick cooking spray or line with a disposable liner.

2 In a medium bowl combine flour, granulated sugar, baking powder, cinnamon, and salt. Add milk and melted butter; stir just until combined. Stir in ½ cup pecans and currants. Spread evenly in the bottom of the prepared cooker.

3 In a medium saucepan combine the water, orange peel, orange juice, brown sugar, and 1 tablespoon butter. Bring to boiling, stirring to dissolve sugar; reduce heat. Boil gently, uncovered, for 2 minutes. Carefully pour over mixture in cooker.

4 Cover and cook on low-heat setting for 4½ to 5 hours (do not use high-heat setting). Remove liner from cooker or turn off cooker. Let stand, uncovered, for about 45 minutes.

5 To serve, spoon pudding cake into dessert dishes. Top with caramel topping and sprinkle with chopped pecans.

nutrition facts per serving: 390 cal., 15 g total fat (6 g sat. fat), 23 mg chol., 255 mg sodium, 61 g carbo., 2 g dietary fiber, 5 g protein.

The addition of cinnamon to chocolate is celebrated in Mexican cuisine. Here the two pair up for a memorable bread pudding.

mexican chocolate
bread pudding

prep: 15 minutes   cook: 4 hours (low) or 2 hours (high)   makes: 6 servings

Nonstick cooking
   spray
1½ cups half-and-half
   or light cream
3 ounces unsweetened
   chocolate, coarsely
   chopped
⅓ cup raisins (optional)
2 eggs, beaten
½ cup sugar
¾ teaspoon ground
   cinnamon
3 cups ½-inch bread
   cubes (about
   4 slices; see note,
   page 465)
Whipped cream
   (optional)
Chopped nuts
   (optional)

1 Lightly coat a 1-quart soufflé dish and a 12-inch square of heavy foil with nonstick cooking spray. In a small saucepan heat half-and-half, chocolate, and if desired, raisins over low heat, stirring until chocolate is melted. Cool slightly.

2 In a medium bowl whisk together eggs, sugar, and cinnamon. Whisk in cream mixture. Gently stir in bread cubes. Pour into prepared soufflé dish. Cover the dish tightly with prepared foil.

3 Tear off two 15x6-inch pieces of heavy foil. Fold each piece in thirds lengthwise. Crisscross the strips and place the soufflé dish in the center. Bringing up foil strips, lift the ends of the strips and transfer the dish and foil to a 3½- to 5-quart slow cooker. (Leave foil strips under dish.) Pour warm water into the cooker around the dish to a depth of 2 inches (about 1 cup).

4 Cover and cook on low-heat setting for about 4 hours or on high-heat setting for about 2 hours or until a knife inserted near the center comes out clean.

5 Using foil strips, carefully lift the dish out of cooker. Serve bread pudding warm or chilled. If desired, top each serving with a dollop of whipped cream and sprinkle with nuts.

nutrition facts per serving: 281 cal., 17 g total fat (8 g sat. fat), 95 mg chol., 124 mg sodium, 31 g carbo., 2.0 g dietary fiber, 7 g protein.

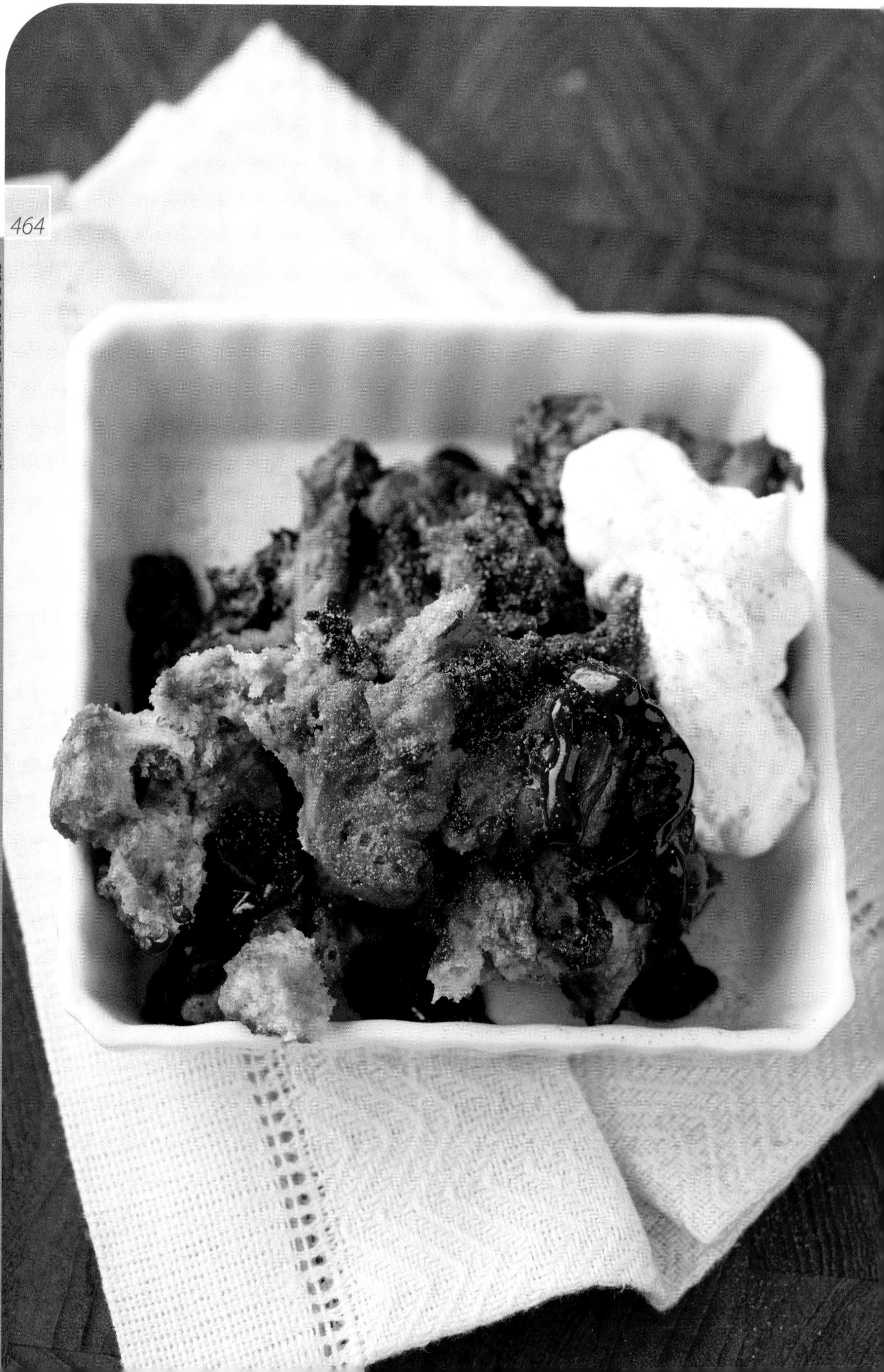

Remember to plan for oven-drying the bread cubes for this bread pudding. It will become one of your favorites, especially when served warm with whipped cream.

semisweet-chocolate
bread pudding

prep: 20 minutes **cook:** 2½ hours (low) **stand:** 30 minutes
makes: 8 servings

Nonstick cooking spray
3 cups milk
¾ cup semisweet chocolate pieces
¾ cup presweetened cocoa powder
3 eggs, lightly beaten
5 cups ½-inch cubes Hawaiian sweet bread or cinnamon swirl bread (no raisins), dried*
Whipped cream (optional)
Presweetened cocoa powder (optional)

1 Lightly coat the inside of a 3½- or 4-quart slow cooker with cooking spray.

2 In a medium saucepan bring milk to simmering; remove from heat. Add chocolate and ¾ cup cocoa powder (do not stir); let stand for 5 minutes. Whisk until smooth; cool slightly (about 10 minutes). In a large bowl whisk together the eggs and chocolate mixture. Gently stir in bread cubes. Spoon bread mixture into the prepared cooker.

3 Cover and cook on low-heat setting for about 2½ hours or until puffed and a knife inserted near center comes out clean (do not use high-heat setting). Turn off cooker. Let stand, uncovered, for 30 minutes (pudding will fall during cooling).

4 To serve, spoon warm pudding into dessert dishes. If desired, top each serving with whipped cream and sprinkle with presweetened cocoa powder.

nutrition facts per serving: 360 cal., 12 g total fat (6 g sat. fat), 95 mg chol., 214 mg sodium, 62 g carbo., 4 g dietary fiber, 9 g protein.

* test kitchen tip: To make dry bread cubes, spread fresh bread cubes in a single layer in a 15x10x1-inch baking pan. Bake, uncovered, in a 300°F oven for 10 to 15 minutes or until dry, stirring twice; cool.

Thanks to this recipe, you can have your cake and pudding too. Rich chocolate infuses this cake and pudding combo. Top with ice cream for a real treat.

brownie pudding cake

prep: 15 minutes   **cook:** 2 hours (high)   **cool:** 30 minutes   **makes:** 8 servings

Nonstick cooking
   spray
1   19.8-ounce package
   brownie mix
½   cup butter or
   margarine, melted
2   eggs
¼   cup water
¾   cup sugar
¾   cup unsweetened
   cocoa powder
3   cups boiling water

1 Lightly coat a 3½- or 4-quart slow cooker with nonstick cooking spray.

2 For batter, in a medium bowl stir together brownie mix, melted butter, eggs, and the ¼ cup water until batter is nearly smooth. Spread brownie batter evenly in the bottom of prepared slow cooker.

3 In another bowl combine sugar and cocoa powder. Gradually stir the 3 cups boiling water into the sugar-cocoa mixture. Pour evenly over batter in slow cooker.

4 Cover and cook on high-heat setting for 2 hours (do not use low-heat setting; center may appear moist but will set up upon standing). Turn off slow cooker. Cool, uncovered, for 30 to 45 minutes.

5 To serve, spoon warm cake into dessert dishes; spoon pudding over cake.

nutrition facts per serving: 534 cal., 25 g total fat (10 g sat. fat), 86 mg chol., 355 mg sodium, 76 g carbo., 0 g dietary fiber, 6 g protein.

Chocolate paired with raspberries is a decadent dessert combination. Dress it up by sprinkling each serving with fresh raspberries and dusting with powdered sugar.

raspberry fudgey brownies

prep: 15 minutes **cook:** 3 to 3½ hours (high) **cool:** 10 minutes
makes: 12 brownie slices

½ cup margarine
   or butter
2 ounces unsweetened
   chocolate
2 eggs
¾ cup sugar
⅓ cup seedless red
   raspberry jam
1 teaspoon vanilla
¾ cup all-purpose flour
¼ teaspoon baking
   powder
Vanilla ice cream
   (optional)
Chocolate ice cream
   topping (optional)
Fresh raspberries
   (optional)

1 Generously grease two 1-pint straight-sided wide-mouth canning jars. Flour the greased jars; set aside.

2 In a saucepan melt margarine and chocolate over low heat. Remove from heat. Stir in eggs, sugar, jam, and vanilla. Using a spoon, beat lightly just until combined. Stir in flour and baking powder. Pour batter into prepared jars. Cover jars tightly with greased foil, greased side down. Place jars in a 3½- or 4-quart slow cooker. Pour 1 cup water around jars.

3 Cover and cook on high-heat setting for 3 to 3½ hours (do not use low-heat setting) or until a toothpick inserted near the centers of brownie rolls comes out clean. Remove jars from cooker; cool for 10 minutes. Using a metal spatula, loosen brownies from sides of jars. Carefully remove rolls from jars. Place rolls on their sides on a wire rack; cool completely. To serve, cut each roll into 6 slices. If desired, serve with ice cream, ice cream topping, and fresh raspberries.

nutrition facts per serving: 204 cal., 11 g total fat (0 g sat. fat), 36 mg chol., 109 mg sodium, 26 g carbo., 1 g dietary fiber, 2 g protein.

A small slow cooker doubles as a fondue pot. Creamy, delightfully rich, and studded with almonds, this fondue will knock your socks off.

candy bar fondue

prep: 15 minutes **cook:** 2 to 2½ hours (low) **makes:** 12 servings

4   1.76-ounce bars
    chocolate-coated
    almond nougat,
    chopped
1   7-ounce bar milk
    chocolate, chopped
1   7-ounce jar
    marshmallow crème
¾   cup whipping cream,
    half-and-half,
    or light cream
¼   cup finely chopped
    almonds, toasted
2   to 3 tablespoons
    almond, hazelnut,
    or raspberry liqueur
    (optional)
    Assorted dippers:
    sugar wafers,
    pound cake cubes,
    strawberries,
    cherries, and/or
    pineapple pieces
    Finely chopped
    toasted almonds,
    toasted coconut,
    miniature semisweet
    chocolate pieces,
    multicolored candy
    sprinkles, and/or
    almond toffee pieces
    (optional)

1 In a 3½-quart slow cooker combine nougat bars, milk chocolate bar, marshmallow crème, and whipping cream.

2 Cover and cook on low-heat setting for 2 to 2½ hours (do not use high-heat setting). Stir until smooth. Stir in the ¼ cup almonds and, if desired, almond liqueur.

3 To serve, if desired, transfer chocolate mixture to a 1½-quart slow cooker. Keep covered on warm setting or low-heat setting for up to 1 hour. Stir occasionally.

4 Spear dippers with fondue forks. Dip into chocolate mixture, swirling as you dip. If desired, dip in coconut, candy pieces, and/or additional almonds to coat.

nutrition facts per serving (fondue only): 294 cal., 16 g total fat (8 g sat. fat), 25 mg chol., 55 mg sodium, 34 g carbo., 1 g dietary fiber, 3 g protein.

index

note: Page numbers in *italics* indicate illustrations.

index

index